IT'S ALL DONE GONE

IT'S ALL DONE GONE

Arkansas Photographs from the Farm Security Administration Collection, 1935–1943

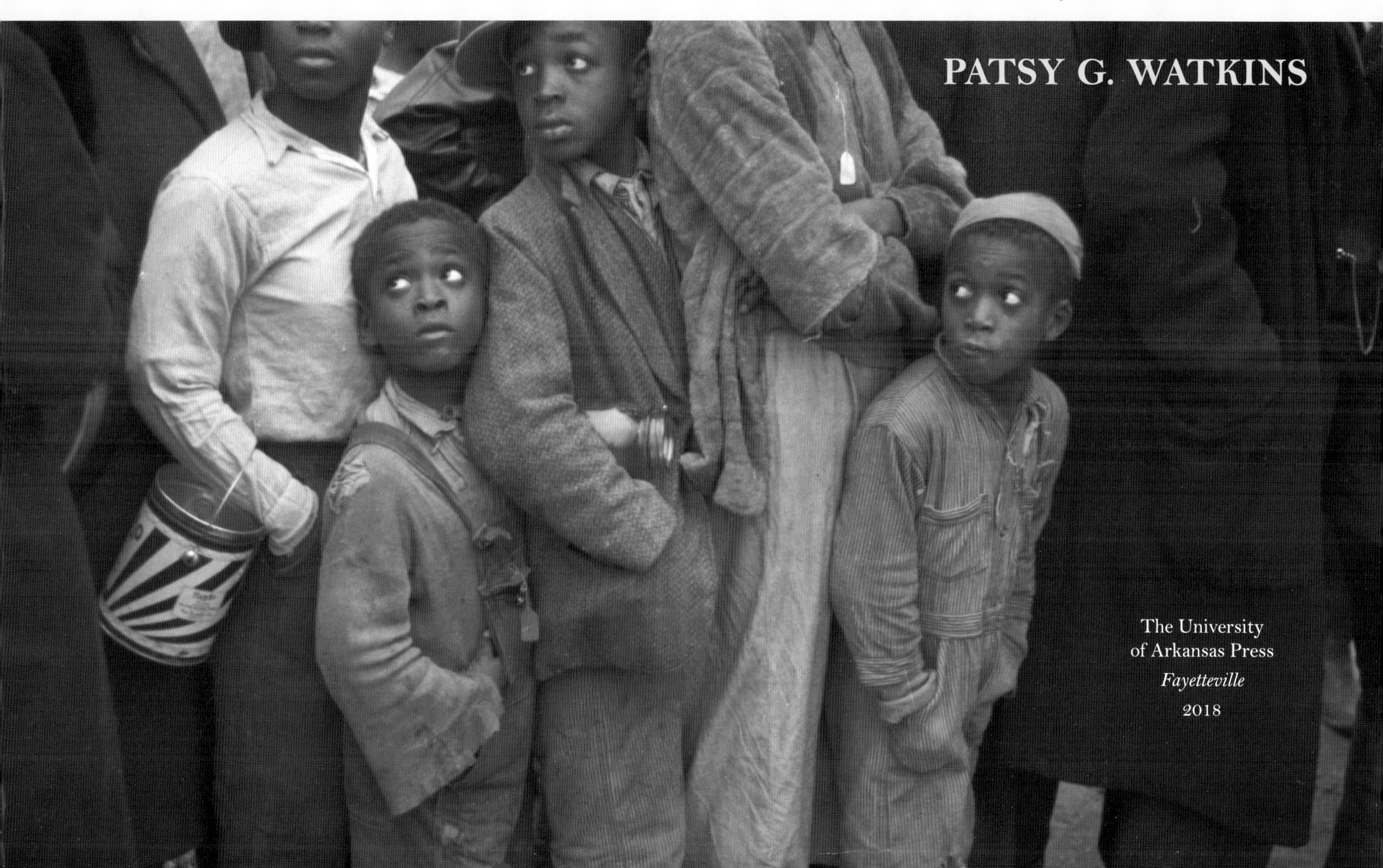

PATSY G. WATKINS

The University of Arkansas Press
Fayetteville
2018

Manufactured in Korea by Pacom
ISBN: 978–1-68226–063-0
eISBN: 978–1-61075–639-6

22 21 20 19 5 4 3 2

Designed by Liz Lester

♾ The paper used in this publication meets the minimum requirements of the American National Standard for Permanence of Paper for Printed Library Materials Z39.48–1984.

Library of Congress Cataloging-in-Publication Data
Names: Watkins, Patsy, 1948– author. | United States. Farm Security Administration.
Title: It's all done gone : Arkansas photographs from the Farm Security Administration collection / Patsy Watkins.
Description: Fayetteville : The University of Arkansas Press, 2018. | Includes bibliographical references. |
Identifiers: LCCN 2017050001 (print) | LCCN 2018007338 (ebook) | ISBN 9781610756396 (electronic) | ISBN 9781682260630 (pbk. : alk. paper)
Subjects: LCSH: Arkansas—Pictorial works. | Arkansas—Social life and customs—Pictorial works.
Classification: LCC F412 (ebook) | LCC F412 .W38 2018 (print) | DDC 976.70022/2--dc23
LC record available at https://lccn.loc.gov/2018007338

To Joseph and Antonie, Pat, Olga, Libbye, Lillian, and Nellie
for their examples of life lived with courage, humor,
and lots of homemade ice cream

Now, none of my children own their land.
It's all done gone, but it raised my family.

—An "Arkansas Hoosier" in Conway,
interviewed by Dorothea Lange

CONTENTS

A NOTE ON THE PHOTOGRAPHS

The photographs in this book are all from the Farm Security Administration—Office of War Information Photograph Collection in the Library of Congress. They were taken in Arkansas from 1935 through 1942 (although the FSA project lasted until 1943, no photographs were taken in Arkansas that year), primarily in the eastern, central, and north-central parts of the state. Anyone wishing to explore the Arkansas photos in the collection can do so easily from any computer with online access. The FSA collection is available through the Library of Congress website, which is free and open to the public with no password or membership required.

Exploring the Arkansas photographs in the collection can begin by searching the phrase "Farm Security Administration / Office of War Information Black-and-White Photographs." On the FSA website, Arkansas photos can be searched by typing in "Arkansas" combined with either a specific county, city, photographer's name, or subject such as "sharecropper." The photos are in the public domain and can be downloaded.

Of sixteen hundred photos in the collection associated with "Arkansas," just over a thousand were actually taken in the state. The rest are shots of Arkansans who had moved to places like California, Oklahoma, or Mississippi. This book includes only photos taken in Arkansas, with the exception of a few shot in Tennessee or Mississippi, particularly of Arkansas sharecroppers evicted for involvement with the Southern Tenant Farmers Union, which is significant in the history of the state in the 1930s.

The photo captions in the book are based on caption information written by the FSA photographers. Though they kept notes on what they shot, often they didn't see proofs of their pictures and write captions until weeks later; the original captions tend to be very brief, sometimes mere labels. Photographers only rarely recorded names of the people they photographed, so subjects are almost never identified in captions.

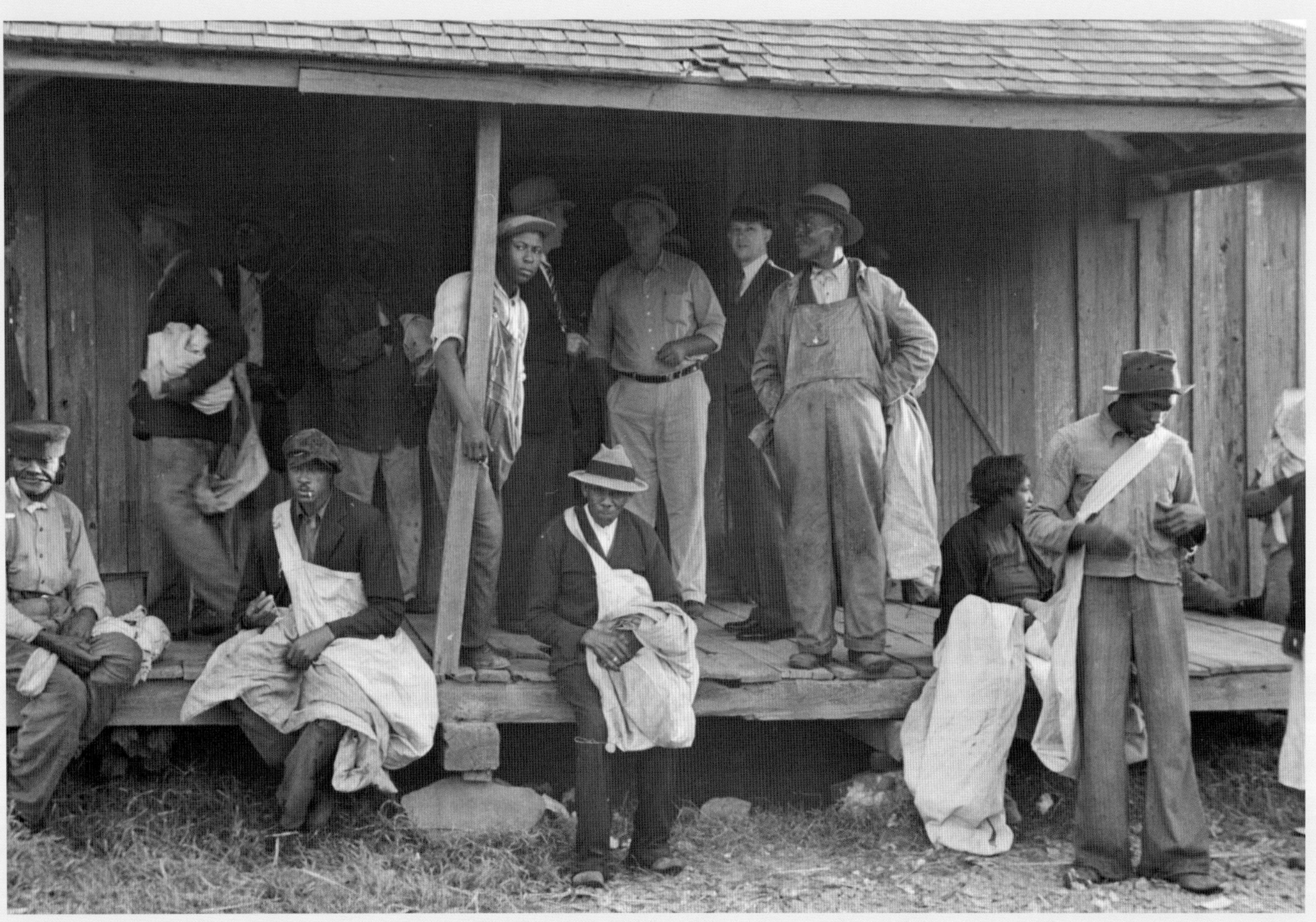

PREFACE

On a cold morning in October 1935, the artist Ben Shahn was in Arkansas, on a trip to find material he could use in designing murals and posters for a New Deal government agency. Shahn had arranged to take pictures of a group of cotton pickers gathering early for the workday in the fields. It was about 6:30 and chilly enough that Shahn could see the pickers' breath.

"The sun was low, just rising, and it was beautiful," Shahn told a Smithsonian historian years later. The pickers were prepared for the hot day to come and had filled large milk cans with water. Shahn began to take photographs, shooting about a dozen frames, some of the whole crew, others of small groups standing around together, and one or two of pickers sitting by themselves.

The pictures Shahn took that day and in his journey across the South were so stunning in their depiction of the destitution that plagued the poorest farmers in the midst of the Great Depression that they were included in a file of photographs used by the government to promote agricultural relief programs. That file, over eight years from 1935 to 1943, accumulated more than a quarter million photographs showing hundreds of thousands of Americans across the country as they coped with the impact of the most severe economic crisis in US history. Since the 1930s, these pictures have become known as the Farm Security Administration (FSA) Photograph Collection and now are the foremost representation of the nation's visual memories of life during the Depression. Many of the photos have become familiar symbols associated with those years, such as Dorothea Lange's picture titled "Migrant Mother" and Arthur Rothstein's shot of a dust storm in Cimarron County (both shown on page xv).

Arkansas is represented in the Farm Security Administration Photograph Collection by about eight hundred pictures, a small percentage of the whole, but among them are many images well known to Americans through their repeated use in books, articles, documentaries, and exhibits about the Depression. The FSA photographers who took them later became some of the most influential documentarists, artists, and photojournalists of the mid-twentieth century—Walker Evans, Dorothea Lange, Ben Shahn, Russell Lee, Arthur Rothstein, Marion Post Wolcott, John Vachon, Carl Mydans, and Edwin Locke.

The FSA was a government agency in charge of farm relief and assistance projects; in the alphabet

opposite: Cotton pickers gather at 6:30 a.m., waiting to be trucked to the fields at a farm in Pulaski County. In the center of the photo, in the shadow of the porch, are company representatives.

(Ben Shahn, October 1935) Farm Security Administration Photograph Collection, Prints & Photographs Division, Library of Congress, LC-USF33–006027–M5

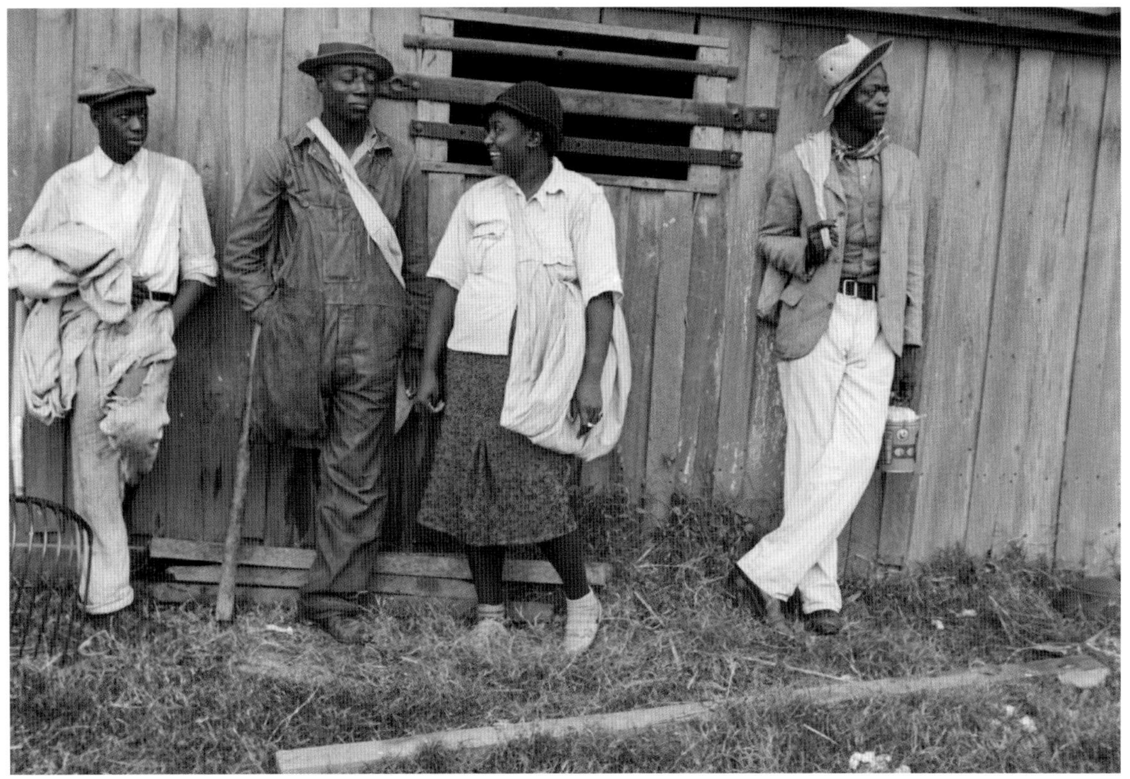

Shahn's photo recognized the distinctive individuality of each of the cotton pickers, expressed in their posture, their clothes, and their demeanor.

(Ben Shahn, October 1935) Farm Security Administration Photograph Collection, Prints & Photographs Division, Library of Congress, LC-USF33–006028–M3

soup of New Deal programs, it had evolved from an earlier agency, the Resettlement Administration (RA), which was created to tackle the crisis in agriculture. The leadership of the RA maintained the photographs were intended to be public information, to inform Americans about the extent and severity of rural poverty and document the federal projects designed to address the problems effectively. However, critics of the RA—and later the FSA as well—attacked the photos as propaganda meant to unfairly manipulate opinion.

The RA/FSA photographers, in recording the extreme poverty conditions they discovered in their assignments, developed a style later called "social documentary," defined as pictures that were factually accurate in depicting those who were poor and disadvantaged, but taken with a sensitivity to their humanity. Few photographers at the time had attempted to use their pictures to call attention to the unseen "one-third" in American society, those referred to by Franklin Roosevelt in his second inaugural address as the "one-third of a nation ill-housed, ill-clad, ill-nourished"; therefore, the approach was unfamiliar to people. The style became associated closely with RA/FSA photographs and proved to be key to their endurance as powerful images that have resonated with viewers over more than three-quarters of a century.

The approach can be seen in Shahn's early morning photographs of the Pulaski County cotton pickers. In 1935, these pickers were likely day laborers, people without jobs and no regular means of support. They made five cents an hour, or sixty cents for a twelve-hour day, according to Shahn. They could have been evicted sharecroppers, kicked off farms when the government instituted cotton production controls in 1933. This meant they were on the very bottom rung of the socioeconomic ladder and represented the poorest farmers and laborers.

To Nicholas Natanson, who has studied Depression-era American photography and closely examined the RA/FSA photographs, Shahn presented the cotton pickers "carefully and respectfully," recognizing each of them as worthy of individual attention, in their dress, their demeanor, and even the way they held their cotton sacks. He wrote that "Shahn's camera reveals a realm of experience not determined simply by occupational and income status." Each of the pickers had a life and identity beyond the cotton fields, not defined solely by the lowly job of wage laborer. Rather than treating the pickers as only part of the mass of workers who labored in the cotton fields, Shahn identified in each of them an "individual spirit" that the system overlooked.

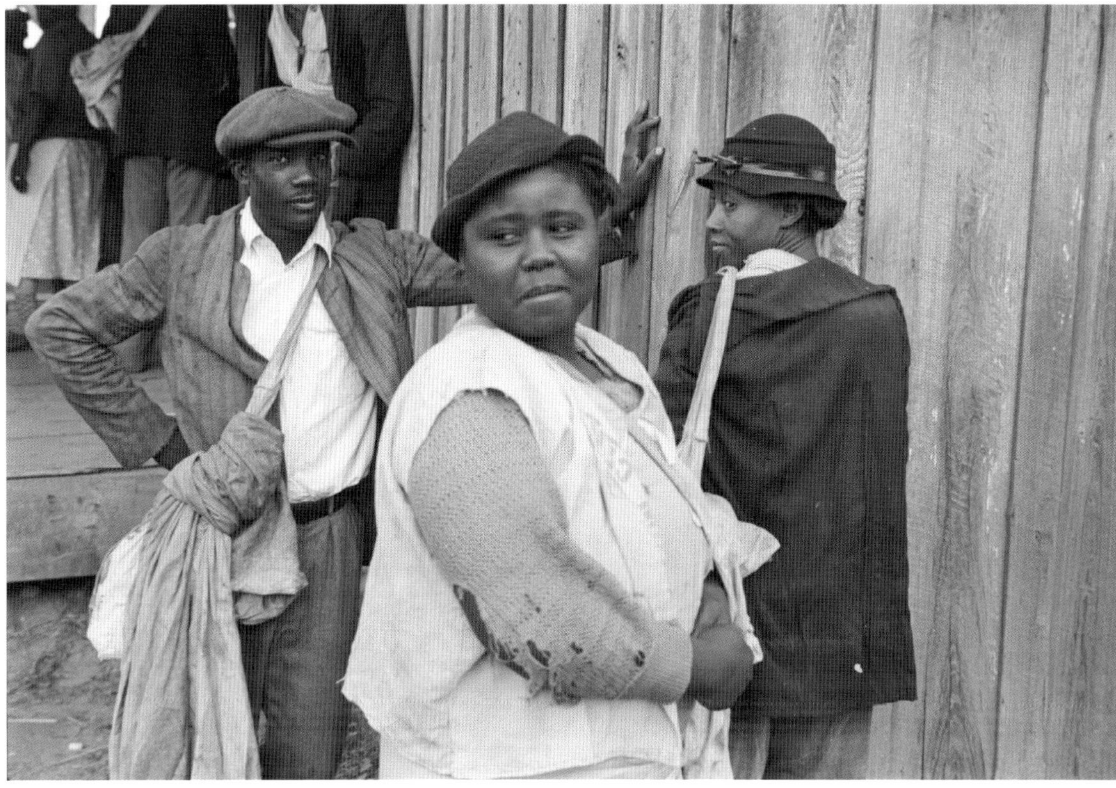

Shahn's use of a right-angle viewfinder enabled him to take a photo while looking in a different direction. By doing this, he caught people off guard, unaware they were being photographed.

(Ben Shahn, October 1935) Farm Security Administration Photograph Collection, Prints & Photographs Division, Library of Congress, LC-USF33–006028–M2

The RA/FSA photographs from Arkansas are extraordinary. Some are among the very best work done by the RA/FSA photographers. Dorothea Lange, Ben Shahn, Walker Evans, and Russell Lee all captured certain distinctive images with a glimpse of life in Arkansas that can strike a viewer with a sudden moment of recognition and connection with the past. Unfortunately, most Arkansans may be unaware that the FSA photographs exist; those who have seen a few of the pictures likely know very little about the photo project and the environment of political, economic, and social tensions and divisions that made it possible. This book is intended to introduce the FSA photos to Arkansans with this collection of some of its most memorable and meaningful images of Arkansas and place them in a historical, cultural, and photographic framework. This background can help readers understand and more fully appreciate the significance of the pictures—why they were taken, who took them, and how they were used.

The history of the FSA Photography Project and its political, economic, and cultural context are provided in an introductory essay, followed by chapters that represent the topics covered most often in the Arkansas photographs, including cotton, tenancy, resettlement farms, African Americans, houses, food, children, small-town life, the 1937 flood, and portraits. A short essay opens each chapter, and captions explain more about the pictures, as well as provide information on the photographers, the dates of the photos, and their identification numbers in the Library of Congress. This book is not a comprehensive visual history of the 1930s in Arkansas; it is instead a collection of photos from a certain period in the state's history. Also, readers should keep in mind that the FSA photos taken in Arkansas were not meant to be a full coverage of the state and all its people. The FSA photo project was part of a federal program steeped in the politics of the 1930s, and the kinds of pictures it included were intended to serve a particular purpose.

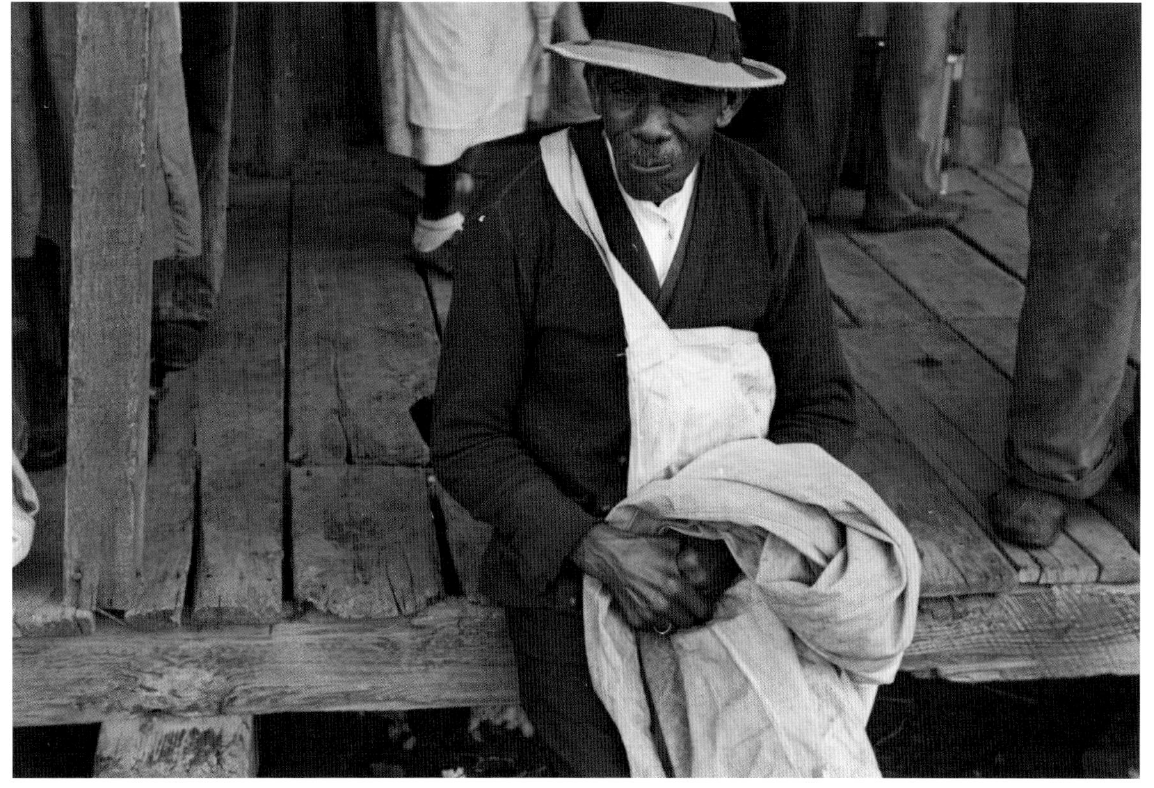

Shahn's portraits of the cotton pickers that morning are worthy of careful study for the clues to their lives that can be read in the details.

(Ben Shahn, October 1935) Farm Security Administration Photograph Collection, Prints & Photographs Division, Library of Congress, LC-USF33–006029–M5

For those who would like to delve deeper into the story of Arkansas during the Depression or into the FSA Photograph Collection, a bibliographic essay discusses the primary sources for the book that are referred to in its pages. Instructions are also provided for searching the FSA collection online through the Library of Congress website to find more Arkansas photos.

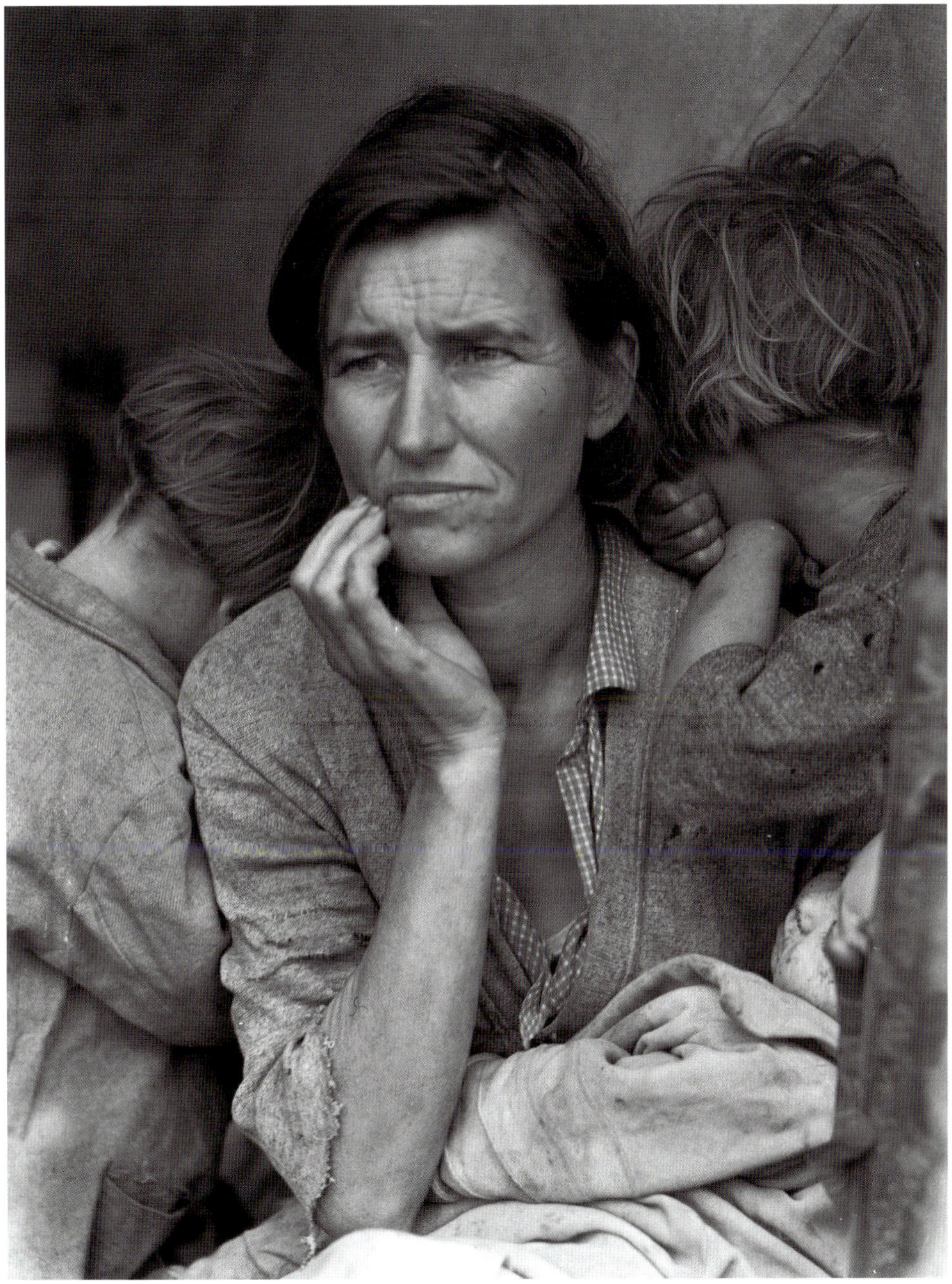

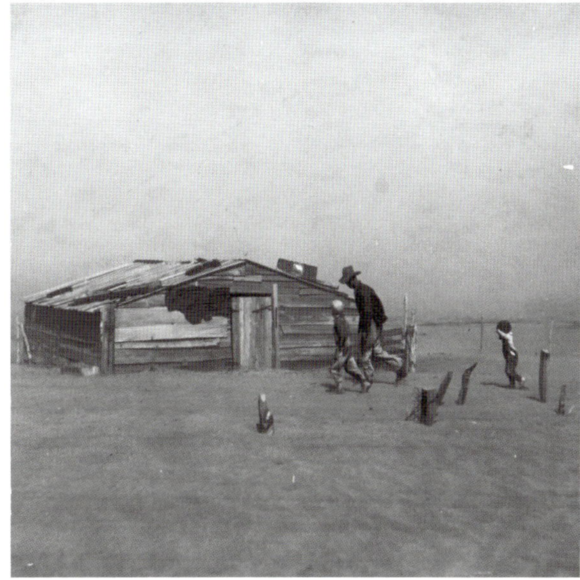

above: This is likely Arthur Rothstein's best-known photograph, taken in Cimarron County, Oklahoma, as a dust storm arose and drove a man and his sons to shelter. The picture has become a symbol of the devastation of the Dust Bowl in the 1930s.

(Arthur Rothstein, April 1936) Farm Security Administration Photograph Collection, Prints & Photographs Division, Library of Congress, LC-USF34 001052 Lot 521

left: This photo by Dorothea Lange is widely known as "Migrant Mother," though her notes for the caption describe a family of destitute pea pickers in Nipomo, California. The mother, age thirty-two, was left by the death of her husband with seven children.

(Dorothea Lange, March 1936) Farm Security Administration Photograph Collection, Prints & Photographs Division, Library of Congress, LC-USF34–009058–C

IT'S ALL DONE GONE

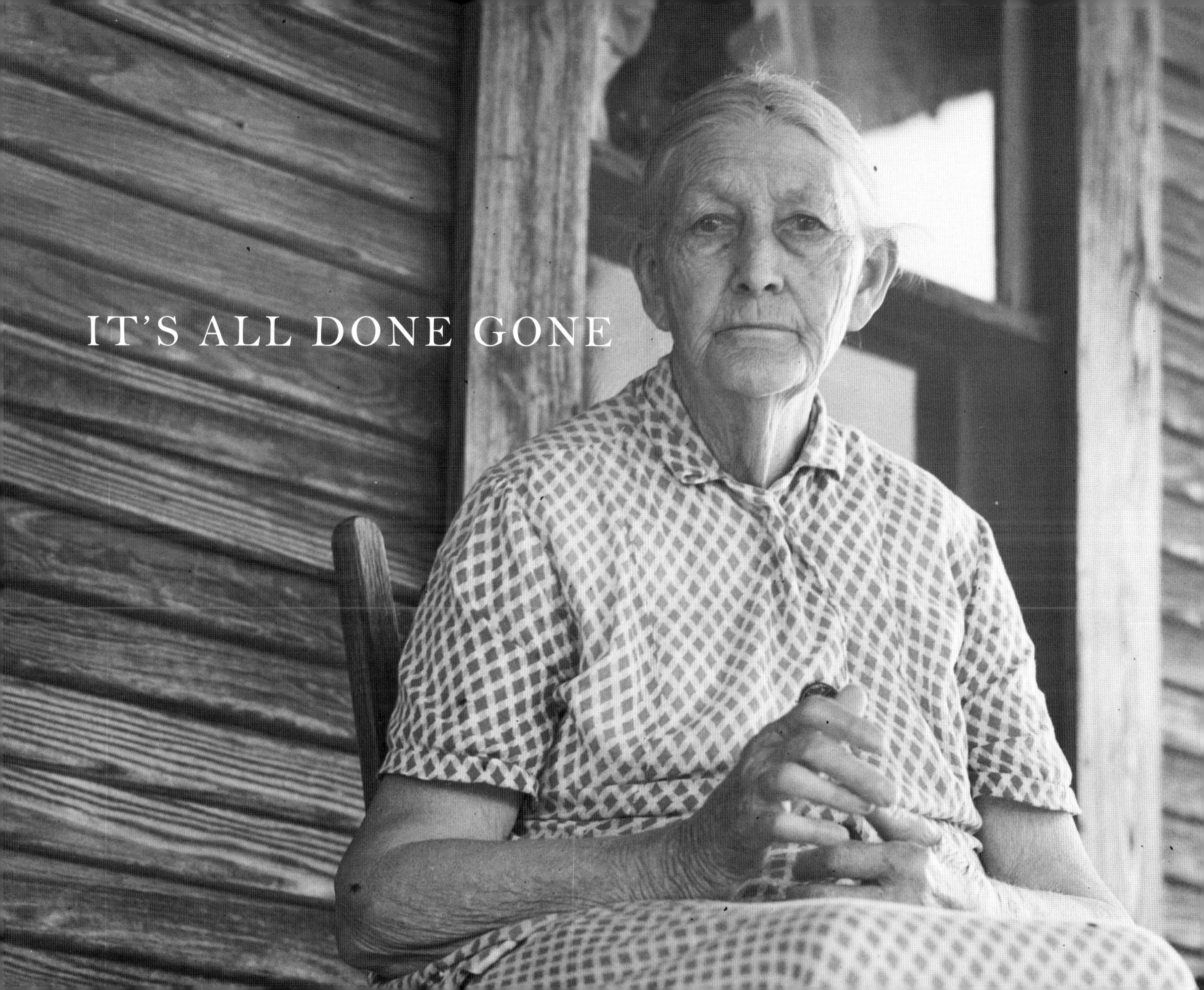

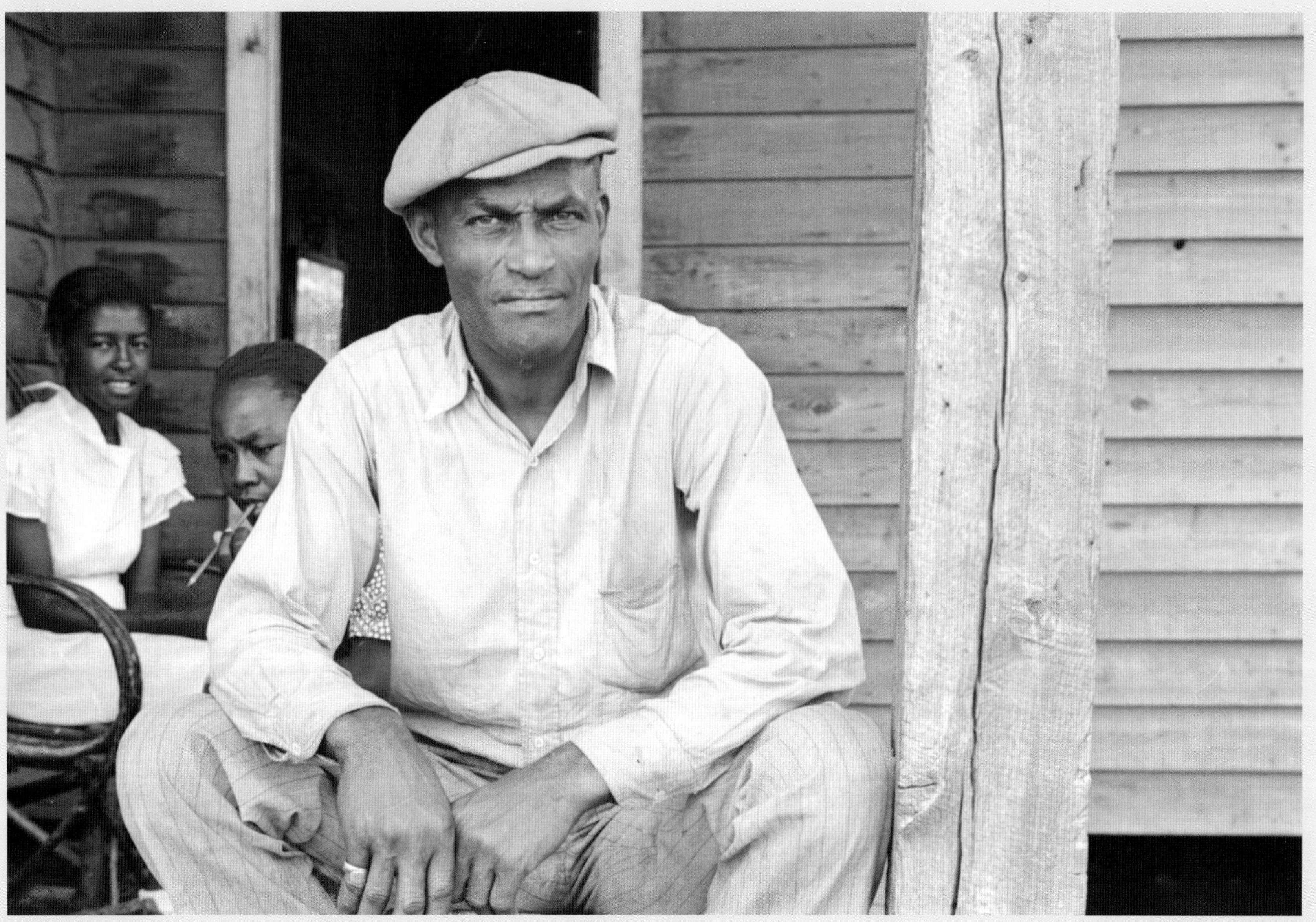

INTRODUCTION

The US economy grew rapidly during the twenties; the production of new goods and technology, such as radios and automobiles, boomed, stimulating a new consumer culture. But it all ended suddenly for millions of Americans in October 1929. The impact of the stock market crash was like "glass shattering," according to the great Harvard economist John Kenneth Galbraith. In one day billions of dollars of wealth were wiped out, simply and dramatically. Consumer spending dropped immediately, beginning a cascade of failures in the US financial system, bank closings, a drop in industrial production, and record unemployment.

Experts may debate the complexity of factors that resulted in the Great Depression, but they agree that the dramatic events on Wall Street in October 1929 signaled the end of the prosperity of the Roaring Twenties and the beginning of a severe economic slide that lasted for most of the following decade.

For farmers, however, the economic crash had started years earlier. Because of new competition from world markets and the development of synthetic fibers, the high prices brought by wheat, cotton, and corn during and after World War I had begun to fall by 1925—from 22 cents a pound for cotton to a low of 5 cents in 1932. Exports of US farm products plummeted and farm income across the nation fell by 75 percent; small farmers who might have made $1,500 a year in 1920 would see earnings drop below $500 by 1932.

In Arkansas, where 60 percent of the population lived on farms and cotton was the dominant crop in all but eight counties, farmers were hit hard. Small cotton growers were especially vulnerable. Cotton paid off once a year, in late fall when the crops came in. For nine to ten months, farmers had to live off the income from the previous year plus the credit extended by local merchants and banks. If cotton prices were low at market time, farmers were in trouble, and by the late 1920s foreclosure was all too common.

Many of these farmers became tenants on large-scale plantation-like cotton farms common to eastern Arkansas that depended heavily on cheap manual labor in the years before widespread mechanization. In the tenancy system workers provided fieldwork in exchange for a house, a portion of the

opposite: This photograph of a sharecropper at home on Sunday somewhere near Little Rock was among the first batch of pictures taken by a Farm Security Administration photographer in Arkansas. Sharecroppers led lives of uncertainty, moving frequently in the constant search for better conditions.

(Ben Shahn, October 1935) Farm Security Administration Photograph Collection, Prints & Photographs Division, Library of Congress, LC-USF33–006026–M1

crops when they were sold at the end of the season, and credit during the year for purchasing food and other necessities. The portion of the crops that went to the tenant farmer varied depending on how much he could bring to the arrangement with the landlord; the more the landlord provided—the "furnish," such as a mule, feed, and tools—the less the tenant could earn. The poverty of sharecroppers, the poorest tenants, was often so extreme they rarely had anything to contribute and therefore could earn little of the crop.

The tenancy system developed out of the sharecropping arrangement planters and freedmen established after the Civil War. Jeannie Whayne, in *The New Plantation South: Land, Labor, and Federal Favor in Twentieth-Century Arkansas*, explains the agreement grew from the postwar predicament in which landowners needed cheap labor to replace freed slaves, and former slaves needed land and work. Consequently, sharecroppers were primarily African American until the late nineteenth century when economic crises drove growing numbers of white farmers into tenancy for survival.

As the agricultural crisis of the 1920s and 1930s struck hundreds of thousands of small farmers across the South leaving them landless and penniless, tenancy grew to encompass 1.8 million farmers by 1935. In the Lower Mississippi Valley of Arkansas, Mississippi, and Louisiana, more than half of the farmers in tenancy were sharecroppers. According to government reports, white tenant farmers outnumbered African American tenants by two to one in the 1930s, but the tenancy rate among African American farmers was higher—nearly four out of five.

The term *tenancy* came to refer broadly to both tenants and sharecroppers, though history, tradition, and law distinguished among them. Under the law, tenants were owners of their portion of the crops; sharecroppers, however, were considered to be mere laborers and not owners. Through history and tradition, tenancy represented a social and economic class structure that divided landowners from workers and tenants from sharecroppers, and even separated tenants into levels. In practice, landowners recognized little difference between tenants and sharecroppers and treated them much the same; that is, with similar lack of respect for their dignity and even humanity.

The temptation to abuse the tenancy system was more than some landowners could bear. According to *The Collapse of Cotton Tenancy* (by Charles S. Johnson, Edwin R. Embree, and W. W. Alexander), the landowner had much control over his tenant—particularly sharecroppers, who often weren't given written tenancy agreements. He told them what, when, and how to plant, and since the landowner kept the records of the amounts tenants and sharecroppers owed him, they had no idea of their financial standing throughout the year, depending completely on his sense of fairness. Less honorable landlords could keep a tenant or sharecropper mired in a cycle of perpetual debt, never able to get ahead.

In addition, houses provided by landowners were often shacks, poorly maintained by either landowners or tenants, who tended to move often anyway, spending perhaps only one or two years on a farm. Historians have suggested this was an attempt to establish some control over their lives, as well as a strategy for avoiding mounting debt to landowners. Additionally, as Whayne points out, the frequent relocating discouraged tenants and sharecroppers' prospects for voting and possible involvement in local politics, in effect disenfranchising them.

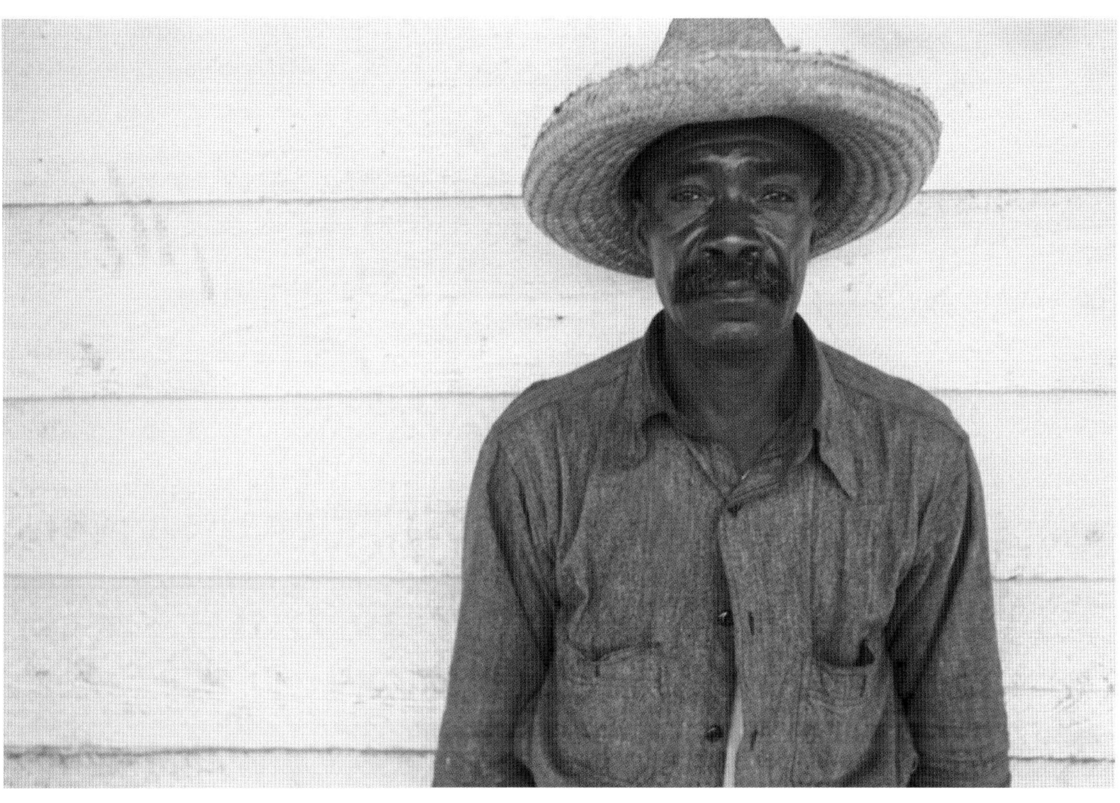

The photographer Ben Shahn identified this man as a sharecropper living in the Ozark Mountains. This is unlikely as sharecropping was common in the Delta region but not on small hill farms. Shahn may have been confused by the terminology around sharecropping and tenancy.

(Ben Shahn, October 1935) Farm Security Administration Photograph Collection, Prints & Photographs Division, Library of Congress, LC-USF33–006163–M3

Tenancy became part of the larger social and economic order in southern life throughout the first decades of the twentieth century. The conflicts arising from the vastly different interests of landowners and laborers and which involved issues of race and class, hardened into political divisions in the 1930s. They coalesced around the two naturally opposing groups: the large farm operations allied with the powerful American Farm Bureau Federation, and the poor farmers, tenants, and sharecroppers who had drawn the attention of certain New Deal agency administrators. These deeply held racial and class animosities would underlie political struggles that continued throughout the financial strains of the Depression years.

As plunging farm commodity prices wreaked havoc on farmers in the 1920s and early 1930s, a series of natural disasters struck Arkansas beginning with a flood that inundated the Mississippi and Ohio river valleys in 1927. Donald Holley in *Uncle Sam's Farmers* describes the devastation in eastern Arkansas as catastrophic. Muddy waters covered 4.3 million acres of the state, forced 40,000 people from their homes, and caused nearly 15 million dollars of property damage. The flood was followed by the killer drought of 1930–1931 and the dust storms that began in 1933 to sweep across the plains from the Texas and Oklahoma panhandles north to the Dakotas.

In Arkansas record-setting heat and dry weather destroyed crops as well as the home gardens that farm families grew to provide their food for the coming year. By the winter of 1930–1931, one-third of the Arkansas population—more than 600,000—faced starvation. One day in January 1931 a group of Lonoke County farmers converged on England, Arkansas, demanding food for their hungry families. To avert a rebellion, merchants opened their doors to the farmers, after being assured of reimbursement by the Red Cross. The event, known as the "England Food Riot," drew national attention, as did similar demonstrations in Iowa and other farming regions across the country. The crisis in agriculture compounded the financial chaos facing the nation as it approached the presidential election of 1932.

Roosevelt, Farm Policy, and Rexford Tugwell

Franklin Roosevelt began his 1932 campaign for the presidency on the Democratic ticket by assembling a team of advisers to develop a strategy for addressing the mounting desperation over the country's economic crisis. Among his core think-tank experts on agricultural policy was a young economics professor from Columbia University named Rexford G. Tugwell, who shared much of Roosevelt's outlook on the economy. When Roosevelt was elected as the thirty-second president, Tugwell joined the administration as undersecretary in the Department of Agriculture where he became one of the major architects of the New Deal farm program—including the agency that was eventually home to the FSA photography project.

The New Deal programs Tugwell advocated were driven by his economic philosophy that favored central planning by the government. To Tugwell, the Depression represented an unbalanced economy that could be righted by instituting a system of government controls and planning, according to Paul Conkin. In *Tomorrow a New World: The New Deal Community Program*, Conkin explains that Tugwell viewed American political and economic traditions as outdated, "rooted in [a] past of rural values, in individualism and independence" that no longer served a nation in the modern era of manufacturing growth and the development of a mass society. He believed that uncontrolled capitalism had glorified achievement and damaged the US economy through its constant competitive drive. The "unscrupulous few" had profited at the expense of the many, dividing rather than unifying American society and exploiting both human and natural resources in the ever striving to achieve.

Tugwell concluded the resulting unequal distribution of income had contributed significantly to the Depression. While wealth was concentrated in the hands of the few, too many people, including poor farmers, lacked purchasing power to buy the manufactured goods produced by expanding American industries, leading to surpluses that undercut industrial progress. Resolving this imbalance required a new, updated approach that called for a complete turn-around of the situation, putting money in the pockets of poor farmers to convert them into consumers, reversing the exploitation of water and land, and creating a more egalitarian society. This meant favoring agricultural programs that provided relief and rehabilitation to poor farmers, tenants, and sharecroppers, a position that in effect challenged the tenancy system and would make enemies for Tugwell of large landowners as well as the Farm Bureau, at both its national and state levels. Through his appointment in the Department of Agriculture and his relationship with Roosevelt, he held a choice position for influencing the administration's farm policies.

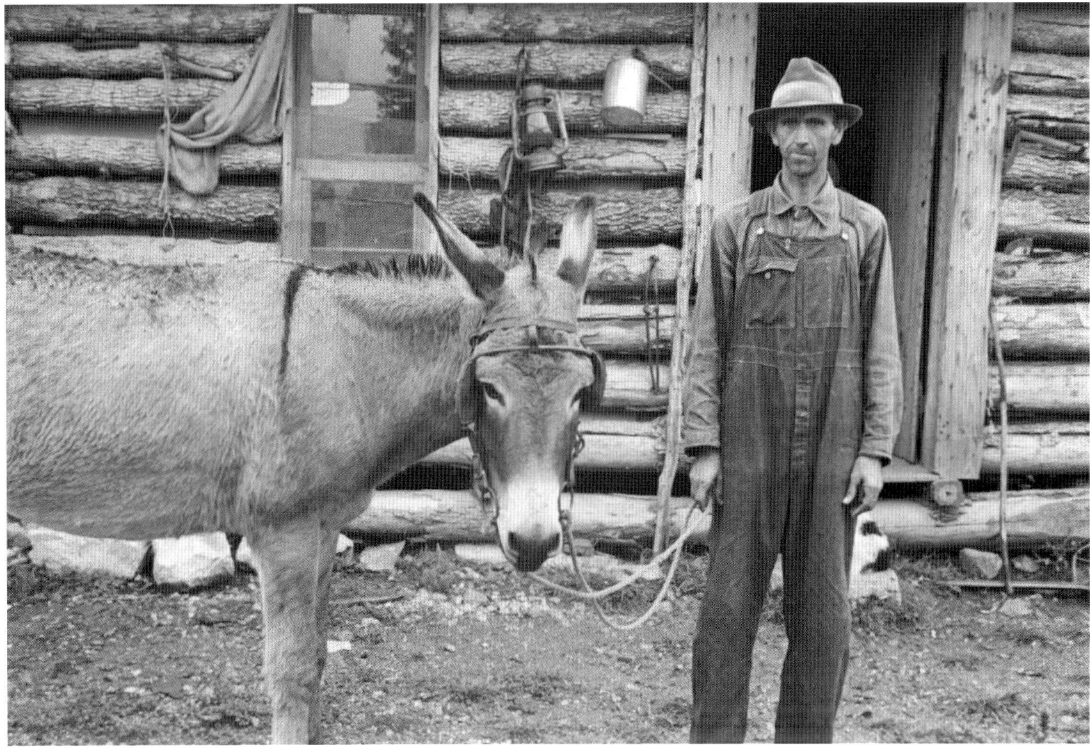

The series of photos Shahn took of this rehabilitation client with his family's cabin in Boone County suggests they were relatively better off than many others. They have a mule, the cabin's windows are covered, and the property seems to be in good condition.

(Ben Shahn, October 1935) Farm Security Administration Photograph Collection, Prints & Photographs Division, Library of Congress, LC-USF33–006033–M4

Roosevelt took office on March 4, 1933, and immediately pushed for a farm bill that created the Agricultural Adjustment Administration (AAA). According to Keith Volanto, forecasts predicted dropping cotton prices that spring, to a level below the 1932 disastrously low rates of 6.1 cents a pound. Volanto points out in "The AAA Cotton Plow-Up Campaign in Arkansas" (*Arkansas Historical Quarterly*) that falling cotton prices would ripple through the economy of Arkansas, affecting everybody connected to the cotton trade. The goal of the AAA was to prevent this blow to the economy by stabilizing prices. It would limit production of certain commodity crops, such as cotton, thus creating a false scarcity that would drive up prices. Government contracts would guarantee subsidies to farmers who volunteered to limit cotton cultivation by planting fewer acres.

The legislation moved slowly through Congress, however, and Roosevelt didn't sign the bill until May 12. According to Volanto, farmers who couldn't wait for the government to act had gone ahead with spring planting, crops had come up, and the growing season had begun. AAA officials realized that to make their price-stabilization plan work, they would have to reduce production by persuading cotton growers to destroy crops. They announced a campaign to pay farmers to plow up from 25 to 40 percent of their cotton acreage. Land that wasn't used for cotton could be planted in other crops that weren't sold on the open market. The government assigned Arkansas a plow-up target of roughly 1 million acres

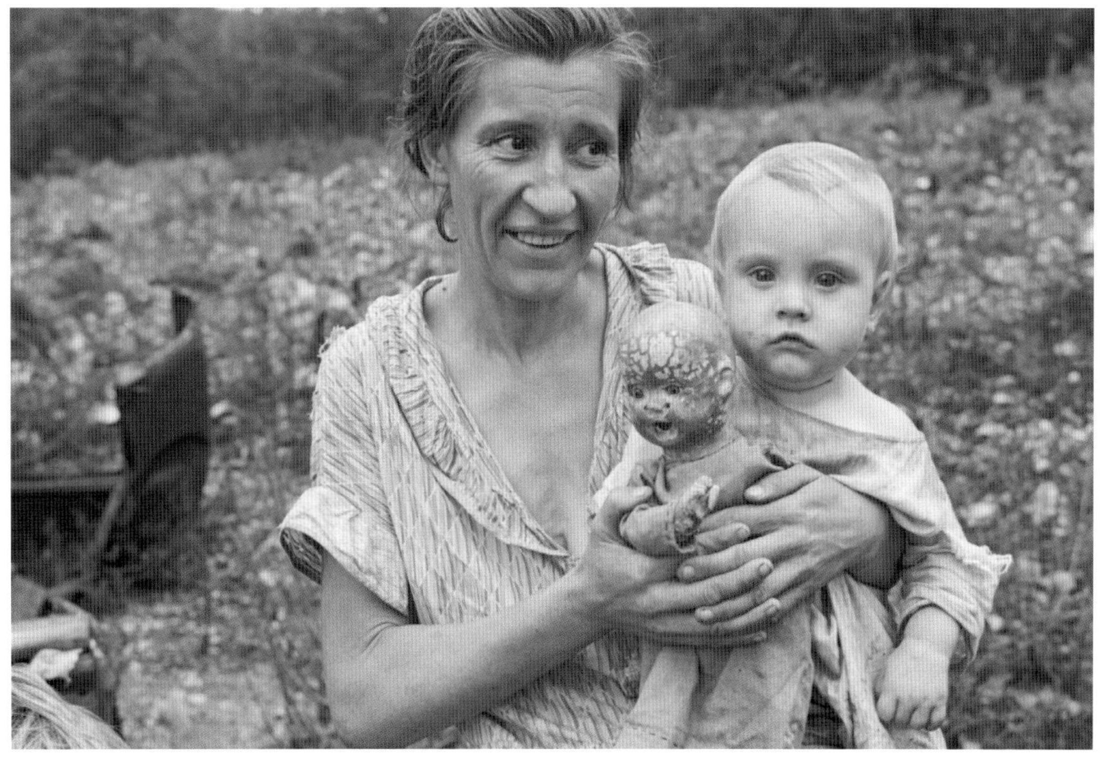

Shahn's "portraits" of three members of a sharecropper family—mother, child, and doll.

(Ben Shahn, October 1935) Farm Security Administration Photograph Collection, Prints & Photographs Division, Library of Congress, LC-USF33–006032–M1

out of the 3,341,000 planted in cotton that spring. Eventually, 97,000 Arkansas farmers agreed to destroy about 930,000 acres.

The AAA's plow-up campaign worked; the price of cotton stabilized at 10 cents a pound by the end of 1933. Volanto reports that the government paid tens of thousands of Arkansas cotton farmers $10.8 million under the plan, bringing them needed relief and optimism about the new administration's ability to fix the economy.

Not everyone was pleased with the way things worked out, however. Tenants and sharecroppers complained that they were treated unfairly, a situation that Jeannie Whayne addresses in *A New Plantation South*. Crop reduction and the plow-up had left tenants and sharecroppers without crops to tend and therefore no income. Though the law required large farm operators to pass along a portion of the production control subsidies to their tenant workers, many reneged and held on to all of the payments. Moreover, the crops landowners planted instead of cotton were often less labor intensive, requiring fewer workers. All of these factors, along with the increasing mechanization on large farms, signaled a significant transformation had begun in labor needs on large farms. Planters who had depended on tenants and sharecroppers' labor in cotton fields were less reliant on tenancy and more open to wage labor. With less land to farm, landowners began evicting tenant families whom they no longer needed.

In the Lower Mississippi Valley, including the Arkansas Delta, the plight of these evicted tenants and sharecroppers became desperate. The resulting outrage overrode long-standing racial antagonisms and spurred African American and white tenants and sharecroppers to unite in organizing a union. In July 1934 in Tyronza, Arkansas, the interracial Southern Tenant Farmers Union (STFU) was founded with the goals of halting the evictions if possible and gaining some leverage with the landlords, according to Whayne. Within eighteen months, membership in the union had grown to about thirty thousand in

Arkansas, Oklahoma, Texas, Missouri, Mississippi, and Tennessee, and the STFU had organized a cotton workers strike for better wages. The union movement was met with violence from eastern Arkansas landowners who struck back against the STFU by harassing and even killing members. Some STFU farmers fled Arkansas to relocate on the Hillhouse cooperative farm in Mississippi, where government photographs by Dorothea Lange show them making a new home for themselves.

By the spring of 1935 the conflict between landowners and tenants and sharecroppers in eastern Arkansas had grown to such a degree of intensity that the *New York Times* sent a reporter to investigate the matter. In April, F. Raymond Daniell produced a five-part series detailing the role of the AAA in the controversy and its effect on the "Meager Incomes" of "Share Croppers," the evictions, and the landowners' actions to "Foment Trouble to Eliminate Any Attempts at Unionism."

The Agricultural Adjustment Act did steady crop prices, but instead of helping all farmers, it primarily benefited the wealthy and displaced the poorest ones, contributing to evictions and the formation of the STFU. Tugwell, frustrated by the AAA's failure on behalf of poor farmers, proposed a new agency that would focus specifically on assistance programs for rural poverty. Roosevelt responded by creating the Resettlement Administration (RA) independent of the Department of Agriculture, generously funding it and appointing Tugwell as its director. In using an executive order, he bypassed the need for congressional approval and gave Tugwell the position and power to try his ideas for agricultural reform. However, angry opposition to the RA from entrenched large farm interests and their congressional representatives led to Tugwell's resignation and the RA's demise within two and a half years.

The Resettlement Administration

The clash was fundamentally about the philosophy and issues of class and power at the national and local levels; it played out as a conflict over federal funding to assist farming and who deserved it—the wealthy whose prosperity was a mark of their merit, or the poor who were starving and desperate for help. Tugwell explained to an interviewer in 1965 that in his view, a poor man should not automatically be held responsible for his condition. "There was always a reason why a man was poor," he told Richard Doud, a historian for the Smithsonian's Archives of American Art.

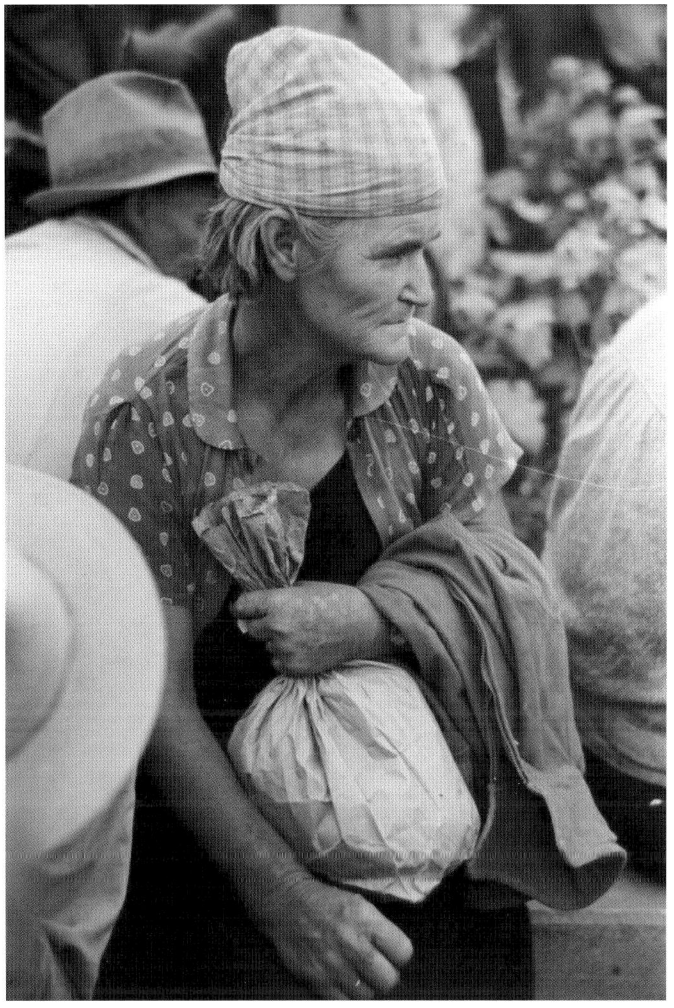

Day laborers, such as this woman, could get a job as an extra fieldhand during cotton-picking season. She worked on the Lake Dick resettlement project where she was paid by the day according to the amount of cotton she picked.

(Russell Lee, September 1938) Farm Security Administration Photograph Collection, Prints & Photographs Division, Library of Congress, LC-USF33–011683–M2

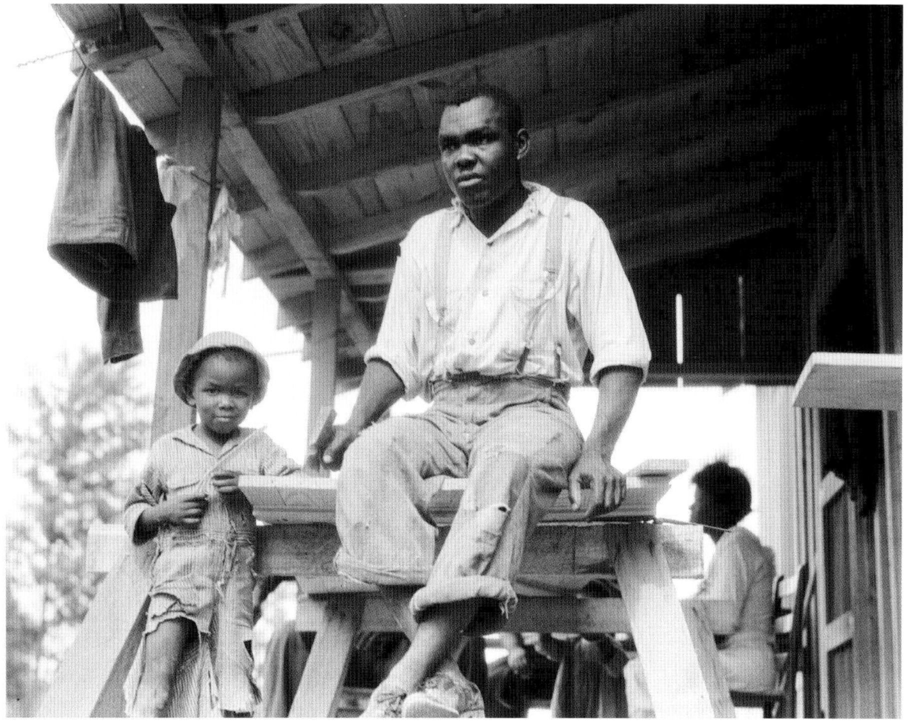

This former Arkansas sharecropper was evicted for his activity with the Southern Tenant Farmers Union. Like other Arkansas STFU members who were harassed, he fled to the Hillhouse settlement in Mississippi and built a new home.

(Dorothea Lange, July 1936) Farm Security Administration Photograph Collection, Prints & Photographs Division, Library of Congress, LC-USF34–009549–C

Perhaps he was "poor human material," but more often it was because of drought or difficulties with the land, such as erosion, or "his land perhaps had worn out."

Tugwell's belief that poor farmers were worthy and deserved assistance directly contradicted the perspective of the farm organizations and the most prosperous farmers, who saw them as unworthy and indolent. "They said these were shiftless people and they don't deserve anything," Tugwell explained to Doud. "[W]hat do you do things for them for? If you want to do anything for people, do it for us. They wanted all the help there was going. This was our worst trouble."

Tugwell sought two fundamental purposes with the RA programs, reform the agricultural system and rehabilitate farmers, according to Paul Conkin in *Tomorrow a New World*. Reforming agriculture meant "rearrangement": remove poor farmers from submarginal land where they couldn't make a living and resettle them on good, productive land that offered them a chance of success. Land that was no good for farming could be converted for other uses, such as forests or recreation. Such a substantial effort, based on Tugwell's ideas of central control and planning, would require time to accomplish and would be expensive. The rehabilitation and rural assistance programs, however, were designed to take effect much more quickly. They were aimed at a much broader target of poor farmers, tenants, and sharecroppers and intended to provide immediate relief by putting money in farmers' pockets at once through a system of loans, grants, and debt-adjustment arrangements.

From the beginning, the RA ran into problems—opposition from large, prosperous farmers and their representatives in Congress, as well as in-house management issues and even lawsuits. The job of dealing with the controversies and promoting the RA programs fell to its Division of Information, which prepared and distributed information on the agency's work. By the 1930s, federal agencies were increasingly using "government publicity men," in-house specialists in preparing reports for the press and others, as described in a study published in 1939 by James McCamy (*Government Publicity: Its Practices in Federal Administration*). The RA's Division of Information therefore was responsible for presenting Tugwell's programs to serve the disadvantaged to the public, to the large farm interests, and to Congress. This meant making the case about the rural poverty crisis and justifying government spending on the poor.

Rural resettlement, which relocated poor farm families to better, more productive land, was the most controversial program in the RA. The new resettlement farms included individual, "scattered" units and projects referred to as farm "communities" comprised of clusters of adjacent tracts of land. According to Conkin, a typical farm community was in the South, and might include one hundred or fewer separate farm units, settled by either African American or white tenants, but not both. Farms ranged from forty to one hundred acres and included a house, usually wood-frame construction with three to five rooms, some with indoor plumbing and electricity. The government bought the land and built the farms, leasing them to the resettled farmers; resident government administrators supervised each farm project. The "community" atmosphere was served by public facilities such as a general store, a school, a cotton gin, and various enterprises that required collaboration by the project's farmers.

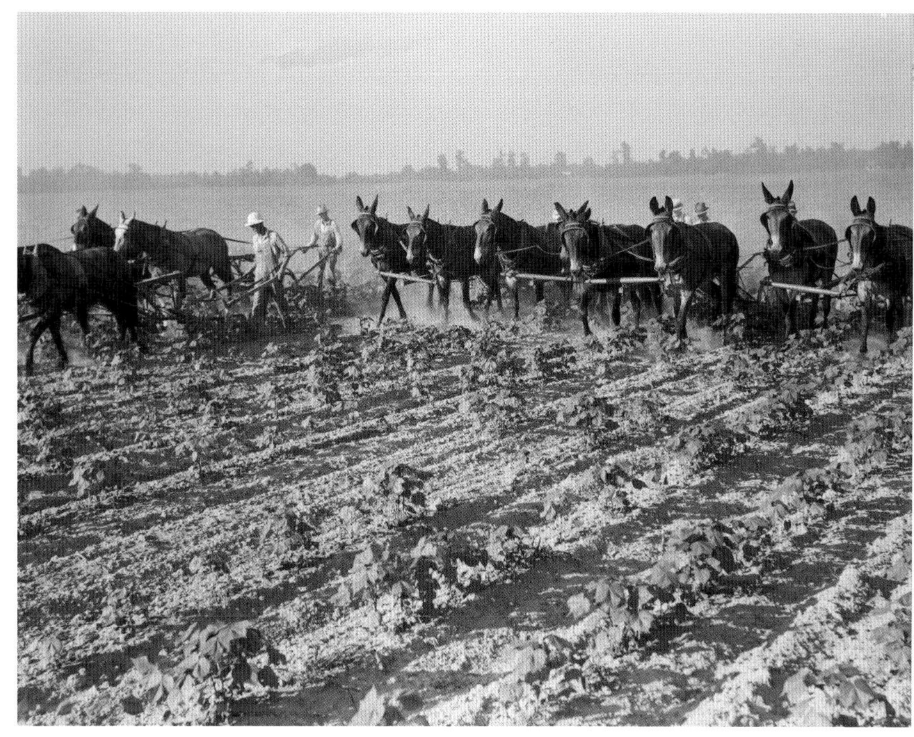

Farmers at the Lake Dick resettlement project use mule teams to cultivate a field. Lake Dick was one of the few resettlement farm projects run as a cooperative where members shared in the work and in the profits when produce was sold.

(Dorothea Lange, June 1938) Farm Security Administration Photograph Collection, Prints & Photographs Division, Library of Congress, LC-USF34–018161–C

Two issues were most significant in the controversy over the resettlement farms, their expense and the operation of some farms as cooperatives. Purchasing land, building new farms, and relocating settlers cost the government millions of dollars. Though the RA argued that the funds would be recouped when settlers eventually bought the farms, the government never made back the investment and took a heavy loss. A select few of the farms, including Lake Dick in Arkansas, were organized as cooperatives where farmers shared the land, the labor, and the profits. They worked fields side by side as well as managing a dairy and other enterprises that brought income to the settlement. To critics, especially in Congress, this was collectivism and "communistic."

Out of two hundred farm resettlement projects nationwide, sixteen were located in Arkansas and involved approximately fourteen hundred new farms. This was the largest number of resettlement projects situated in any one state, according to Donald Holley in *Uncle Sam's Farmers*. Five of the Arkansas farm projects were documented in the photo project: Chicot Farms (Chicot and Drew counties), Dyess

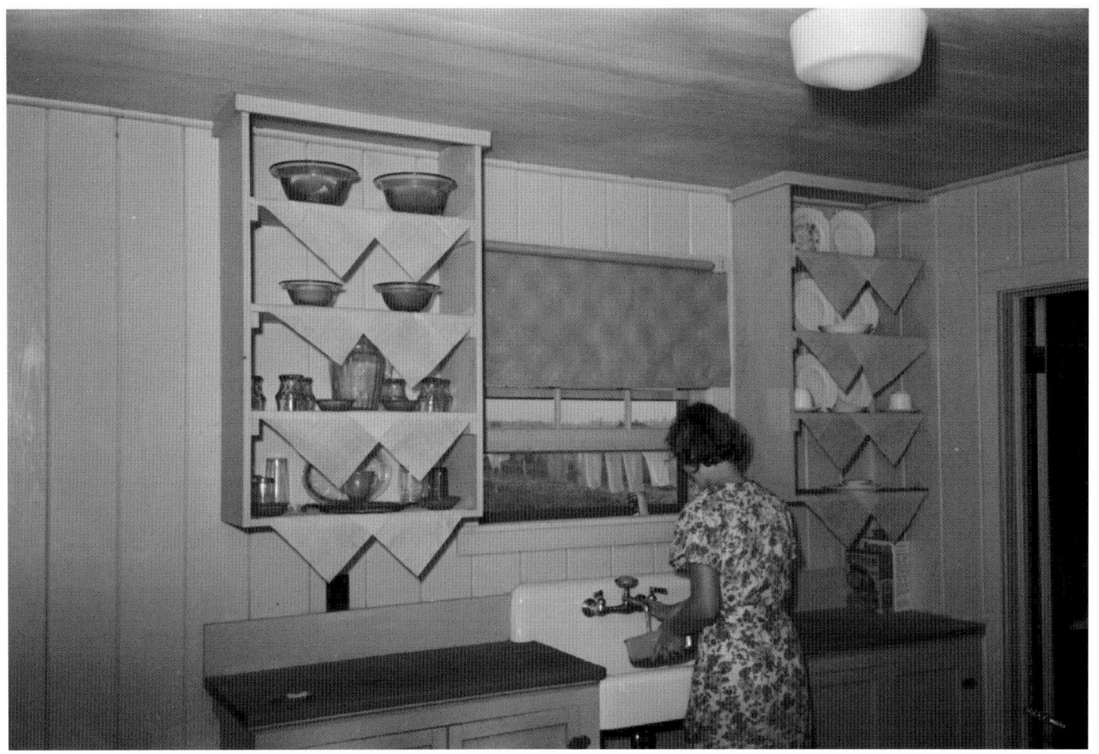

The photograph clearly was taken to show some of the amenities built into this farmhouse kitchen on the Lake Dick resettlement project—the running water in the sink and the electric light in the ceiling. The decoration on the shelves was likely added by the farmwife.

(Russell Lee, September 1938) Farm Security Administration Photograph Collection, Prints & Photographs Division, Library of Congress, LC-USF33–011665–M4

Colony (Mississippi County), Lake Dick (Jefferson County), Lakeview (Phillips County), and Plum Bayou (Jefferson County). The Dyess Colony was the first in the state, developed in 1934 under an early federal subsistence program, and was intended to resettle five hundred farm families. Named for Arkansas politician William R. Dyess, it is perhaps best known now as the home of country music legend Johnny Cash and his family, who were among the early resettled families.

The purpose behind the resettlement projects went beyond the farm families' economic rehabilitation, however. Conkin reports that they were planned to be "demonstration[s] of a better type of rural life." By placing these families in comfortable and secure living conditions with the prospects of improving their financial situation, and training them to better manage their affairs, the government's goal was to change their attitudes, ambitions, and behaviors in order to raise their level of sophistication and sense of class expectations. No matter how well meaning the idea may have seemed, its effort at social control went much too far for some settlers.

Resettlement generated a number of controversies involving its expense, legal challenges, management problems, settlers' dissatisfactions, and accusations of collectivism and communism. Congressmen, representing the interests of large farm owners and the powerful American Farm Bureau Federation, vigorously criticized resettlement and the RA as a whole, turning the agency into an issue in the election of 1936. By the end of that year, the RA was dismantled and Tugwell resigned. Nine months later, in September 1937, the government created the Farm Security Administration (FSA), assigning it to oversee essentially the same programs begun by the RA albeit with some changes.

Though Congress had opposed many of the provisions in the RA, the government had come to recognize that tenancy was a serious issue requiring attention. The FSA was established therefore with directions to continue in completing resettlement projects but forbidden from beginning new ones; it also included a tenant purchase program that offered long purchase terms. Like many federal programs to aid poor farmers, however, it was limited by its availability only to tenants with specific qualifications, which excluded those who were poorest and neediest.

Tugwell's RA challenged the large farm operators and their interests by providing major government funding assistance to poor farmers. By offering alternatives to this disadvantaged group, the agency essentially undercut the tenancy system and threatened the ready availability of cheap labor to landowners, who had little concern for the welfare of tenants, sharecroppers, and small farmers. In addition, Tugwell's ideas were "anathema" to landowners, according to Conkin. They represented the antithesis of the traditional myth of the American farmer and his individualism, whose success depended on the strength of his own merit and his staunch independence. To those who opposed him, Tugwell's approach was dangerously socialistic; by using government controls he intended to change the balance in society, to equalize the divisions created by wealth and class.

The FSA, Roy Stryker, and the Photography Project

In developing the structure of the RA in 1935, Tugwell had paid particular attention to the Division of Information and especially to one of its branches called the Historical Section. This modest office was charged with copying documents and compiling a historical record of RA activities, including photographs that might be supplied to the press and others. In a step that led eventually to the creation of the Farm Security Administration Photography Project, Tugwell appointed Roy E. Stryker, his former graduate assistant at Columbia, as head of the section.

As an economics instructor at Columbia, Tugwell had packed his lectures with graphs and photographs, having found that visual examples of abstract ideas at work helped students understand unfamiliar material more easily. Consequently, when he wrote an economics textbook, Tugwell wanted lots of illustrations and hired Stryker to help him find pictures. Stryker shared a confidence in the communication potential of photographs with Tugwell, and became particularly adept at spotting images that were effective in expressing just the right message—a skill he was to apply to great effect in his job with the Historical Section. No doubt this was Tugwell's intention in hiring Stryker for a job where he might develop photography into a larger part of the information division's promotional operation.

Stories vary in explaining how Stryker transformed the Historical Section into a collection of 250,000 photographs, but all agree that Stryker was an energetic entrepreneur who had an eye for opportunities to expand the photographic work of his office amid the chaos and excitement of organizing a new federal agency. He was a likable, talkative, and friendly fellow, curious about everything and everybody, and intensely interested in photography. Though not a photographer himself, he believed that pictures could be powerful instruments of information. Through good fortune, his own assertiveness, and Tugwell's support, Stryker within weeks redirected the section from copying documents into a photo service for the RA with its own staff of photographers.

Stryker led the Historical Section for eight years (1935–1943), developing its role as a resource for photos rather than for copying documents. By the time the section was absorbed by the Office of War Information after the US entry into World War II, the file had become enormous and covered not only government projects but also rural life, farming, mining, migrants, small towns, and life in cities such as Chicago and New York.

According to the Library of Congress, most of the images were taken by a core group of sixteen photographers, with contributions from as many as seventy-six others. Funding for the RA/FSA was often a political battle, so the photo staff size periodically went up and down, depending on the budget for the agency. The photographer Russell Lee recalled that Stryker usually had ten or twelve photographers on staff, but at times as few as two.

The job paid a salary of about $500 a month, plus $5 per diem and 5 cents a mile when photographers were on the road, which they were most of the time. Their specific assignments came from photo requests by federal agencies as well as the press. However, as Stryker evolved his own idea about what the photo file might become, he began suggesting photo topics. He envisioned the photo file as developing into a fuller record of American life during the Depression years, a documentation of its transformation from a nation of farmers into the modern, urban state. Sensing a personal nostalgia for the small-town life that he saw fading away, Stryker enlisted the photographers in capturing it on film; he gave them lists of images to look for in the towns they visited while on assignments—signs in store windows, people visiting on street corners. Thus, as Stryker expanded the scope and nature of the photo file, it began to reflect a broader view of America.

The FSA Photographic Style

Other New Deal agencies had photo staffs and collections, but none has drawn the attention given the FSA photographs in the 1930s and in decades since for their distinctive quality in content and style. Numerous books and articles about the collection have examined every aspect of the photographs—their subjects, their style, and their evolution over the project's eight years; the emphasis adjusting to shifting political winds in Congress, the series of agency administrators who followed Tugwell, and to Stryker's own changing ideas about what the project might become. The consequences can be seen in the photographs themselves.

In the early years of the project under the RA (1935–1936), when Tugwell needed support to justify the agency, the photographs focused on problems of rural poverty and Tugwell's agenda of programs designed to solve them. He had told Stryker that photos were needed to educate the public, not only about the government's rural assistance efforts but also about the people they were created to help. Tugwell had said that the photos had a role, "to try to tell the rest of the world that here is a lower third, and that they are human beings like the rest of us." But in 1937 after Tugwell left and the FSA was created, the agenda changed and new leadership in the Division of Information shifted attention to a more positive, uplifting message, documenting the success of the government's programs in changing lives of the rural poor for the better.

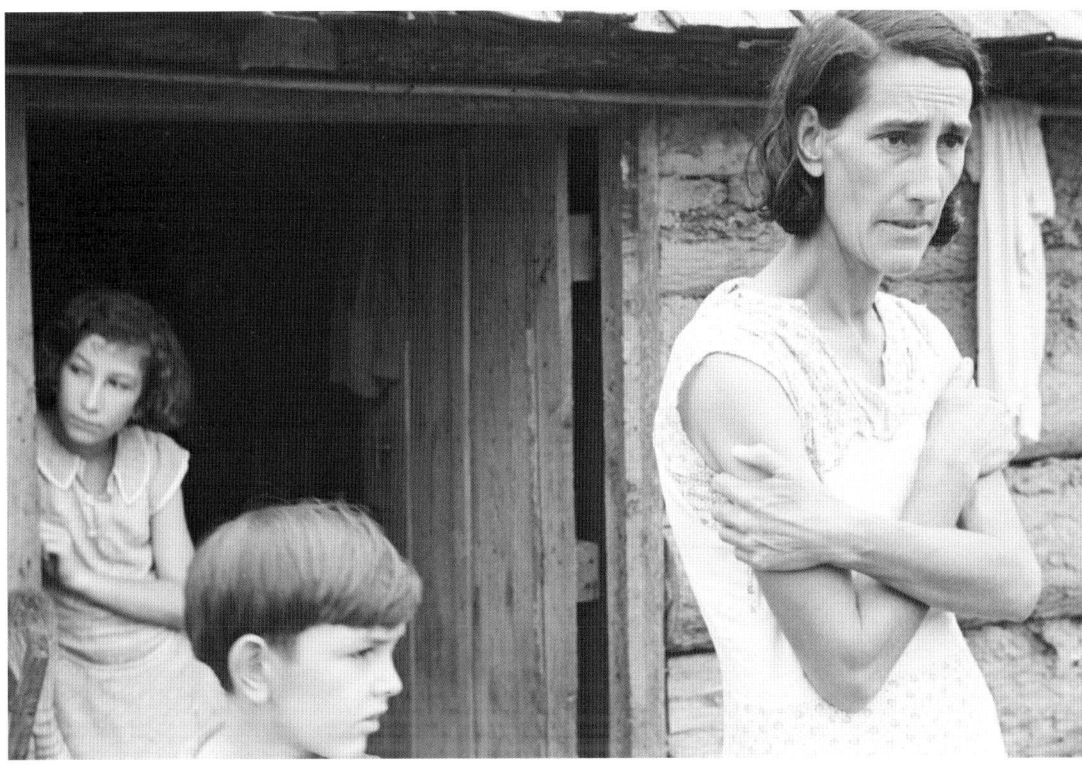

This Shahn photo of the family of a rehabilitation client is a good example of his unconventional approach to composition. Here he divides the photo frame almost in half with the mother "boxed in" to one side and the children positioned against the darkness of the doorway.

(Ben Shahn, October 1935) Farm Security Administration Photograph Collection, Prints & Photographs Division, Library of Congress, LC-USF33–006035–M4

Despite the public information efforts by the RA and FSA, it's difficult to know whether the photos had any impact on Americans' opinions in the 1930s and how widespread that impact might have been. Cara Finnegan in her book *Picturing Poverty* pointed out that newspapers published the project photos only occasionally, and *Life* and *Look*, the major photo magazines that began in the 1930s, rarely ran them. They were used more often by small, special-interest magazines, such as the *Survey Graphic*, and in traveling exhibits sponsored by the government. Edwin Rosskam, an editor with the Historical Section, estimated that out of the quarter million FSA photos, perhaps only 10 percent were ever published or seen by the public. Of those 25,000, the pictures most often associated with the FSA collection and its photographic style in documenting poverty would number even fewer.

The public did have one specific opportunity to give direct feedback on RA/FSA photos, however—the First International Photographic Exposition held in New York in 1938. Over the course of a week, more than one hundred thousand people viewed the show of about three thousand photographs from all genres, as John Raeburn writes in *A Staggering Revolution: A Cultural History of Thirties Photography*. Critics, reporters, and other photographers praised the selection of FSA photos included in the exposition, but more interesting were the handwritten comments from nearly five hundred viewers. The 1939 *U.S. Camera Annual* published seventy-one of the comments. Some viewers' notes were more political—observations such as "Portrayal of life as it is!" and "Subversive propaganda." Others were empathetic: "Touched me to the point where I would like to quit everything in order to help these stricken people . . ." and "Why the hell isn't something done about it?" Raeburn, however, sums up the comments, noting that while some were disparaging, most viewers admired the "esthetic distinction" of the photos and claimed they were the highlight of the exposition.

Understanding this "FSA style" is key to appreciating the photos. It has been described as straightforward and direct, yet personal in the depiction of the poor and downtrodden; a mix of factual photography with a sense of social responsibility and individual artistic sensibility. Edwin Rosskam, Stryker's assistant, offered a clue to the approach in his explanation that photographers knew their job was to produce "visual evidence," depictions of the social conditions targeted by the RA. That is, they focused on visible facts, but facts selected with a purpose. As Raeburn notes, indications were that Stryker and his staff were on board with the reform goals of the RA, sharing a belief "that their work could help foster social renewal." Dorothea Lange expressed it as a sense of "social consciousness" in an interview with Richard Doud. The staff might play down the artistic reputation of the FSA photos, but the pictures' undeniable esthetic strength made a powerful case in their submission to editors.

Historically, only two principal photographers had focused on poverty as a social issue before the Depression. Jack Hurley wrote that Stryker, in his work for Tugwell at Columbia University, had become familiar with Jacob Riis's photographs of immigrants in New York slums in the late 1800s, and Lewis Hine's pictures of child labor in factories in the early 1900s. His admiration for Hine's style and his sensitivity to his subjects no doubt affected the way Stryker thought about the photo project. Hine's approach can be seen in the best of the FSA photos—in their combination of artistry with an awareness of social problems—and contributed to their powerful resonance with Americans over decades. The Smithsonian historian Richard Doud, who interviewed many of the FSA photographers in the 1960s, labeled this group of photographs the "immortal pictures."

Stryker encouraged this style through a collaborative relationship with the photographers on his staff, discussing photographs with them, trading ideas. Based on Raeburn's book, Stryker's comments to Jack Hurley, and Richard Doud's interviews with photographers, these conversations were about the directions they should take in the photographs—what and how they should photograph—in order to promote the goals of the RA. Stryker claimed their focus was not on the "art" of their work but on its social meaning and on the strict technical quality standards that he set for FSA photos.

In the development of the FSA style, Stryker was also very fortunate in the remarkable talent of the FSA photographers, especially those who contributed the earliest photos to the Historical Section—Arthur Rothstein, Walker Evans, Ben Shahn, and Dorothea Lange. Stryker provided general oversight and direction while allowing them wide latitude to use their own creative vision in the field. In turn he demanded that they understand the mechanical issues of photography and submit technically flawless pictures, and that they study and thoroughly know the subjects they covered. To give photographers a sense of the scope and tone needed in the assignments, he gave them reading material, compiled lists of photo possibilities (known as "shooting scripts"), and kept up a voluminous correspondence with them while they were on the road—sometimes for two or three months at a time—checking on them, sending reminders, and offering encouragement.

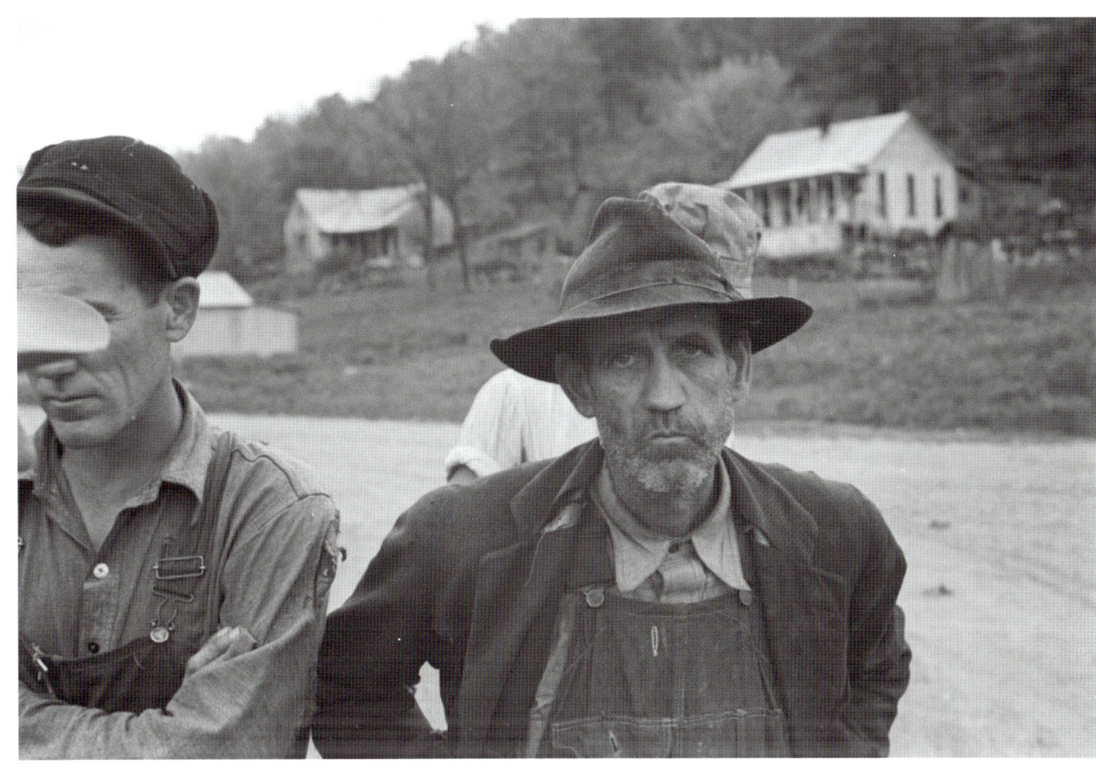

This picture of a group of citizens from Zinc—described by Shahn as a "deserted mining town"—is usually cropped to focus specifically on the man looking directly into the camera.

(Ben Shahn, October 1935) Farm Security Administration Photograph Collection, Prints & Photographs Division, Library of Congress, LC-USF33–006036–M5

Beverly Brannan, curator of twentieth-century documentary photography at the Library of Congress, proposed that the nature of the job—"photographing people living in difficult circumstances, while trying to understand and explain the crisis"—shaped the nature of the FSA photographs. Dorothea Lange, among other FSA photographers, agreed. Lange, originally a portrait photographer on the West Coast, had independently started taking pictures of the migrant workers and families in California. She was invited to join the FSA project in 1935. Lange told Doud that in working alone in the field, she could often feel the weight of her role to help the public see through her pictures, the conditions that existed. She said Stryker made photographers feel that "what you were doing was important, . . . that you had a responsibility"—a feeling that deepened for photographers such as Shahn, Lange, and Russell Lee during their constant exposure to the conditions they found around the country.

This style of photographing poverty in a straightforward but sensitive manner was classified as "documentary," one of the variety of genres that developed with the introduction of new and inexpensive camera and printing technology in the early twentieth century and the explosion of international interest in photography. William Stott explained the genre in his study of *Documentary Expression in Thirties America*. He wrote that documentary photography went beyond the conventional definition of an objective presentation of facts, that would make a picture simply a historical record, evidence of how things looked at a particular time and place. The documentary photo could also be a "human" document, a record of the subject's personal experience that gave the picture an "emotional truth" as well, "a glimpse . . . of an inner existence." Thus, documentary photos could be understood both through the facts they pictured and through the feelings they generated. The photographer and historian Gilles Mora, in *FSA: The American Vision,* considered the sense of social responsibility the FSA photographers brought to the job and qualified the term, calling the FSA style "social documentary"; that is, a "bearing witness," factual approach combined with a social purpose.

Whatever the label and its definition, critics over the years have accused Stryker and the photographers of taking unfair advantage of viewers through emotional manipulation. The photographs were called propaganda beginning in the 1930s when the term was an insidious reference to the state-run information campaigns of communist Russia and Nazi Germany. Historians have pointed out, however, that at the time using such extreme language was often a strategy for indirectly attacking Roosevelt, and the photographers have always had their defenders. Hartley Howe, for example, wrote in *Survey Graphic* magazine in 1940 that the photo project was well within the limits of legitimate, government-sponsored publicity. Recent, more detached assessments of the photos by Michael Carlebach and Eugene Provenzo, have pointed out that though they were indeed government publicity, the images were unretouched and did depict real life.

African Americans and the Photograph Collection

Of all the specific assignments and photo suggestions made by Stryker, one subject was rarely if ever mentioned—the African Americans who were the very poorest of farm laborers. Though Stryker occasionally suggested photos of federal projects targeted at African Americans, more often ideas for these photo stories came from photographers such as Marion Post Wolcott, Russell Lee, Walker Evans, and Dorothea Lange. Stryker rarely approved them; these photos were just not useful to the section's work.

White newspapers and magazines were not interested in pictures of poor African Americans. Research has documented that the white press in the 1930s rarely ran photos of African Americans, and when it did, the images tended to be demeaning stereotypes. But there were requests for African American pictures from the black press, the thriving network of newspapers that served African

American communities around the nation in cities like Chicago, Memphis, New Orleans, Philadelphia, and San Francisco. Stryker did respond to those requests. Though he was likely as sensitive to race issues as many other individuals in the Roosevelt administration, he had to deal with political realities that affected the funding for the photo project. This meant avoiding anything that could attract negative attention and become politically explosive. And race was definitely a volatile issue in 1930s America.

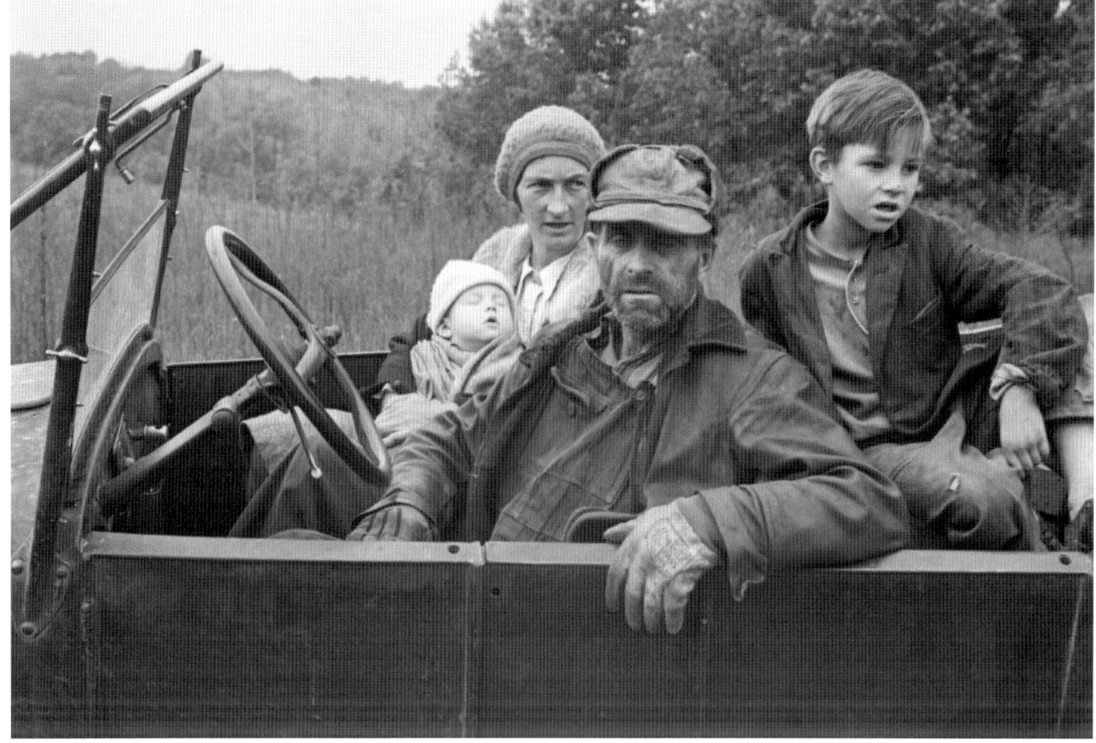

Shahn took a series of pictures of this family, which he labeled "destitute . . . Ozark Mountains area." This photo is among his better-known images from Arkansas.

(Ben Shahn, October 1935) Farm Security Administration Photograph Collection, Prints & Photographs Division, Library of Congress, LC-USF33–006071–M4

Most African Americans still lived in the South in 1930, where the power base—including large landowners—believed race to be a state issue. Influential southern congressmen such as Arkansas senator Joe T. Robinson adamantly contended that states' rights precluded federal interference in race issues. The political strength of these congressmen complicated any federal government effort on behalf of African Americans in the South, which was strictly segregated, highly prejudiccd, and opprcssivc for blacks. Lynching was still a menace, and disenfranchisement by poll tax, literacy tests, and intimidation kept them from developing any political power, according to Nancy Weiss in *Farewell to the Party of Lincoln*. African Americans were at the bottom of any economic, cultural, educational, or other standings and had limited prospects for advancement. Any move made by the Roosevelt administration to address racial equality issues—and jeopardize states' rights—would be met with threats to scuttle his New Deal legislation from Senator Robinson and other powerful southern congressmen.

The antilynching bill pushed by African American leaders at the beginning of Roosevelt's first term was just such an issue. Though African Americans had a long list of pressing concerns, the antilynching measure was at the top. Lynching was a racial terror perversity that had plagued the South since Reconstruction. In 2015, the Equal Justice Initiative counted more than 4,000 lynchings between 1877 and 1950 in twelve states of the old Confederacy. Leading all other counties in these states was Phillips

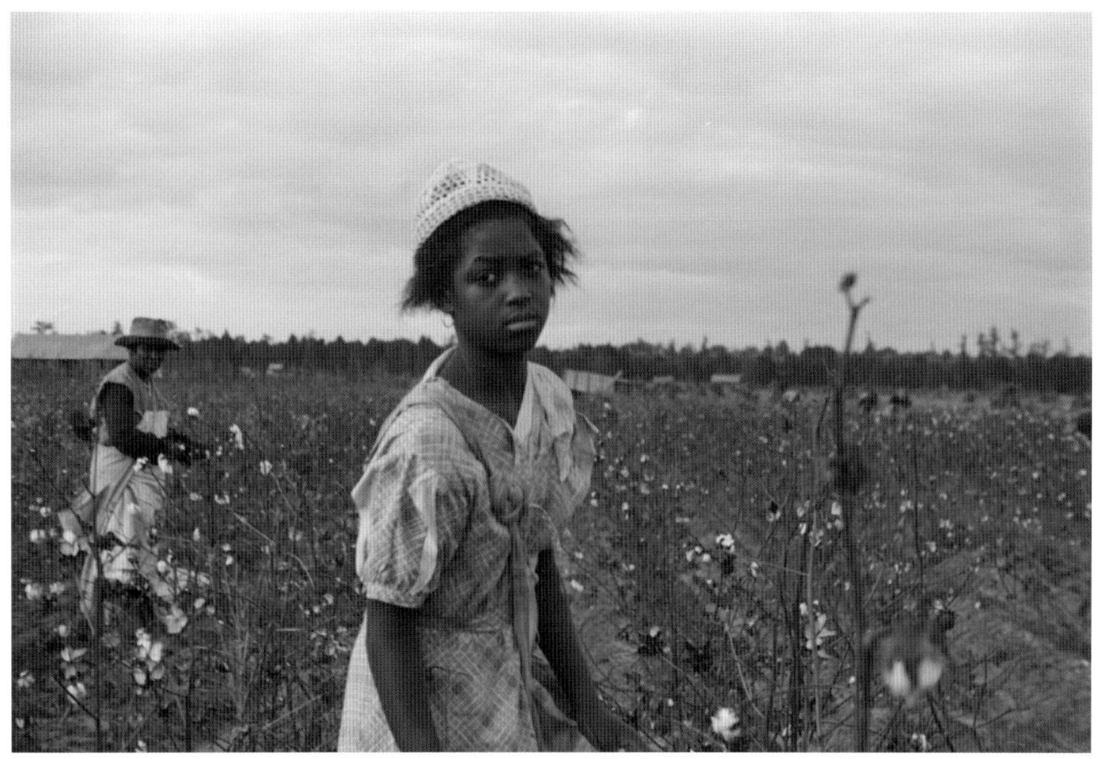

Shahn took a series of photos of this young girl as she picked cotton. He and other RA/FSA photographers emphasized the age range of fieldworkers.

(Ben Shahn, October 1935) Farm Security Administration Photograph Collection, Prints & Photographs Division, Library of Congress, LC-USF33–006218–M3

County, Arkansas, with 254 lynchings; in second place were two Louisiana parishes with 51 lynchings each. Weiss writes that from 1932 on, southern congressmen blocked every attempt to pass antilynching legislation on the basis that it would represent federal intervention in a state's right of local law enforcement. Roosevelt judiciously kept his distance from the proposed legislation despite intense efforts by African American leaders to lobby him.

He did try to secure coverage of rural African Americans under his New Deal by issuing an official pronouncement to forbid discrimination in farm assistance and work relief programs, according to Weiss. But there were plenty of loopholes in the administration of the programs. Decisions about who got assistance and how much were made at the local level by committees and boards whose members didn't hesitate to approve benefits to applicants based on the customary local prejudices. Therefore, African Americans in the South wound up getting the least and the lowest quality of relief. "[T]he administration of relief . . . could just as well be handled by the K.K.K," complained a 1933 letter to the editor of a prominent black newspaper, as quoted by Weiss.

African Americans knew they were getting less economic help than whites, but, as Weiss notes, the point for them was that they were at least getting something, and that kept many people from starving. Moreover, by not actively excluding African Americans from New Deal programs, Roosevelt appeared to be their benefactor. African American leaders may have been frustrated in their efforts to seek civil rights through legislation, but for the African Americans at the bottom, economic problems were more pressing than racial issues. According to Weiss, "The struggle to survive took precedence over the struggle for equality. And in the struggle to survive, many New Deal programs made a critical difference."

In 1930s Arkansas, more than a quarter of the population was African American (about half a million people). Six out of ten lived in rural areas, mostly in eastern counties in the cotton-growing

Mississippi Delta, center of slave ownership in the state before the Civil War. In 1860 there were nine thousand slaves living in Phillips County, according to M. Langley Biegart in the *Journal of Southern History*. Biegart describes a pattern of resistance that developed in central east Arkansas going back to the 1860s and continuing through efforts to unionize during Reconstruction, typically followed by violent suppression. Phillips County had been the site of the most violent racial conflict in the state's history in 1919, near the little town of Elaine. Grif Stockley in his 2001 book about the incident, *Blood in Their Eyes,* estimates that between 20 to 856 African Americans were killed following a shootout at a sharecroppers' union meeting. White mobs, possibly joined by US troops from Camp Pike, reportedly hunted down and slaughtered the African American farmers. The sharecroppers, in their effort to organize and seek a better deal from landowners, represented a threat to whites.

Fifteen years later in 1934, unionizing activity in the same region led farmers to found the interracial Southern Tenant Farmers Union in Tyronza, in Poinsett County about one hundred miles north of Elaine. The following year, as the STFU was organizing a cotton workers' strike, the first FSA photographers to visit Arkansas showed up—Arthur Rothstein in August and Ben Shahn in the fall. Shahn stopped briefly in Marked Tree, a small town about eight miles from Tyronza where confrontations between the union and landowners had driven up the tension. In these trips, he and Rothstein were responsible for shooting the earliest of roughly four hundred photographs of African Americans in the Arkansas FSA collection, images mainly of tenants, sharecroppers, and day laborers.

Years later Shahn recalled the racism toward African Americans that he encountered in Arkansas, extending even to staff members at the RA local and regional offices. In Pulaski County, he toured the area briefly with Senator Joe T. Robinson as well as local guides who appalled him with their crude language in referring to African Americans. Shahn was not one to shy away from confrontation, as is evident in photos he took in other states earlier in his trip. However, Nicholas Natanson observes in *The Black Image in the New Deal* that Shahn approached photographing Arkansas African Americans differently from his other work. Natanson credited Shahn with focusing on his subjects' individuality and giving them a "sense of self"— offering "subtle insights that challenged misleading assumptions on both the right and the left about African Americans."

Principal RA/FSA Photographers in Arkansas

Five photographers whose work has been mentioned in this introduction—Ben Shahn, Arthur Rothstein, Dorothea Lange, Walker Evans, and Russell Lee—took the majority of the FSA photos in Arkansas, as well as some of the best and most memorable. Richard Doud, the Smithsonian historian, interviewed all of these photographers except Walker Evans, and others have written books and articles

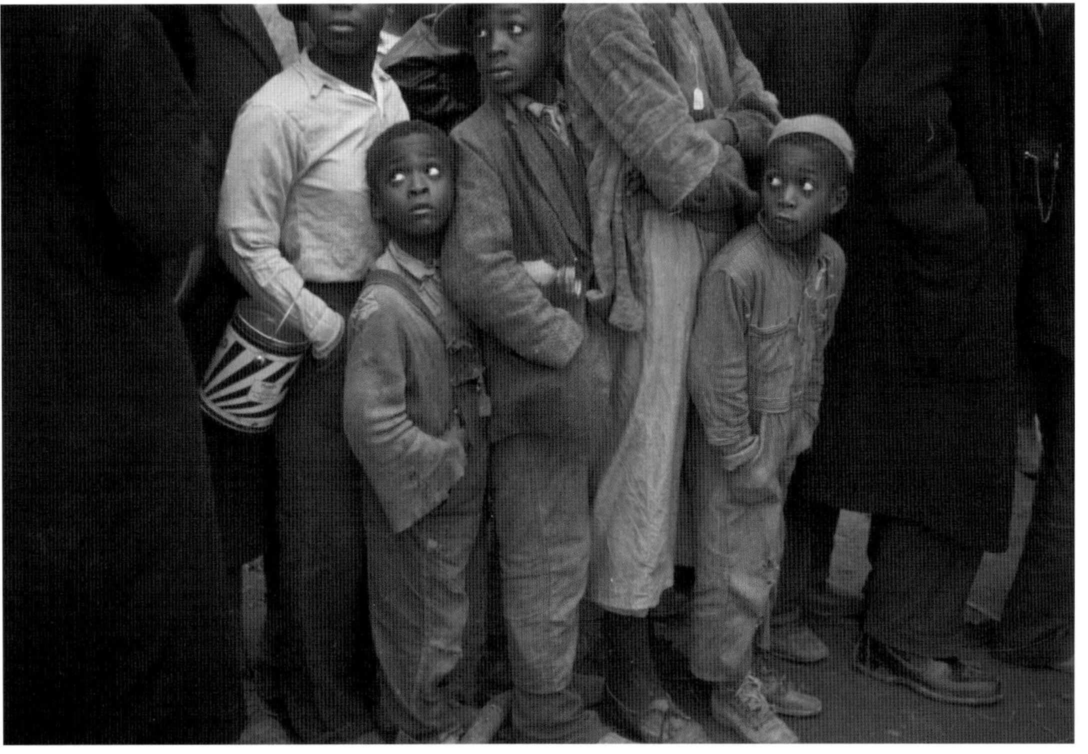

In the aftermath of the 1937 flood of the Mississippi and the Ohio rivers, the American Red Cross set up segregated camps in Arkansas for refugees. These children squeeze into a line of people waiting for one of the two daily meals served in the camp.

(Walker Evans, February 1937) Farm Security Administration Photograph Collection, Prints & Photographs Division, Library of Congress, LC-USF33–009231–M1

about their work during and after the FSA. Here is a brief look at their stories and their photography in Arkansas.

Ben Shahn is perhaps better known as an artist and printmaker than as a photographer. His 1935 trip through the South and into Arkansas was to gather material for the murals he had been hired to paint by the RA's Special Skills Division, and he used a camera as a kind of mechanical sketchpad. Stryker paid for Shahn's film and later included the photos in the FSA collection. To Shahn, who grew up in New York and studied art in Europe, the South was a "revelation," where his deep moral consciousness was offended by his impression of the exploitation of poor farmers. Though he contributed a small number of pictures to the collection, Shahn influenced its direction in conversations with Stryker. He told Doud that once, when Stryker admired a photo of eroded soil, Shahn explained to him that the picture would have little impact on viewers: "Look, Roy, you're not going to move anybody with this eroded soil—but the effect this eroded soil has on a kid who looks starved, this is going to move people."

On his trip through the South, Shahn took about 800 photos, of which 261 were in Arkansas. He stopped briefly in West Memphis and Marked Tree before moving on through Pulaski County and up to the Ozarks. In Pulaski County Shahn took a series of photos of African Americans picking cotton, gathering on a front porch on a day off and visiting outside church on Sunday. His Ozarks photos capture rehabilitation clients in front of log cabins, citizens of a deserted mining town, and a destitute family taking to the road in their old car.

Shahn used a small Leica camera with a right-angle viewfinder, which meant he could look in a different direction while taking a photo of someone. This no doubt contributed to the personal, unguarded moments he was able to catch in many of his portraits. But then, people and their predicaments were key to Shahn's pictures; a few images from the Arkansas photos do appear in his later paintings.

Arthur Rothstein visited Arkansas in August 1935, a month or so earlier than Shahn. He was the first photographer employed in the Historical Section, hired by Stryker to manage the photo lab and make copies of documents. Rothstein had been a premed student at Columbia, and the government job looked like a way to make money to pay for medical school while developing his hobby of photography. He was eager to escape the photo lab, though, and take photographs himself; the trip that took him through Arkansas was one of his first in the field. He took 119 pictures in the state—of Dyess Colony, the Plum Bayou resettlement farm, sharecroppers on plantations, and rehabilitation clients in the Ozarks—where he used a technique he described to Richard Doud as the "unobtrusive camera." By distracting people or hanging around until they forgot about him, Rothstein could take pictures that he felt gave him a more truthful image of them.

After World War II Rothstein became director of photography for *Look* magazine, but was also known for inadvertently causing a major public relations crisis for the RA. While on assignment in South Dakota in 1936, he took five shots of an old bleached cow skull on a parched alkali flat, repositioning the skull for lighting and different angles. A few months later, in the midst of an anti-Roosevelt political flap in the Dakotas, a local newspaper charged that Rothstein's photos were fake since he had moved the skull around. The story snowballed into accusations questioning the integrity of not only the photography project, but the whole RA agency. Jack Hurley wrote that though Stryker managed the crisis and was able to get retractions from a number of papers, people in the Midwest continued to associate the RA with "faked" photos for years.

Walker Evans is recognized as being perhaps the best of the FSA photographers, though after eighteen months with the Historical Section, he was fired—mainly for his low productivity in a federal agency that had to justify its budget in terms of quantity. Born in Missouri and educated on the East Coast, Evans's evolution as a photographer occurred in Paris in the 1920s where he was heavily influenced by Eugene Atget's hundreds of photos taken to document Paris in the late 1800s.

Evans's approach differed from other FSA photographers. His pictures were suffused less with a sense of social consciousness and more with the goal of creating a visual documentation of America—much as Atget had done in Paris. The photos often did not include people but instead showed the evidence of their lives through details of their environment. Where other FSA photographers looked for the candid shot—the revealing, authentic moment—Evans, according to William Stott, did not "glimpse but frankly, interminably, stare." Evans was deliberate in framing his photos, taking time and producing sharp, technically excellent images, which Stott called a "cool disquieting vision of America."

Evans's Arkansas photos do show a sensitivity to human suffering, though. In February of 1937 he

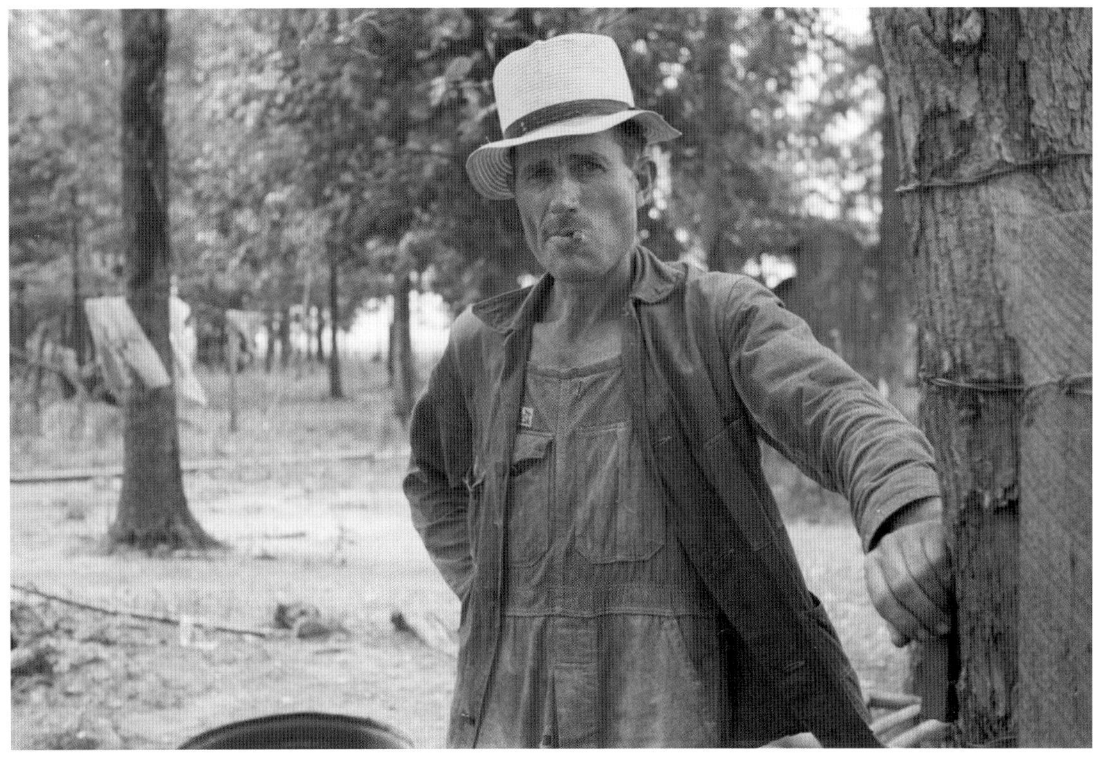

Arthur Rothstein took this photo of a sharecropper on the Wilson plantation. Though most sharecroppers in the 1800s were African American, by the early 1900s the number of white sharecroppers was increasing.

(Arthur Rothstein, August 1935) Farm Security Administration Photograph Collection, Prints & Photographs Division, Library of Congress, LC-USF33–002011–M3

and Edwin Locke were sent to Marianna and Forrest City to photograph the thousands of flood refugees in Red Cross camps. Evans shot 131 pictures, multiple scenes of African American and white refugees looking stunned and bedraggled. One of these photos has become an iconic image associated with the FSA and the Depression. In it, the bodies of several African Americans press together tightly in a food line, hands holding a tin plate and a chipped enamel bowl for the meal to be ladled into, the image of patience imposed by a dull routine.

Evans may be best known today for a project he undertook in summer 1936 with James Agee. Stryker had given him a two-month release to take photos for an article Agee was researching for *Fortune* magazine on Alabama tenant farmers. The book that resulted from the project, *Let Us Now Praise Famous Men* (1941), includes forty or more of Evans's pictures, depending on the edition. The photographs are archived in the Library of Congress.

Dorothea Lange was one of the most admired of the FSA photographers and certainly one of the best. Her personal warmth and ability to connect with her subjects infused many of her images, which then drew an emotional response from viewers. She likely developed the skill during her years as a portrait photographer on the West Coast, a job she abandoned to record the impact of the Depression on the growing numbers of people she saw out of work and standing in bread lines. Stryker was initially attracted to Lange's photographs of migrant workers in California, a topic not covered in the photo project. He hired her in 1935, and they worked together for months before meeting face to face when she was able to travel to Washington.

Lange tended to write extended, lengthy captions for her photos as opposed to the short notes made by other FSA photographers. As Anne Whiston Spirn explained in *Daring to Look*, Lange had a firm belief in the importance of combining words with images, and that together the two provided a greater clarity of meaning. Lange's captions included background on the people she photographed, where they came from and what had happened to them. She spent time with people, talking with them and drawing out their stories. She told Doud that she would ask for a drink of water and then sip it slowly while she chatted, establishing a connection before asking to photograph them. As Stott wrote, the result was portraits that often suggest an "emotional complexity" unexpected in a photo taken within perhaps only few minutes of photographer and subject having met.

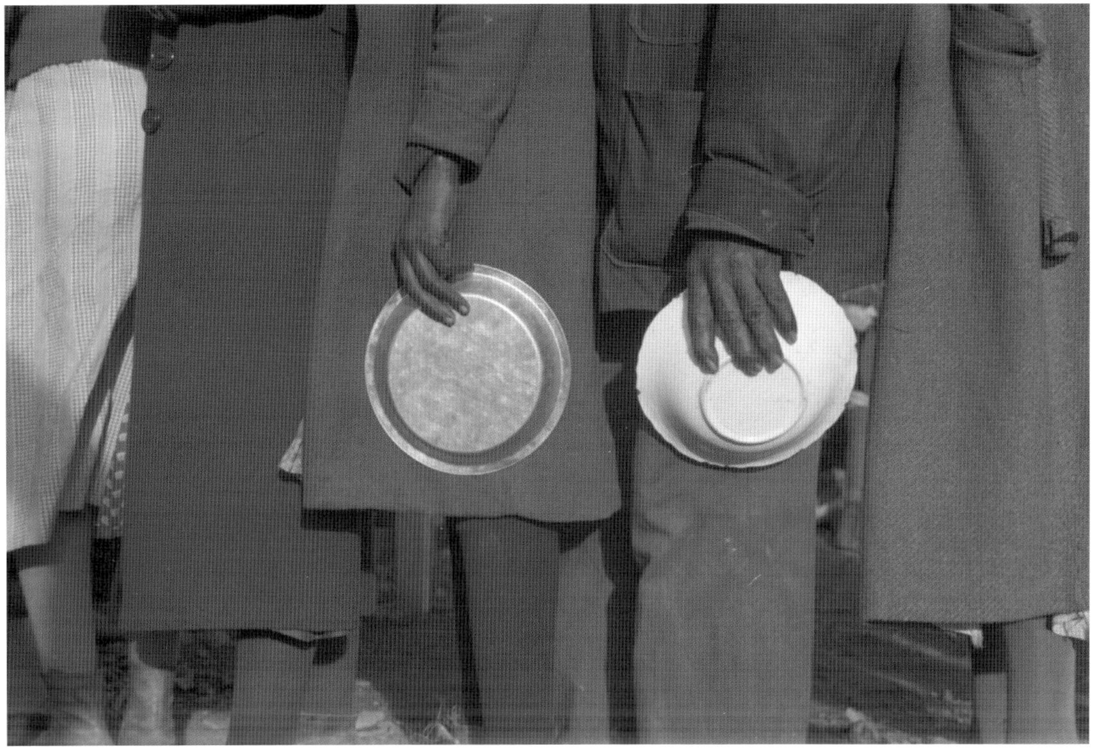

This approach can be seen in her portraits of Arkansans, such as the "Arkansas hoosier" sitting on her front porch in Conway, and the three sharecroppers on a wagon, heading home near Blytheville. Though the FSA archive lists 119 Arkansas photos for Lange, only 57 were taken in the state; the rest are of Arkansans on the road, in California migrant camps, or resettled at Hillhouse in Mississippi after eviction from Arkansas plantations because of their activities with the Southern Tenant Farmers Union. Lange's travels in Arkansas ranged from West Memphis, across the north part of the state on Highway 62, to Rogers and Fayetteville in the northwest, and Faulkner and Jefferson counties in the center. In subject matter, they included very personal portraits, the routine "project" photos taken on resettlement farms, and a series of shots of African American wage laborers packed into the backs of trucks to be driven to Arkansas plantations for a day's work.

This photograph, one of Walker Evans's best-known shots, shows refugees from the 1937 flood in the lineup for food at mealtime in the Forrest City Red Cross camp.

(Walker Evans, February 1937) Farm Security Administration Photograph Collection, Prints & Photographs Division, Library of Congress, LC-USF33–009217–M3

Russell Lee was perhaps the most prolific of the FSA photographers; in the six years he worked for the project, he took more than 23,000 pictures, 450 of them in Arkansas, which is about half of all the FSA photos taken in the state. Lee trained as a chemical engineer and studied art briefly before becoming fascinated with photography. He was very congenial and, like Lange, had great personal warmth. According to J. B. Colson, Lee's colleague at the University of Texas, where he taught photography

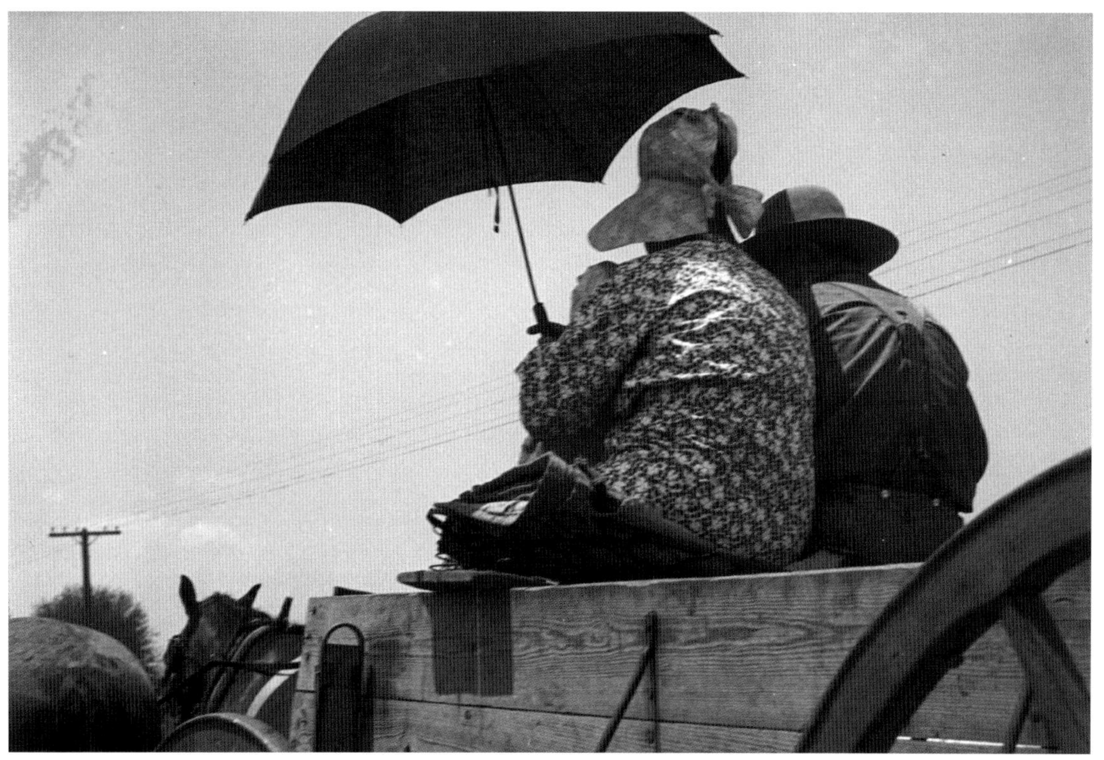

Dorothea Lange labeled this photo very simply "Arkansas farm folk."

(Dorothea Lange, August 1936) Farm Security Administration Photograph Collection, Prints & Photographs Division, Library of Congress, LC-USF34–009735–E

in the art program later in life, Lee had "a genuine sympathy for people and a natural charisma that is unexplainable, but I saw it often when he interacted with strangers." Also, much like Lange, Lee had a knack for engaging with people who at first were skeptical about having their picture taken by a government photographer, and he was able to overcome their resistance through his sympathy, warmth, and honesty.

Colson, who directed the UT photojournalism program, described Lee's images as "beautiful and precise and so natural that the critics can't seem to take them seriously." Jack Hurley and others have noted the "stark, almost glaring light" in Lee's photos, a result of the on-the-camera flash he used that brought out a wealth of detail in his pictures, especially interiors. Lee told Hurley of his interest in learning how people lived through the details of the environments they created around themselves: "I'd go into a bedroom and maybe I'd see something on a bedside table that would interest me. The things people kept around them could tell you an awful lot about the antecedents of these people."

This attention to detail is apparent in many of Lee's photos of resettlement farms in Arkansas, which comprise much of his work in the state. He spent several weeks during the fall and early winter of 1938–1939, staying for a time in Hot Springs, traveling back and forth to Mississippi and Louisiana, and photographing resettlement farms at Lake Dick, Lakeview, and Chicot, a total of 329 images. Thanks to Lee's penchant for capturing the detail of people's lives, there is an extensive visual record of the farmhouses and the schools built by the federal government on the resettlement projects. These photos document the government's idea of what a farmhouse should be, for example, as well as the way that farm families would try to make the space their own with personal touches such as pictures and curtains.

The activities of the FSA photographers are well documented as well as the pervasive sense of a social responsibility to the people they photographed and sympathy for their plight. However, there is scant information about the subjects of the pictures, not even their names, much less how they felt about being photographed when approached by someone identifying him- or herself as a government photographer. The issues of socioeconomic class and race placed them at a disadvantage in the dynamics of the photographer-subject relationship, especially when the photographer represented the government. Though evidently some people had the option to refuse to be photographed—and chose not to be—many others were not given a choice. Richard Doud raised this issue with Stryker, asking, "What did these people think when your photographers were taking their pictures under certain really unnatural or undesirable conditions? How did these people react to being photographed in these surroundings?"

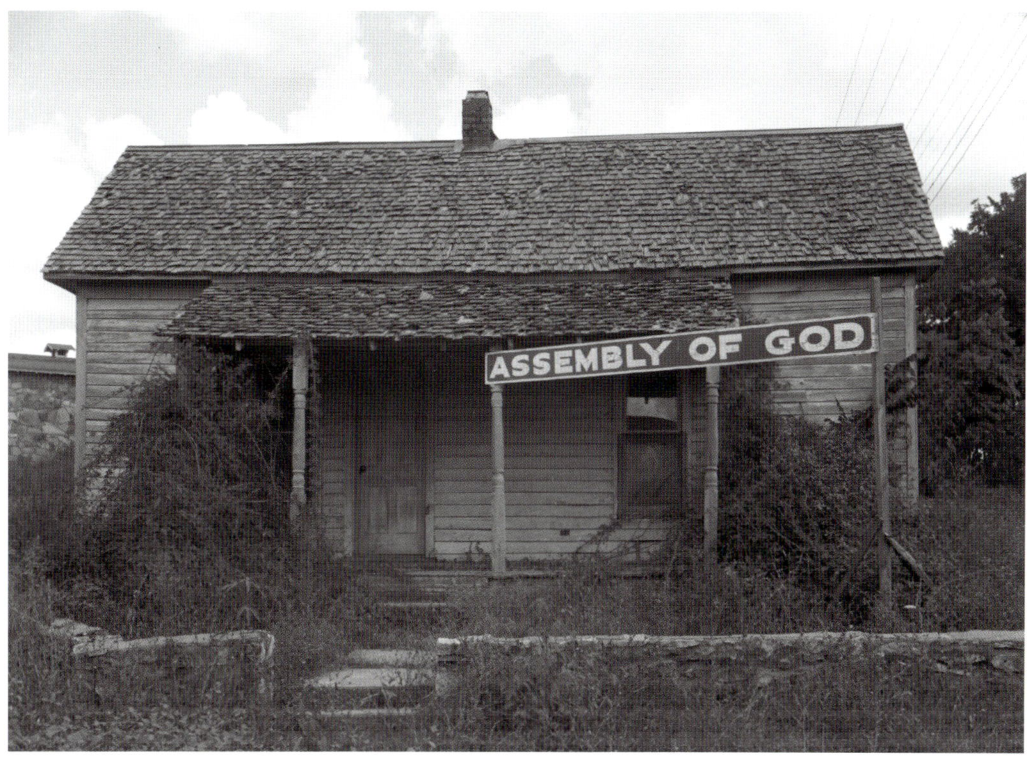

Driving US 62 across northern Arkansas in 1938, Dorothea Lange came across this apparently abandoned house and noted, "Migrants carry this sect to California."

(Dorothea Lange, August 1938) Farm Security Administration Photograph Collection, Prints & Photographs Division, Library of Congress, LC-USF34–018971–E

Stryker maintained that the photographers were consistently respectful of their subjects and had a "sincere, passionate love" of people. He could not recall any photographer at any time ridiculing or taking advantage of people, but he admitted that he really didn't know since he was rarely with the photographers in the field. Stryker described on one occasion watching Russell Lee interact with an elderly woman who had at first told him he couldn't take her picture. Lee's approach was sympathetic. He explained that "a lot of people think that you represent a bunch of lazy good-for-nothings," but that he didn't agree. In fact, he wanted to tell those people about "who you are and what your problems are." The woman agreed to the photo.

Stryker said Ben Shahn's technique was to talk "to them in terms of what he knew were their problems." Shahn also used a right-angle viewfinder that enabled him to take pictures without people knowing they were being photographed. Stryker did imply that Shahn may have provoked irritation and frustration in subjects, which might be noticeable in some photos, but he didn't think Shahn was being dishonest. Dorothea Lange, however, could warm up anyone; Stryker, who always praised Lange, said

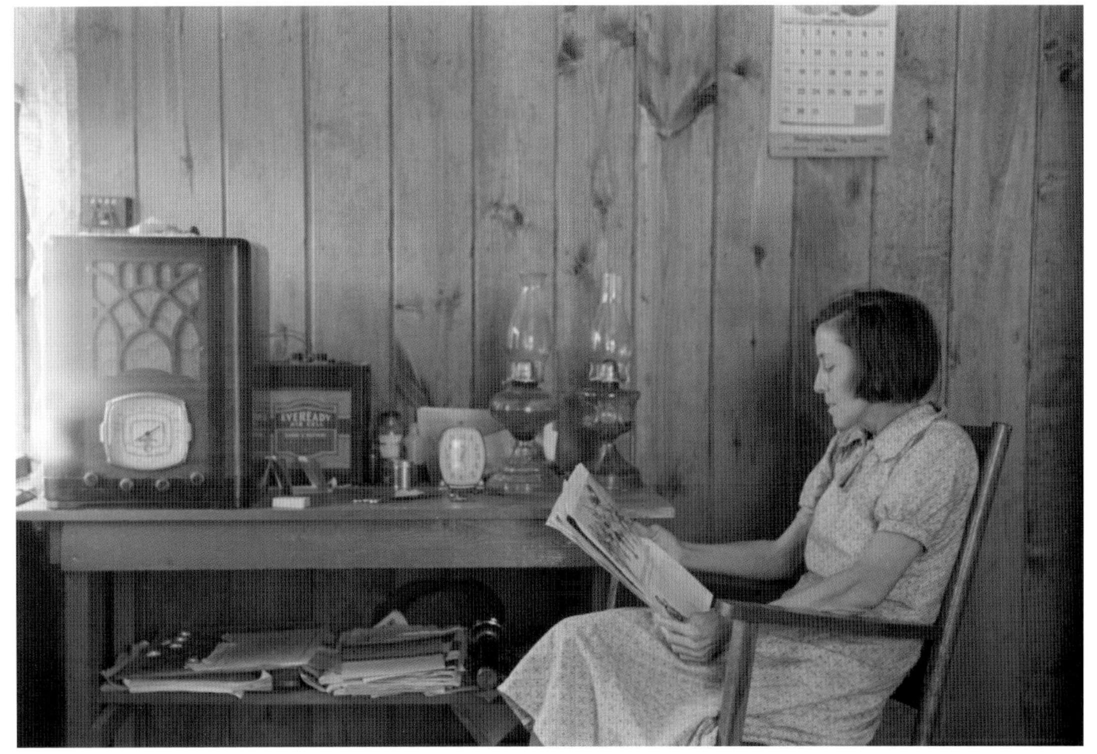

Russell Lee, who liked to capture the details of a person's environment, shows this housewife from the Chicot resettlement farm reading in her living room, with a display of the family's possessions nearby. The composition of the photo is reminiscent of the 1871 painting by James Whistler known as "Whistler's Mother."

(Russell Lee, January 1939) Farm Security Administration Photograph Collection, Prints & Photographs Division, Library of Congress, LC-USF33–011935–M2

she must have "sparked a great deal of simpatico, a great deal of rapport" with people.

Nevertheless, the potential for exploiting the poor and powerless clearly bothered Stryker. At the end of his final interview with Doud, he said, "Dick, look, there have been times when I wanted to throw the whole Goddamned thing up and get out. . . . There's times when I said, 'Jesus Christ, is it right to be taking these pictures?'" Though Stryker of course had no control over how the FSA photos were used once they were distributed, he believed that they had, for the most part, been used correctly. Still the potential for the exploitation of the photo subjects and the desperation of their lives clearly troubled him.

In the end, however, the proof of the sincerity of the photographers has to lie in the photographs themselves. In a collection of more than a quarter million images, there are indeed examples that treat people unfairly—a few of them were taken in Arkansas—but those photos are rarely if ever seen. Instead, by and large, the FSA collection allows people their dignity in a direct and honest way, and because of that, it has continued to intrigue generations since the 1930s with its witnessing to American life during the Depression.

ONE | COTTON

ROUGHLY ONE-FOURTH OF the FSA photographs taken in Arkansas deal with cotton—cotton piled on the front porch of a house, cotton fields, people picking cotton, the operation of a cotton gin, cotton plantations, and workers loaded into trucks to be driven to cotton fields. Cotton had permeated southern agriculture so deeply and for so long that it defined the culture and determined the course of lives. In Arkansas cotton was grown extensively across the state—in all but eight counties—but it truly was "king cotton" on the large plantations of the Delta where it spawned a cotton culture.

Before cotton cultivation was mechanized in the middle and late 1930s, it relied heavily on manual labor for chopping and picking. This dependency had led to the tenancy system, which provided large planters with cheap labor, and poor, landless farmers with a means to make a living, though not a very good one. Because cotton supported the agricultural economy of an area, it became the pivot point of life for everyone in a cotton community, but particularly for workers who had the most intimate and constant contact with the crop.

Sidney Baldwin (*Poverty and Politics*) points to Frank Tannenbaum's characterization of cotton as the tyrant of the South. Tannenbaum, labor activist and historian, meant cotton had spawned a tenancy system based on ensuring cheap, available labor that enabled large farm operations to function at a profit but kept tenants and sharecroppers in perpetual debt. The rhythms of cotton cultivation shaped workers' lives throughout the year because the fieldwork required the labor of whole families—fathers, mothers, children, and even grandparents, when possible. School schedules were organized by the need to tend to cotton, taking breaks—"cotton vacations"—so children could help chop weeds in the spring and pick cotton in the fall.

The RA/FSA photos of cotton farming in Arkansas focus primarily on the workers—the small farmers, tenants, and sharecroppers whose lives were attuned most closely to cotton and its environment, the land, and the climate. Three photographers—Dorothea Lange, Russell Lee, and Ben Shahn—took most of these photos of cotton workers. Their distinctive personal photographic styles are evident in the pictures, but the work of all three reflects the RA/FSA's message of social responsibility and sensitivity to the predicament of the poorest farmers, making the case for federal government assistance to them. These photographs contrast the view of farm laborers simply as an undifferentiated mass mechanically working the fields, with one that presents them as a collection of unique individuals stuck in a society of unequal opportunity.

Shahn took this approach in his 1935 series of photos from the Alexander plantation, as Nicholas Natanson notes in *The Black Image in the New Deal*. He photographed the cotton workers waiting to be trucked out to the field, focusing on one person or on people sitting and standing in small groups, so that each could be seen clearly as an individual human being. A viewer could "read" each person's face, clothes, and demeanor and was therefore invited to speculate about their personalities and their lives—in effect, to give each an imagined biography.

Shahn followed the group to the field and photographed them throughout the day. His technique was to select one person for study and take several pictures showing the person's actions in picking. In this series, Shahn focused on a young girl as she worked her way through the dry and dusty field and paused for a moment to play with a cotton boll. It is a scene reminiscent of Shahn's suggestion to Roy Stryker that juxtaposing a "kid who looks starved" against eroded soil was the kind of picture that would move people.

Dorothea Lange took a different angle on day laborers in her series of photos from 1937 and 1938 of workers loading onto trucks in Memphis for transportation to Arkansas Delta plantations to chop cotton. According to Lange's extended captions, hundreds of African Americans showed up each morning hoping to get work; they faced a farm labor environment in which reduced cotton acreage had cut back the need for seasonal workers and made jobs scarce. Planters paid truck drivers to recruit workers by offering sixty cents to a dollar a day. Trucks left at five o'clock in the morning—each carrying thirty to fifty workers—to drive the forty-three miles to the Wilson plantation in Arkansas.

Lange's photos show the workers as a mass, faceless as a herd and packed into the truck beds with no concern for safety, much less comfort. She took the pictures from a slight rise, looking down onto the scene. By doing this she suggests an attitude of large landowners that holds workers at a distance, not recognizing their individuality and value except for their work—at five cents an hour.

Russell Lee's photos are from the resettlement farm community at Lake Dick in 1938. He photographed day laborers hired by the Lake Dick farmers to pick their crop. Though Shahn and Lange only photographed African American cotton workers, the photographs Lee took at Lake Dick show both black and white workers. In fact, in Lee's photo of seven pickers bent over nearly double to reach the cotton, the race of the workers is not evident. It is clear, however, that those in charge are white—the man who weighs the cotton sacks, the paymaster, and the overseer on horseback. In these photos, Lee shows the distinctions of race and class made according to those in control and those doing the hard labor. A full sack of cotton could weigh upward of fifty pounds; in one picture a woman strains to drag her sack.

Cotton played a fundamental role in shaping the RA/FSA photo coverage of Arkansas. As a major cash crop that was most efficiently grown on large plantations dependent on tenancy, cotton factored into the story that the RA/FSA wanted to tell about a system of unequal opportunity that exacerbated economic, social, and racial divisions. The photographers' depiction of cotton workers as individuals receiving low wages for debilitating work by large landowners who regarded them as part of the mechanism of cultivation supported this message—which was guaranteed to offend and enrage the coalition of large farming operations and the American Farm Bureau with its state satellites and their representative in Congress.

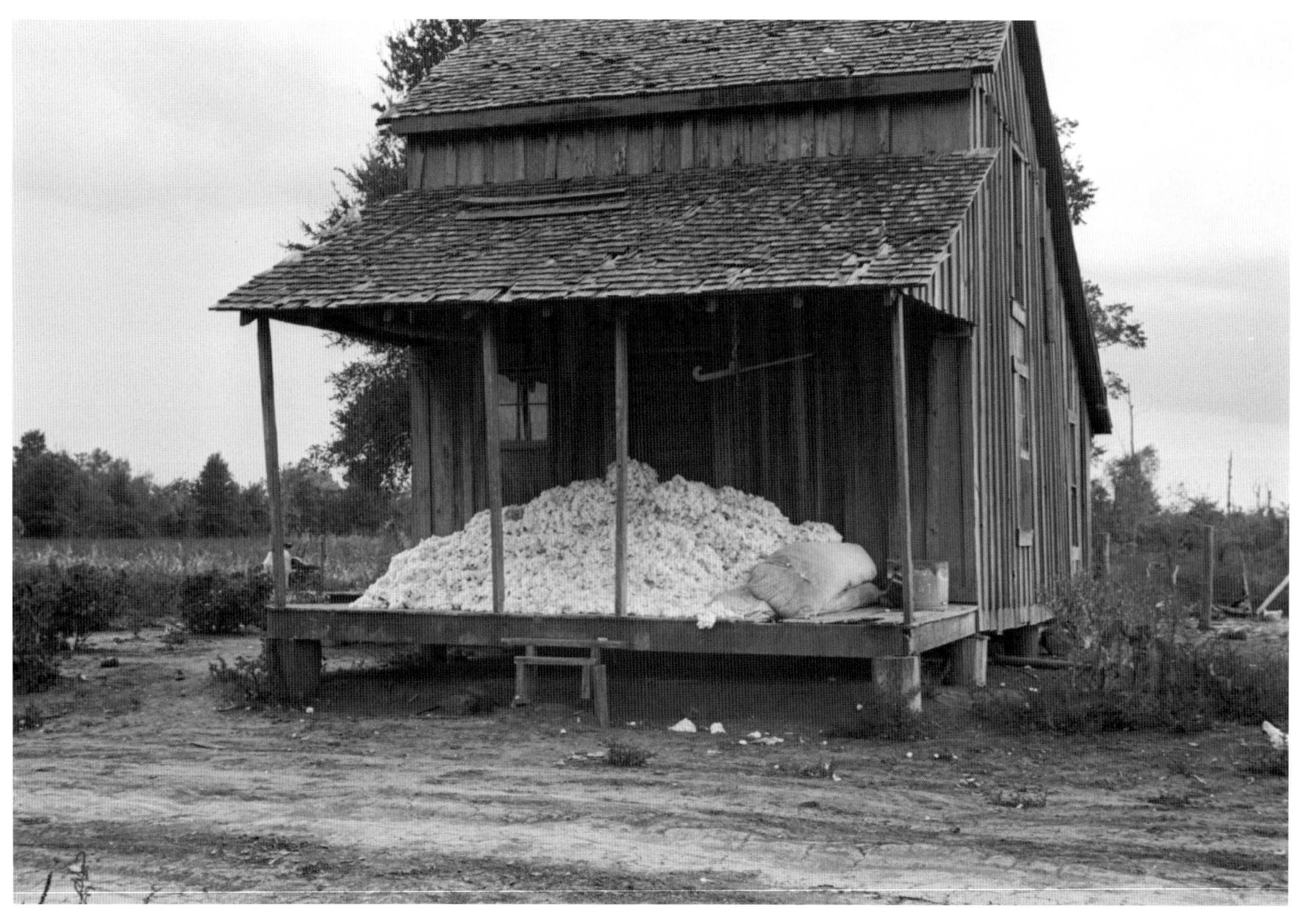

Cotton is piled on the porch of a sharecropper's home on the Maria plantation.

(Ben Shahn, October 1935) Farm Security Administration Photograph Collection, Prints & Photographs Division, Library of Congress, LC-USF33–006050–M4

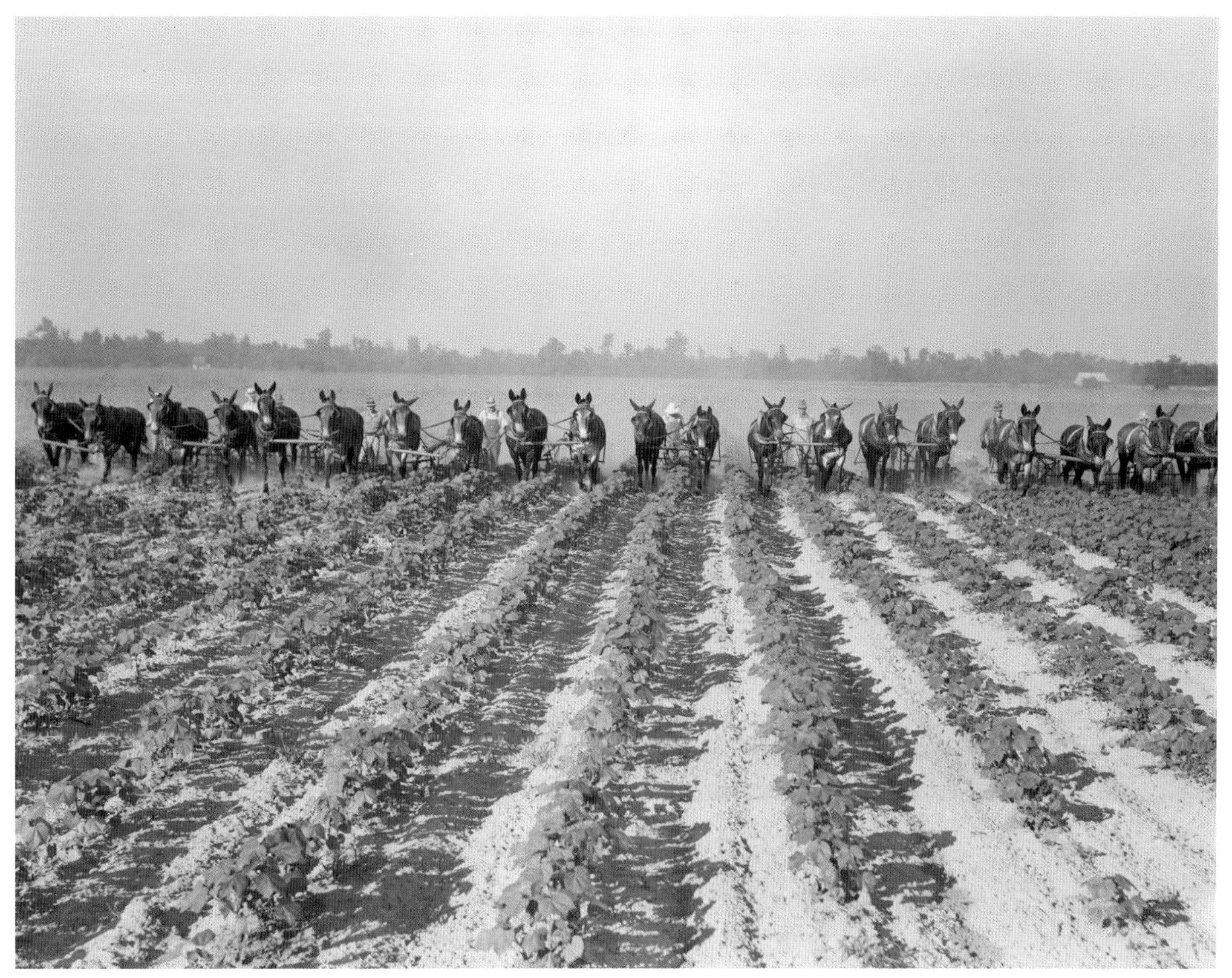

Farmers use mules in cultivating a cotton field at the Lake Dick resettlement project in Jefferson County.

(Dorothea Lange, June 1938) Farm Security Administration Photograph Collection, Prints & Photographs Division, Library of Congress, LC-USF34–018150–C

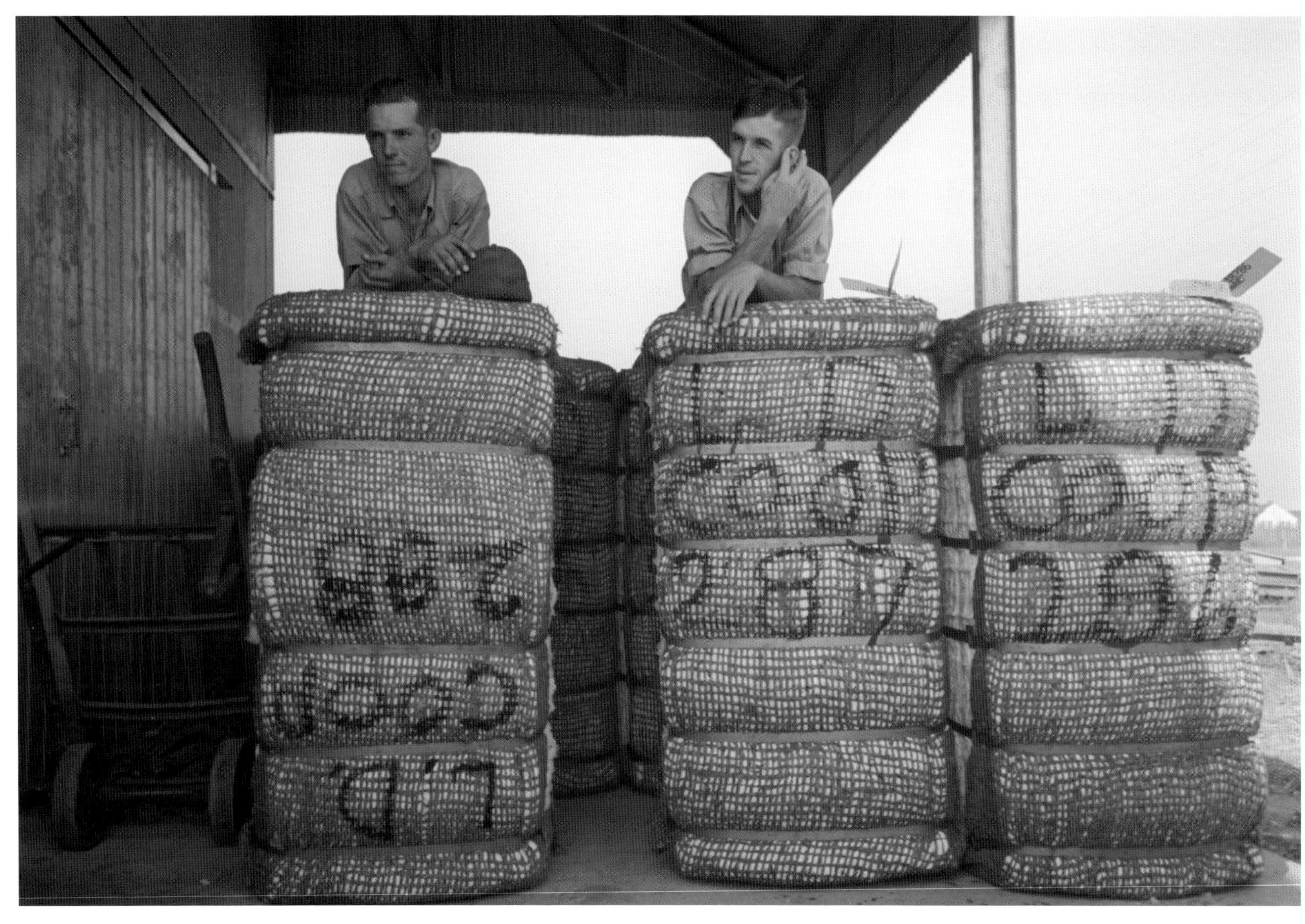

Members of the Lake Dick cooperative farm relax on bales of cotton.

(Russell Lee, September 1938) Farm Security Administration Photograph Collection, Prints & Photographs Division, Library of Congress, LC-USF33–011691–M1

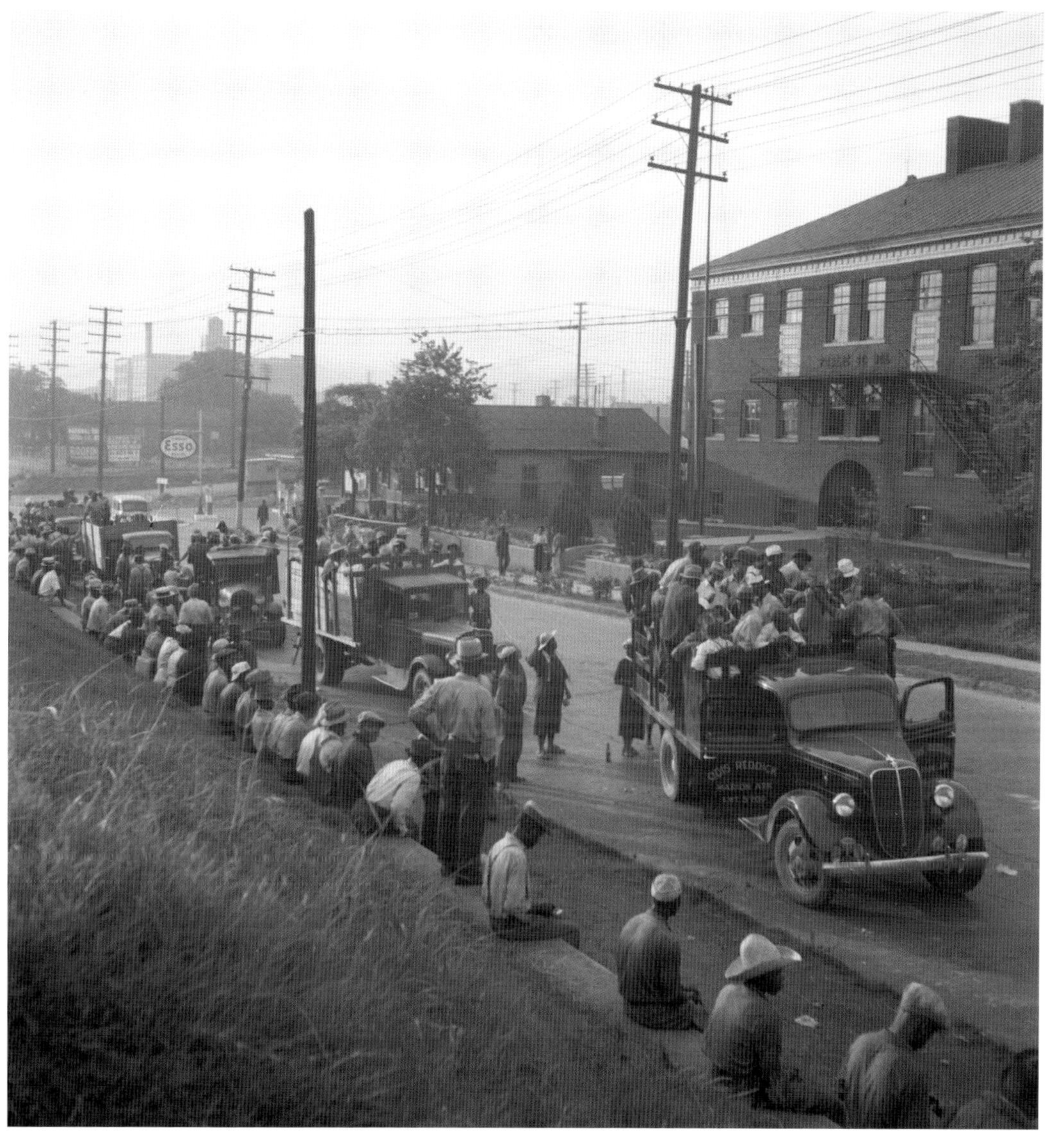

Describing this scene from Memphis, Dorothea Lange wrote, "Cotton hoers are transported to the fields daily during the season. Truck drivers are paid by the planters and serve as 'runners' to recruit the men [and women]. Trucks leave at five o'clock in the morning for the Arkansas Delta plantations."

(Dorothea Lange, June 1937) Farm Security Administration Photograph Collection, Prints & Photographs Division, Library of Congress, LC-USF34–017552–E

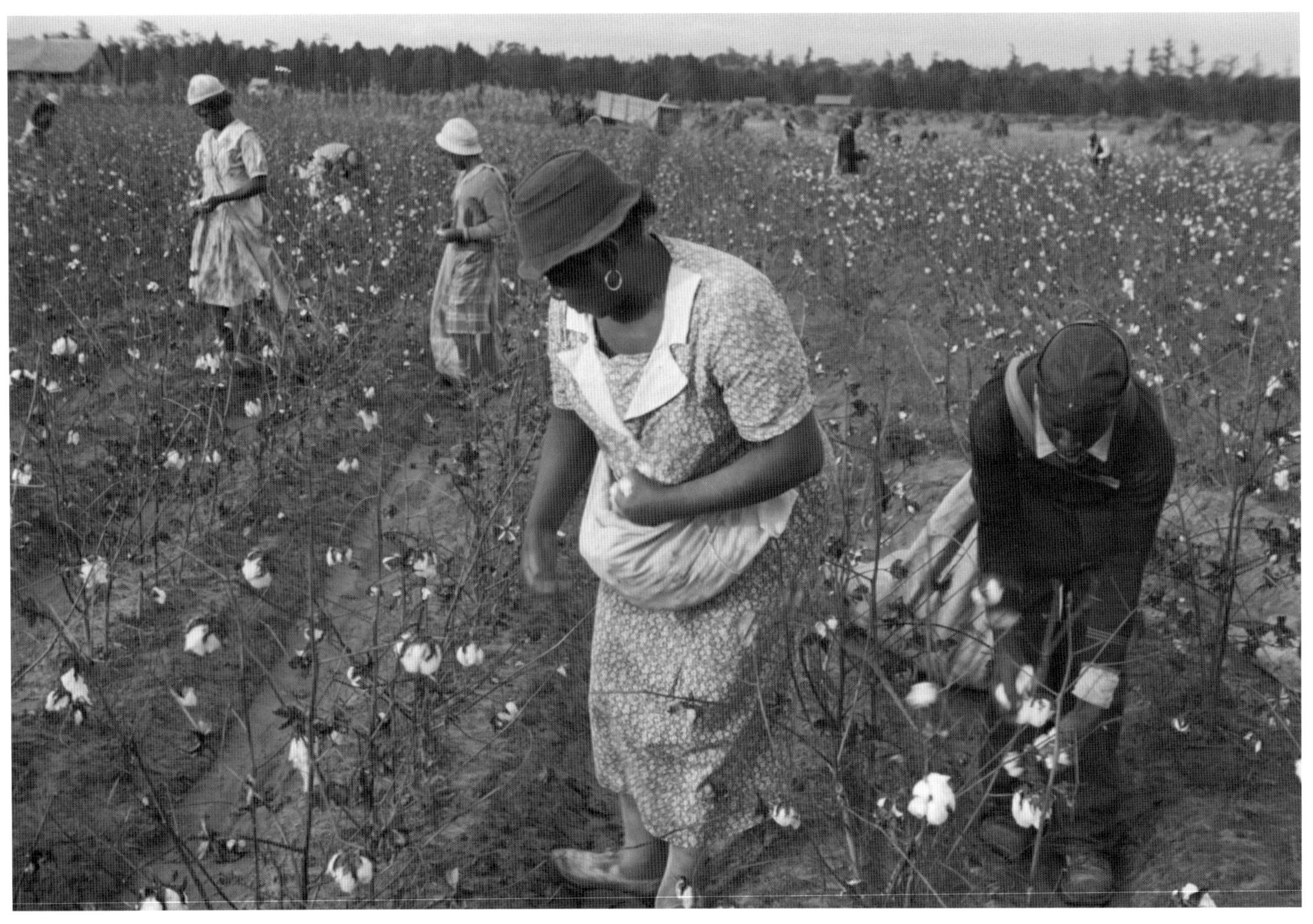

Shahn seemed interested in showing the different ages of cotton pickers working in the fields, as well as their manner of dress.

(Ben Shahn, October 1935) Farm Security Administration Photograph Collection, Prints & Photographs Division, Library of Congress, LC-USF33–006217–M2

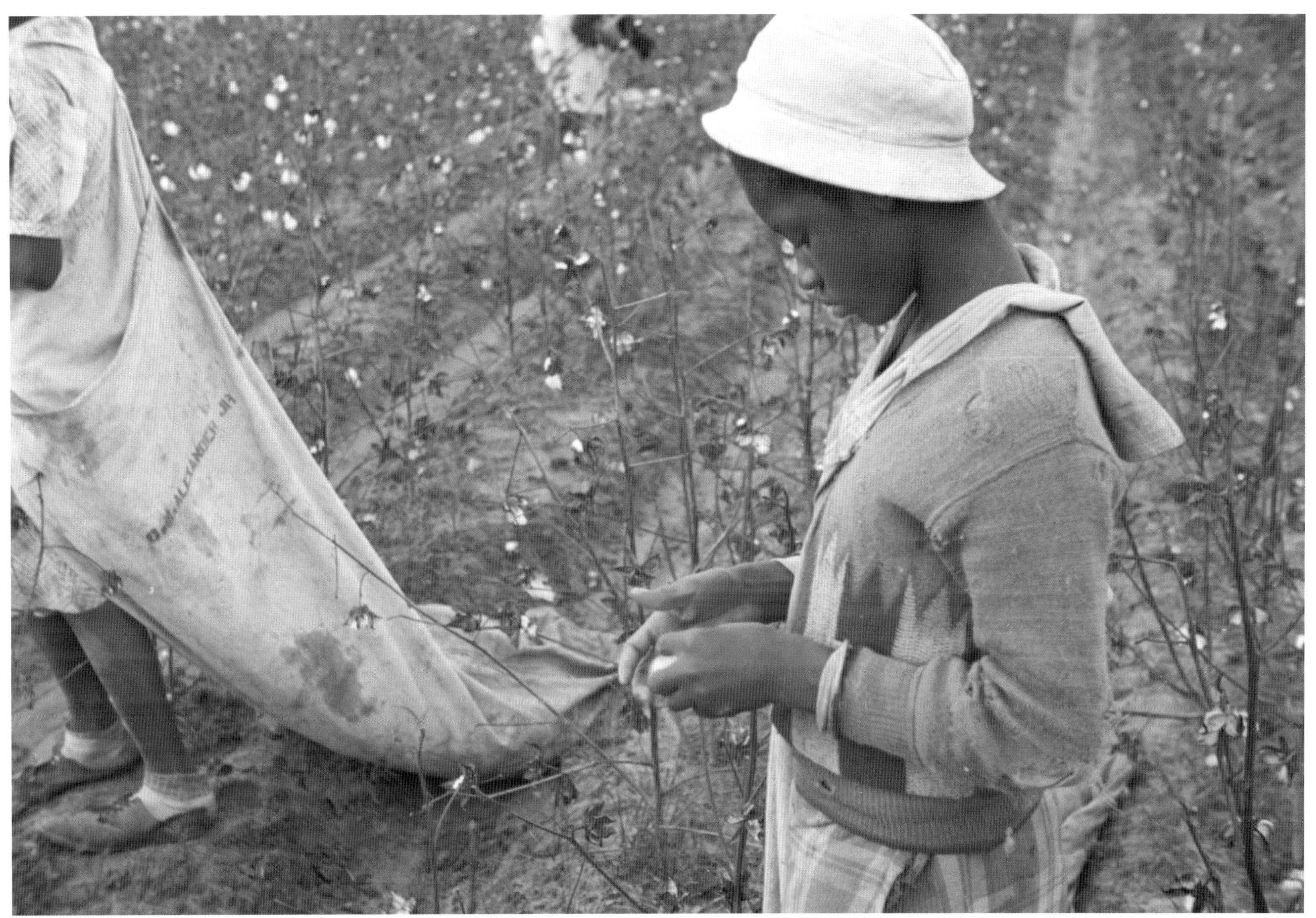

Shahn focused on one young girl at work picking cotton in Arkansas in October. Segregated schools for African American children did not open until January, so as not to interfere with the cotton-picking season.

(Ben Shahn, October 1935) Farm Security Administration Photograph Collection, Prints & Photographs Division, Library of Congress, LC-USF33–006218–M5

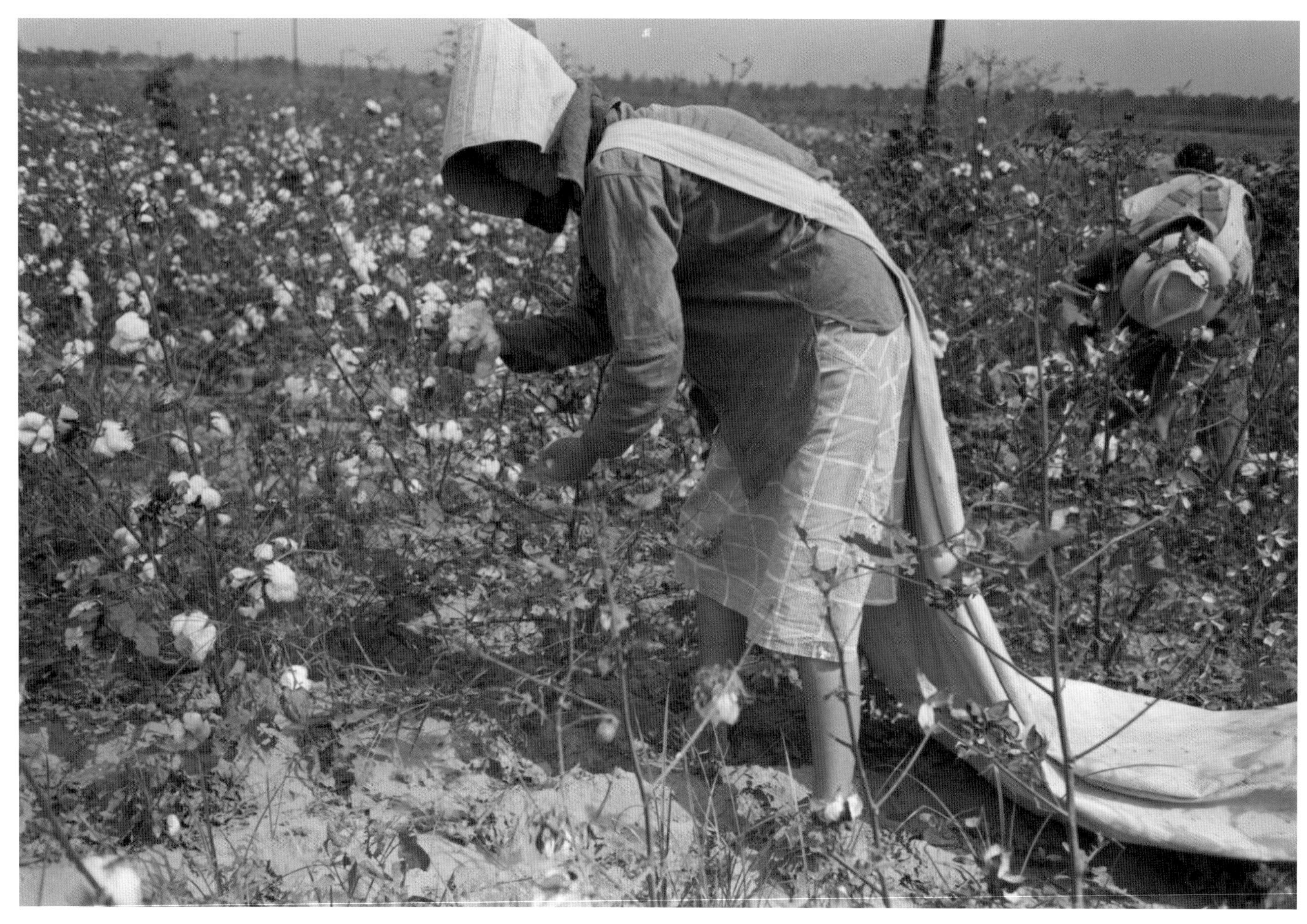

A cotton picker on the Lake Dick Project.

(Russell Lee, September 1938) Farm Security Administration Photograph Collection, Prints & Photographs Division, Library of Congress, LC-USF33–011670–M4

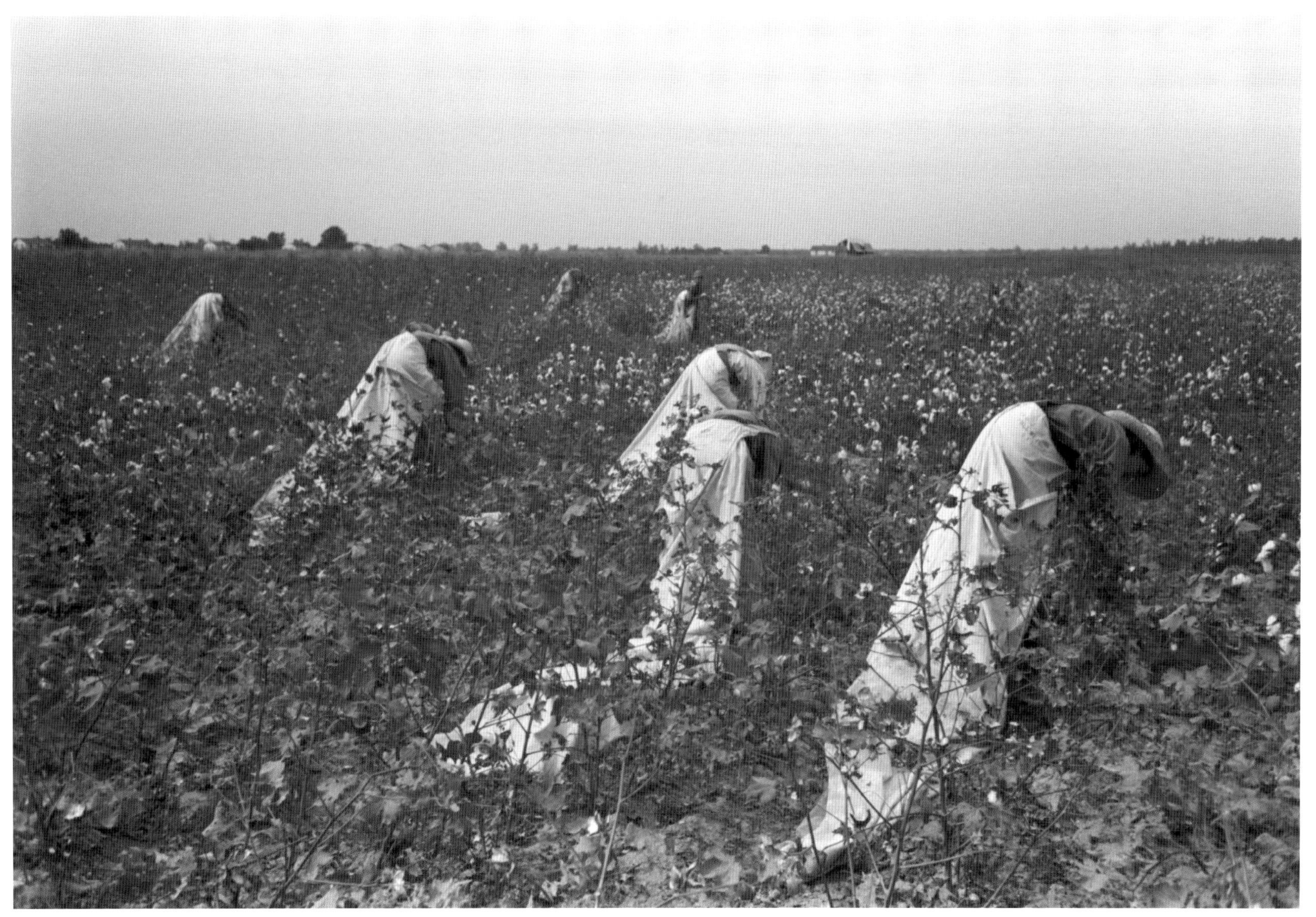

Russell Lee's image of workers bent over to pick cotton suggests a graceful rhythm in the rounded shapes flowing easily into long cotton sacks. However, the job was hot, back-breaking, debilitating labor.

(Russell Lee, September 1938) Farm Security Administration Photograph Collection, Prints & Photographs Division, Library of Congress, LC-USF33–011671–M2

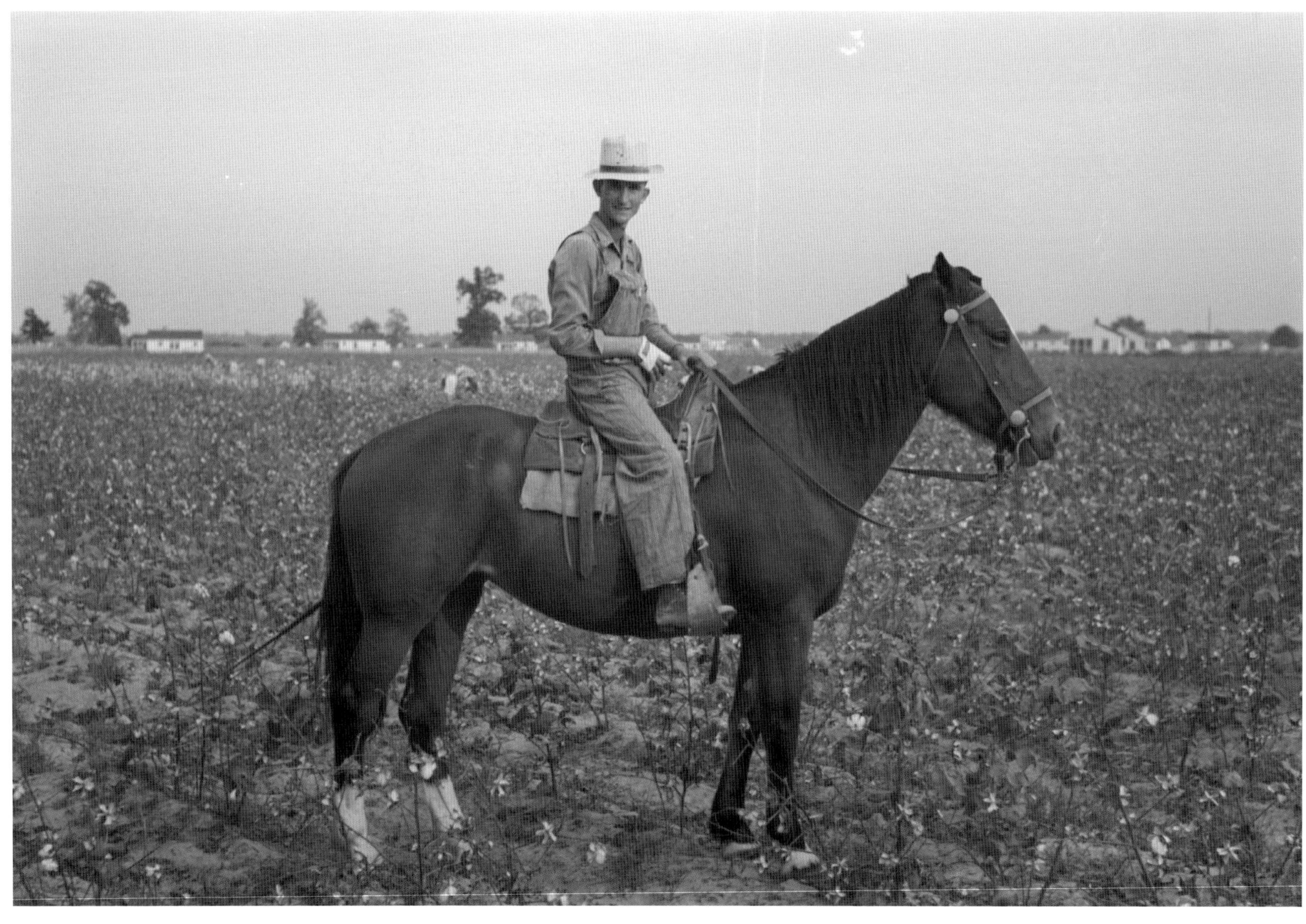

A member of the Lake Dick cooperative association served as overseer of cotton pickers and could ride through the fields to monitor them.

(Russell Lee, September 1938) Farm Security Administration Photograph Collection, Prints & Photographs Division, Library of Congress, LC-USF33–011681–M3

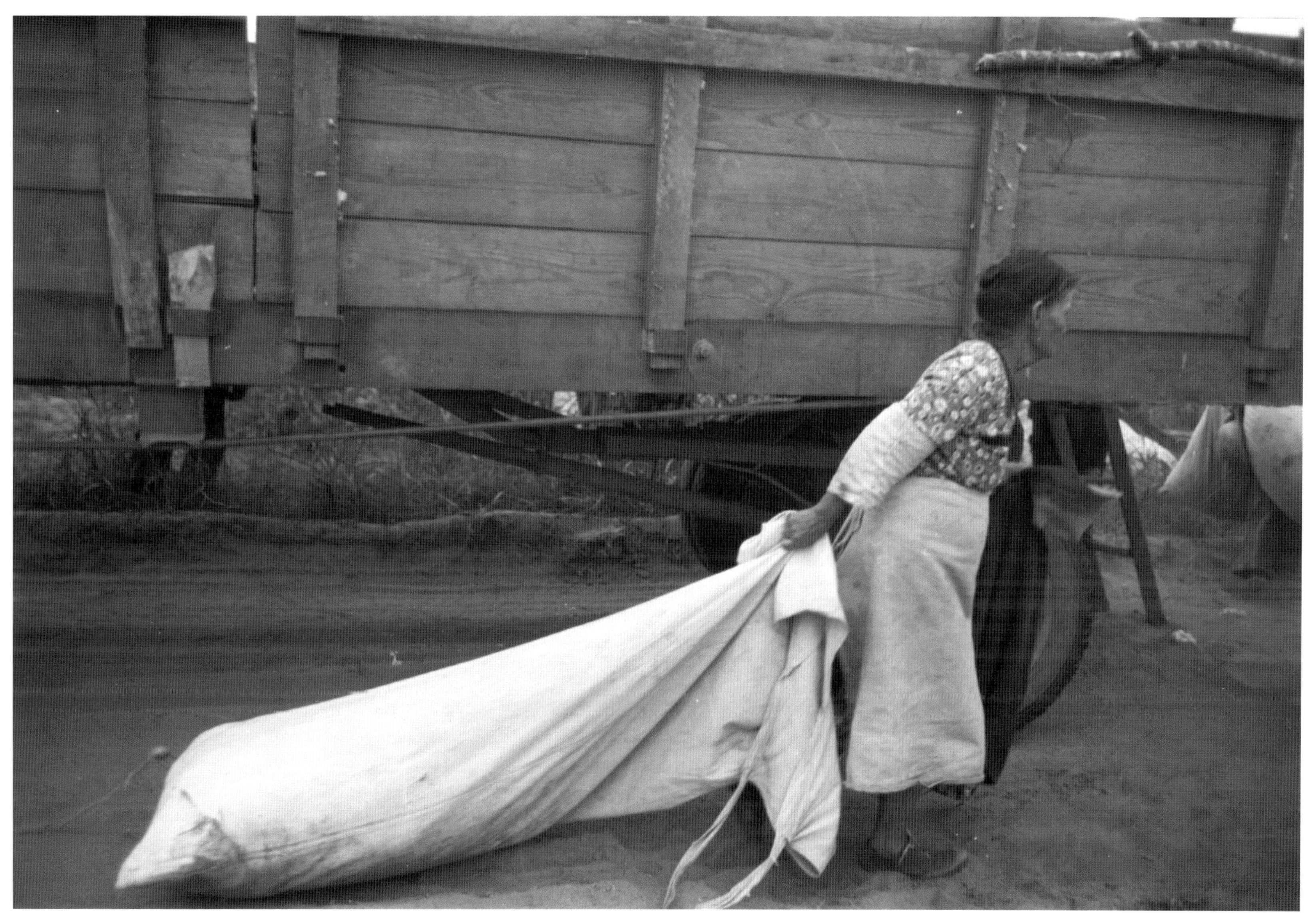

In this picture of a Lake Dick day laborer dragging her bag of cotton, Lee calls attention to the weight and bulk of a full sack.

(Russell Lee, September 1938) Farm Security Administration Photograph Collection, Prints & Photographs Division, Library of Congress, LC-USF33–011688–M3

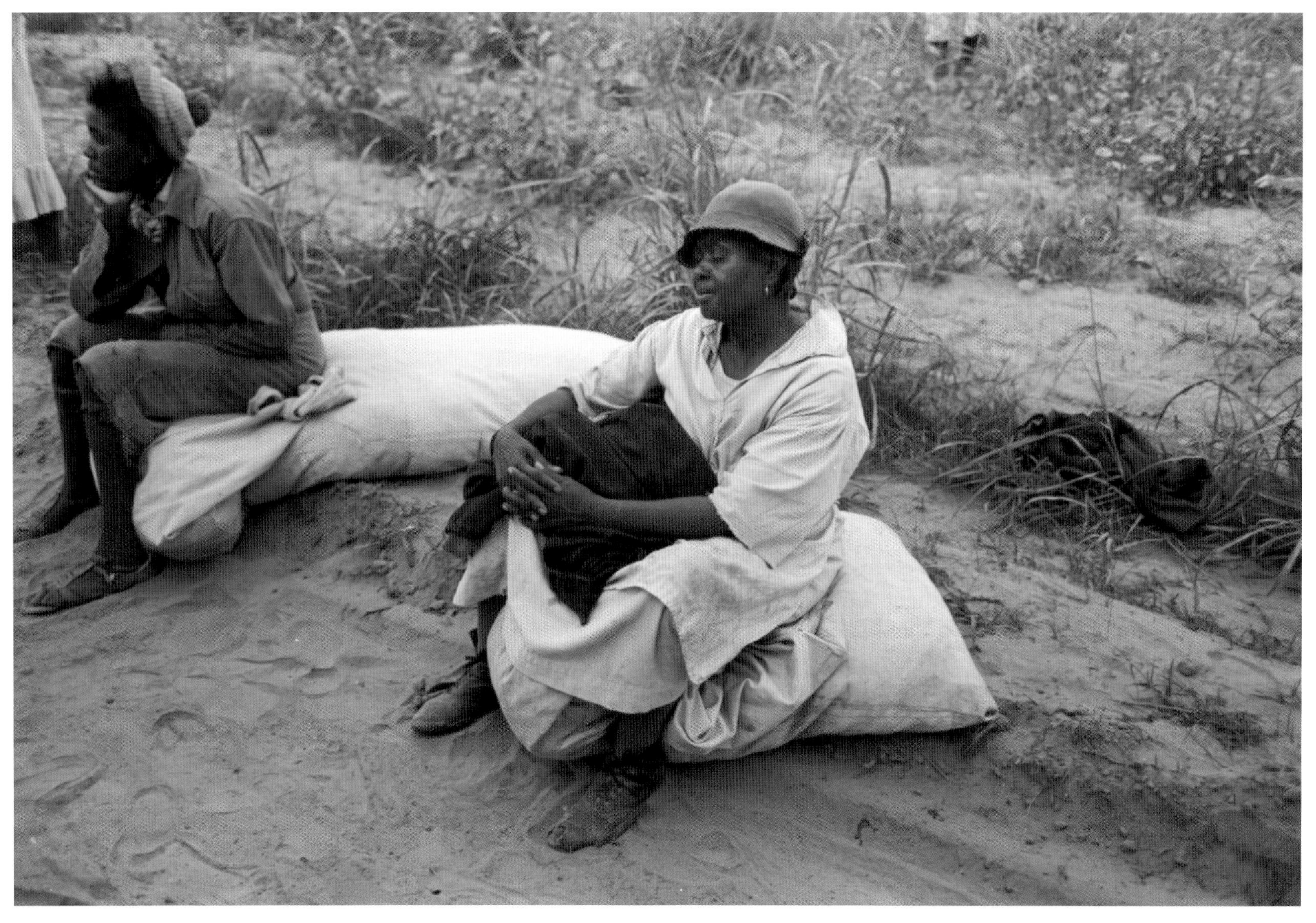

Cotton pickers at the Lake Dick project rest on their filled bags of cotton while waiting to be paid.

(Russell Lee, September 1938) Farm Security Administration Photograph Collection, Prints & Photographs Division, Library of Congress, LC-USF33–011688–M5

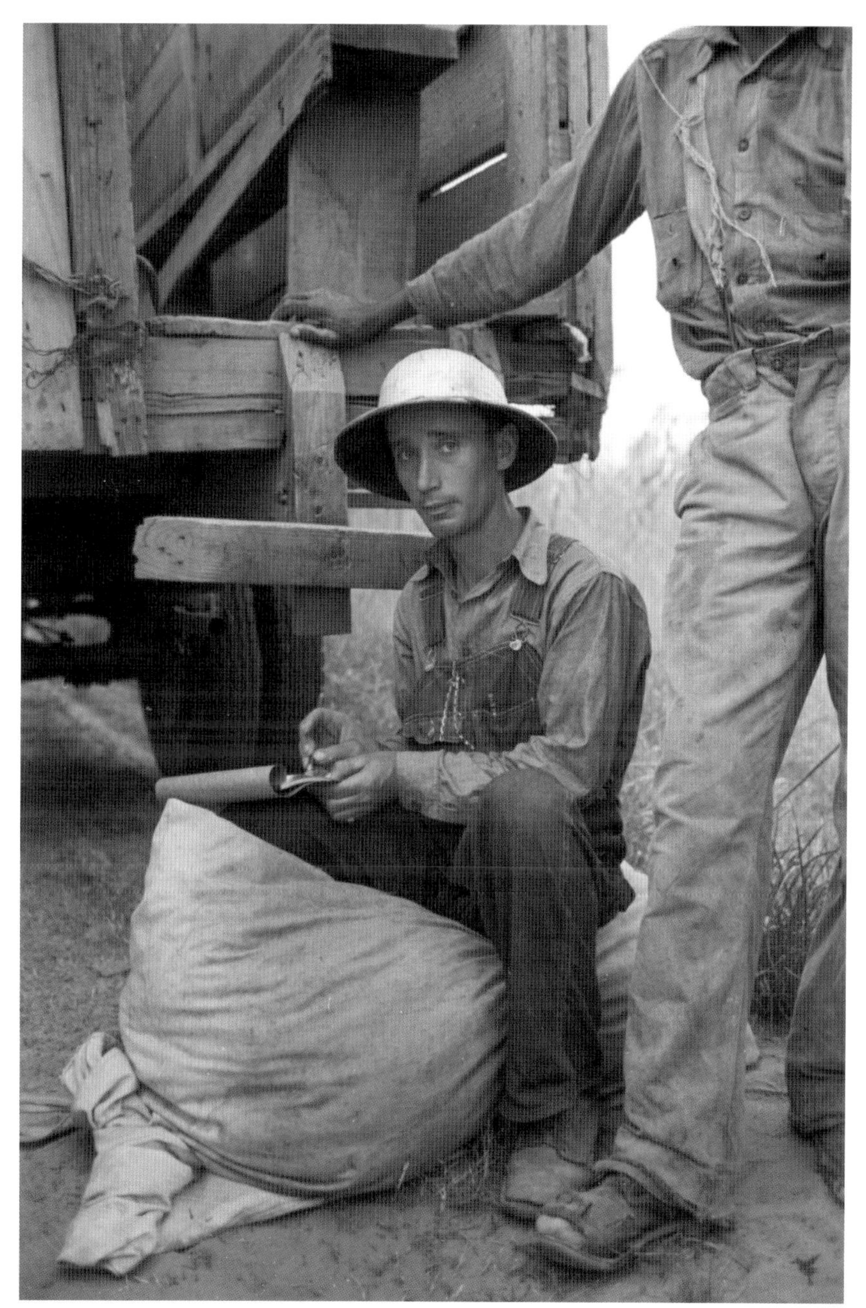

A Lake Dick farmer records the weights of cotton picked by day laborers.

(Russell Lee, September 1938) Farm Security Administration Photograph Collection, Prints & Photographs Division, Library of Congress, LC-USF33–011690–M1

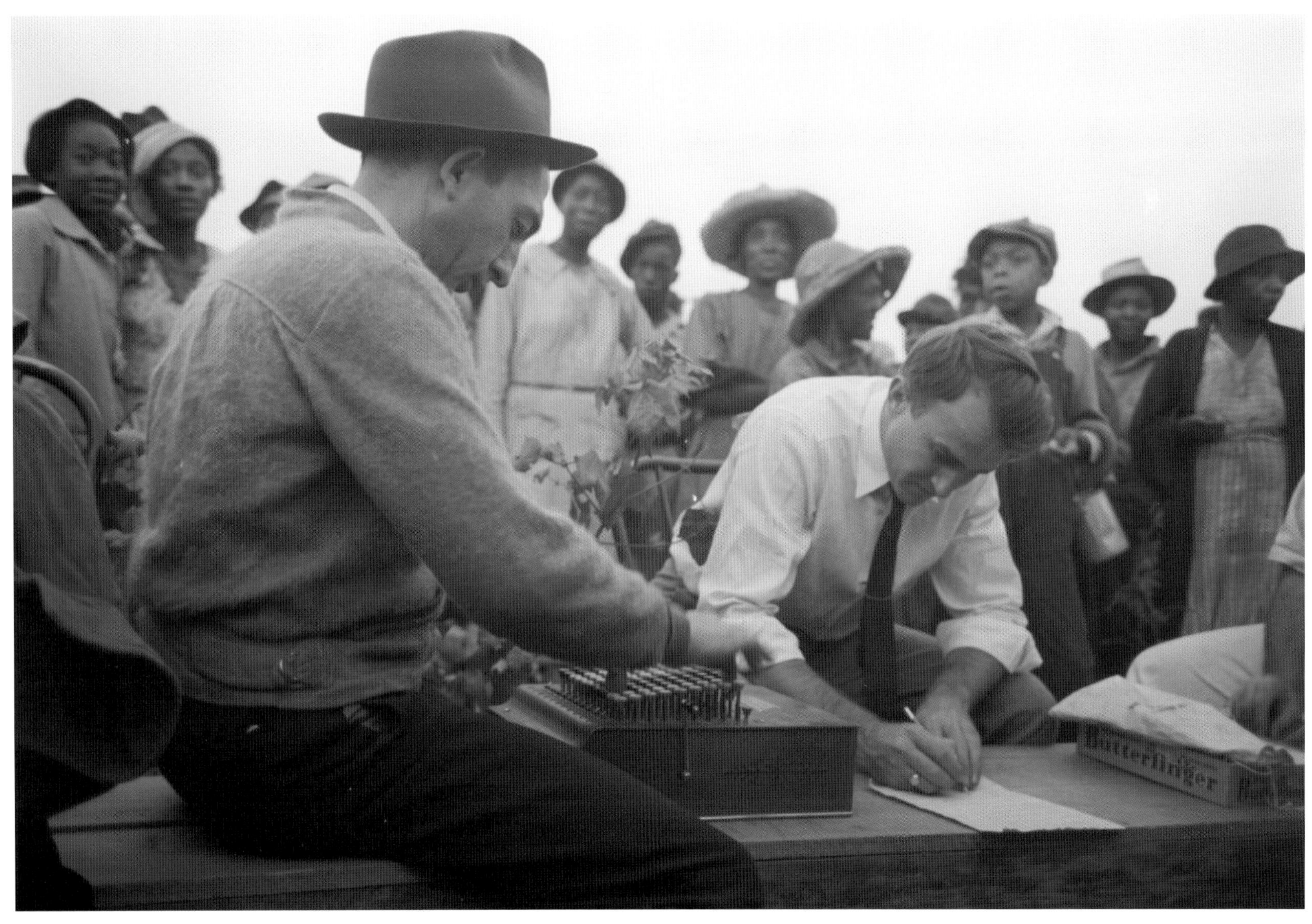

Members of the Lake Dick project pay the day laborers at the end of a day of picking.

(Russell Lee, September 1938) Farm Security Administration Photograph Collection, Prints & Photographs Division, Library of Congress, LC-USF33–011689–M4

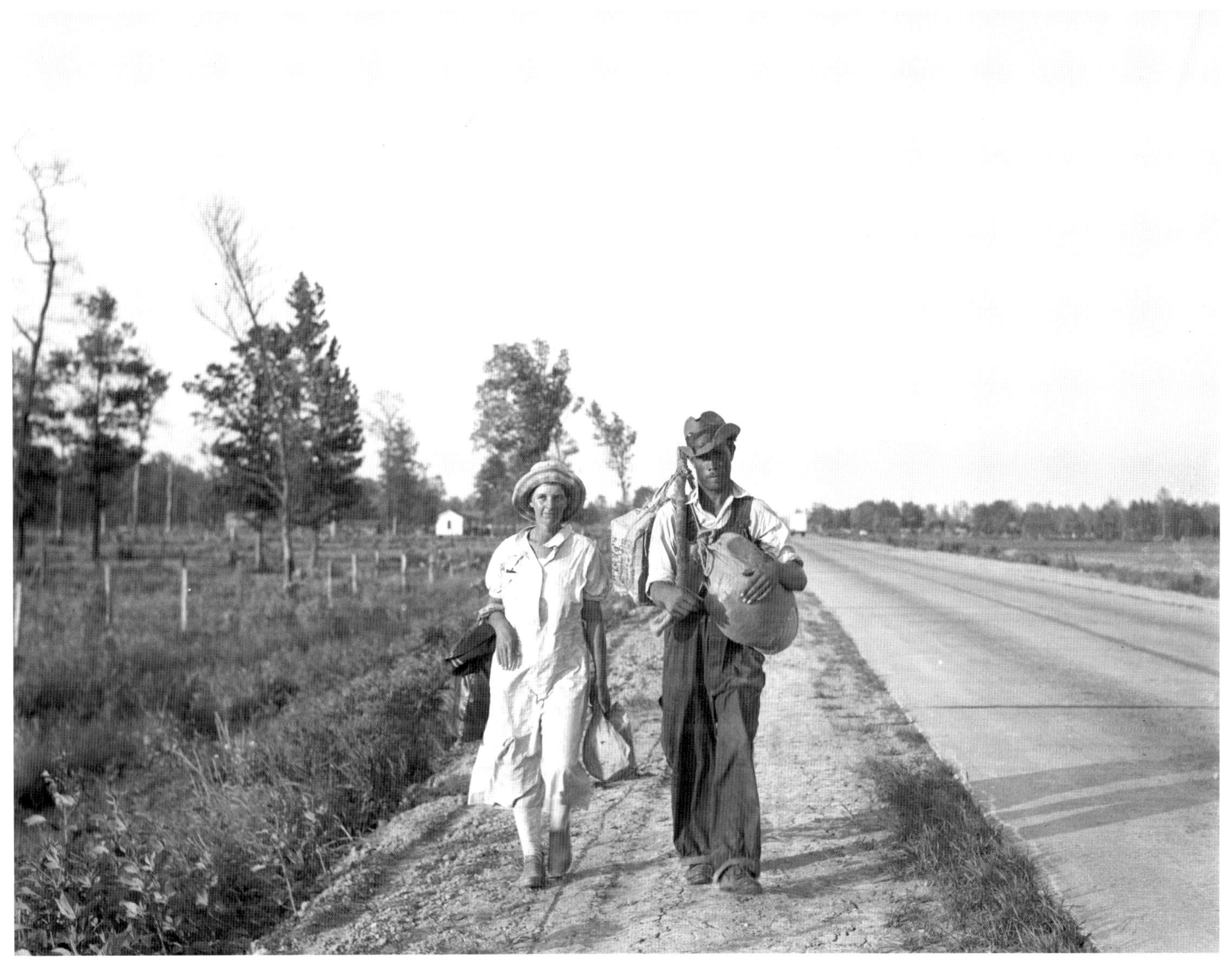

These cotton workers, walking down a road in Crittenden County, carry all they possess in the world. The photographer Carl Mydans wrote about the couple: "Damned if we'll work for what they pay folks hereabouts."

(Carl Mydans, May 1936) Farm Security Administration Photograph Collection, Prints & Photographs Division, Library of Congress, LC-USF34–006322–D

TWO | TENANTS, SHARECROPPERS, AND REHABILITATION CLIENTS

IN 1936 WALKER EVANS and the writer James Agee spent several weeks living with three Alabama sharecropper families to research an article for *Fortune* magazine. Agee later described the families' lives as "a steady shame and insult of discomforts, insecurities, and inferiorities, piecing these together into whatever semblance of comfortable living they can and the whole of it . . . a stark nakedness of makeshifts and the lack of means."

Walker and Agee's effort to accurately document the lives of sharecroppers never made it to the pages of *Fortune*, but was eventually published in 1941 as the book *Let Us Now Praise Famous Men*. The *Fortune* article idea was dropped over Agee's concern about exploiting and trivializing the destitute families, according to Christine Haughney in the *New York Times*. Sidney Baldwin in *Poverty and Politics* wrote that the nation's increasing interest in tenancy in the mid-1930s led journalists, political writers, social critics, and others to turn tenants and sharecroppers into "symbols of America's sense of guilt." To Agee and Evans this "crescendo of concern" about poverty did not indicate either a full understanding or commitment to addressing the problem.

Tenancy was a major theme for the RA/FSA photo project when it was launched in 1935. Through multiple media sources, America had become aware of the evils of southern tenancy—the "discomforts, insecurities, and inferiorities"—and its extent. By 1930 more than 45 percent of American farmers were in tenancy, according to Sidney Baldwin (*Poverty and Politics*). The numbers in Arkansas were high; Donald Holley (*Uncle Sam's Farmers*) reports the state ranked sixth in the nation in tenancy. Many of Arkansas's tenants were African American, nearly 40 percent by 1935, and most of them sharecroppers, as Michael Mehlman wrote in his dissertation about African Americans in New Deal Arkansas. He noted further the especially high tenancy rates in Delta counties such as Mississippi (90 percent), Chicot (87 percent), and Crittenden (94 percent).

National interest was piqued by news coverage of the violence surrounding the attempted suppression of the Arkansas Southern Tenant Farmers Union movement in 1935—as well as by 1930s popular novels about the South from authors such as Erskine Caldwell (*Tobacco Road*, 1932; *God's Little Acre*, 1933). The *New York Times*'s spring 1935 series of articles about violence in eastern Arkansas had drawn attention to towns like Marked Tree, which had seen mob violence in March and April. Ben Shahn stopped in Marked Tree briefly that October, but took only a few pictures of people on main street sidewalks in front of stores.

In response to newspapers and magazines clamoring for pictures of tenant farmers, RA/FSA photo project director Roy Stryker told his photographers: "There is a great demand now for pictures of farm tenancy. We will be able to use everything we can get." However, reflecting the culture of the time, he also cautioned: "I would suggest you take both black and white, but place the emphasis on white tenants, since we know they will receive much wider use."

The RA/FSA photographs in Arkansas document the conditions in which tenants, sharecroppers, and rehabilitation clients lived—the shacks, ragged clothes, and meager possessions. However, as Arthur Rothstein's pictures of a sharecropper and his house on the Wilson cotton plantation show, some tenant housing was in relatively good condition. Windows in the house appear to be screened, which meant they could be opened to breezes without admitting mosquitos and other insects. The house may even have been built professionally, unlike some of the cabins that look like slapdash construction with uneven boards and sagging porches. The quality of housing, as documented by the RA/FSA photos, implies landowners' lack of attention and care accorded to their tenants and sharecroppers.

Though the tenancy system had begun to draw national attention in the mid-1930s, it could be complicated and easily misunderstood by those unfamiliar with rural life. Baldwin explains the system involved variations on a basic structure in which tenants rented land for farming, and paid for its use with either cash rent or a cash share of their crops, or both. There were four kinds of tenancy: cash, share, share-cash, and sharecropping; in the first three, the tenant was relatively independent of the landowner, but the fourth kind intentionally created dependency while at the same time treating sharecroppers as little more than day laborers.

In cash tenancy, the tenant paid rent in a fixed amount of cash or crop and furnished all of his farming needs, such as tools, animals, and other items. Share tenancy meant the tenant furnished all his needs and traded a share of his crop for using the land. The share-cash arrangement, then, was a combination of both share and cash tenancy. In sharecropping the landlord provided everything to the tenant—land, tools, animals, household items, food, and management. The tenant's share was whatever was left after his bills were deducted from the crop sales. Often sharecroppers weren't provided with written tenancy agreements, which left them vulnerable in the relationship with a landlord.

The early RA/FSA photographers were unfamiliar with the tenancy system and thus liable to make mistakes in identifying the subjects of their photos. One such slip-up by Arthur Rothstein in

1935 resulted in embarrassing the RA/FSA a couple of years later when a lawsuit resulted from a misidentification in a photo caption. The incident also demonstrated that Americans, though troubled by tenancy, understood very little about it; oversights were possible not only by a federal government photographer but also the editors of a major national magazine.

In 1935, Arthur Rothstein took photos of Mrs. Gladys Reed and her children and identified them in the caption as the "wife and children of a sharecropper." Two of the photos were published widely and for a couple of years achieved nearly iconic status in newspapers and magazines as symbols of southern poverty. Three years later, in 1938, the *Saturday Evening Post* used one of the pictures with a story about medical care for FSA clients in the Dakotas, adding the photo caption, "'They don't know how to use a doctor; they've never had one.' An Arkansas sharecropper's family." The Reeds sued the *Post* for libel, stating that as they were not sharecroppers, the magazine had defamed them. Though the lawsuit eventually was dropped, the FSA received unwanted attention, which could have caused political problems for an agency whose budget was constantly challenged by Congress.

Despite the agency's often politically tenuous status, RA/FSA photographers did cover controversies that no doubt further irritated the large landowners and their allies. One of those involved the evictions of tenants and sharecroppers in eastern Arkansas for their unionizing activities. In January 1936 John Vachon took pictures of African American sharecroppers evicted from the C. H. Dibble plantation near Parkin; they show families standing along a roadside with all their possessions stacked nearby. Dorothea Lange later that year photographed Arkansas farmers, also evicted from the Dibble plantation, who had relocated to the Hillhouse Delta cooperative farm in Mississippi. One of her more poignant Arkansas images is the portrait of a young African American boy named Clarence Weems, resettled at Hillhouse, whose father had been beaten and then disappeared.

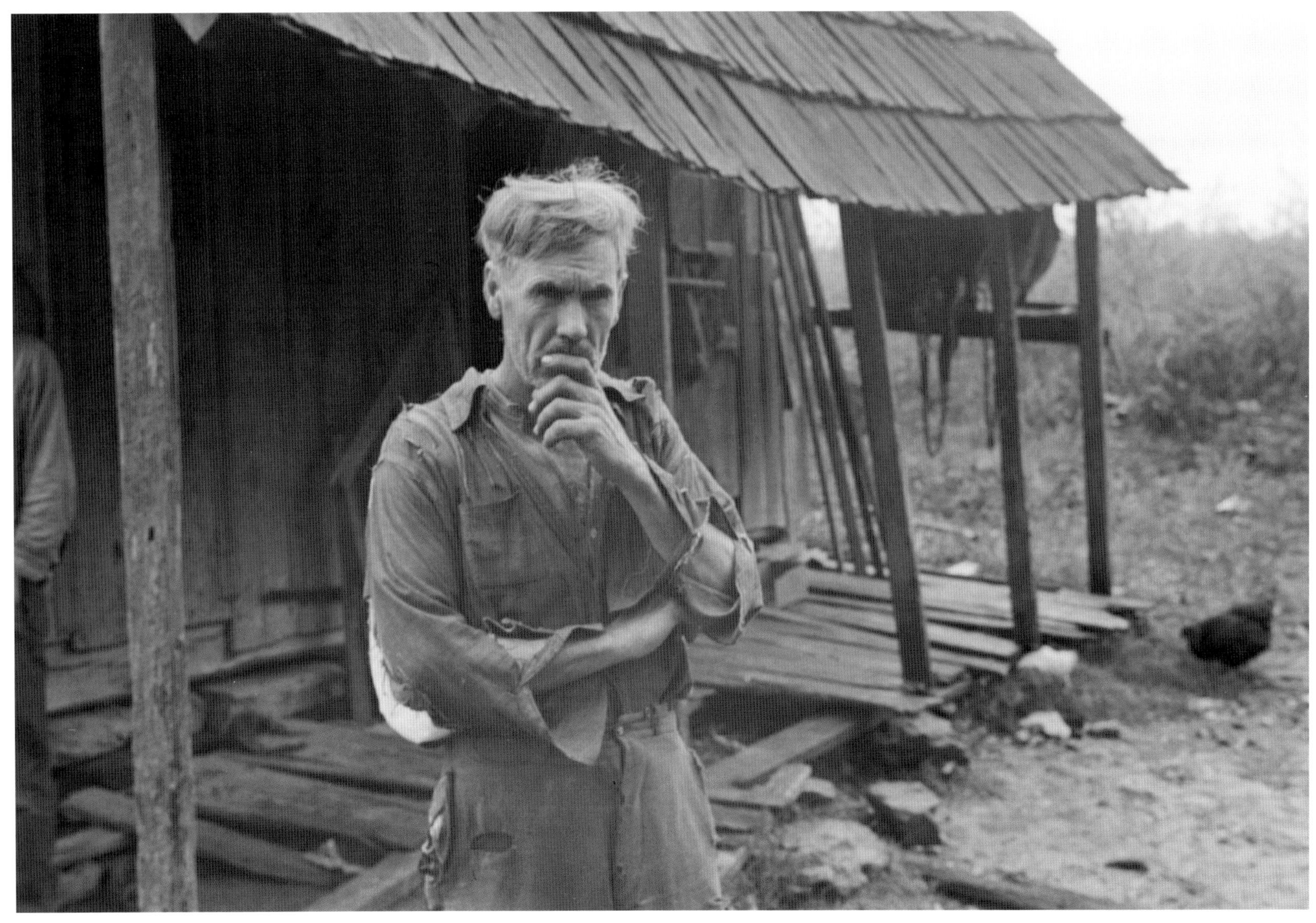

Ben Shahn identified Sam Nichols by name in the caption for this photo in front of Nichols's house. Over the years, FSA photographers rarely identified subjects, though sometimes they used fake names. Nichols was a tenant farmer in Boone County.

(Ben Shahn, October 1935) Farm Security Administration Photograph Collection, Prints & Photographs Division, Library of Congress, LC-USF33–006037–M3

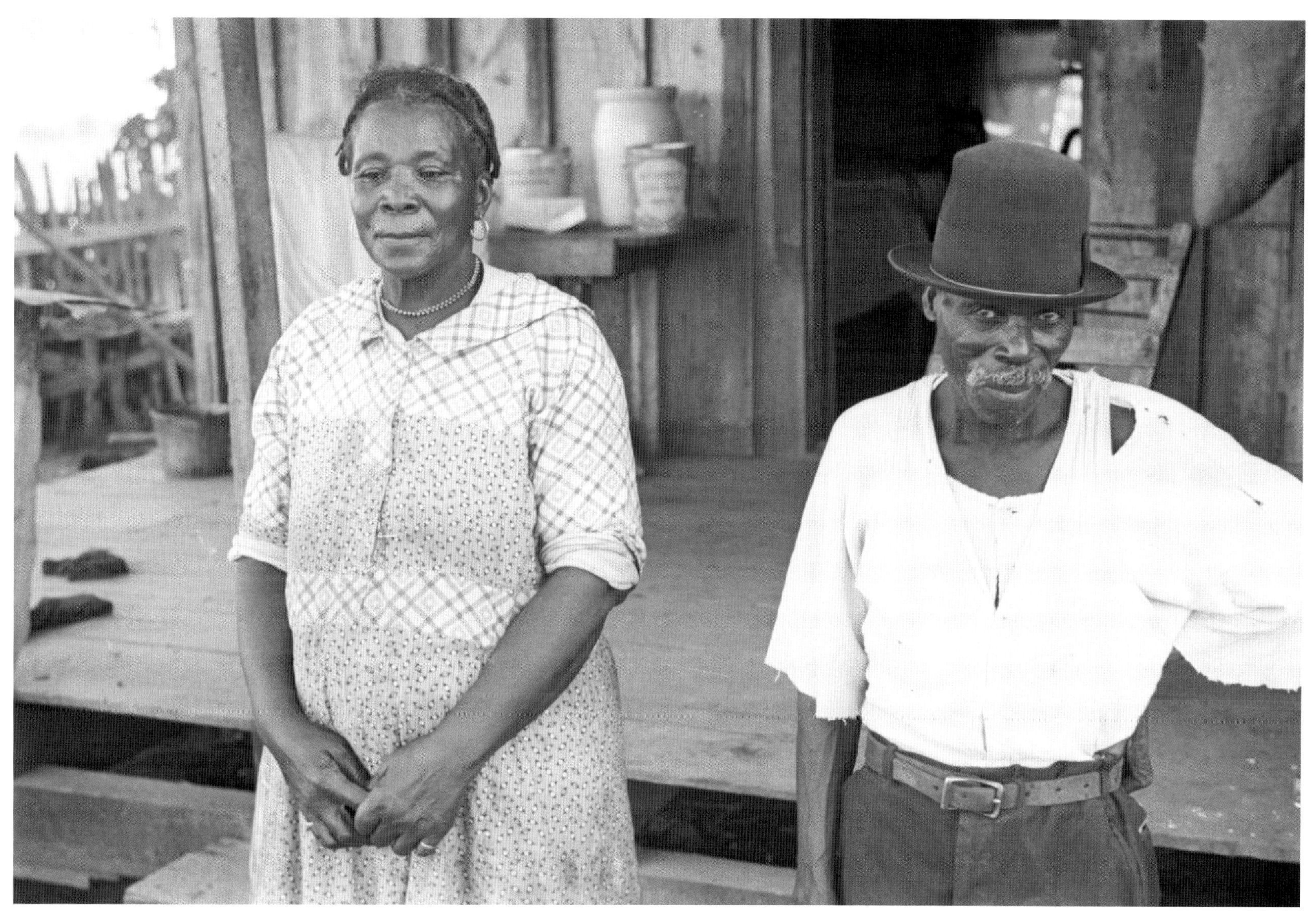

A sharecropper family in Pulaski County.

(Ben Shahn, October 1935) Farm Security Administration Photograph Collection, Prints & Photographs Division, Library of Congress, LC-USF33–006019–M1

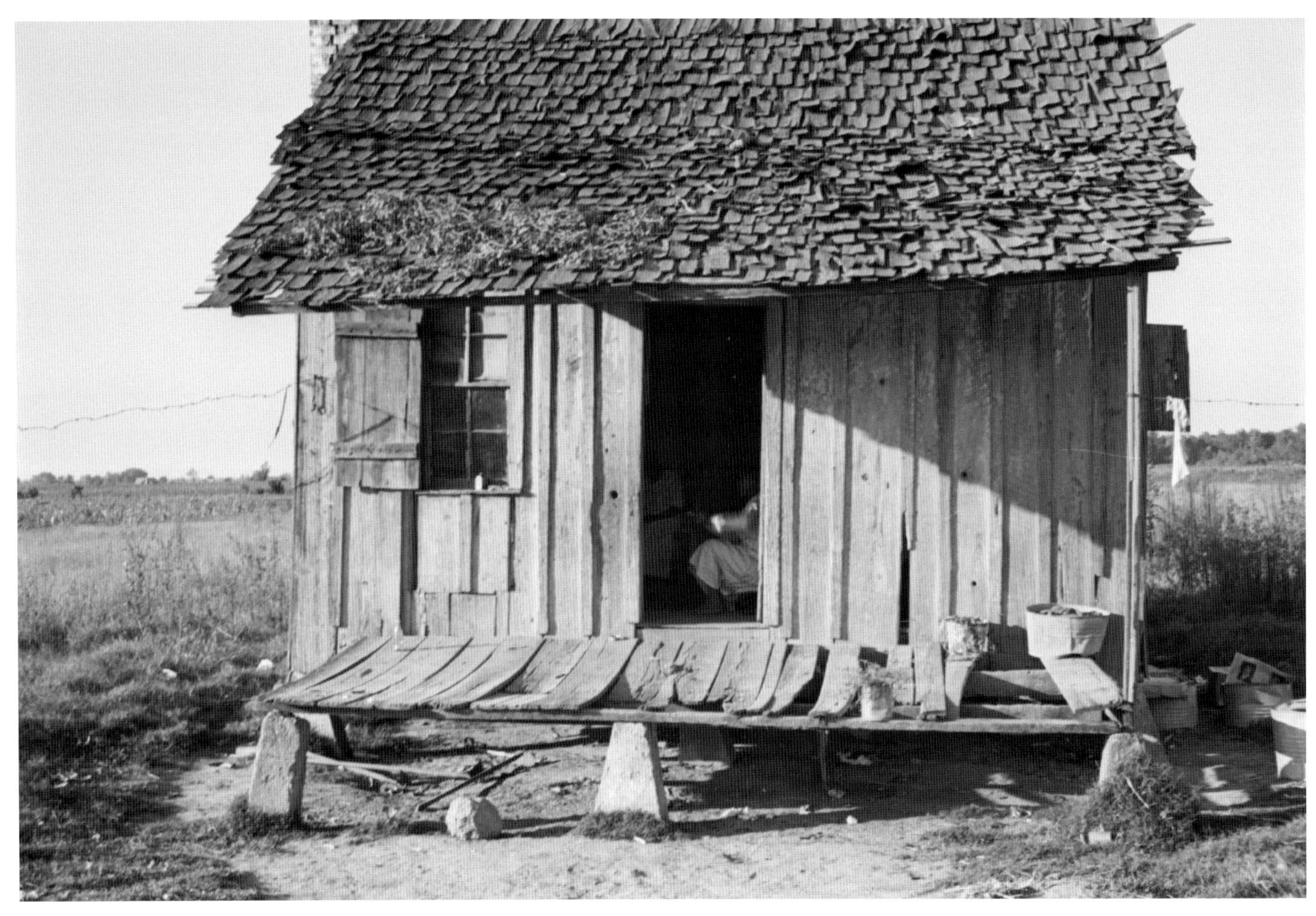

A sharecropper's cabin.

(Ben Shahn, October 1935) Farm Security Administration Photograph Collection, Prints & Photographs Division, Library of Congress, LC-USF33–006106–M4

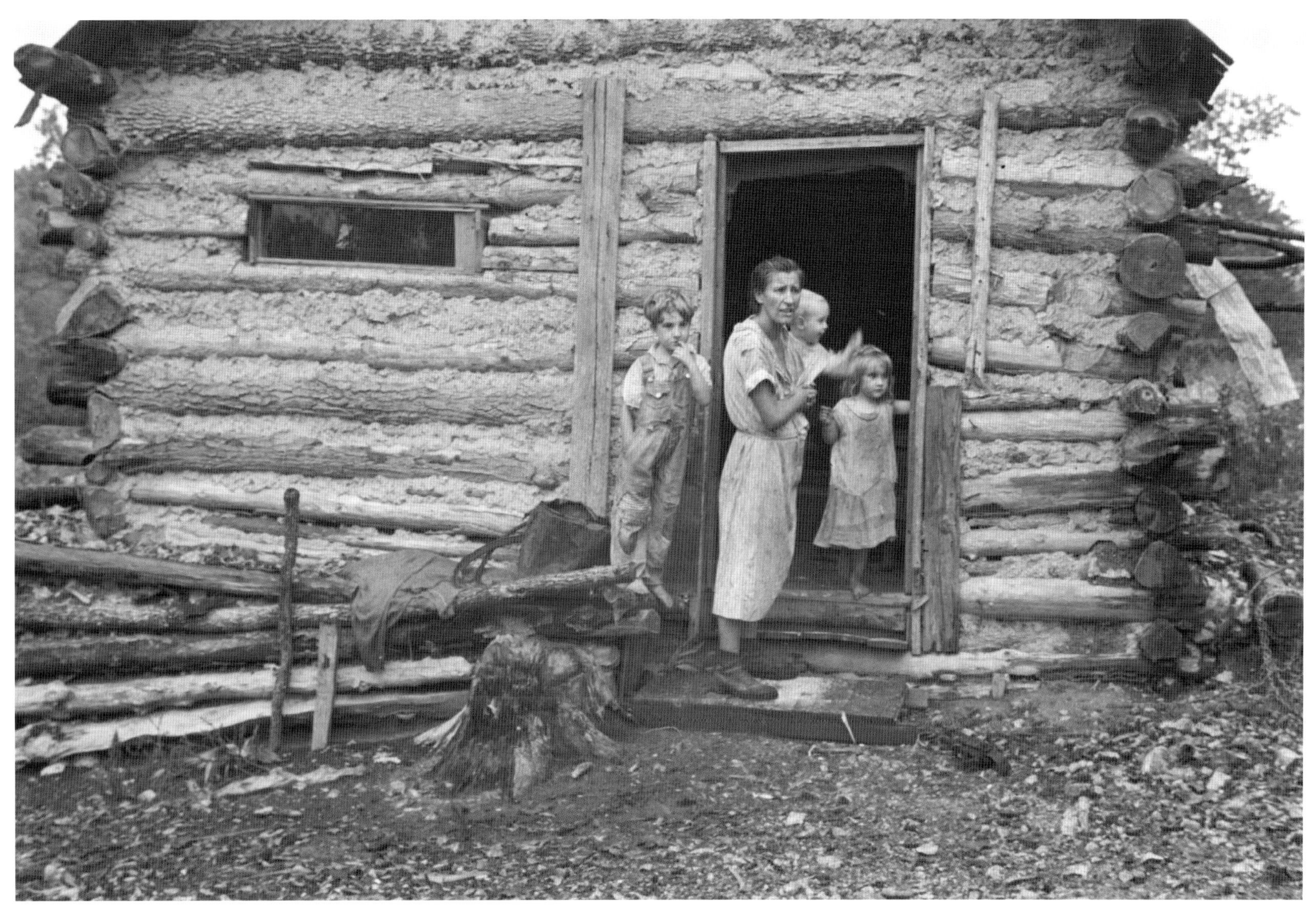

A sharecropper's family and their cabin.

(Ben Shahn, October 1935) Farm Security Administration Photograph Collection, Prints & Photographs Division, Library of Congress, LC-USF33–006069–M1

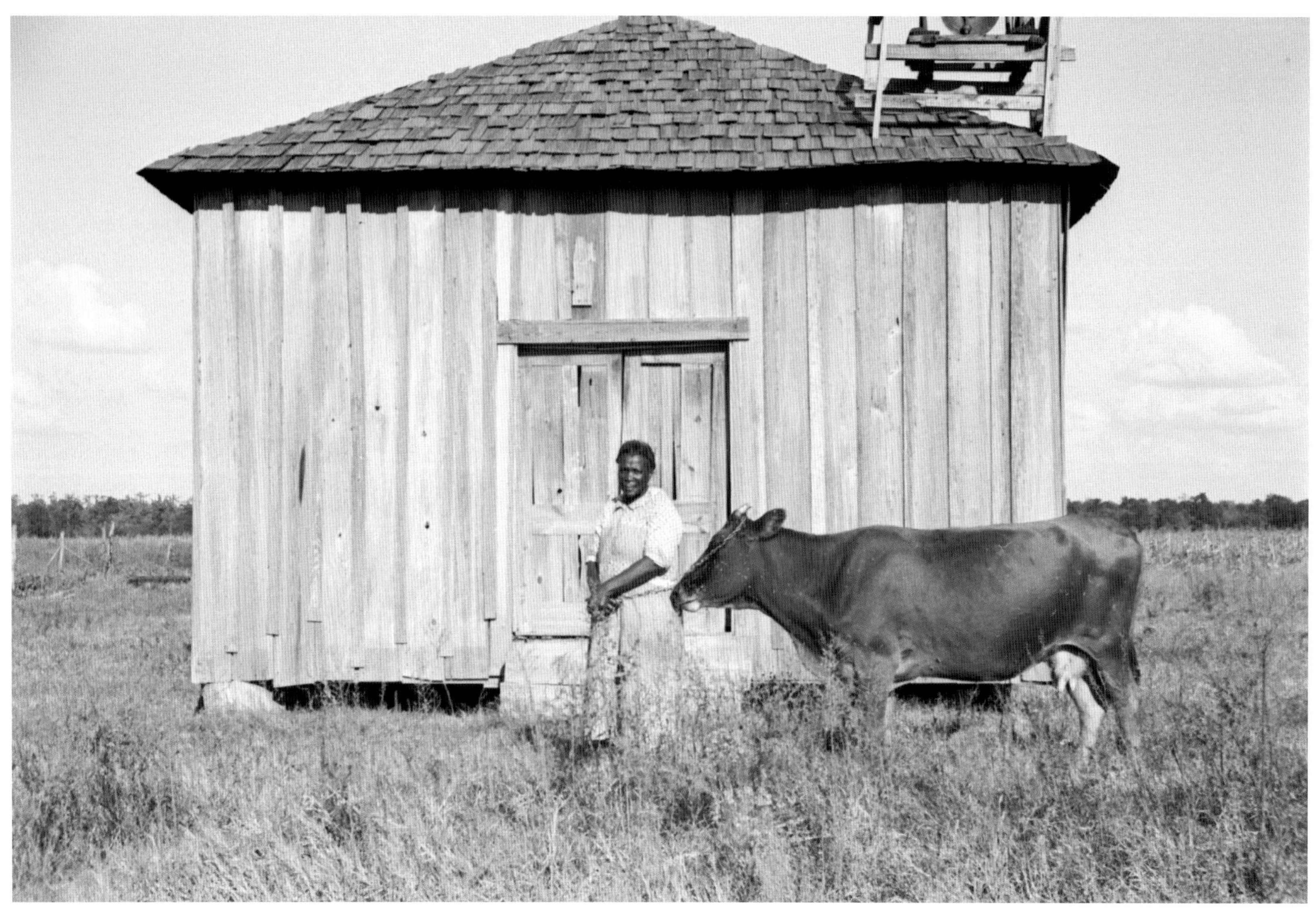

"Mother Lane," a Pulaski County sharecropper, with her house and her cow.

(Ben Shahn, October 1935) Farm Security Administration Photograph Collection, Prints & Photographs Division, Library of Congress, LC-USF33–006105–M5

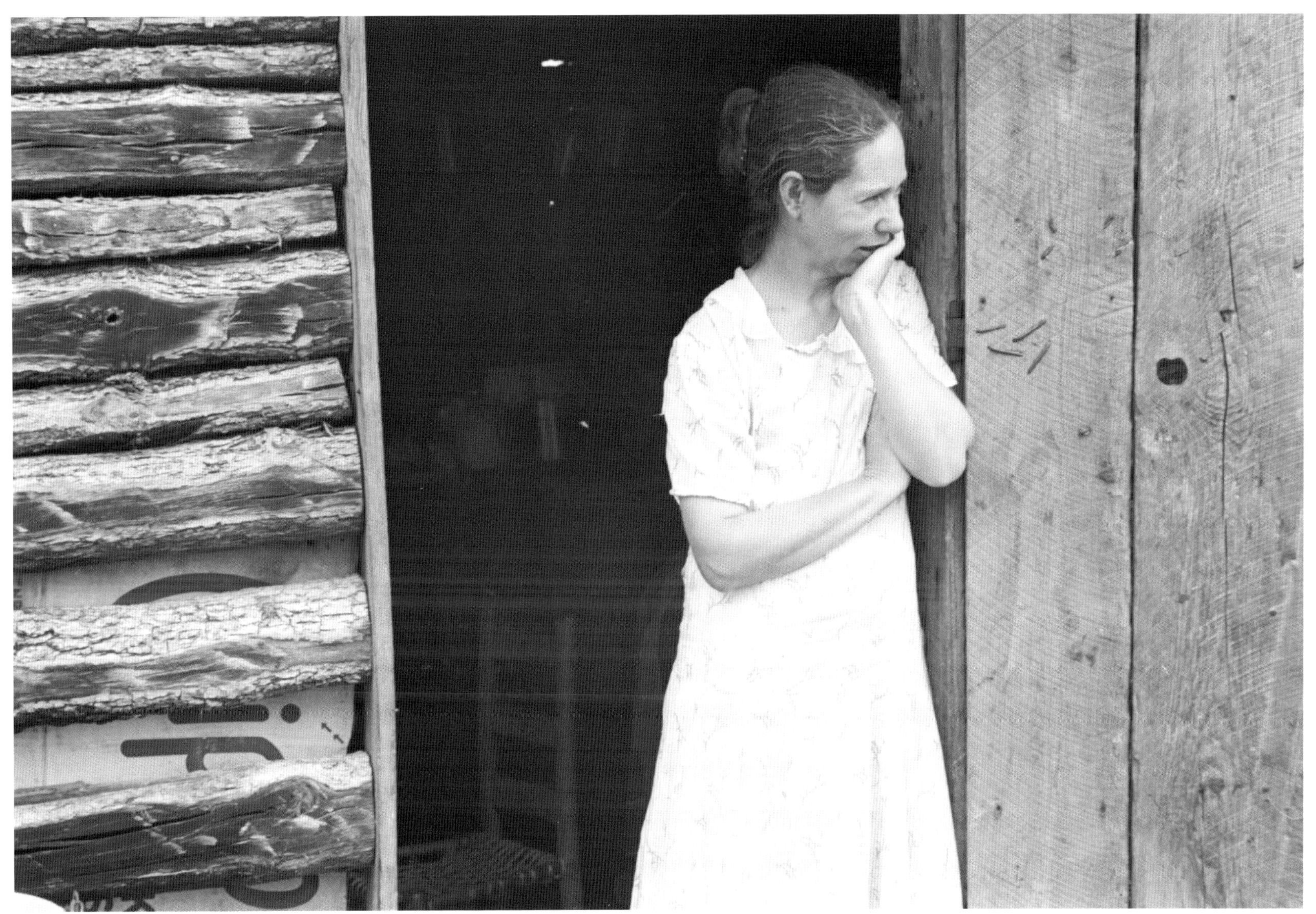

A Boone County rehabilitation client.

(Ben Shahn, October 1935) Farm Security Administration Photograph Collection, Prints & Photographs Division, Library of Congress, LC-USF33–006034–M3

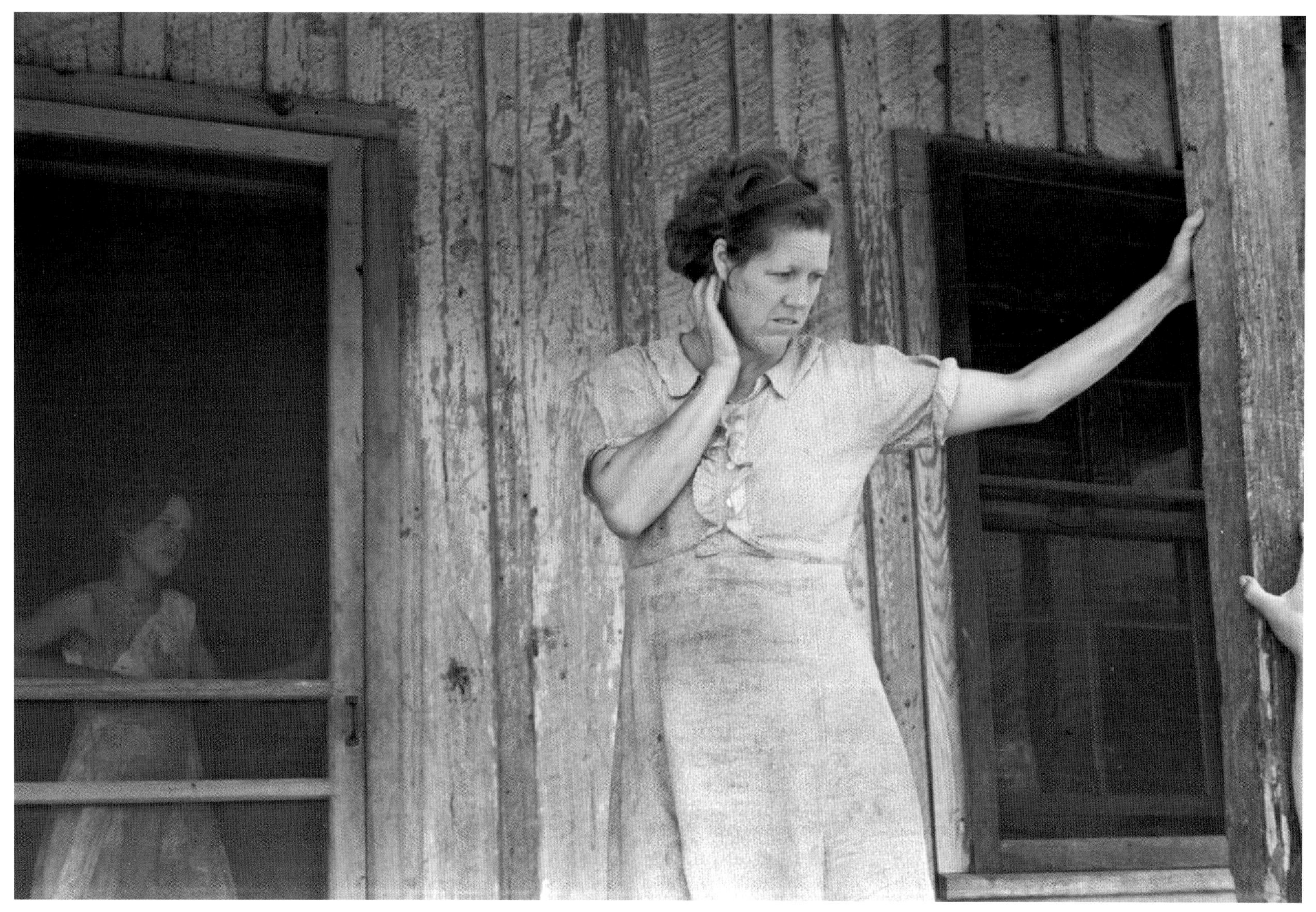

A sharecropper family on the Stortz cotton plantation in Pulaski County.

(Arthur Rothstein, August 1935) Farm Security Administration Photograph Collection, Prints & Photographs Division, Library of Congress, LC-USF33–002028–M1

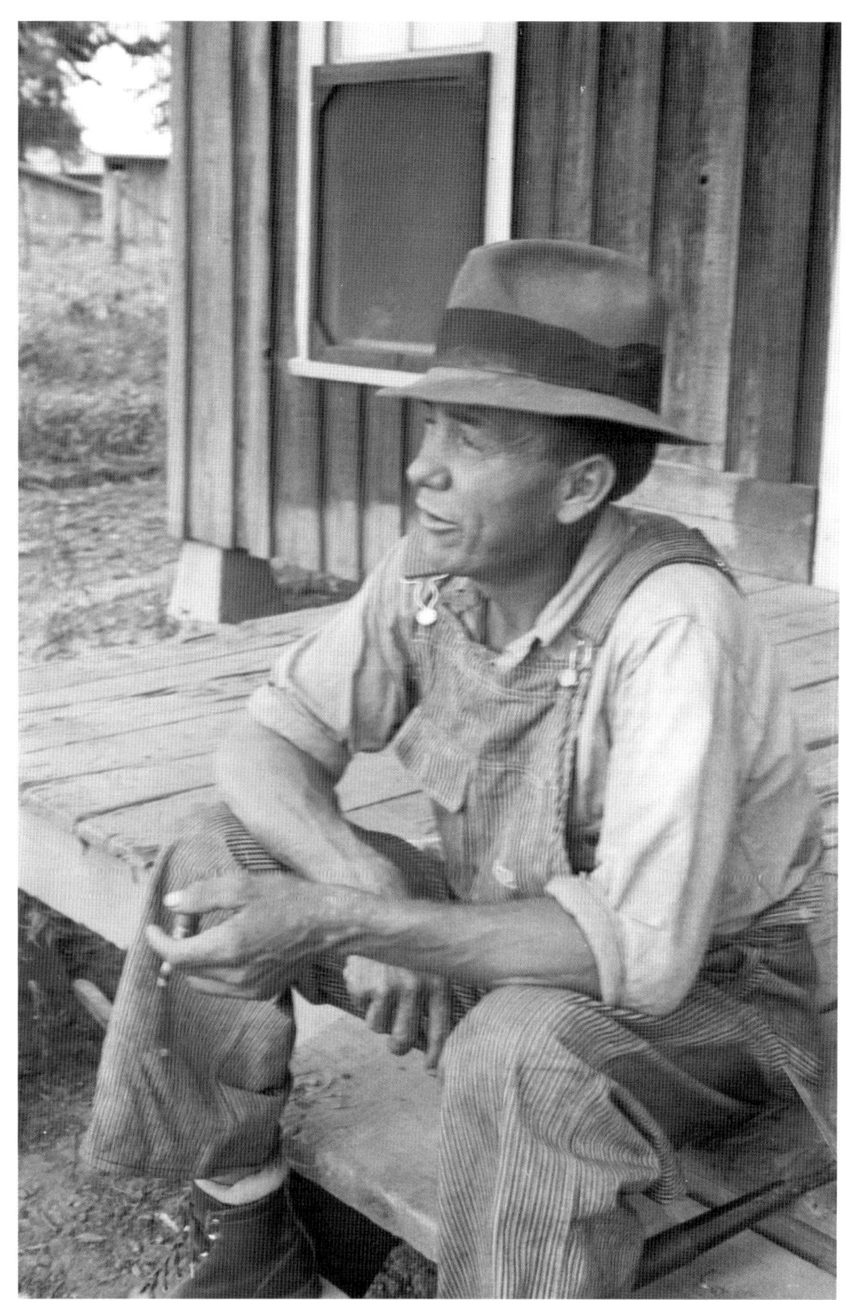

A sharecropper on the front porch of a company house on the Wilson cotton plantation.

(Arthur Rothstein, August 1935) Farm Security Administration Photograph Collection, Prints & Photographs Division, Library of Congress, LC-USF33–002012–M1

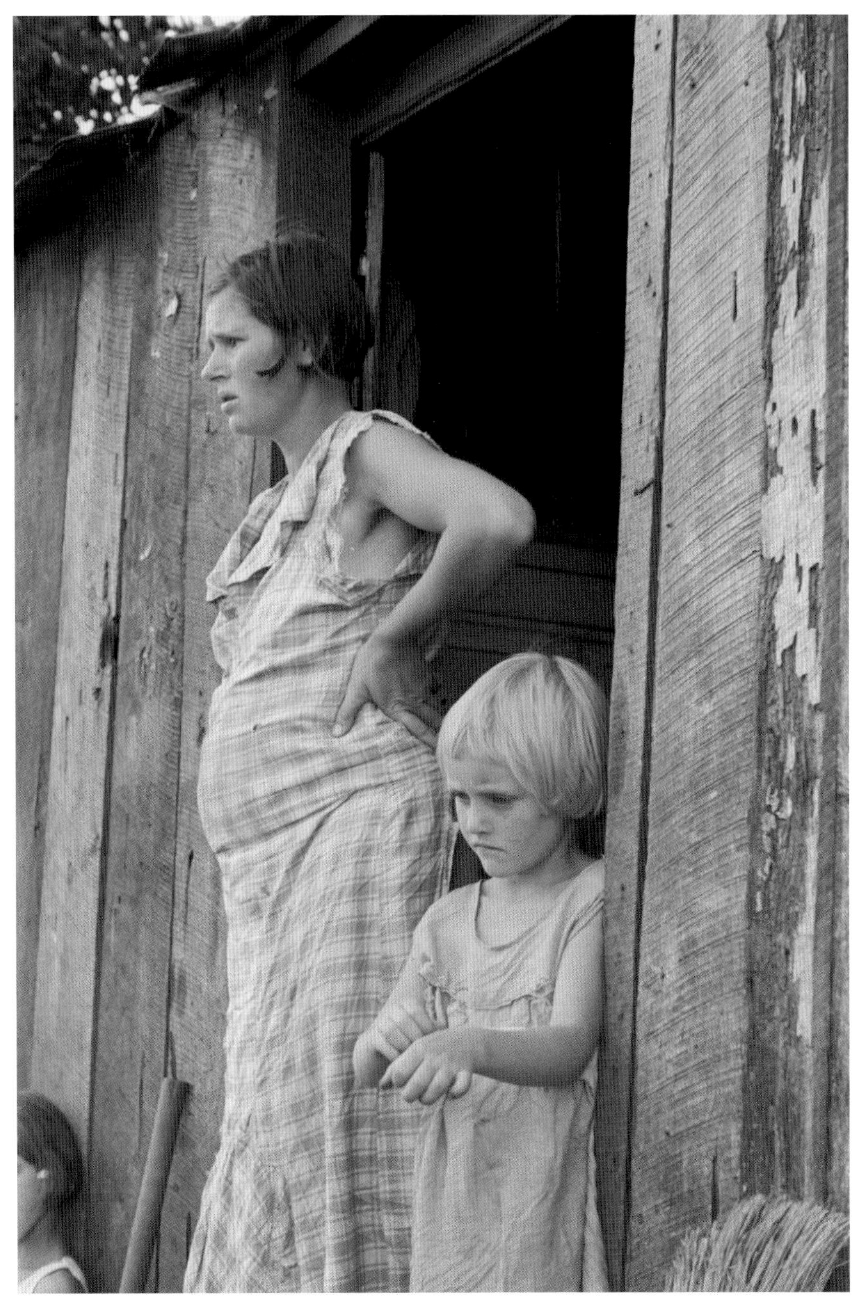

This is one of several photos taken by Arthur Rothstein of Mrs. Gladys Reed and her children that were published widely from 1935 to 1937. *Look* magazine, and others, used the picture as a symbol of southern poverty. Rothstein identified Mrs. Reed and her children as the family of a Washington County sharecropper.

(Arthur Rothstein, August 1935) Farm Security Administration Photograph Collection, Prints & Photographs Division, Library of Congress, LC-USF33–002022–M4

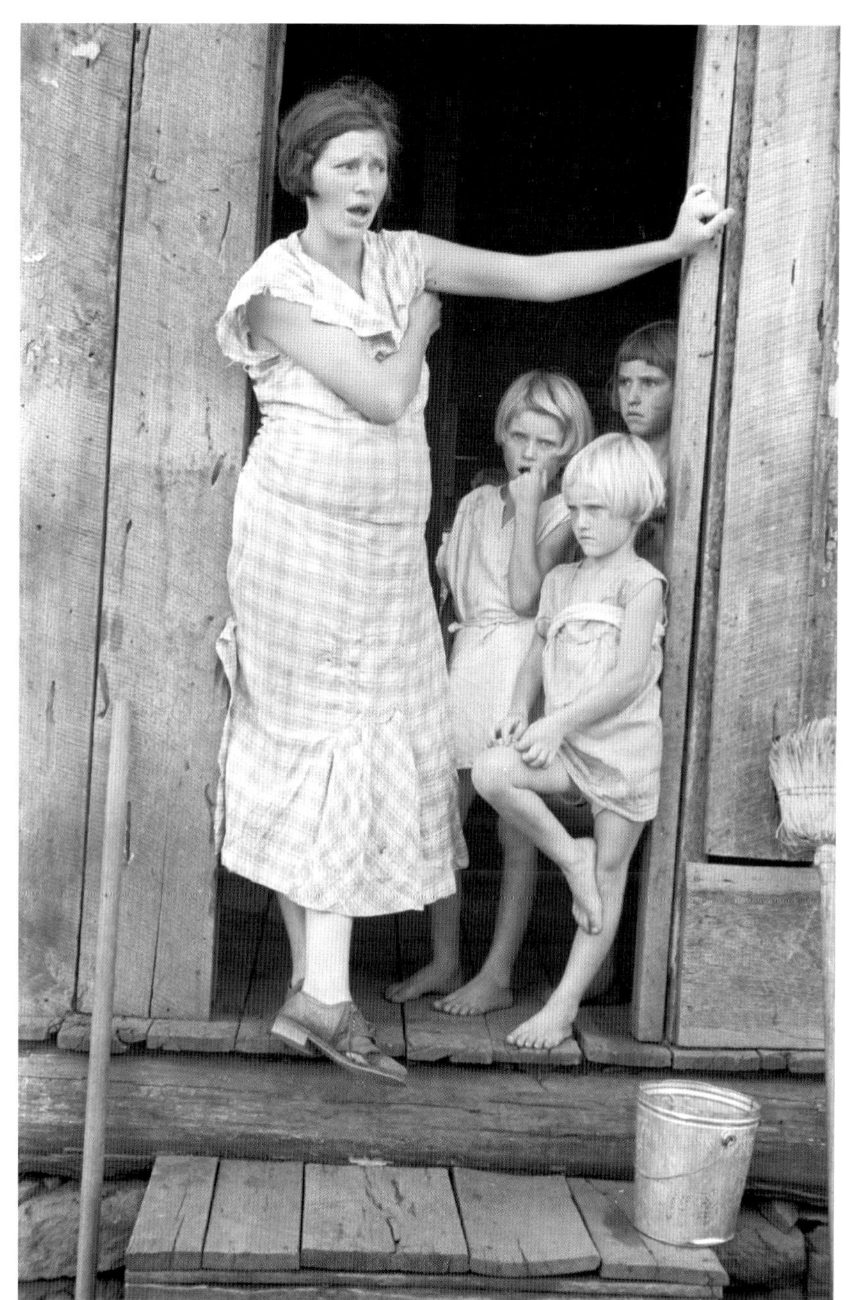

This second Arthur Rothstein photo of Mrs. Reed published by the *Saturday Evening Post* in December 1939 resulted in a libel lawsuit. The Reeds claimed that the *Post*'s identification of them as sharecroppers was incorrect and defamatory.

(Arthur Rothstein, August 1935) Farm Security Administration Photograph Collection, Prints & Photographs Division, Library of Congress, LC-USF33–002021–M2

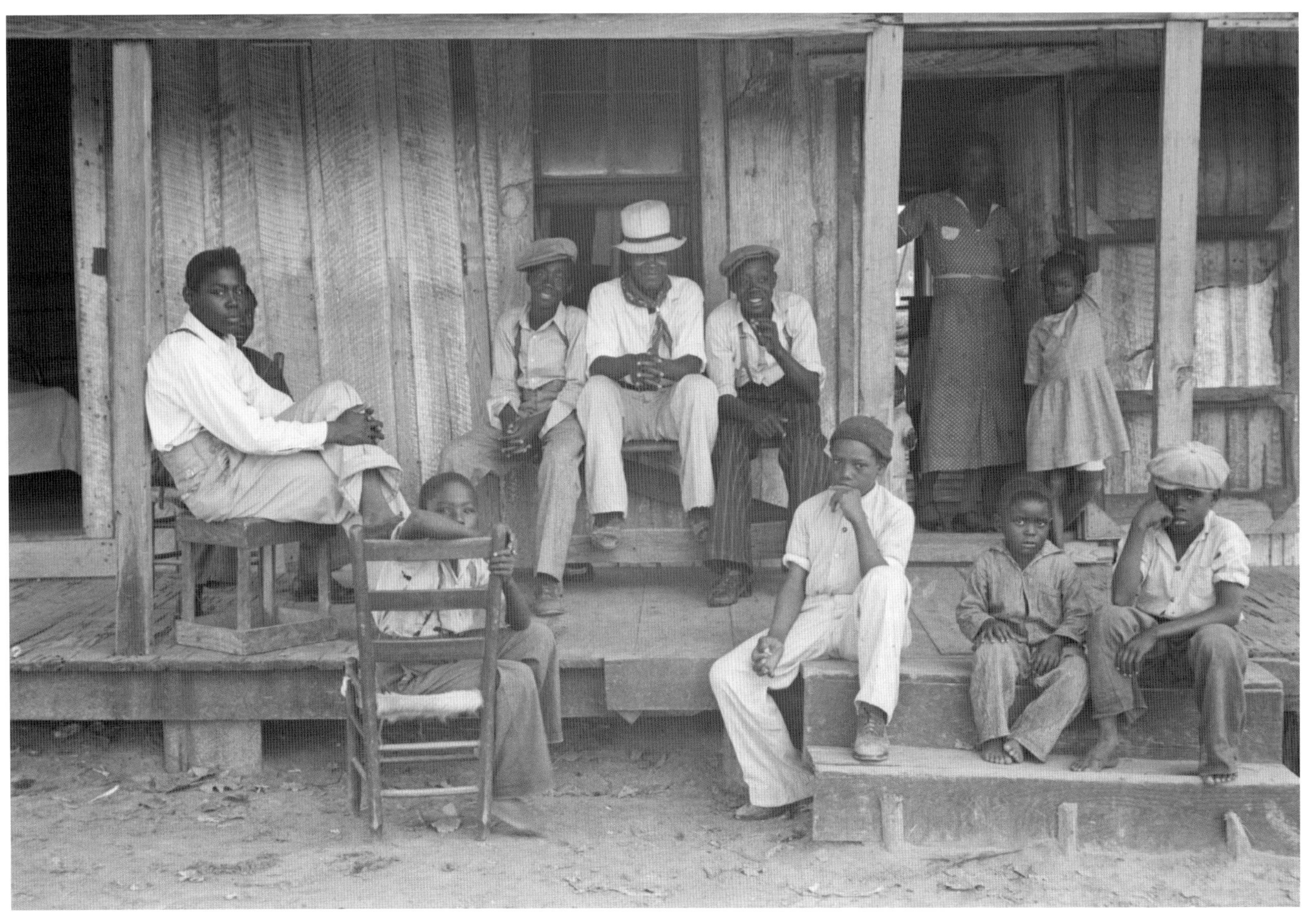

A sharecropper family gathered on their front porch on a day off, taken near Little Rock.

(Ben Shahn, October 1935) Farm Security Administration Photograph Collection, Prints & Photographs Division, Library of Congress, LC-USF33–006025–M3

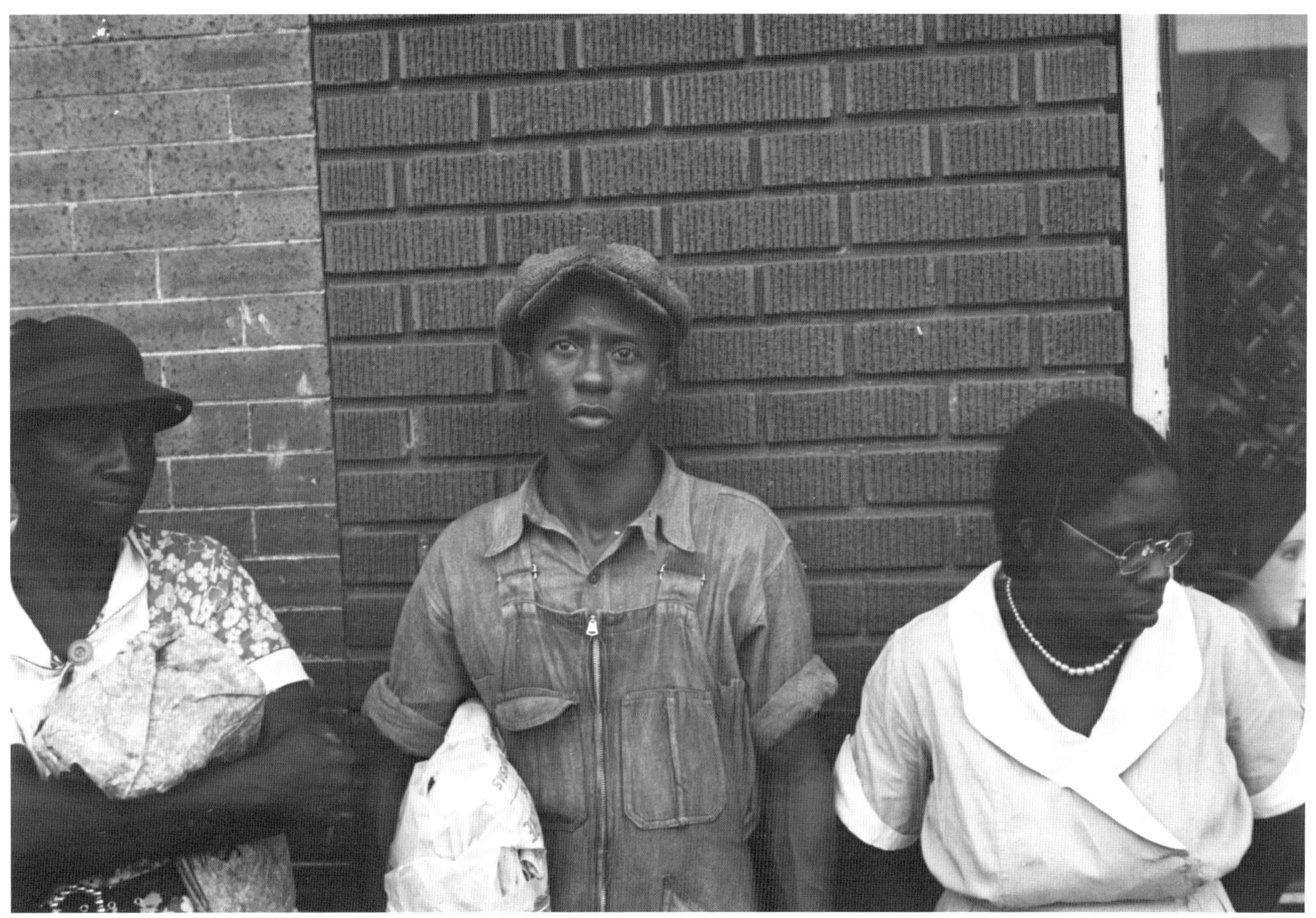

This is one of the few photos Ben Shahn took in his brief stop at Marked Tree in 1935, where violence had erupted against Southern Tenant Farmers Union members in the spring. Shahn identified the people as sharecroppers, but the woman on the right might work as a domestic, judging by her dress.

(Ben Shahn, September 1935) Farm Security Administration Photograph Collection, Prints & Photographs Division, Library of Congress, LC-USF33–006052–M4

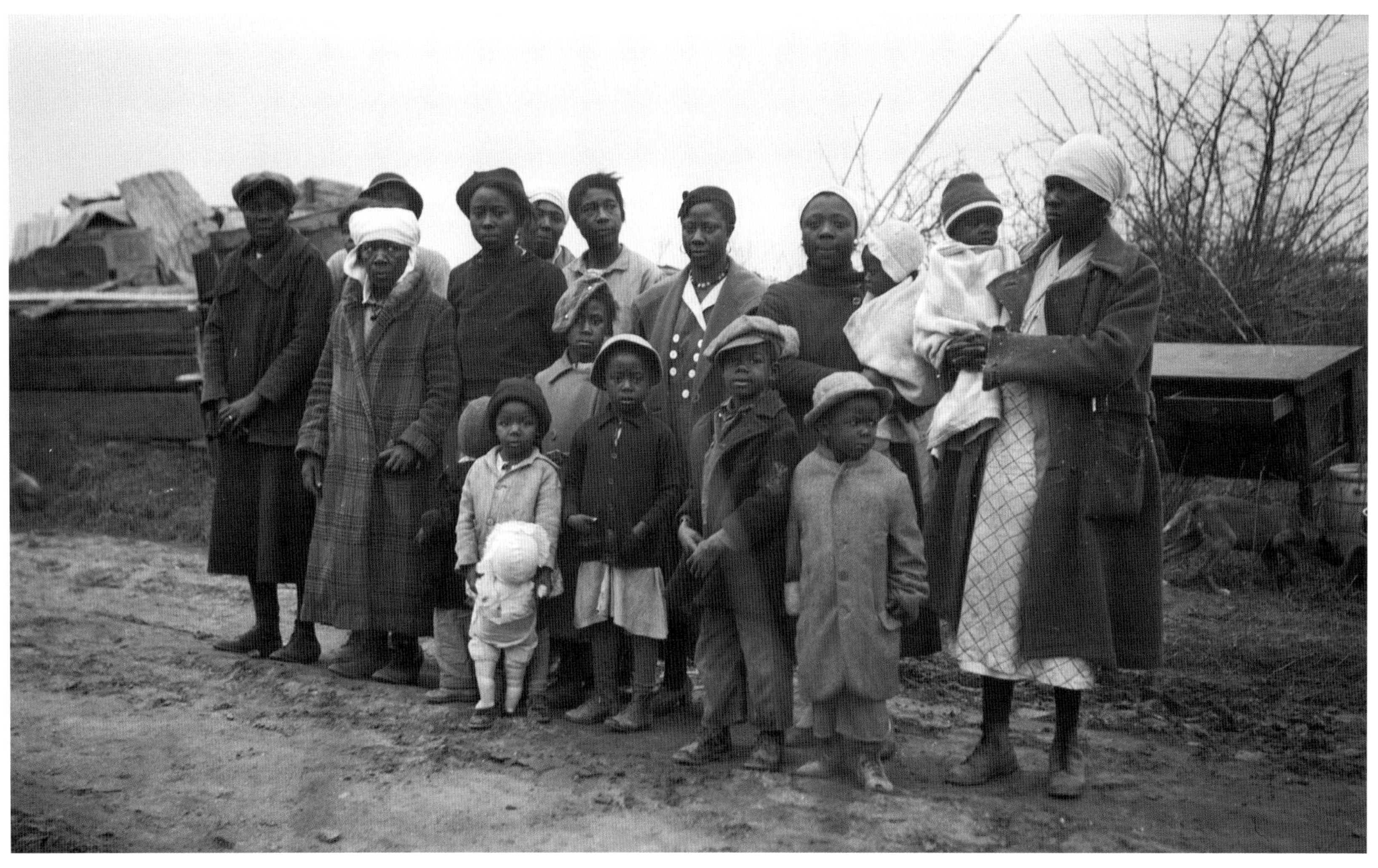

In January of 1936 roughly one hundred sharecropper families were evicted from the C. H. Dibble plantation near Parkin, Arkansas, for unionizing activities. John Vachon photographed several of the families and their possessions before they were moved into a temporary tent colony set up by the Southern Tenant Farmers Union. A group of the families later moved to Mississippi to the Delta cooperative farm known as Hillhouse.

(John Vachon, January 1936) Farm Security Administration Photograph Collection, Prints & Photographs Division, Library of Congress, LC-USF34–014005–E

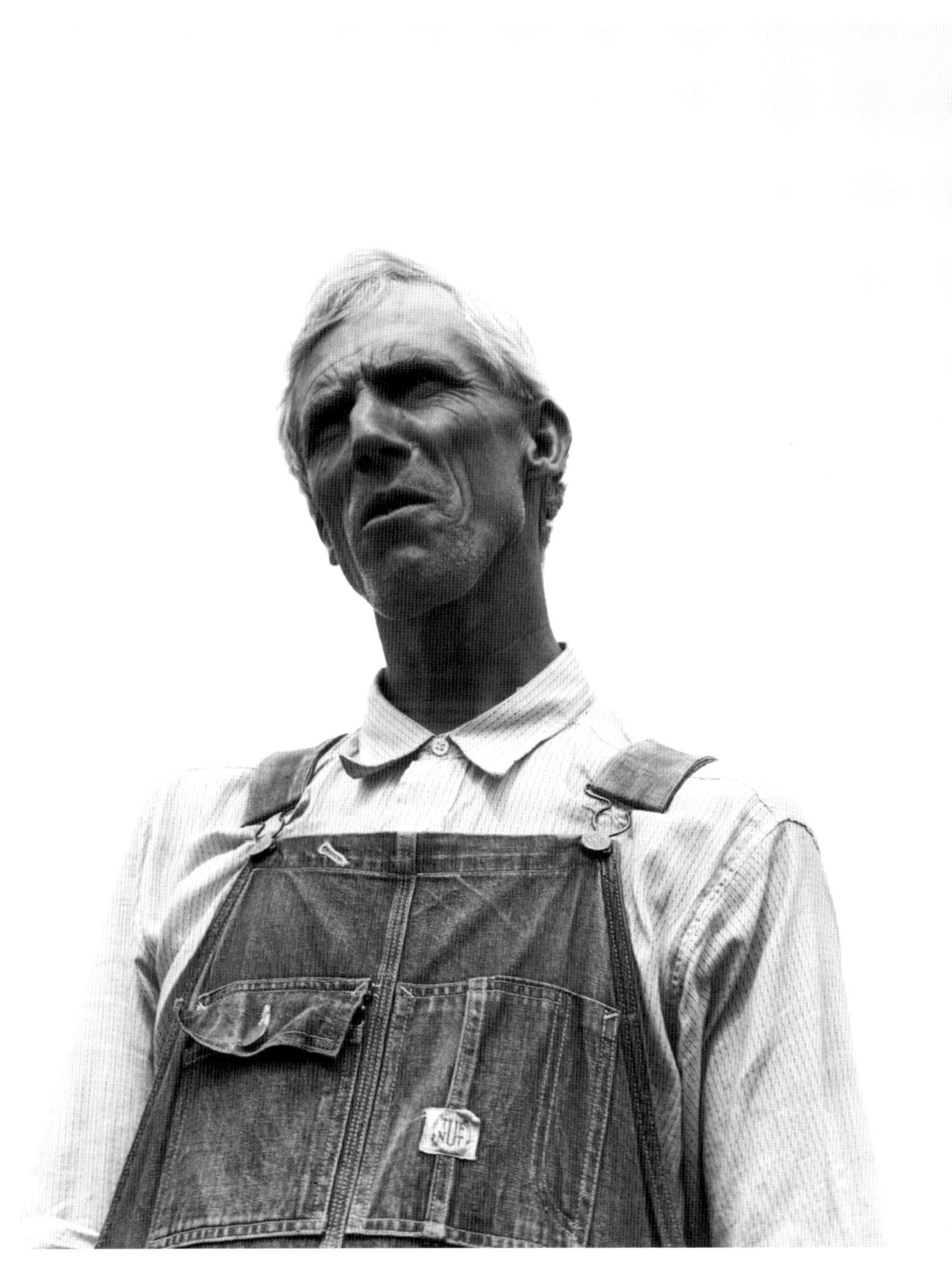

Dorothea Lange visited the cooperative farm at Hillhouse in 1936 and 1937 where she photographed a number of the Arkansas farmers, such as this man, who had been evicted from the Dibble plantation. Hillhouse was settled by both white and African American farmers who shared in the work and in the profits.

(Dorothea Lange, July–September 1936) Farm Security Administration Photograph Collection, Prints & Photographs Division, Library of Congress, LC-USF34–009374–C

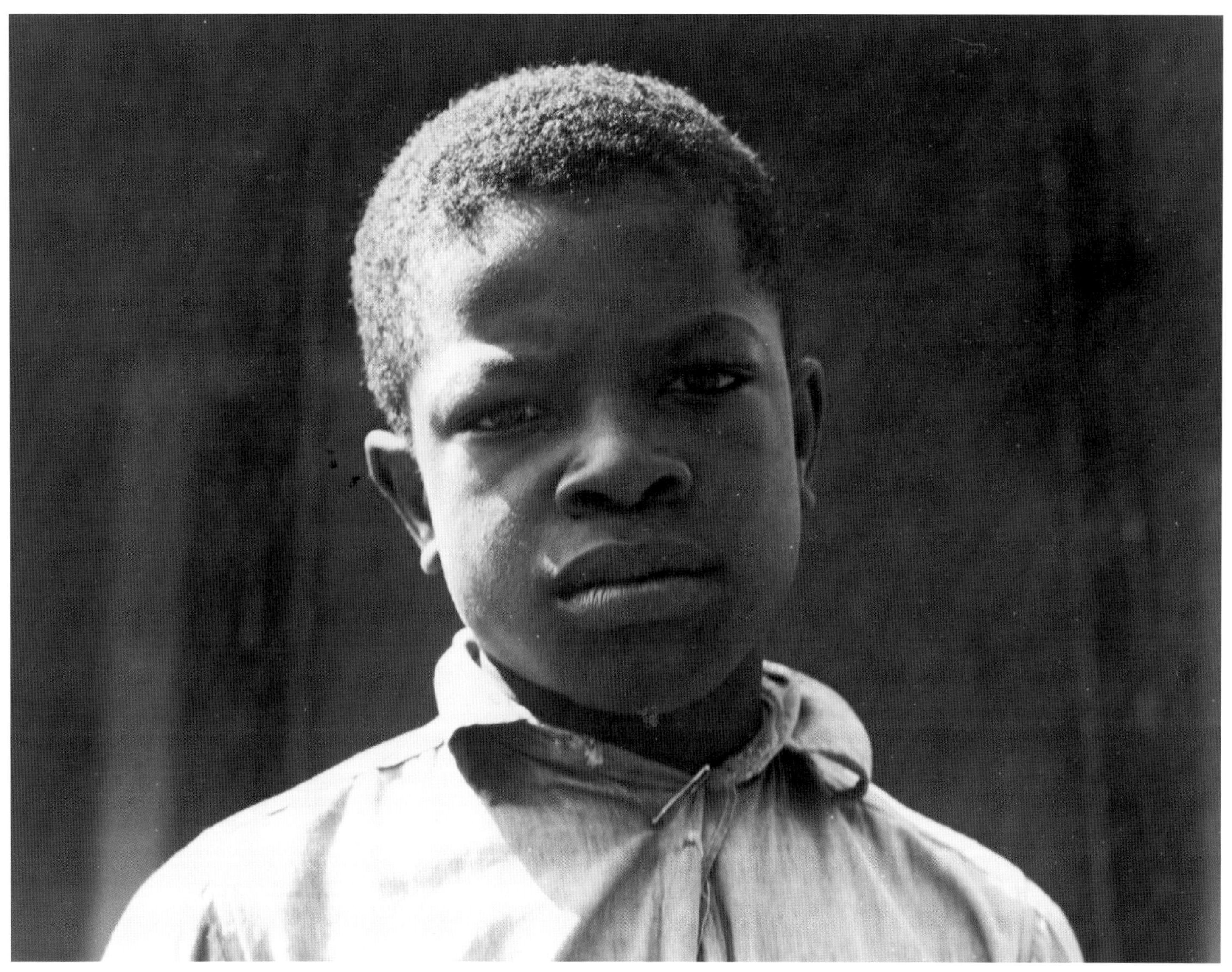

Dorothea Lange wrote that Clarence Weems had been relocated from Arkansas to the Hillhouse Delta cooperative farm in Mississippi, and that he could remember the evictions of farmers' union members in Arkansas, where his father was beaten and then disappeared.

(Dorothea Lange, June 1937) Farm Security Administration Photograph Collection, Prints & Photographs Division, Library of Congress, LC-USF34–017338–C

THREE | RESETTLEMENT FARMS

BEN SHAHN'S 1935 photographs of Arkansas cotton pickers and sharecroppers told a story of destitution and poverty so extreme it strained the imagination. RA/FSA photographs taken three years later of the government's resettlement farms presented a much different message, one of radical change in the lives of poor Arkansas farmers, thanks to the federal relief program that gave them a fresh start. The difference in the photographs reflected the shift in the role of the photo project from awakening Americans to a crisis to demonstrating the government's effectiveness in addressing it.

Of the thousands of Arkansas farmers in dire poverty, the resettlement program affected only a small number, around fourteen hundred; however, at least according to the RA/FSA photos, their lives were immeasurably better. The resettlement farms are heavily covered in the Arkansas photos. In fact, there are more pictures of these farms than almost any other topic—nearly four hundred. Out of the sixteen resettlement projects in the state, the RA/FSA photographers focused on five—Lake Dick, Lakeview, Dyess Colony, Plum Bayou, and Chicot, with the most attention given to Lake Dick.

Rexford Tugwell devised the resettlement farm program as part of his plan to reform the agricultural system by equalizing the opportunities for disadvantaged farmers. He believed, as he had told Richard Doud, that the reasons for rural poverty were more often drought or erosion than that farmers were simply "poor human material." Capitalism's driving competitive force had benefited large landowners but created great obstacles for poor farmers. The depressed economy now needed the stimulus that could come from converting these farmers into consumers, but farmers needed the government's helping hand.

The grim message of the early RA/FSA photos had supported Tugwell's belief that Americans needed education on the reality of rural poverty. But Tugwell had then been forced out and the Resettlement Administration absorbed into the Farm Security Administration; as a consequence, the message of the photos changed to the much more positive story about the success of resettlement, and the resulting transformation of farm families' lives. The photos helped justify the agency and its programs as it came under fire from large farming operations and their allies in the Farm Bureau and in Congress.

Donald Holley in *Uncle Sam's Farmers* explains what it meant for a farm family to relocate on a resettlement project by describing one family's experience at the Dyess Colony in Mississippi County. The colony had been established under the Federal Emergency Relief Administration in 1934 and later transferred to the RA. Too poor to own land, W. H. "Harve" Smith, along with his wife and five children, had rented until the Depression left them with nothing. After proving that their plight was due to circumstances beyond their control, they were accepted at Dyess, which was only seven miles from their home. As Holley writes, the Smiths had been living in a leaky three-room cabin; at Dyess they moved into a new five-room home—"still smelling of fresh paint"—with thirty acres that Harve had to clear before he could plant.

Most resettled families like the Smiths had to go on temporary relief, but they were helped with household items such as beds and a stove, which would be charged to their account. They were given a coupon book for groceries and received advances for buying farming needs like tools and seeds, repayable over three years. Harve, as the head of the family, could work on jobs around the colony to make money until his farm was up and running. A home economist and a farm supervisor worked with families like the Smiths to teach them home, farm, and budget management, as well as how to improve their skills in sewing and canning.

Training programs such as these obviously helped settlers increase their chances of success on the farm projects, but they also created an environment that encouraged behavioral change, a cultural issue involving social and economic class distinctions. There were hints of this in Russell Lee's photographs of Lake Dick farmers supervising the day laborers who pick cotton on the farm (see chapter 1). The Lake Dick farmers may have escaped the fate of day labor themselves by qualifying for resettlement, where they now have become day labor employers.

Resettlement projects could be single, isolated farms or clusters of farms. Dyess was the latter; it was designed to be a community with a town center of businesses such as a barber, café, and general store, as well as a post office and schools. Tracts for five hundred farms radiated out from the business area, with the acreage depending on the size of the family. An Arthur Rothstein photo from 1935 shows a family of six resettled at Dyess standing in front of a sun-dappled, wood-frame white house. It is perhaps the most overtly promotional photograph of a resettlement farm from Arkansas; the family appears neatly dressed but perhaps more prosperous than might be expected after only one year of relocation.

More typical of Arkansas resettlement photographs are those from the Lake Dick farm taken by Russell Lee and Dorothea Lange. RA/FSA administrators were likely very interested in Lake Dick because it was a cooperative, an organizational system used on only a few farm projects. It was a

Tugwell experiment based on his belief that small farmers could compete with large commercial farms if they worked together on "community-type" projects by cooperating in all aspects of the operation from cultivation to sharing in the proceeds. Instead of working on their own tracts of land, they would all farm the same land, shoulder to shoulder. Critics alleged these projects were "collectivist" and vehemently opposed them.

John Fischer, director of the FSA Division of Information, wrote Lee in September 1938, directing him to Lake Dick: "If you have time to stop at Lake Dick we are badly in need of a complete photographic story on this project. It is one of the most cooperative farms in the country and we have very little material on it so far."

The visual style of Lee's photographs has a different quality from the early Rothstein and Shahn pictures. Their photos were "stand-alone" images, documents that focused on individuals and their living conditions, and that could be published individually and still tell a story effectively. Lee's pictures seem intended to be viewed as a group or series, each one representing a part of a broader narrative. They focus less on the experience of individuals and more on the environment of the farms, leaving the people to serve more as anonymous figures in the display of buildings and facilities. Lee had been on the road almost constantly at this time, photographing several resettlement farms; from August 1938 through January 1939 he took pictures of four projects in southeastern Missouri and in Arkansas. Therefore, he may have relied on this almost formulaic approach for its efficiency or, more likely, to meet specific needs for the photos—such as farmers working together, farmwives in their kitchens, children in school, the farm community store, family members in their houses, and a few portraits of individual farmers.

Dorothea Lange also visited Lake Dick in summer 1938, but took only a few pictures, mainly of the farmers. She showed them working the fields both with mule-drawn plows and tractors, as though to document the expensive equipment that was available to project farmers, but unaffordable to single farmers working their own land.

The photographs of Arkansas resettlement farms argue for the success of the government's relief and rescue program. Holley, however, concluded that resettlement was both a success and a failure. The program was very expensive, costing the government millions of dollars to construct the farms with all of their community buildings, facilities, farmhouses, equipment, supplies, and relocation expenses. Theoretically, the government was to recover most of its investment when farmers finally paid off their loans; unfortunately, that didn't happen and the government eventually lost about half of its initial outlay. Holley and Marion Clawson, a government economist who examined the resettlement program in 1941, both declared the plan was doomed by poor planning and poor administration. Farm families were allowed to take on too much debt, which many of them could not pay back, and they wound up being evicted; others left, unhappy with the operation of the farms or simply discouraged, unable to adjust to life on the projects.

Holley found a bright lining in the resettlement farms, however. He pointed out that they did make a difference in the lives of those farm families who participated, giving them a "renewed hope for the future," which was not to be discounted given the many discouragements during the Depression. This view was shared by others at the time. Holley quotes the *Memphis Commercial Appeal*, which wrote in 1943 that the "original purpose of the FSA—to aid worthy farmers in establishing themselves on their own farms—was valid." Moreover, the paper stated, "The idea was good; the administration of it, terrible."

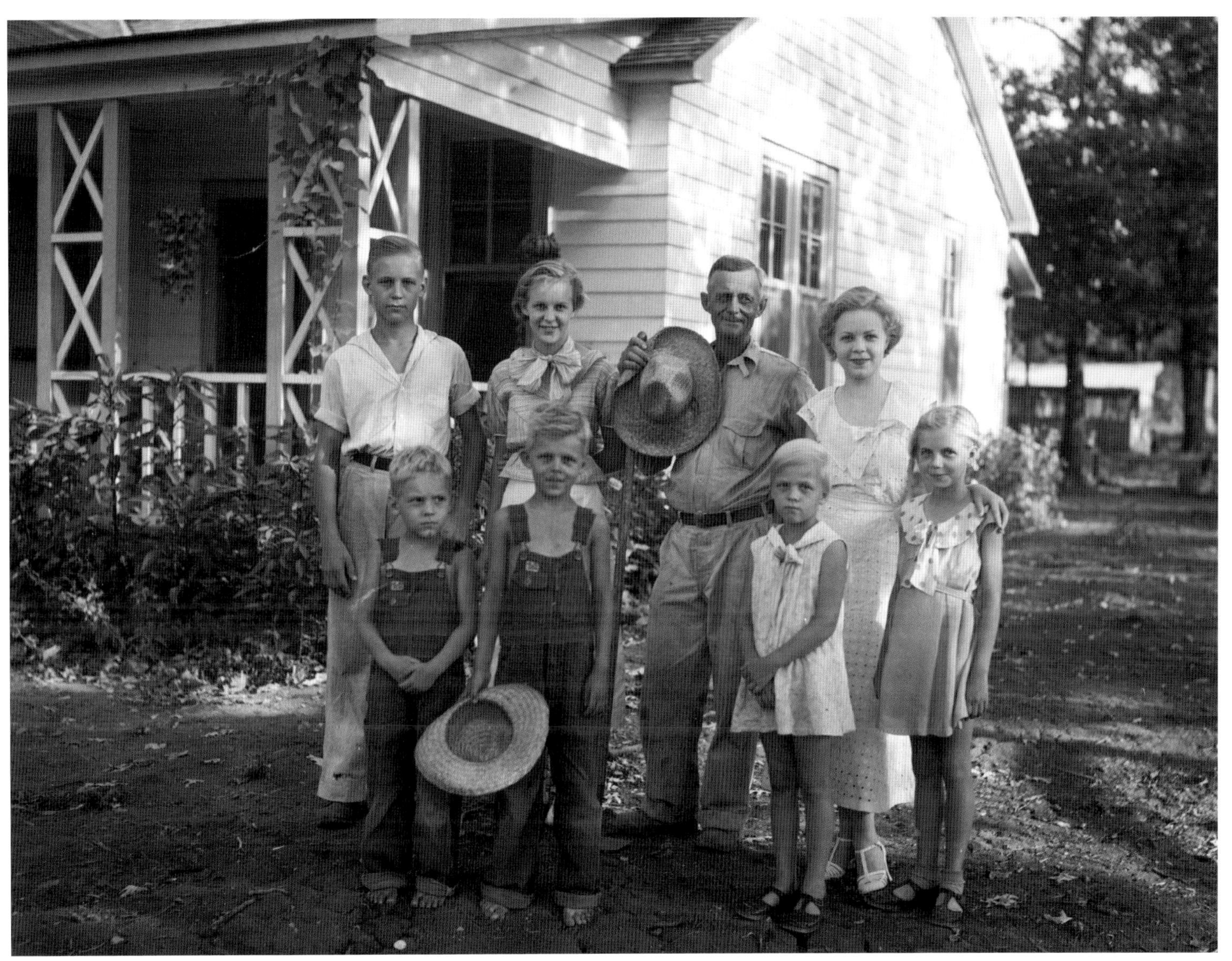

A farm family resettled at the Dyess Colony.

(Arthur Rothstein, August 1935) Farm Security Administration Photograph Collection, Prints & Photographs Division, Library of Congress, LC-USF34–000429–D

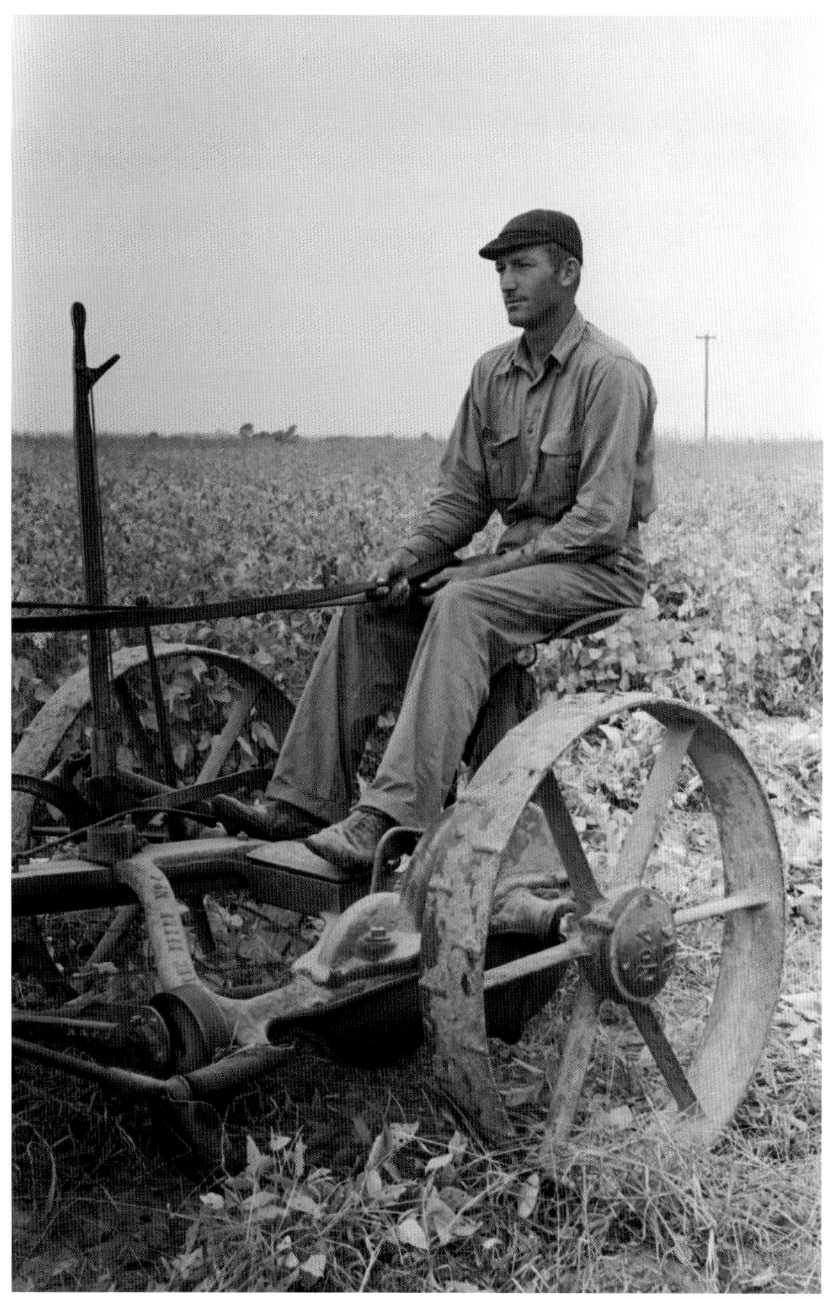

A farmer resettled at Lake Dick using nonmechanized equipment.

(Russell Lee, September 1938) Farm Security Administration Photograph Collection, Prints & Photographs Division, Library of Congress, LC-USF33–011680–M5

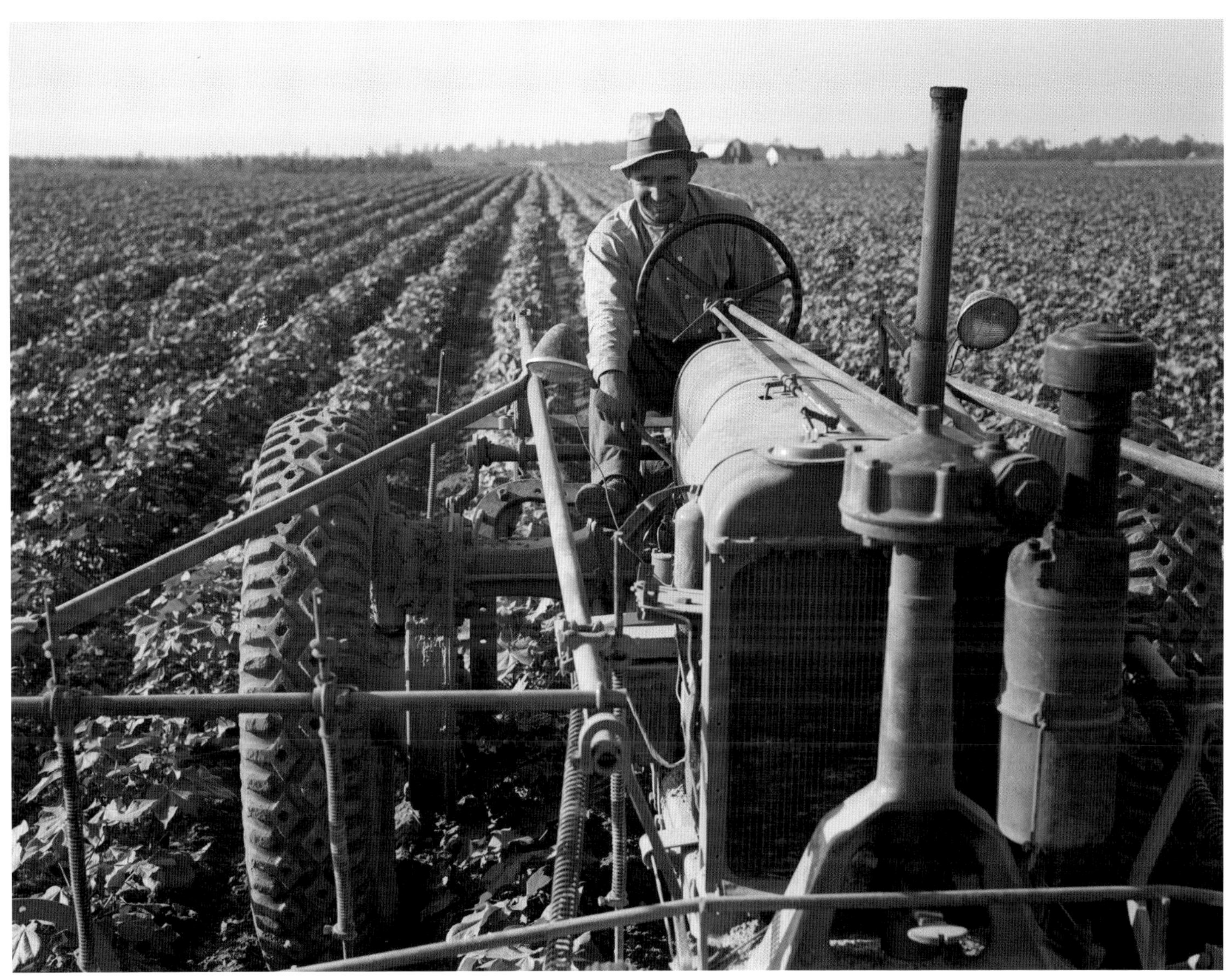

Dorothea Lange's photo shows that Lake Dick farmers also had access to mechanized equipment.

(Dorothea Lange, June 1938) Farm Security Administration Photograph Collection, Prints & Photographs Division, Library of Congress, LC-USF34–018162–C

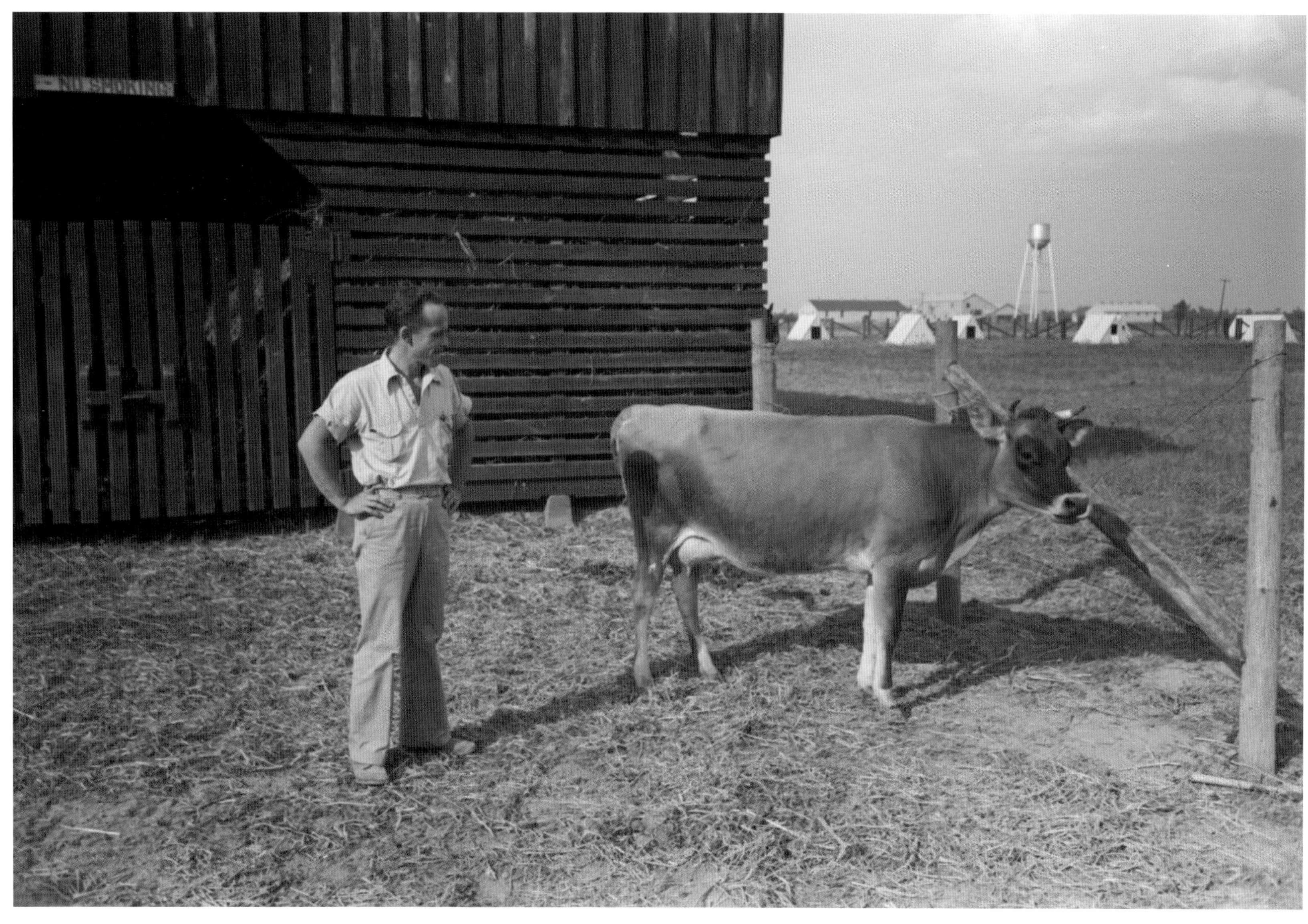

The Lake Dick resettlement farm included operations such as a dairy, a cotton gin, and sorghum processing, and settlers shared the work in all of them.

(Russell Lee, October 1938) Farm Security Administration Photograph Collection, Prints & Photographs Division, Library of Congress, LC-USF33–011686–M2

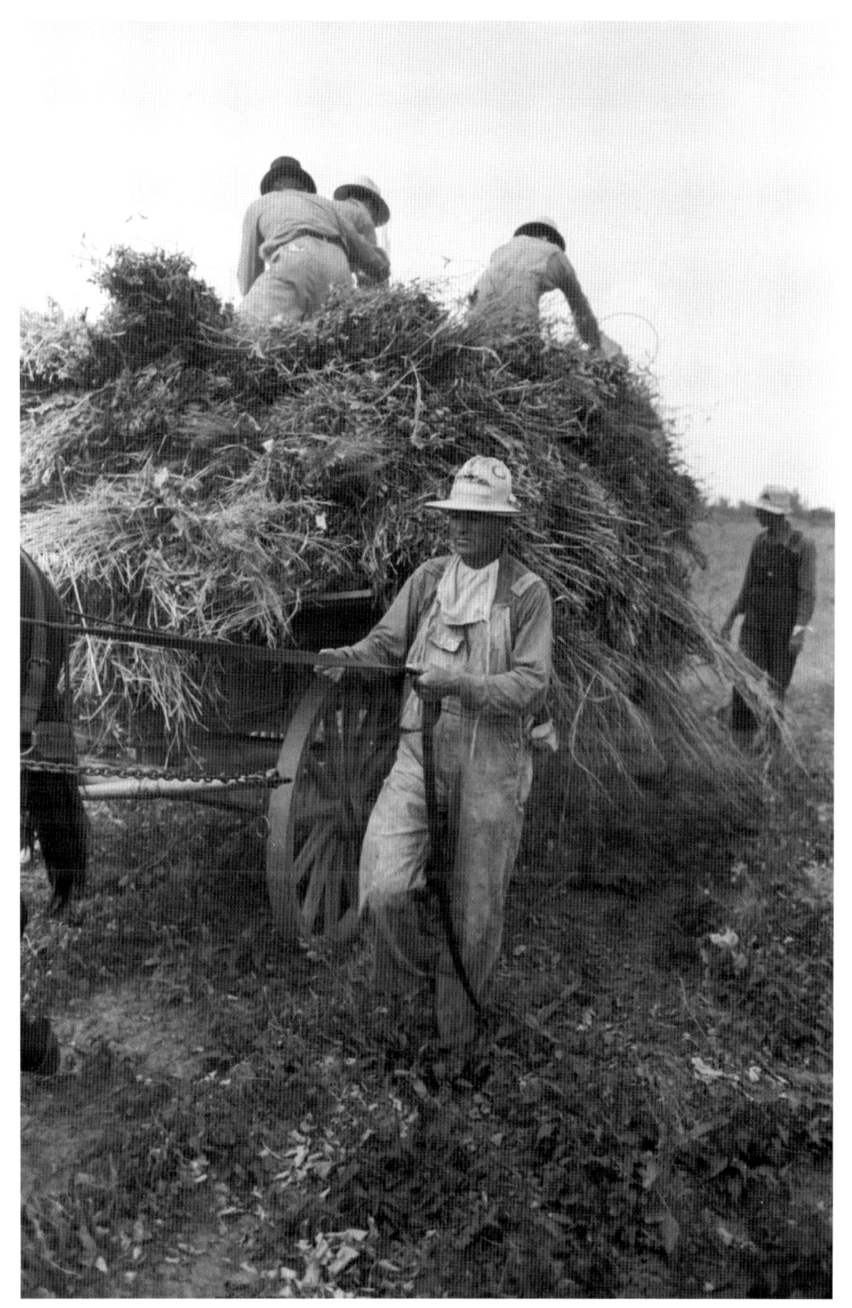

Men are putting up soybean hay at Lake Dick. The man driving the mule is president of the cooperative association at the project.

(Russell Lee, September 1938) Farm Security Administration Photograph Collection, Prints & Photographs Division, Library of Congress, LC-USF33–011675–M4

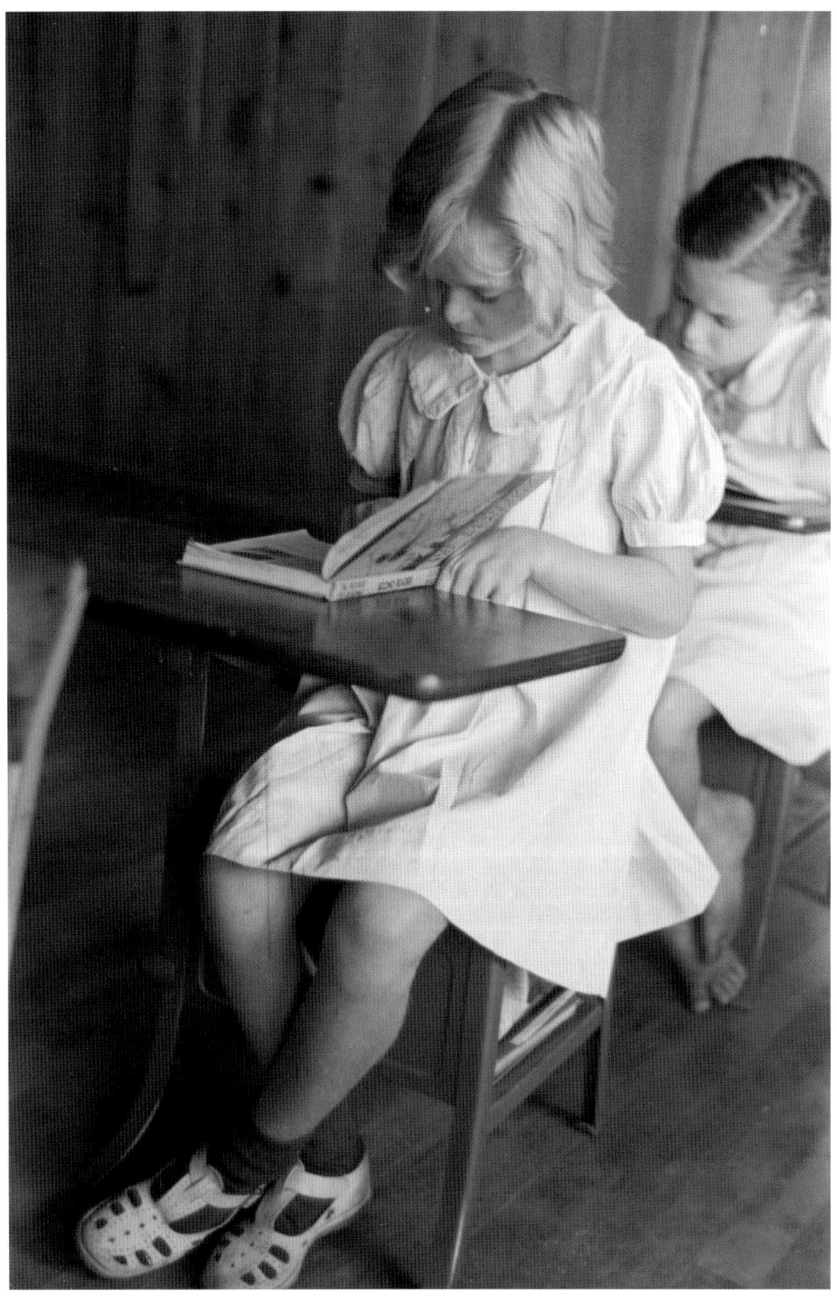

Children in a classroom at the Lake Dick resettlement project school.

(Russell Lee, October 1938) Farm Security Administration Photograph Collection, Prints & Photographs Division, Library of Congress, LC-USF33–011698–M2

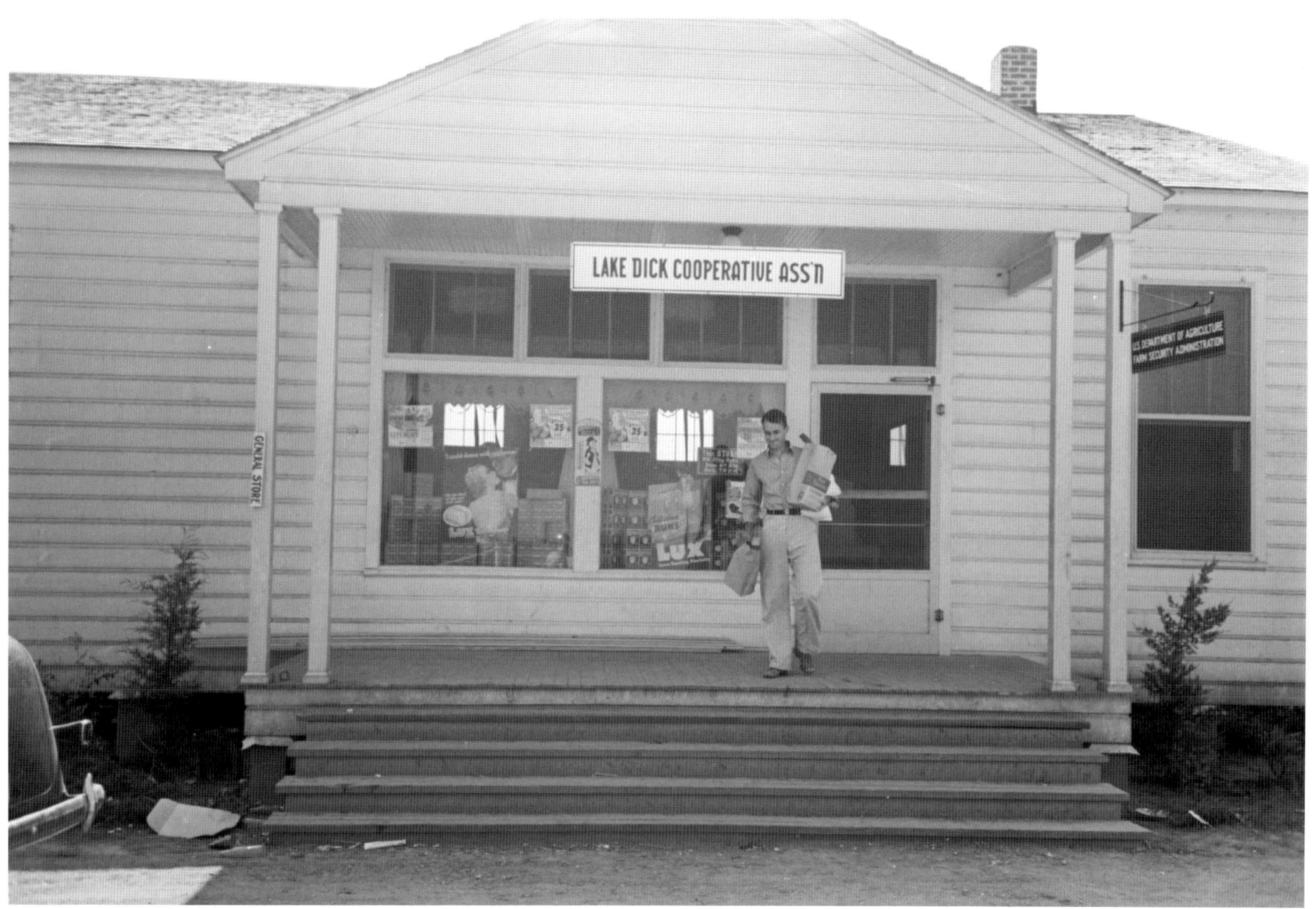

Resettlement families could purchase groceries and other goods in the general stores that were a feature of the farms.

(Russell Lee, October 1938) Farm Security Administration Photograph Collection, Prints & Photographs Division, Library of Congress, LC-USF33–011663–M1

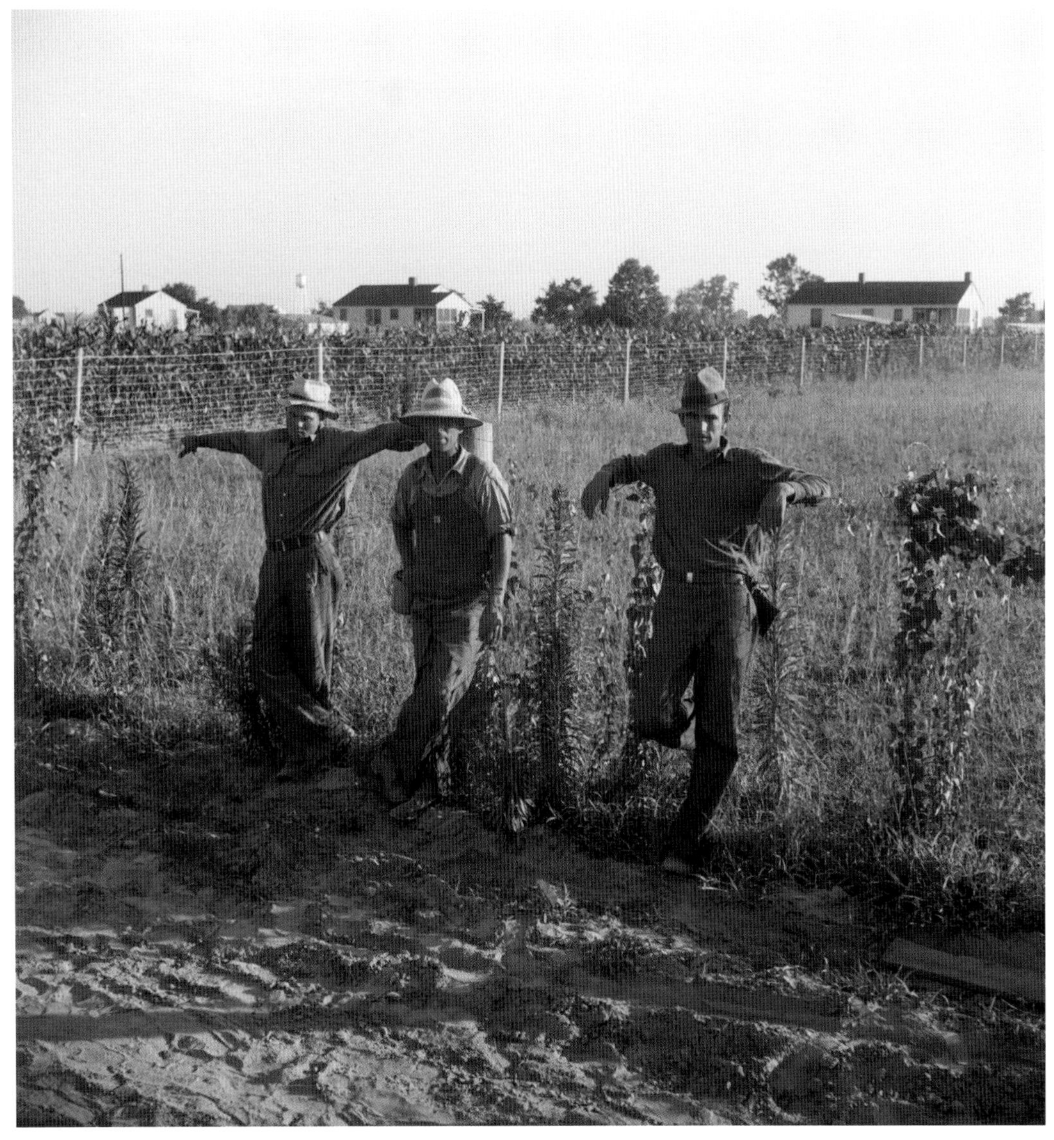

Dorothea Lange wrote that farmers on the Lake Dick project were young Arkansans selected from all parts of the state.

(Dorothea Lange, June 1939) Farm Security Administration Photograph Collection, Prints & Photographs Division, Library of Congress, LC-USF34–018945–E

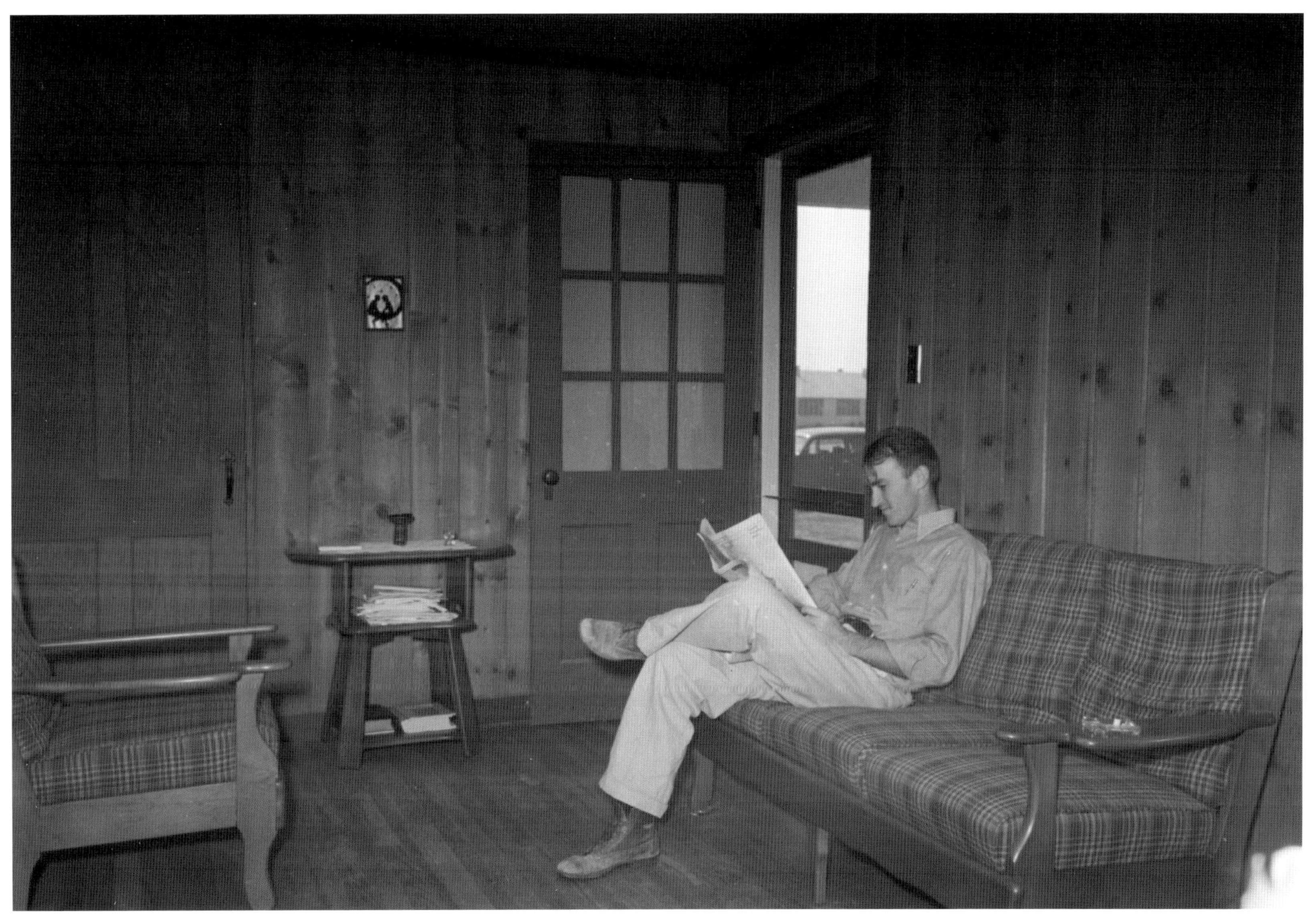

Lee's picture of a Lake Dick farmer relaxing with a newspaper in his sparse but comfortable living room suggests that farmers at the cooperative not only had leisure time, but could spend it reading in houses that were well furnished and had screen doors and multiple rooms.

(Russell Lee, September 1938) Farm Security Administration Photograph Collection, Prints & Photographs Division, Library of Congress, LC-USF33–011662–M3

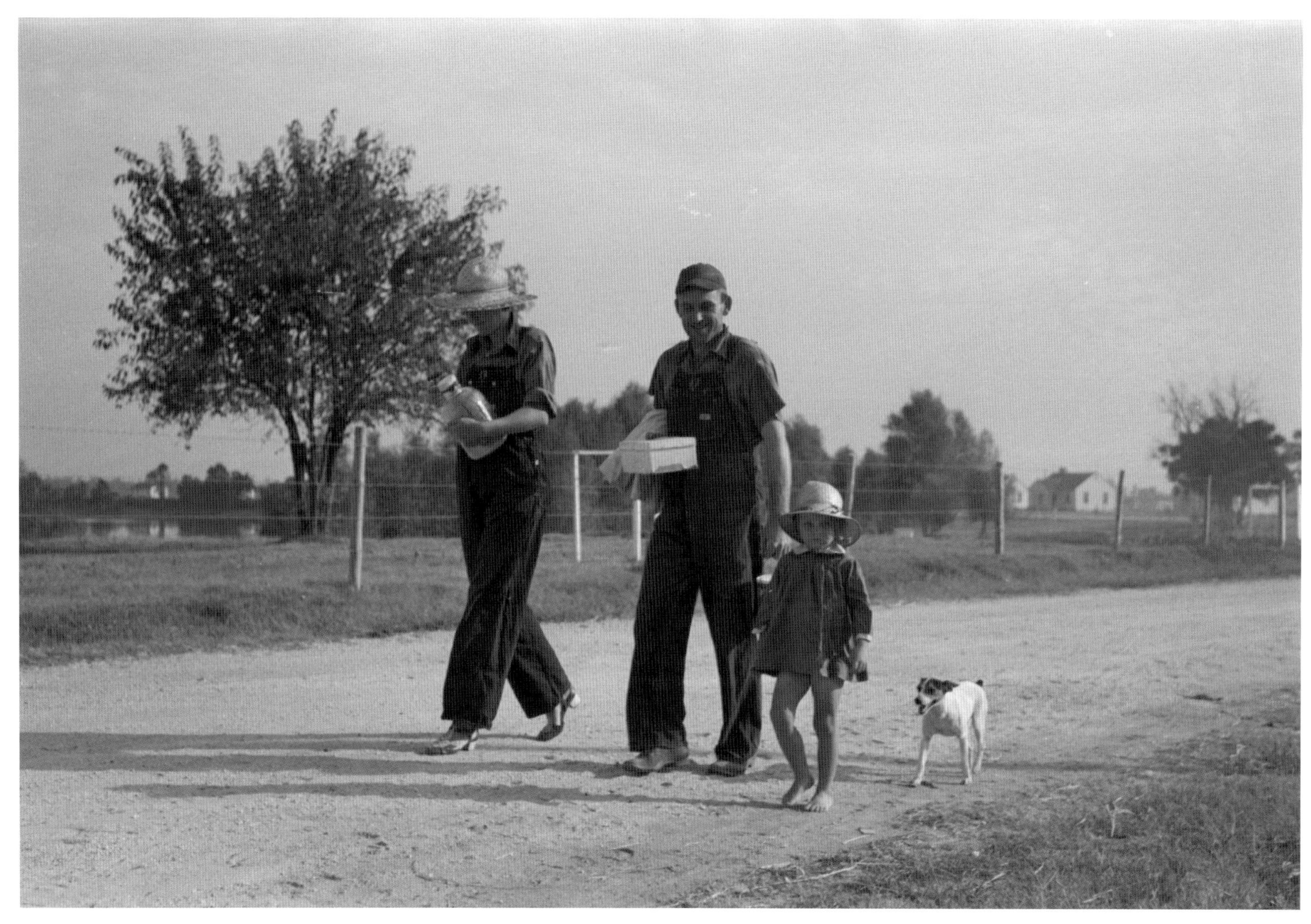

A young homesteader family at Lake Dick.

(Russell Lee, September–October 1938) Farm Security Administration Photograph Collection, Prints & Photographs Division, Library of Congress, LC-USF33–011698–M4

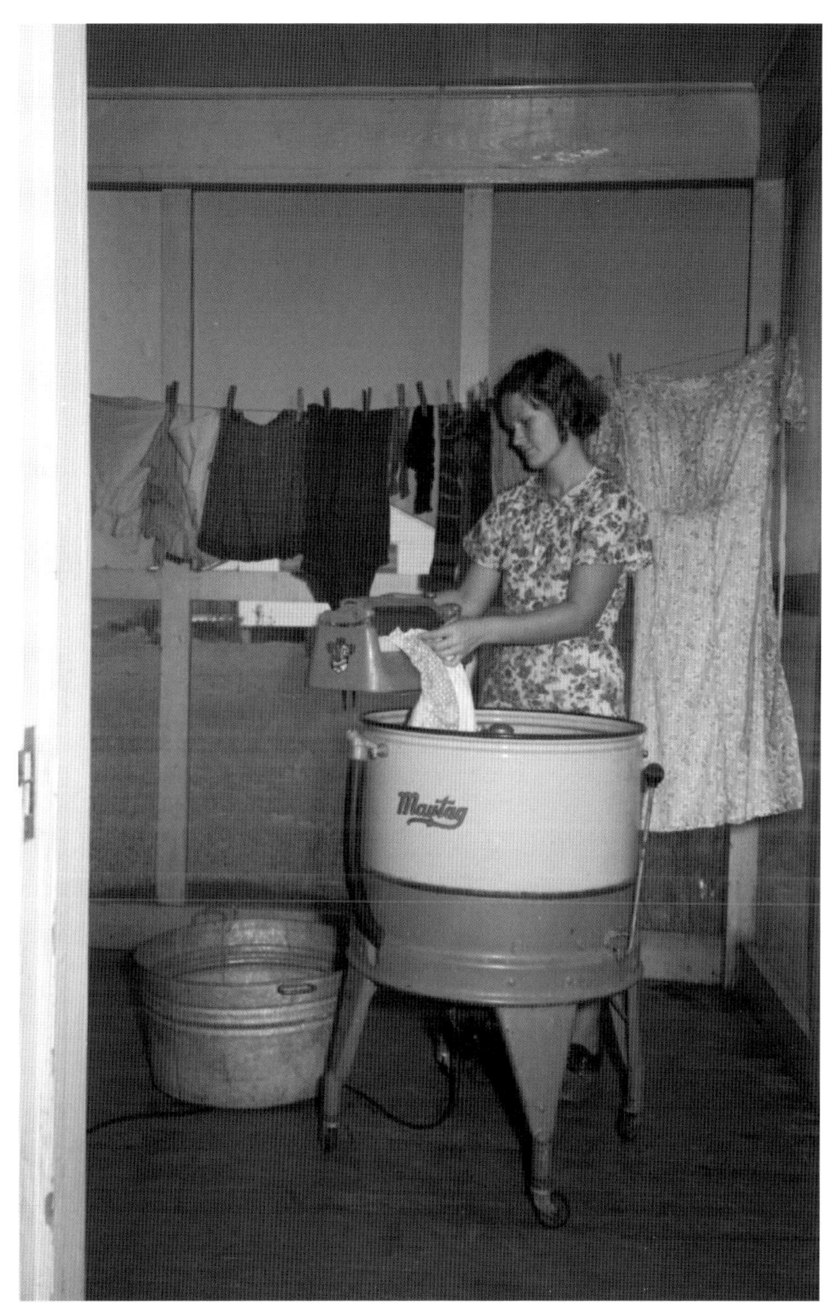

Farmhouses at the Lake Dick settlement farm were outfitted with new appliances, such as washing machines.

(Russell Lee, September 1938) Farm Security Administration Photograph Collection, Prints & Photographs Division, Library of Congress, LC-USF33–011665–M3

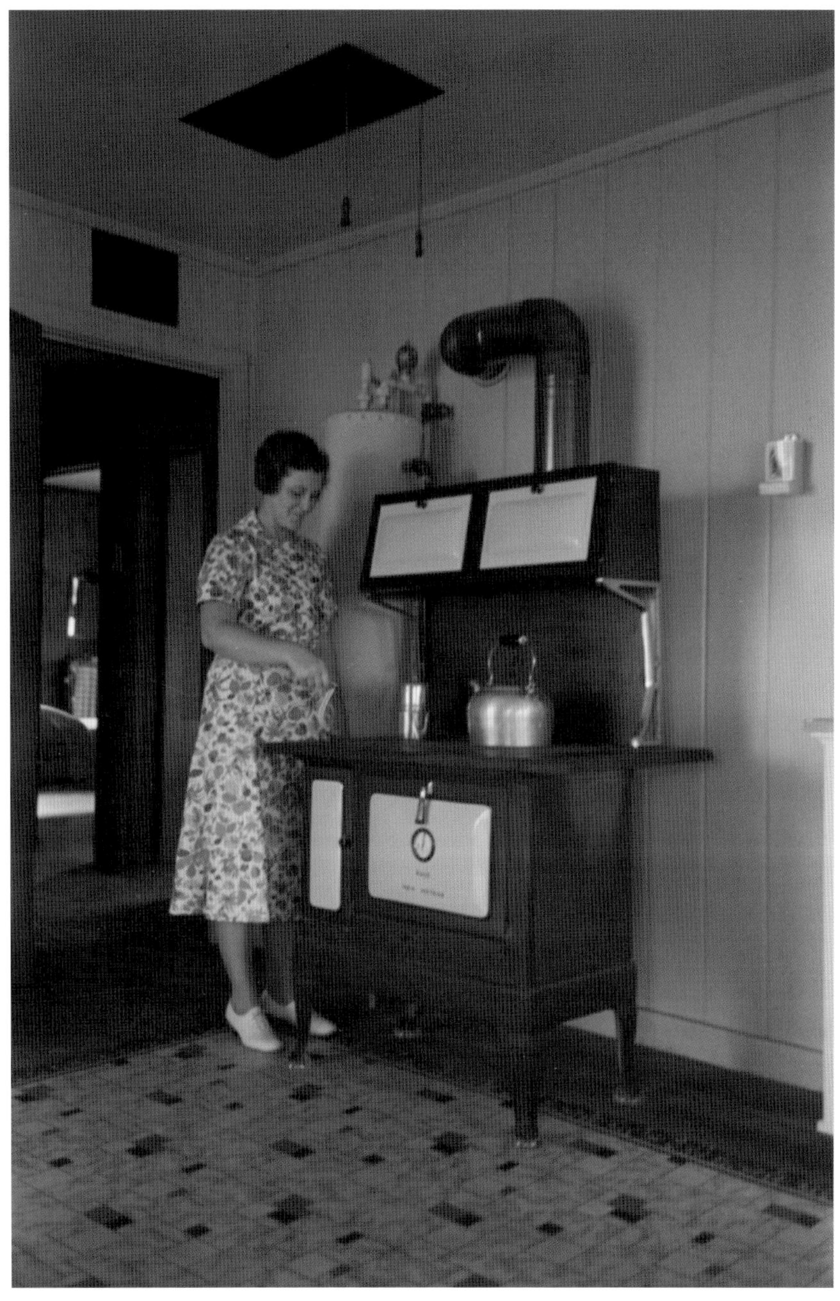

A kitchen in a Lake Dick farmhouse with amenities including a new stove, hot water heater, linoleum, and white-washed walls.

(Russell Lee, September 1938) Farm Security Administration Photograph Collection, Prints & Photographs Division, Library of Congress, LC-USF33–011672–M3

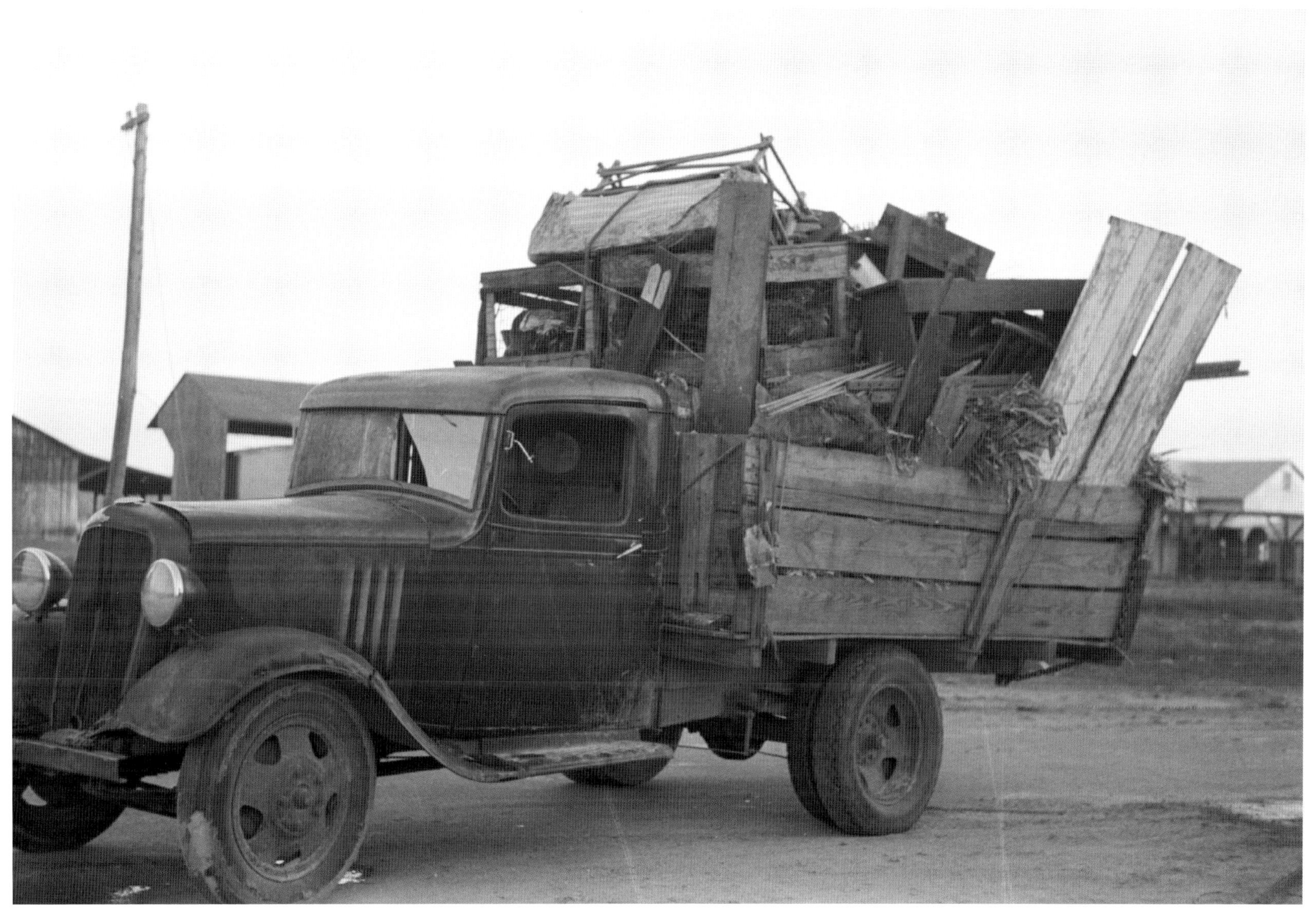

A family's belongings piled into the back of a truck at the Chicot resettlement farm.

(Russell Lee, January 1939) Farm Security Administration Photograph Collection, Prints & Photographs Division, Library of Congress, LC-USF33–011922–M3

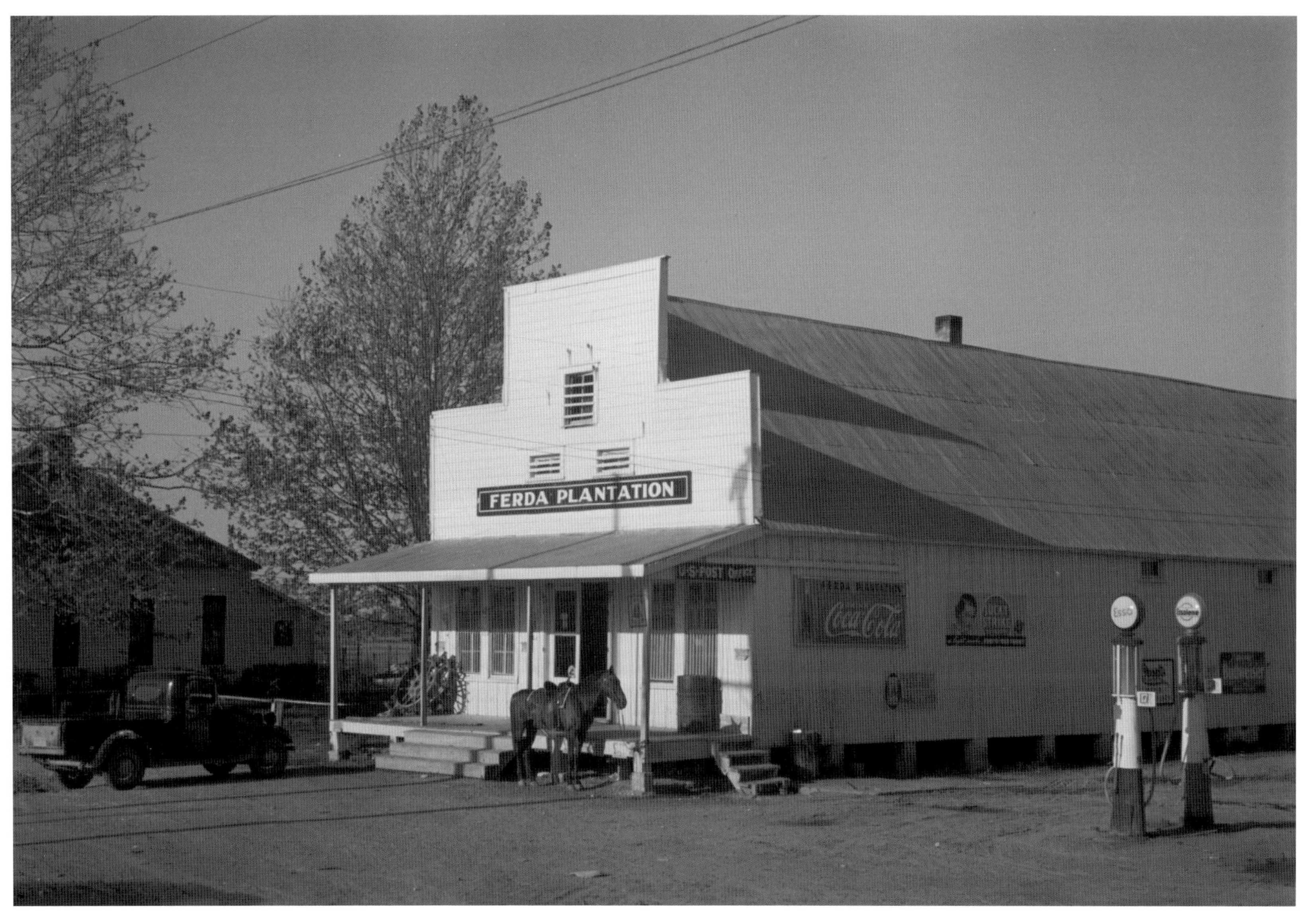

The general store at the Plum Bayou project served multiple purposes, such as post office and gas station.

(Arthur Rothstein, 1937) Farm Security Administration Photograph Collection, Prints & Photographs Division, Library of Congress, LC-USF33–002429–M1

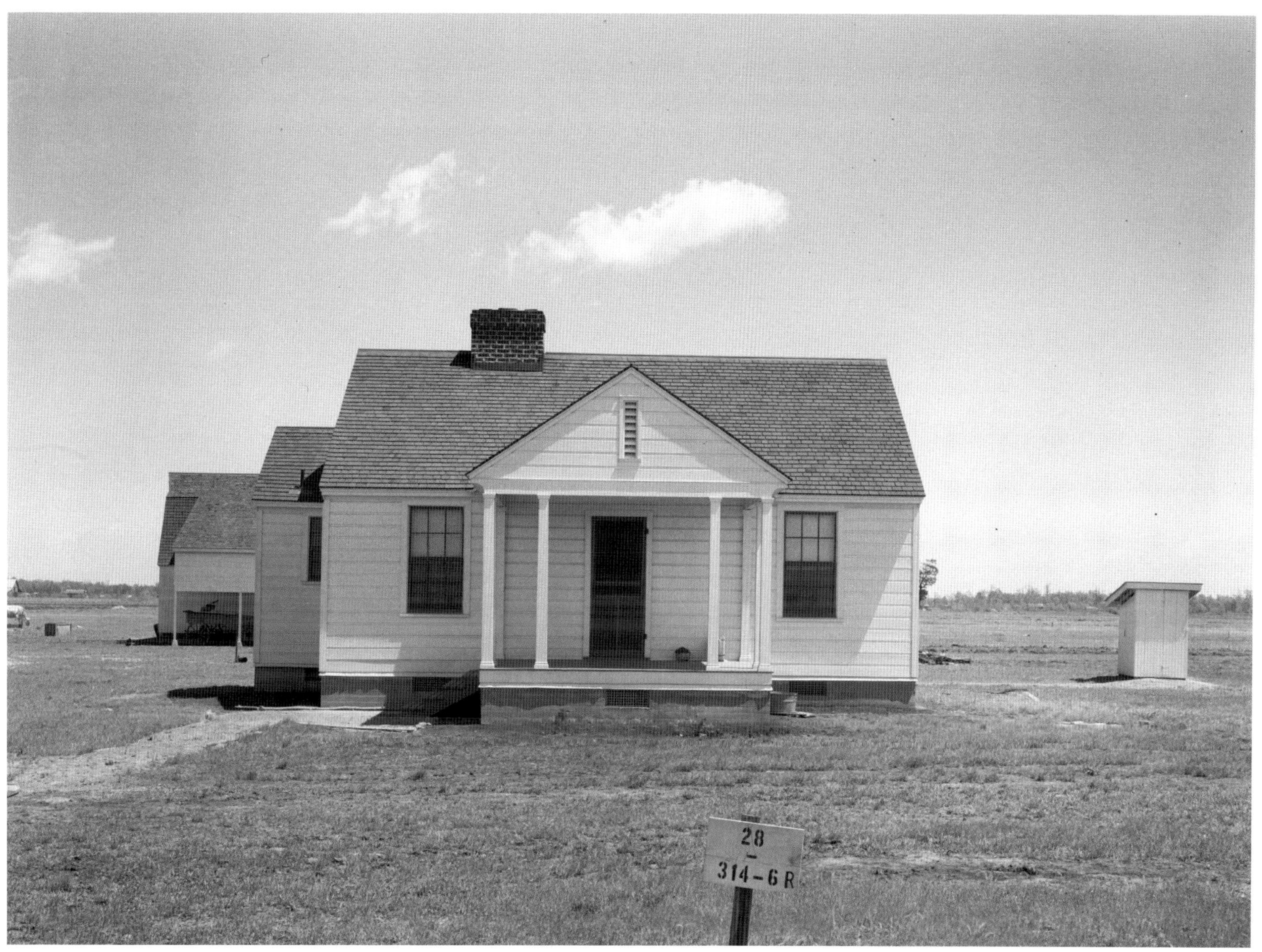

A Plum Bayou farmhouse in a style typical of those built on Arkansas resettlement farms, including screened windows and doors, a front porch with decorative columns, and a chimney.

(Arthur Rothstein, April 1937) Farm Security Administration Photograph Collection, Prints & Photographs Division, Library of Congress, LC-USF34–025326–D

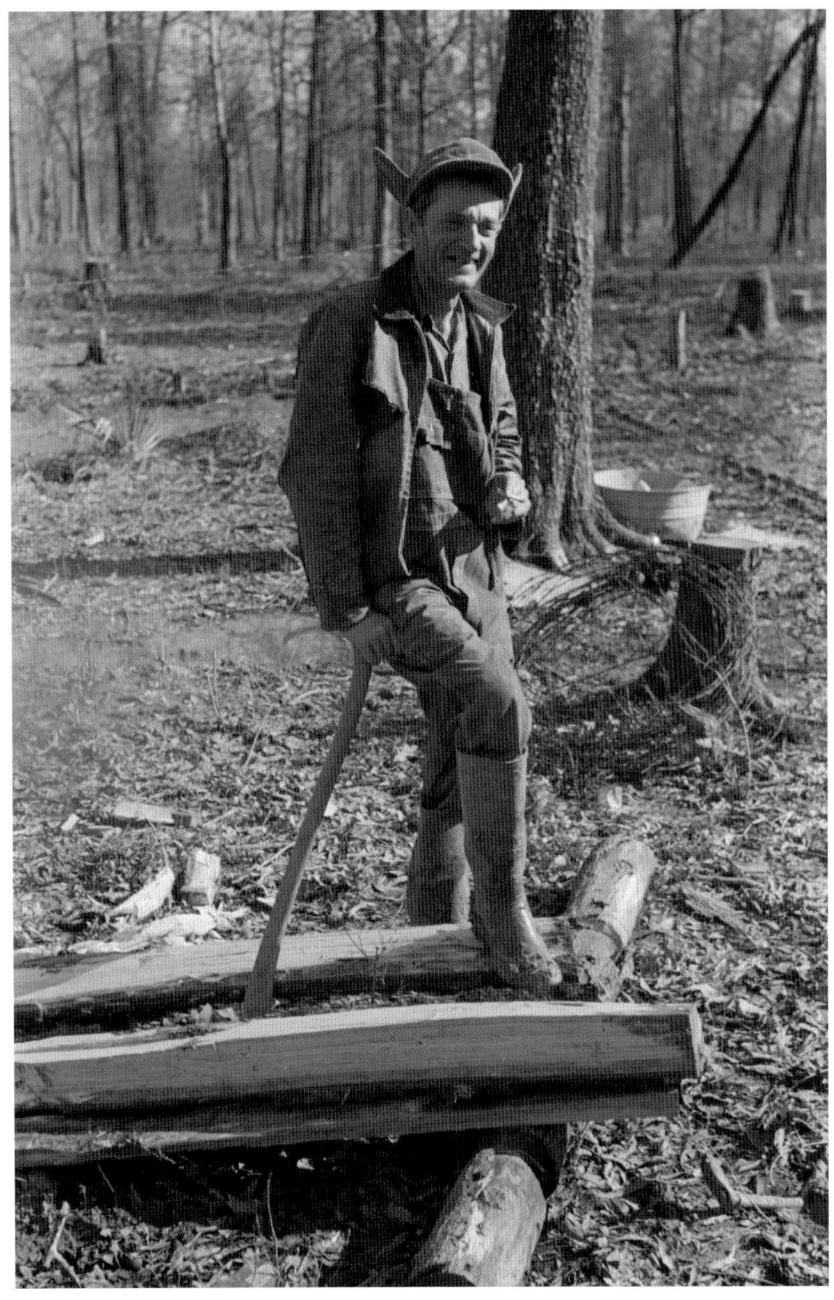

A farmer at the Chicot resettlement project.

(Russell Lee, January 1939) Farm Security Administration Photograph Collection, Prints & Photographs Division, Library of Congress, LC-USF33–011919–M1

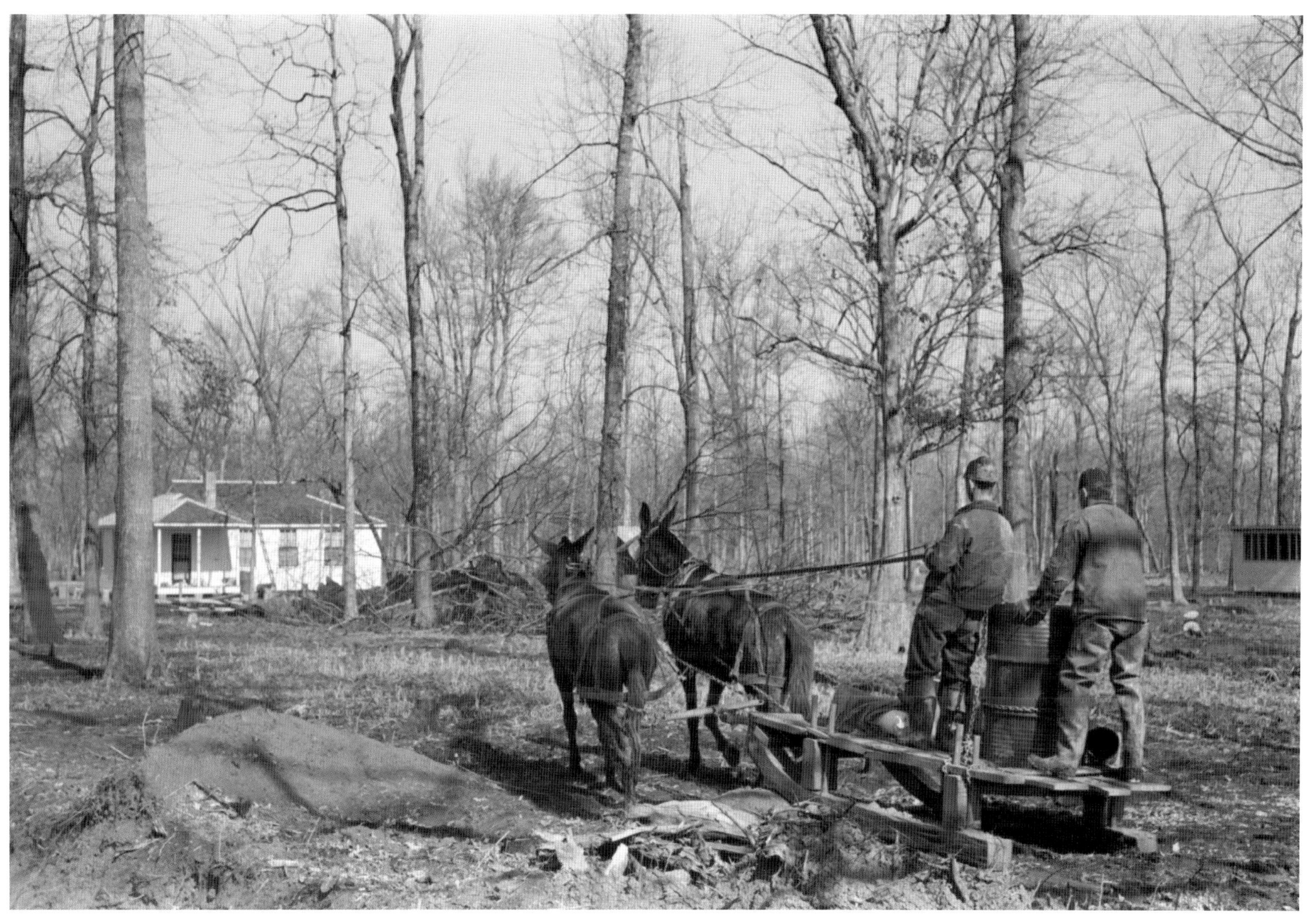

Mud sleds were needed to transport supplies to a homestead at Chicot Farms because of the wet January weather.

(Russell Lee, January 1939) Farm Security Administration Photograph Collection, Prints & Photographs Division, Library of Congress, LC-USF33–011933–M1

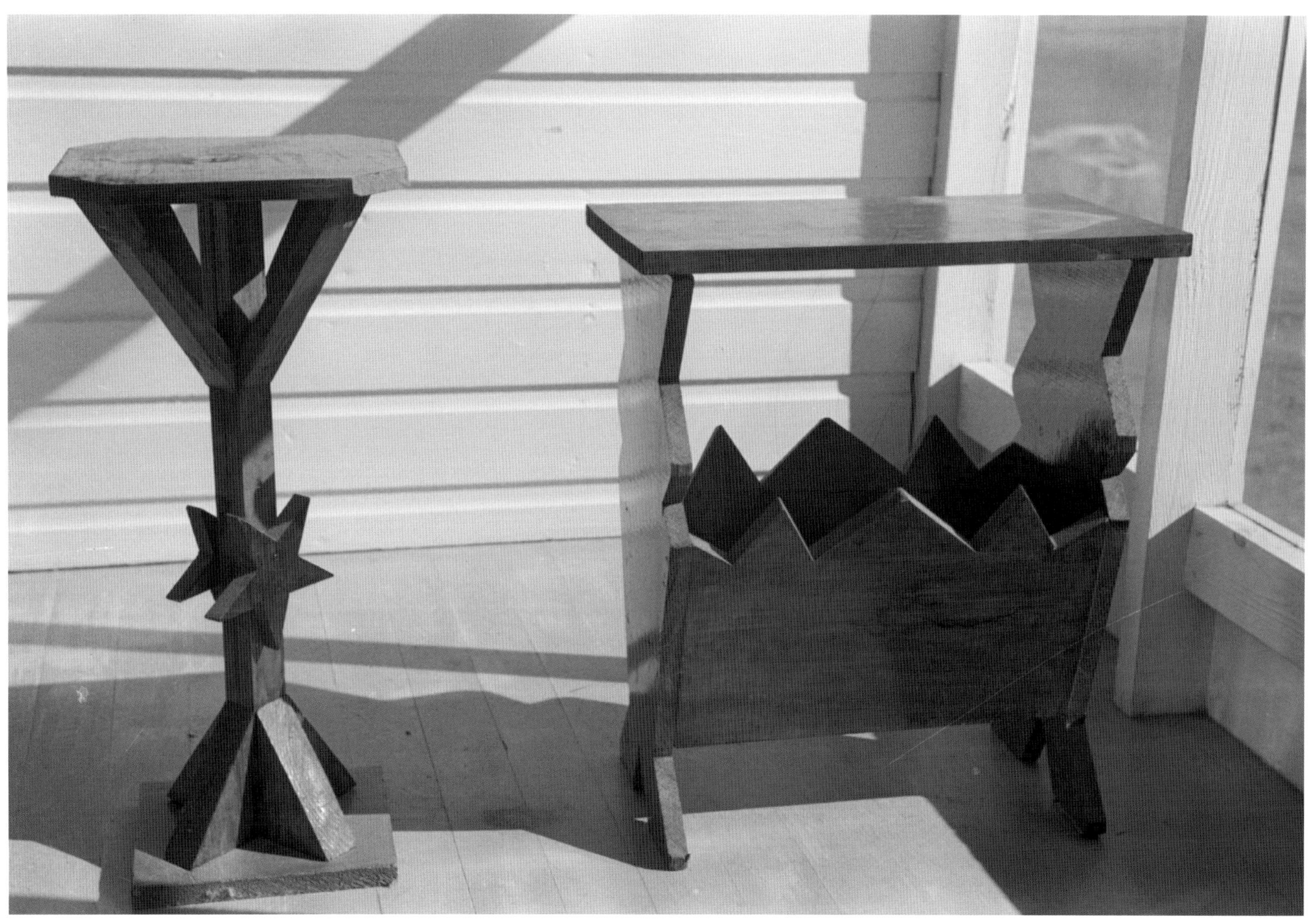

Farmers at the Chicot project could make money in the off-season working at a small factory that produced furniture for homes on the farm.

(Russell Lee, January 1939) Farm Security Administration Photograph Collection, Prints & Photographs Division, Library of Congress, LC-USF33–011917–M4

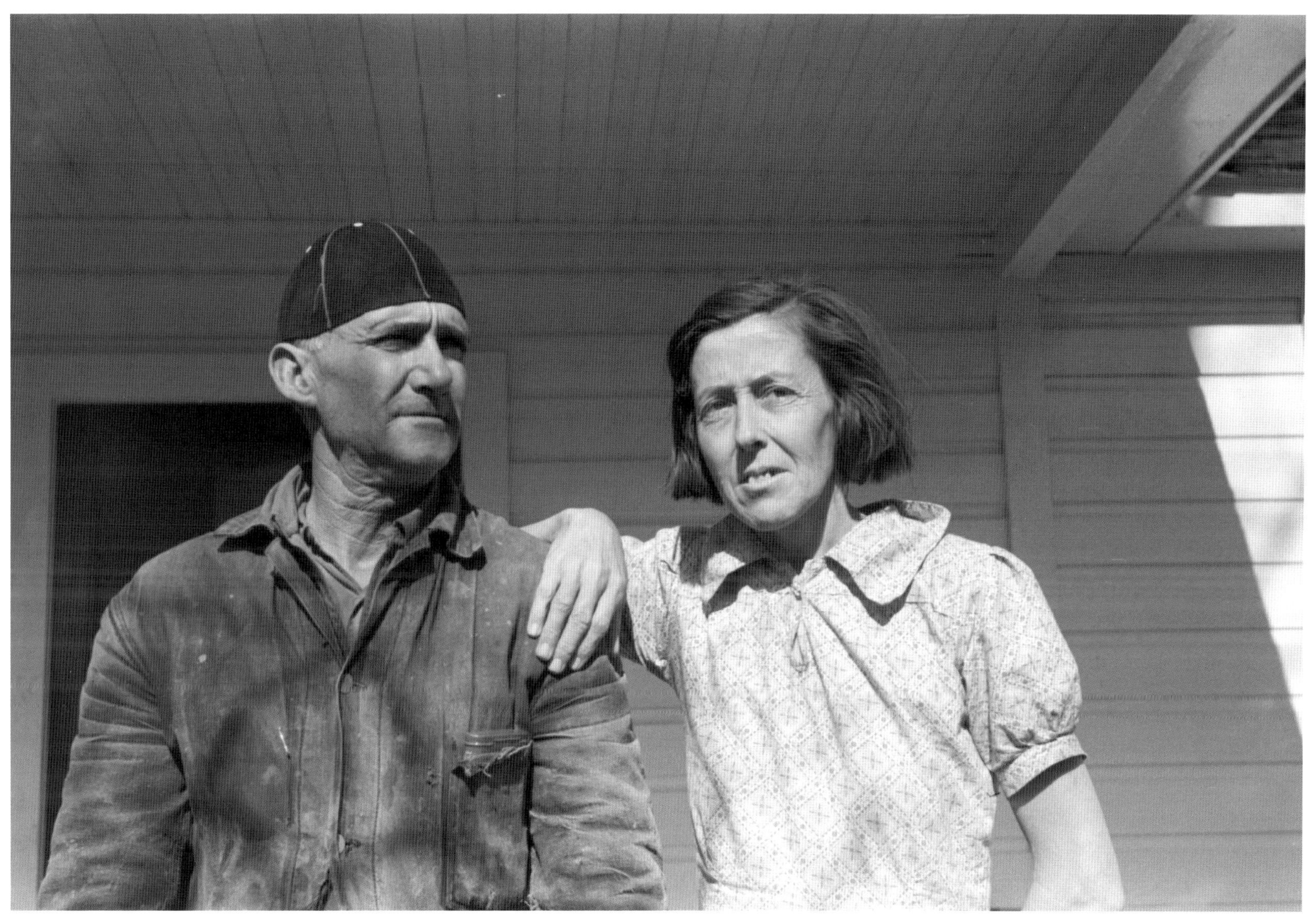

A couple homesteading at Chicot Farms, on the front porch of their house.

(Russell Lee, January 1939) Farm Security Administration Photograph Collection, Prints & Photographs Division, Library of Congress, LC-USF33–011934–M2

FOUR | ARKANSAS AFRICAN AMERICANS

THE RA/FSA PHOTOGRAPHS of African American Arkansans in the 1930s show lives bound by the labor demands of cotton farming. Throughout the collection are pictures of people picking cotton, being trucked to and from cotton fields or waiting to be paid at the end of the day. Everyone worked in the fields: men, women, old, young, and even children of seven or eight, mostly as day laborers or sharecroppers, which meant they were poorly paid, had no job security, and got work where and when they could.

However, the racism that permeated the state as well as the nation is not overtly evident in the Arkansas RA/FSA pictures. Nicholas Natanson, who studied media images of African Americans in the Depression, observed that RA/FSA photographers did not "shoot more of the controversial material," perhaps because of an implicit New Deal strategy that "deemphasized the fundamental racial imbalances and conflicts lying beneath the surface." Though some RA/FSA photographers suggested more coverage of these issues, administrators were cautious. The intensity of southern racial attitudes had stalled antilynching legislation as well as led to inequities and tensions in the management of government relief programs in several states, as described in a dissertation by Michael Mehlman on Arkansas tenant farmers.

The roughly four hundred RA/FSA photographs of Arkansas African Americans cover three topics most extensively, sharecroppers in the Delta and Pulaski County, the Lakeview resettlement farm in Phillips County, and refugees from the 1937 flood in the Mississippi River Valley. Ben Shahn took most of the pictures of sharecroppers in 1935, and Russell Lee was responsible for coverage of the Lakeview farm. Unfortunately, the technical quality of Lee's photos of Lakeview hinders their reproduction here. The 1937 flood refugee camps were photographed by Walker Evans and Edwin Locke and show black and white refugees about equally. Notably, in addition to these are about fifteen pictures by Dorothea Lange and John Vachon of African American farmers evicted for unionizing activities; some are shown in their new homes on the interracial Hillhouse farm in Mississippi.

In a state with a population of nearly two million in 1930, the African American population comprised 25.8 percent, or almost half a million people. Nearly two-thirds lived on farms or in rural areas

—mostly in conditions of desperate poverty—concentrated along the eastern side of the state, in the cotton-growing Mississippi Delta, and in some southern and central counties. African American citizens were segregated in "colored" sections of towns and in rural areas, in badly constructed houses that rarely had indoor toilets or electricity. Generally, they had little access to education and made less than $500 a year. Given their inadequate nutrition and medical care, the black population in Arkansas tended to have persistent health problems—with one consequence a high infant mortality rate, twice that of white babies, according to government reports. The RA/FSA photos in Arkansas very clearly portray the level of poverty African Americans faced and even occasionally hint at the racism prevalent across the region. African American citizens are rarely shown in positions of authority. In most cases where people of more than one race are represented in an image, African Americans are shown as dependent on a white person—the manager of a resettlement farm store, the supervisor weighing cotton sacks at the end of the day, or the truck driver transporting workers to and from the fieldss.

Roy Stryker had told photographers that the white press had little interest in photos of African Americans, a fact which Natanson confirmed in his book *The Black Image in the New Deal,* stating that African Americans were largely invisible in the white mainstream media in the 1930s. He viewed the RA/FSA's photo coverage of African Americans as conservative in depicting the conditions of black lives, but concluded that it still "achieved a range and depth of black coverage that was rare in government or private photography." Though the white press published few of these RA/FSA pictures, there was great demand from the two hundred or so black newspapers around the country. Natanson quoted an RA/FSA regional public information officer in North Carolina who wrote, "Black newspaper editors wanted any pictures, showing improvement in black lives, they could get. I never even had to suggest stories to them."

Constance Daniel, RA/FSA special assistant for information services, was assigned to cater specifically to the black press, according to Natanson, to feed them RA/FSA-generated stories and photos on the progress of "Negro borrowers or projects." Mrs. Daniel also was a member of the Federal Council of Negro Affairs, often referred to as the "black cabinet," an informal group of New Deal advisers and administrators.

One story that did get coverage in both the black and white press described the Lakeview resettlement farm project in Phillips County, one of three all-black RA/FSA resettlement farms in Arkansas; the other two were Desha and Townes. Lakeview was a large resettlement farm of about one hundred units built during 1936 and 1937 on fifty-six hundred acres fifteen miles southwest of Helena, along the bow of Old Town Lake, a fishing and water recreation area. It was also not far from Elaine, site of the 1919 racial conflict, though news stories about Lakeview didn't mention that.

An *Arkansas Democrat* August 1939 story about Lakeview ("FSA Seeks 'Way Out' for Negro

Sharecroppers") reported that it was intended to be a model demonstration of how "worthy negro tenants and sharecroppers" could become successful independent farmers with appropriate government assistance. Lakeview was opened officially with a formal dedication ceremony in November 1938 that featured speeches by none other than W. W. Alexander, head of the Farm Security Administration, and Dr. Frederick Douglass Patterson, the president of Tuskegee Institute, and was covered by one of the leading black newspapers, the *Chicago Defender*. "Each farm unit averages 56 acres, and is provided with a farm cottage of modern design, necessary barns, outhouses and sanitary facilities and drilled wells," the *Defender* reported.

RA/FSA photographer Russell Lee visited Lakeview in December 1938. His forty-eight photos provide a limited overview of the farm operation, showing a few farmers shopping in the general store and farmwives canning food in their kitchens. Instead, most of the pictures show children and teachers in the Lakeview school, which the government had heavily promoted in introducing the project, noting its vocational orientation and its direction by the State Department of Vocational Education. White leaders did not encourage African American schools, but did find vocational training acceptable as it emphasized skills that were useful at home and on the farm.

The Lakeview school was designed to accommodate 250 students in all twelve grades plus a nursery—one of the few in the nation for African American children. It was housed in a new building with facilities that included an auditorium, a sewing room, a model kitchen, and a shop. Lee's photos seemed to emphasize the vocational training in the school as well as the instruction in good health practices and appropriate social behavior, especially with nursery school children. His pictures show children taking a daily dose of cod liver oil, washing their hands, eating lunch together at small tables, and taking naps. Older students were photographed learning to cook, sew, and build furniture. One photo shows a group of students using typewriters to work on the school newspaper.

The eventual success of the Lakeview project provides an interesting coda to the story. By 1943 most of the Lakeview farms had been paid off by the resettled families; the farm community was incorporated as a town in 1972 and in 1988 celebrated its fiftieth anniversary, achieving a stability that had eluded many white resettlement projects around the country. In 1992 the school district, which had become known as Lake View, became the center of a lawsuit against the State of Arkansas over public school funding, claiming it was inequitable and inadequate under both the state and the US constitutions. Repeated court filings kept the issue unresolved until 2006 legislation in the Arkansas General Assembly that addressed public school funding and a 2012 Arkansas Supreme Court ruling on the dispersal of property tax revenue.

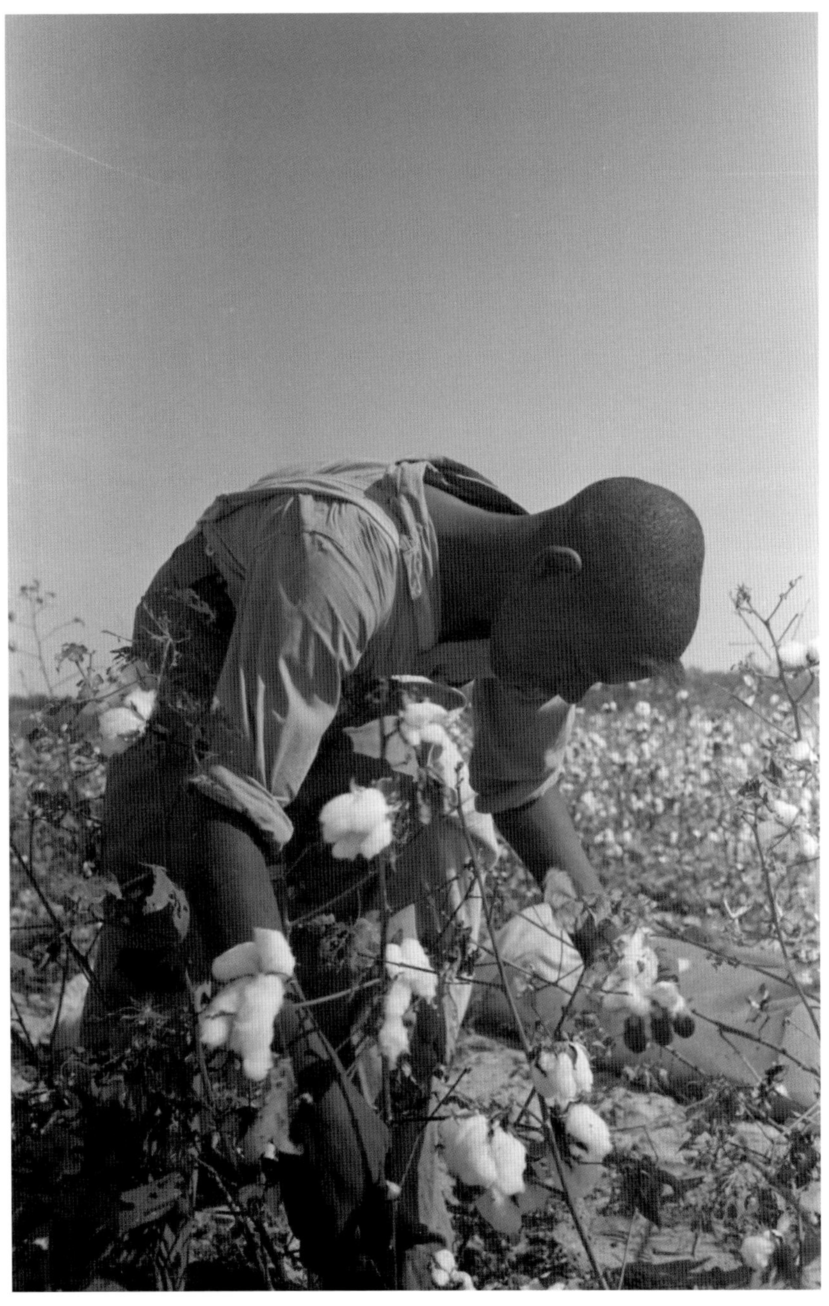

A young boy picks cotton at the Lake Dick resettlement farm.

(Russell Lee, September 1938) Farm Security Administration Photograph Collection, Prints & Photographs Division, Library of Congress, LC-USF33–011667–M4

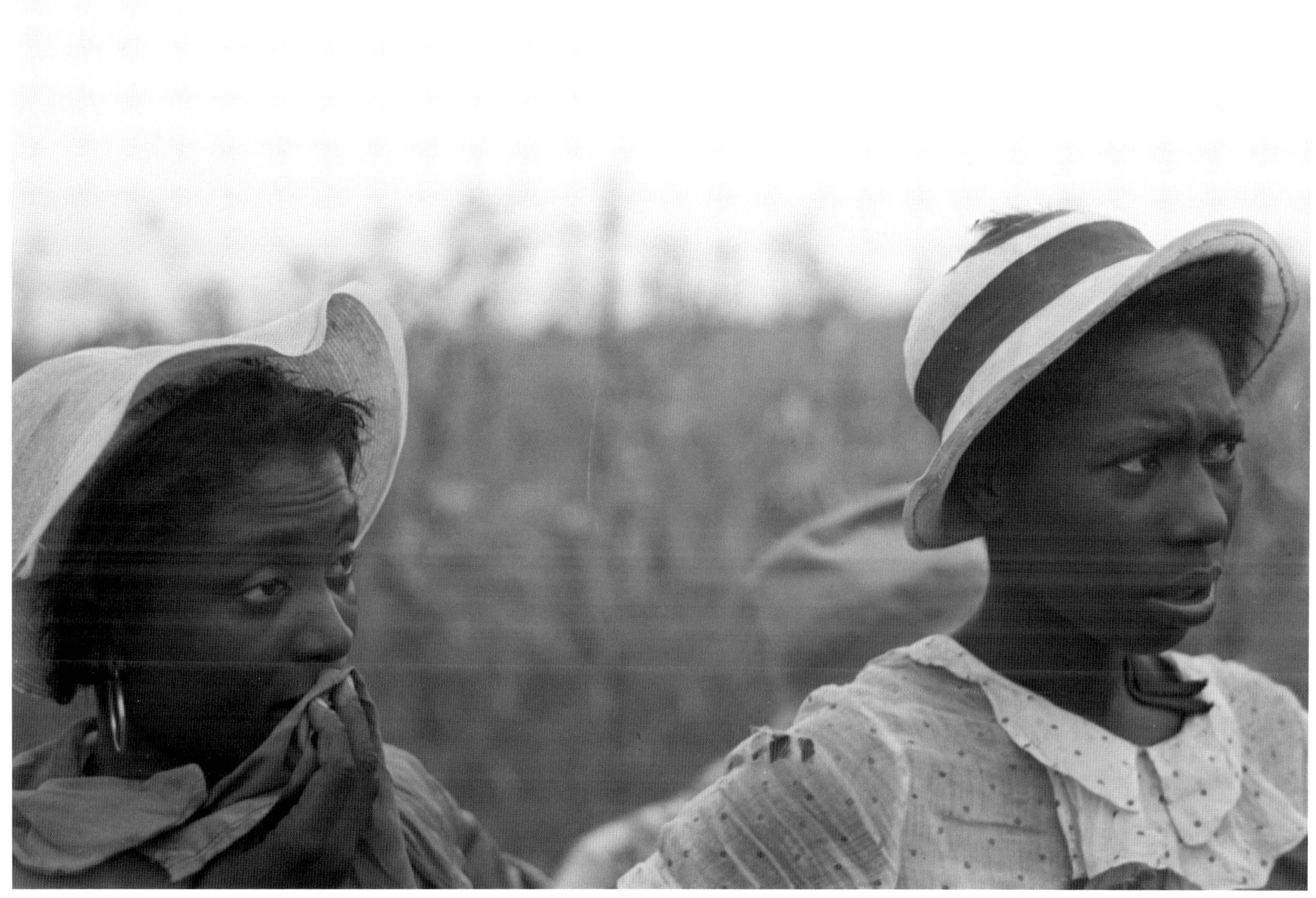

Girls work as day laborers picking cotton at the Lake Dick resettlement farm.

(Russell Lee, September 1938) Farm Security Administration Photograph Collection, Prints & Photographs Division, Library of Congress, LC-USF33–011683–M3

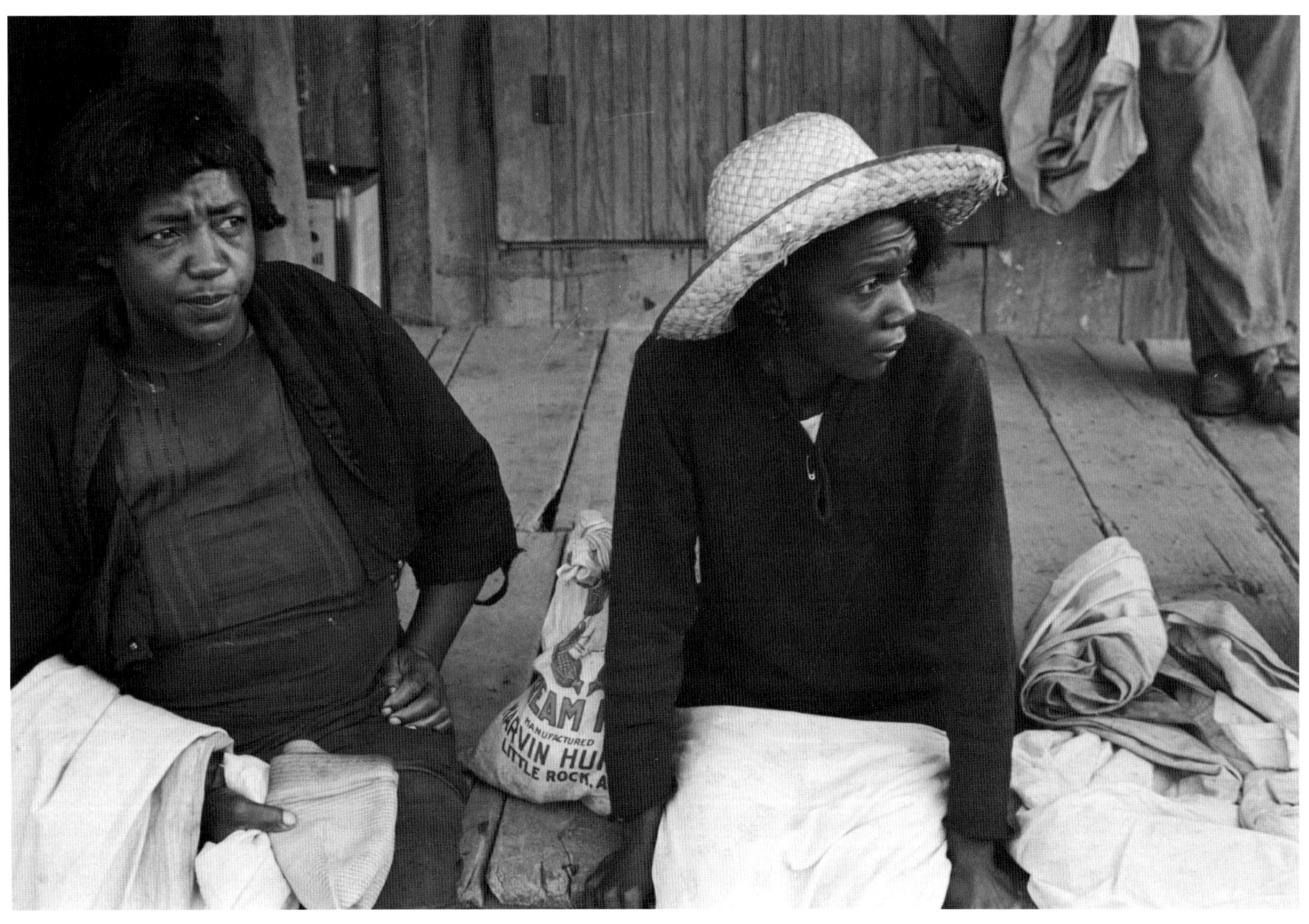

Day laborers in Pulaski County wait to be transported to the fields to pick cotton.

(Ben Shahn, October 1935) Farm Security Administration Photograph Collection, Prints & Photographs Division, Library of Congress, LC-USF33–006028–M1

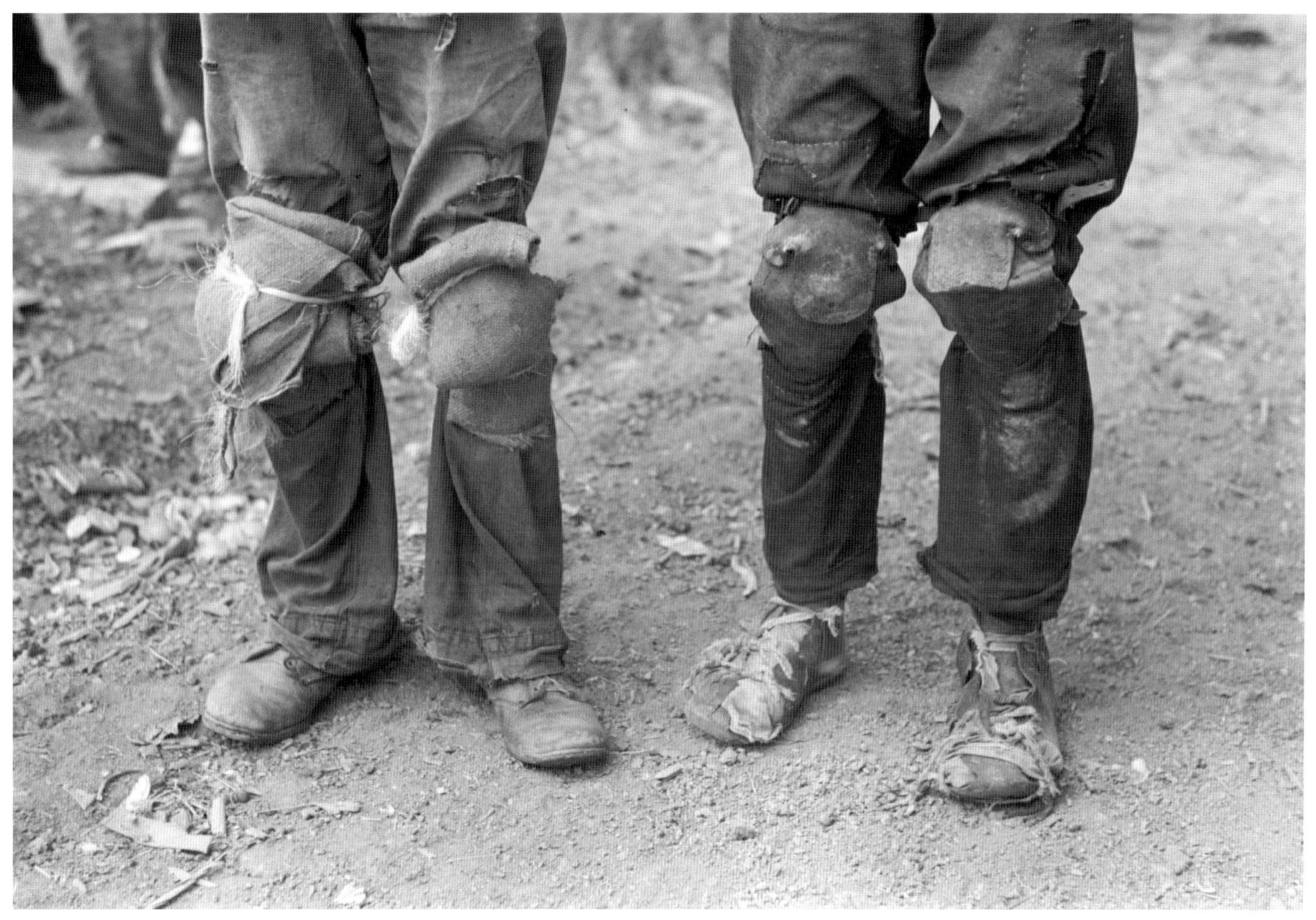

Cotton pickers fashion homemade knee pads for fieldwork at Lehi in Crittenden County.

(Russell Lee, September 1938) Farm Security Administration Photograph Collection, Prints & Photographs Division, Library of Congress, LC-USF33–011620–M1

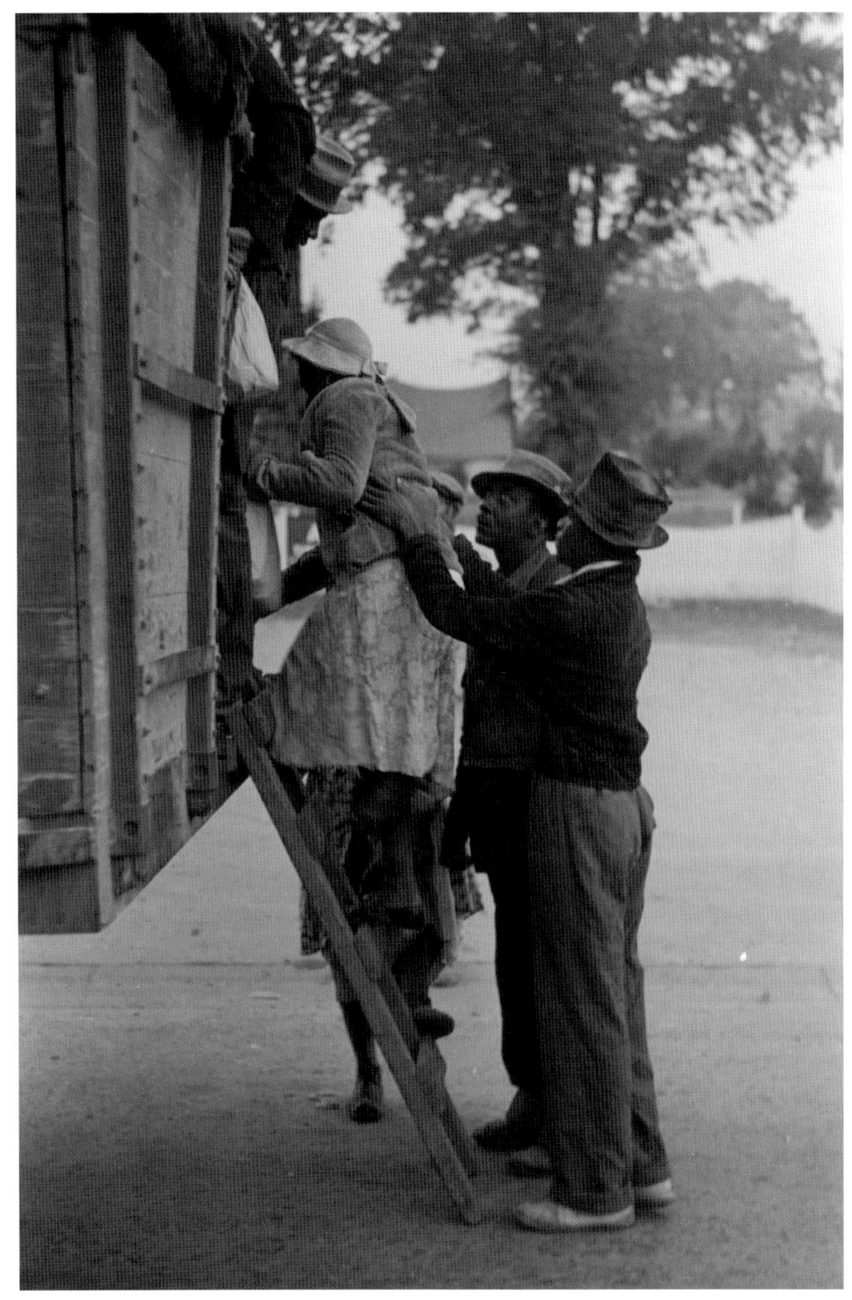

Men help a woman board the truck that will take workers to the cotton fields near Pine Bluff.

(Russell Lee, September–October 1938) Farm Security Administration Photograph Collection, Prints & Photographs Division, Library of Congress, LC-USF33–011697–M4

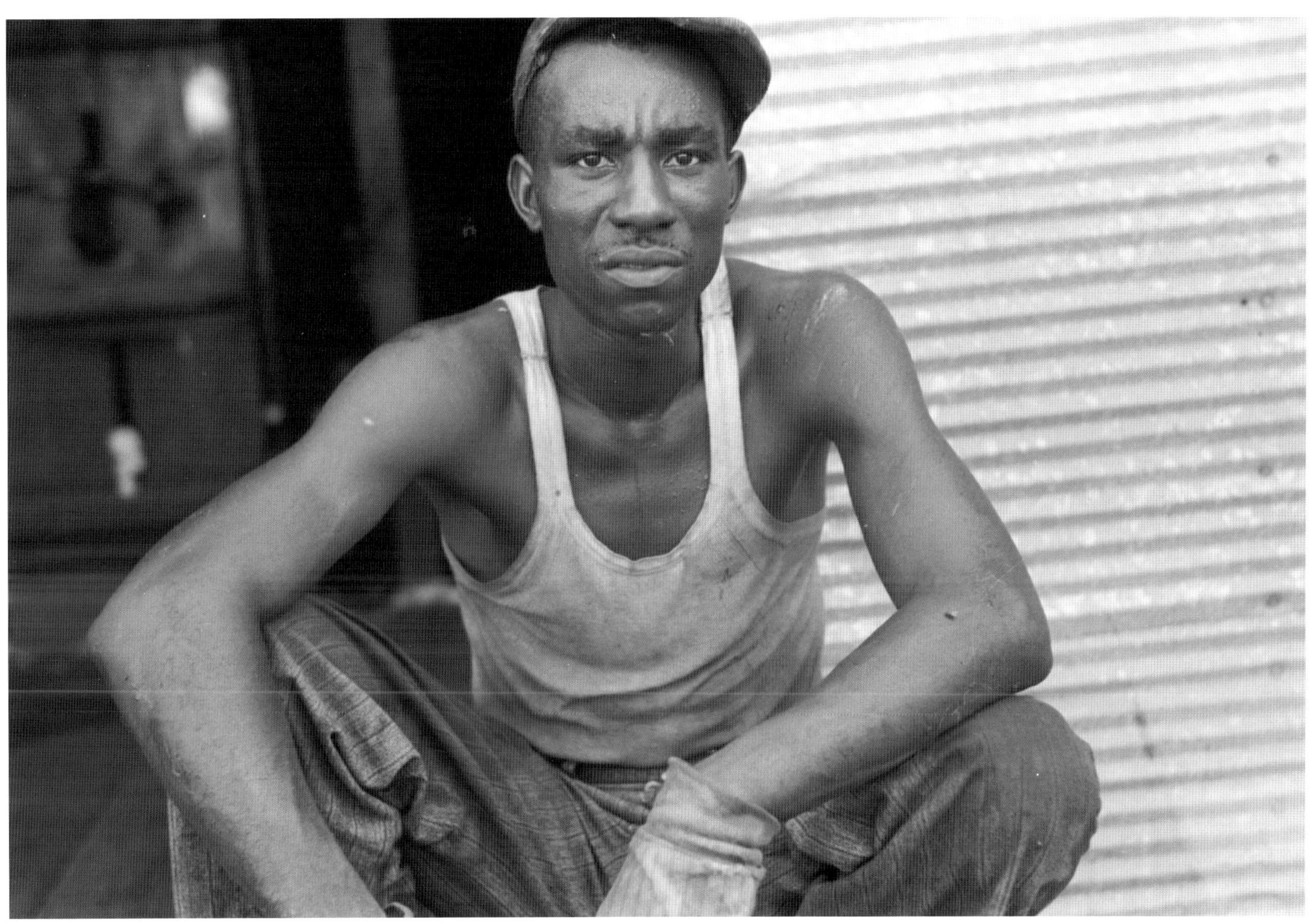

Employee in a Lehi cotton gin.

(Russell Lee, September 1938) Farm Security Administration Photograph Collection, Prints & Photographs Division, Library of Congress, LC-USF33–011624–M5

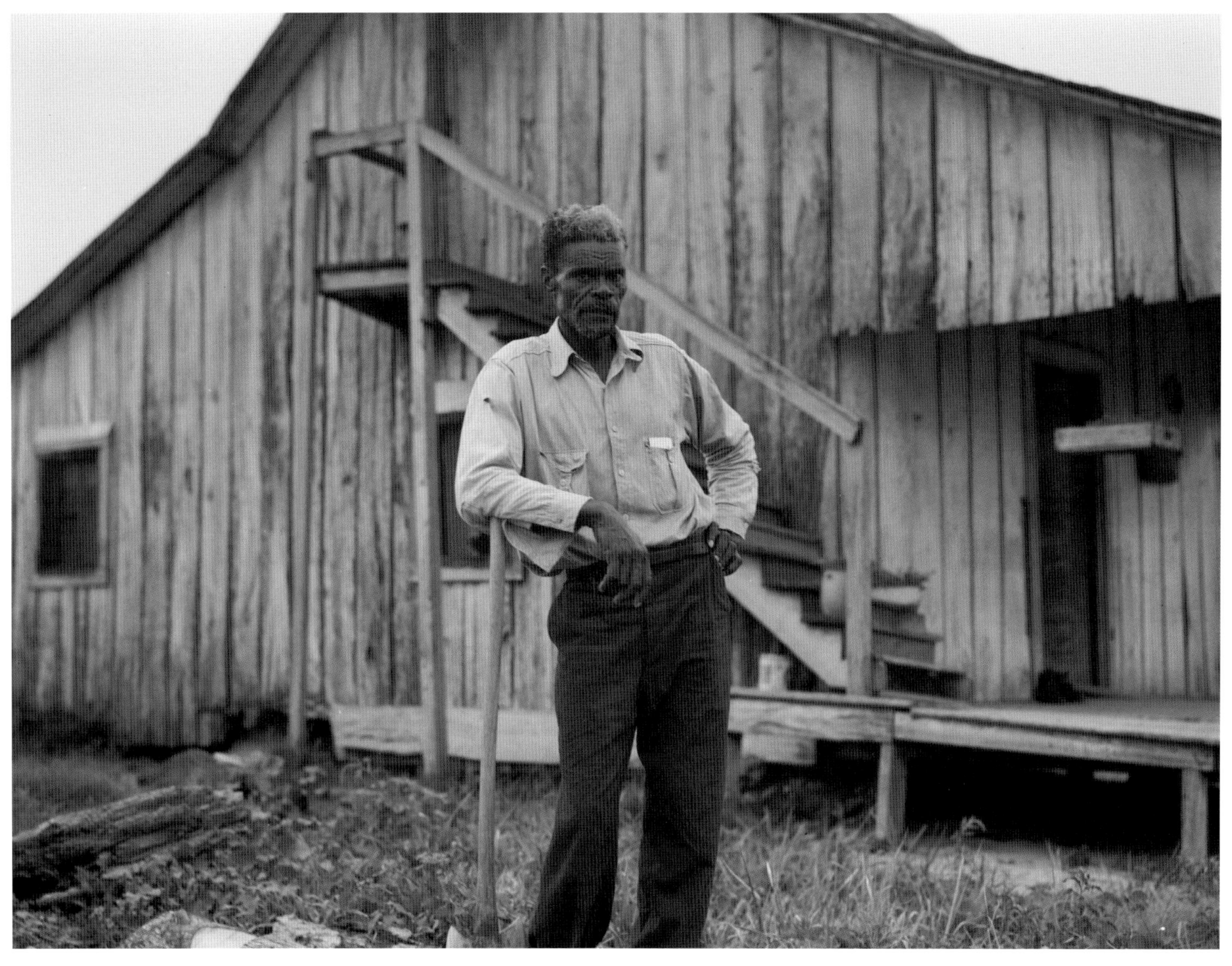

Dorothea Lange wrote that this cotton worker was dressed in Sunday clothes.

(Dorothea Lange, June 1937) Farm Security Administration Photograph Collection, Prints & Photographs Division, Library of Congress, LC-USF34–017363–C

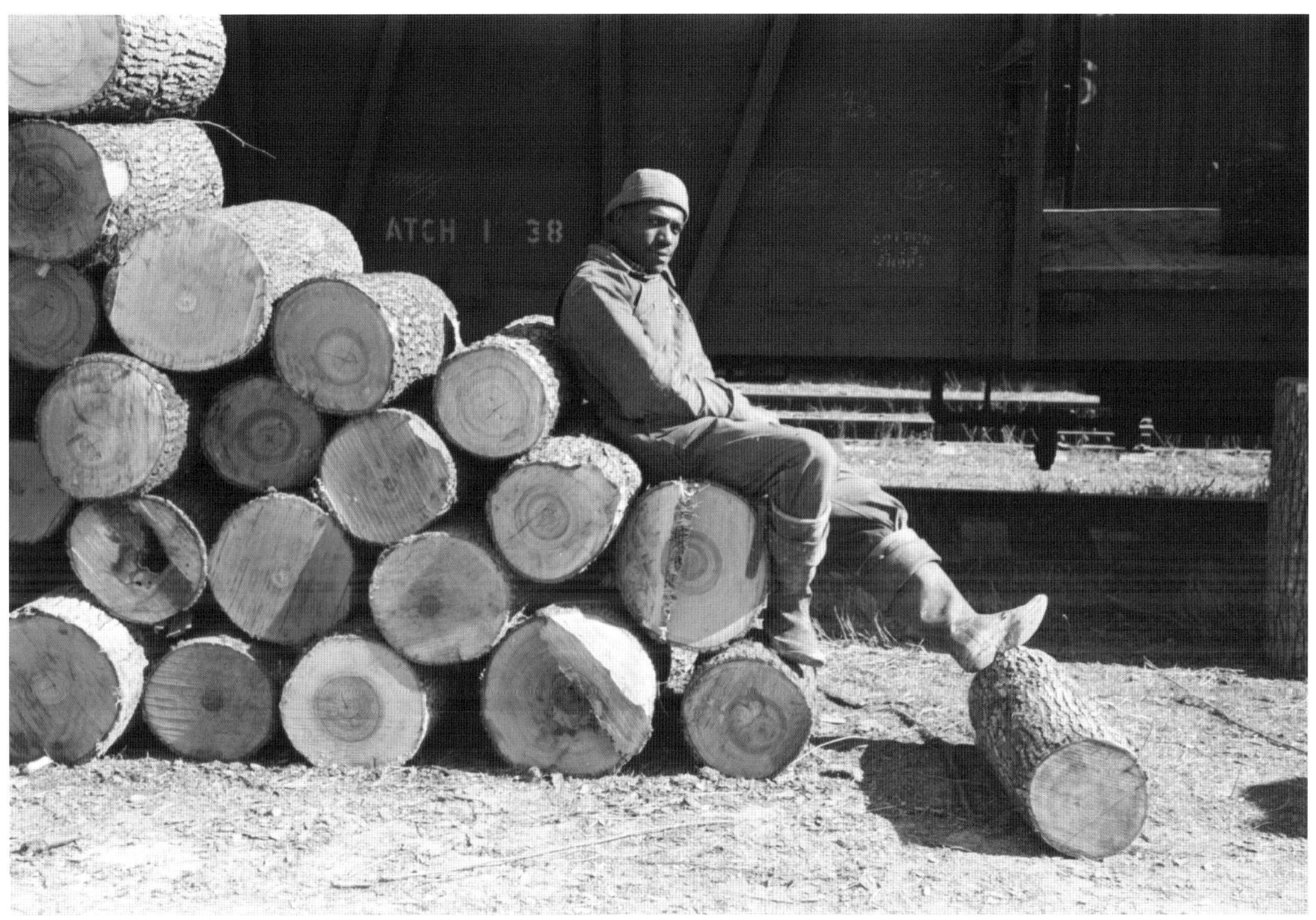

Worker whose job was loading logs into boxcars at Eudora for shipping to Tallulah, Louisiana, to be made into barrel staves.

(Russell Lee, January 1939) Farm Security Administration Photograph Collection, Prints & Photographs Division, Library of Congress, LC-USF33–011970–M3

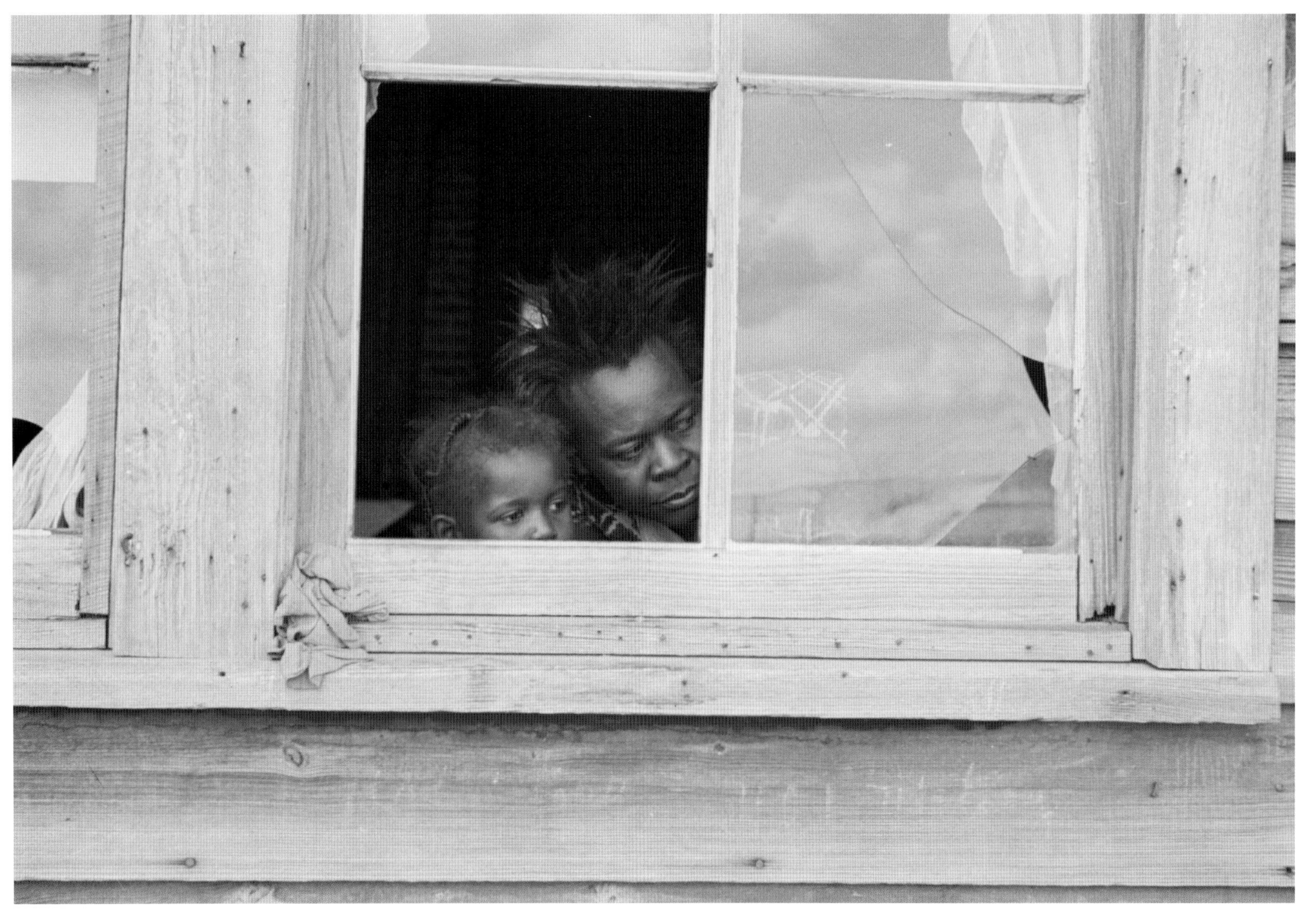

Woman and child in a sharecropper's cabin.

(Ben Shahn, October 1935) Farm Security Administration Photograph Collection, Prints & Photographs Division, Library of Congress, LC-USF33–006026–M5

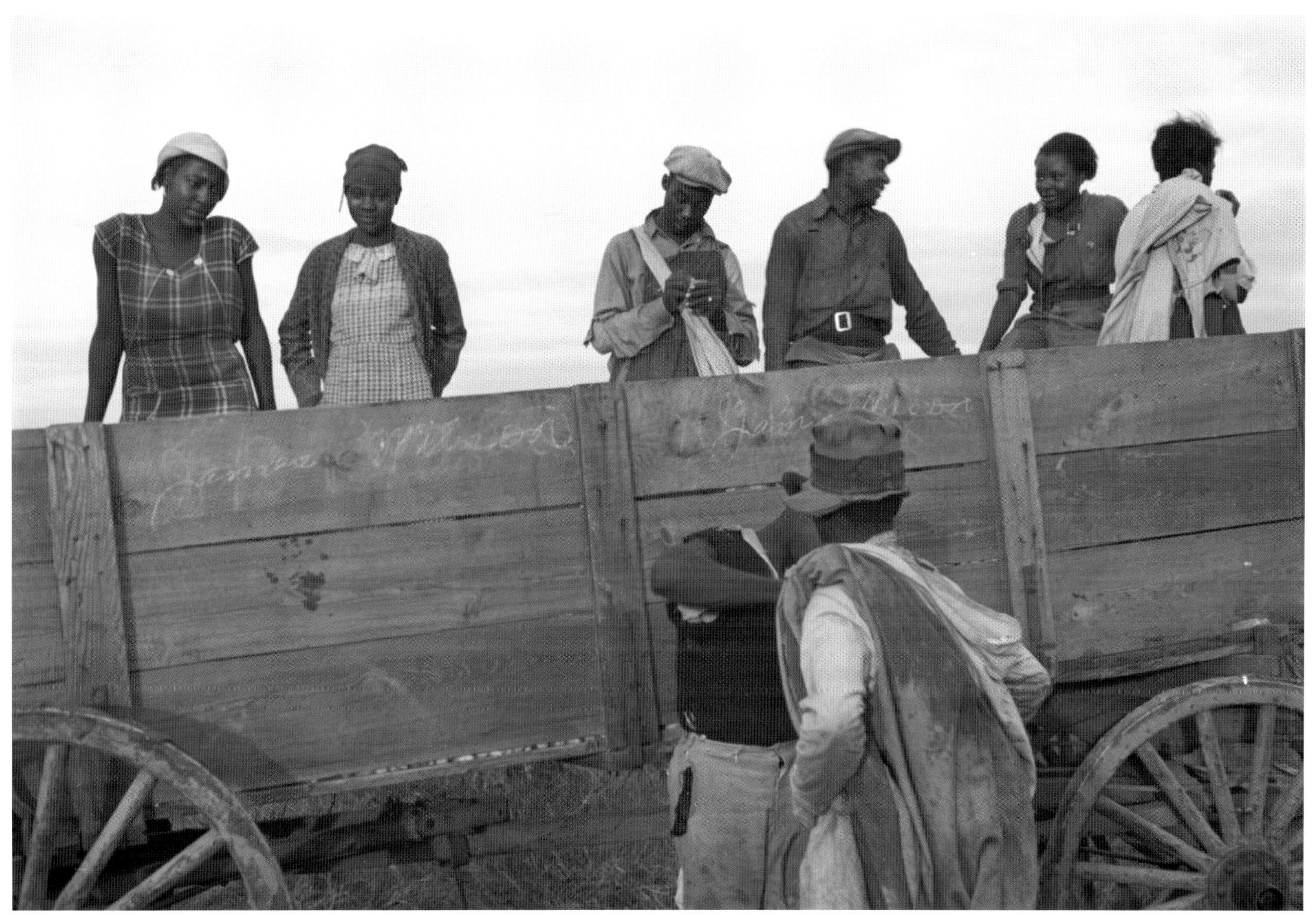

Cotton pickers loaded into a wagon at the end of the day to be taken home from the field.

(Ben Shahn, October 1935) Farm Security Administration Photograph Collection, Prints & Photographs Division, Library of Congress, LC-USF33–006218–M1

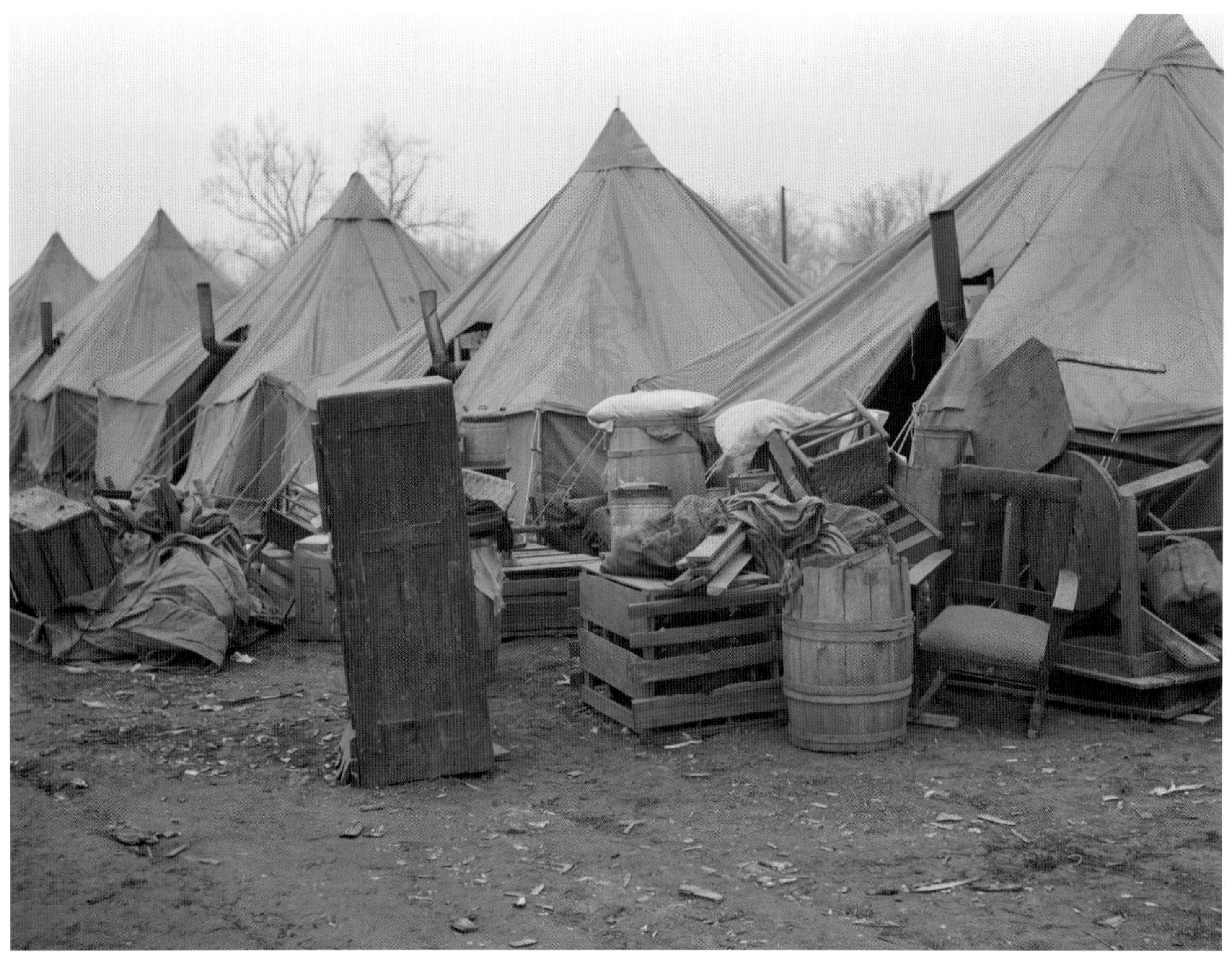

African American farmers' possessions outside tents in the camp set up for refugees from the 1937 flood in the Mississippi Valley.

(Edwin Locke, February 1937) Farm Security Administration Photograph Collection, Prints & Photographs Division, Library of Congress, LC-USF34–013152–D

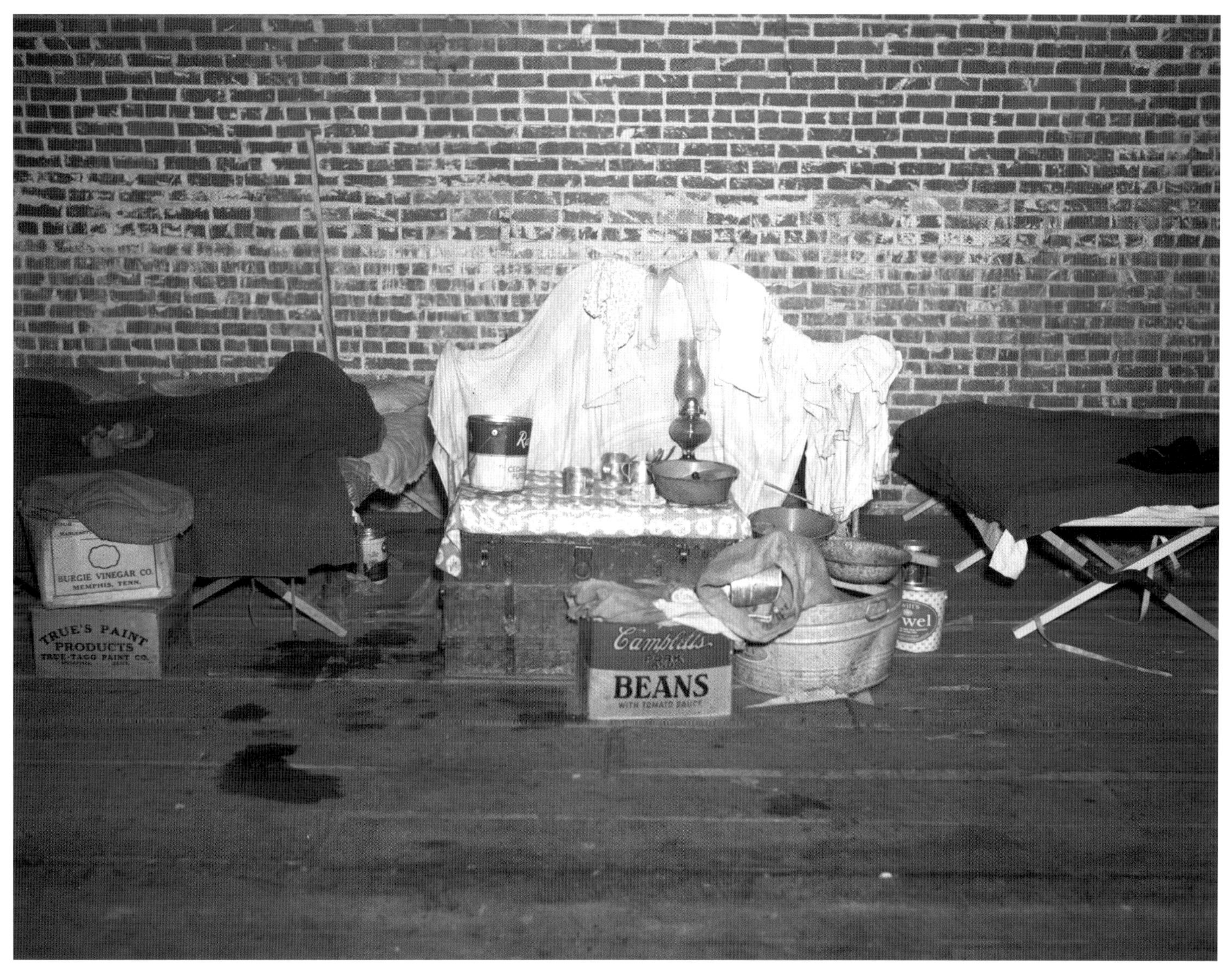

Possessions of African American flood refugees kept in temporary housing in a cotton compress at Forrest City.

(Walker Evans, February 1937) Farm Security Administration Photograph Collection, Prints & Photographs Division, Library of Congress, LC-USF34–008204–C

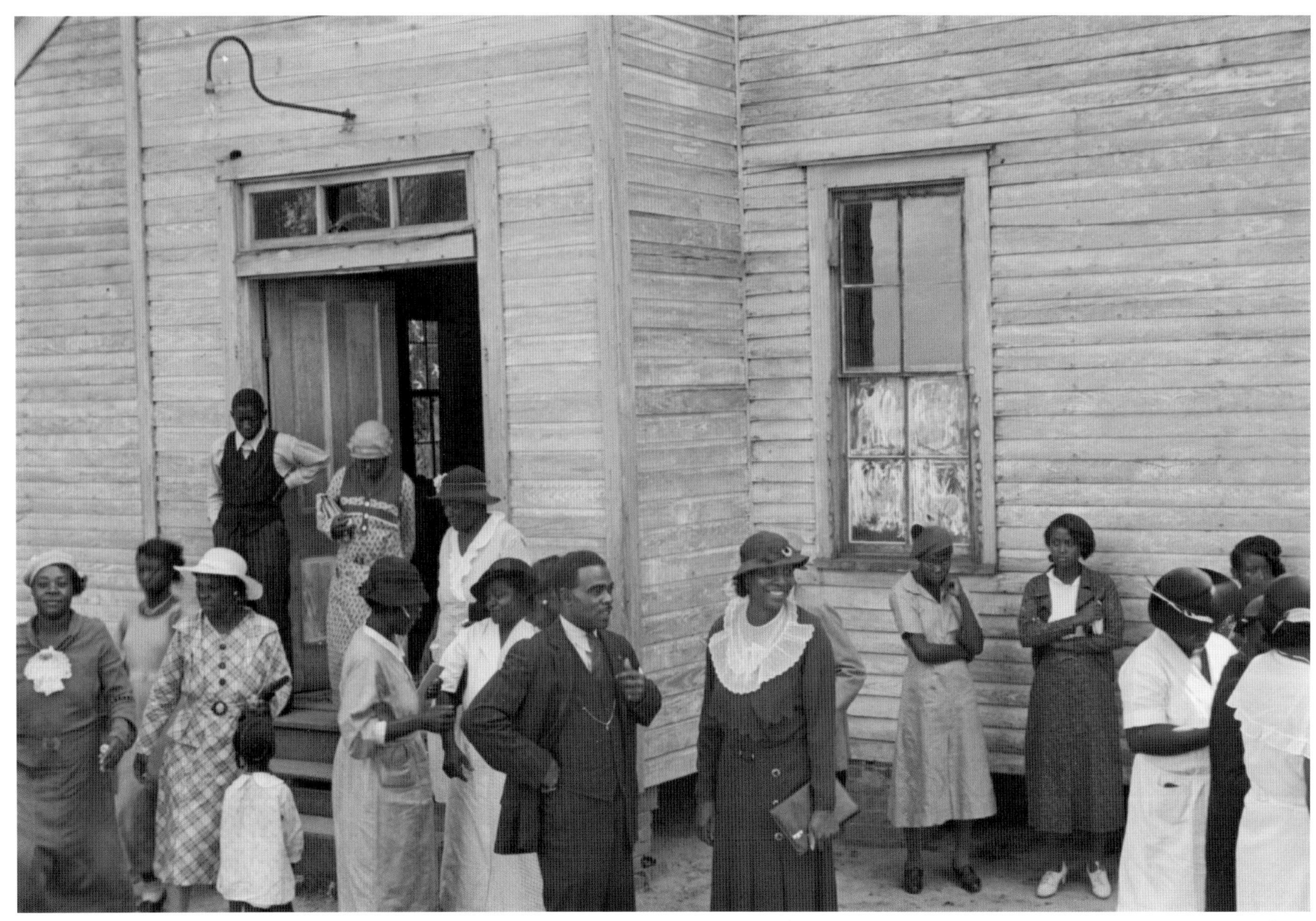

Parishioners mingle outside church on Sunday in Little Rock.

(Ben Shahn, October 1935) Farm Security Administration Photograph Collection, Prints & Photographs Division, Library of Congress, LC-USF33–006023–M3

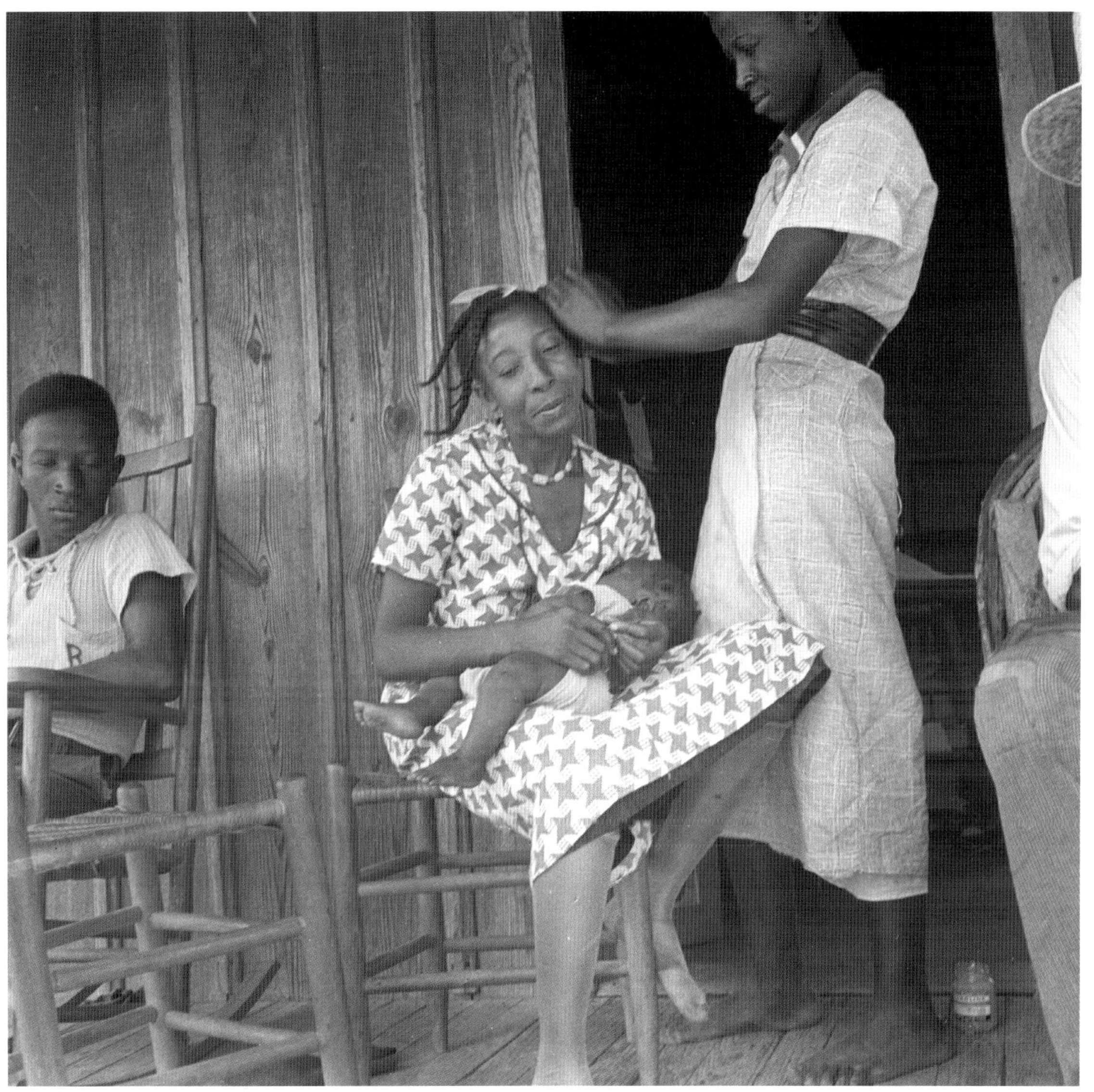

A sharecropper family on the porch of their cabin near Earle.

(Dorothea Lange, July 1936) Farm Security Administration Photograph Collection, Prints & Photographs Division, Library of Congress, LC-USF34–009765–E

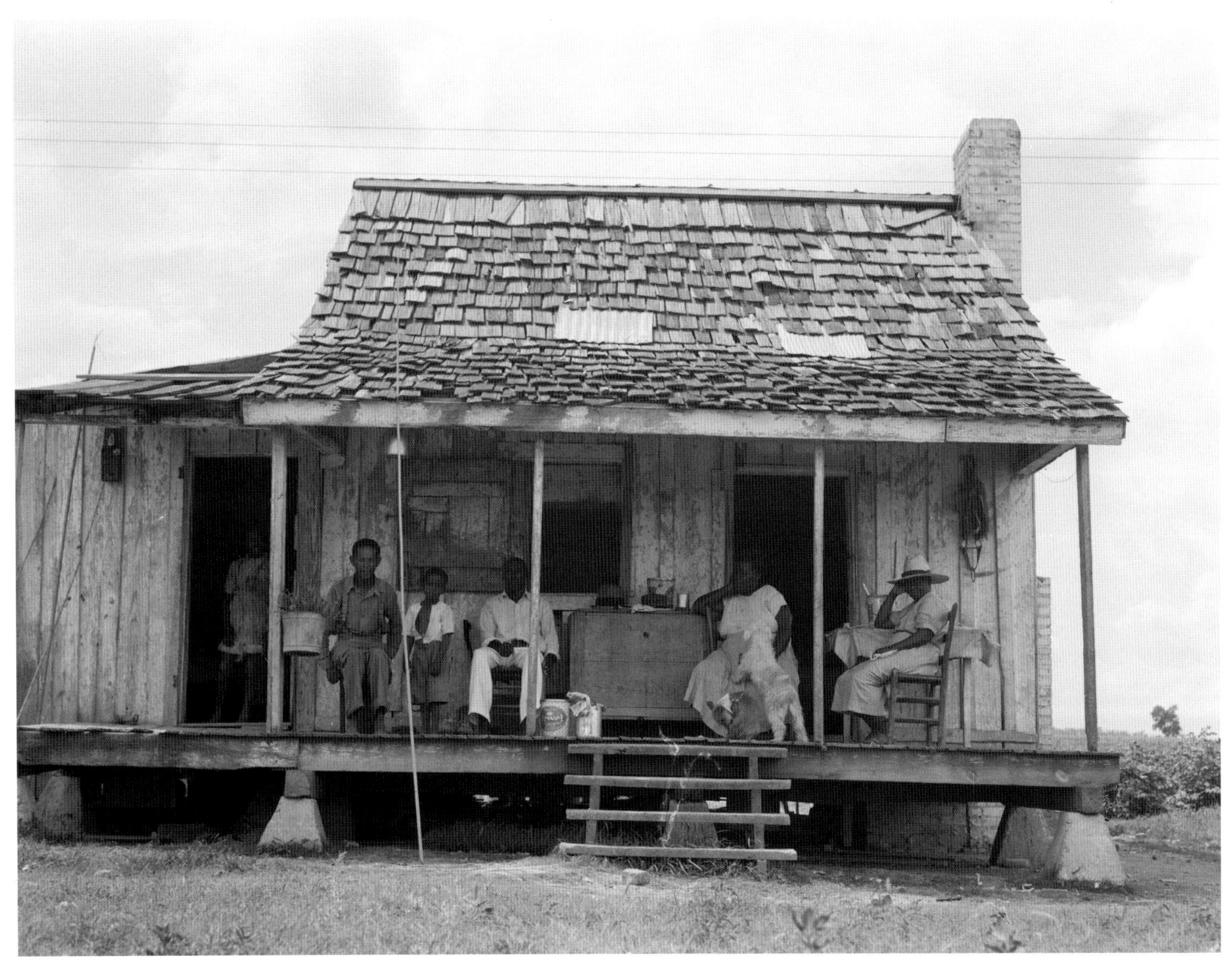

A sharecropper family on their front porch during a summer Saturday afternoon on an Arkansas Delta plantation.

(Dorothea Lange, August 1938) Farm Security Administration Photograph Collection, Prints & Photographs Division, Library of Congress, LC-USF34–018343–D

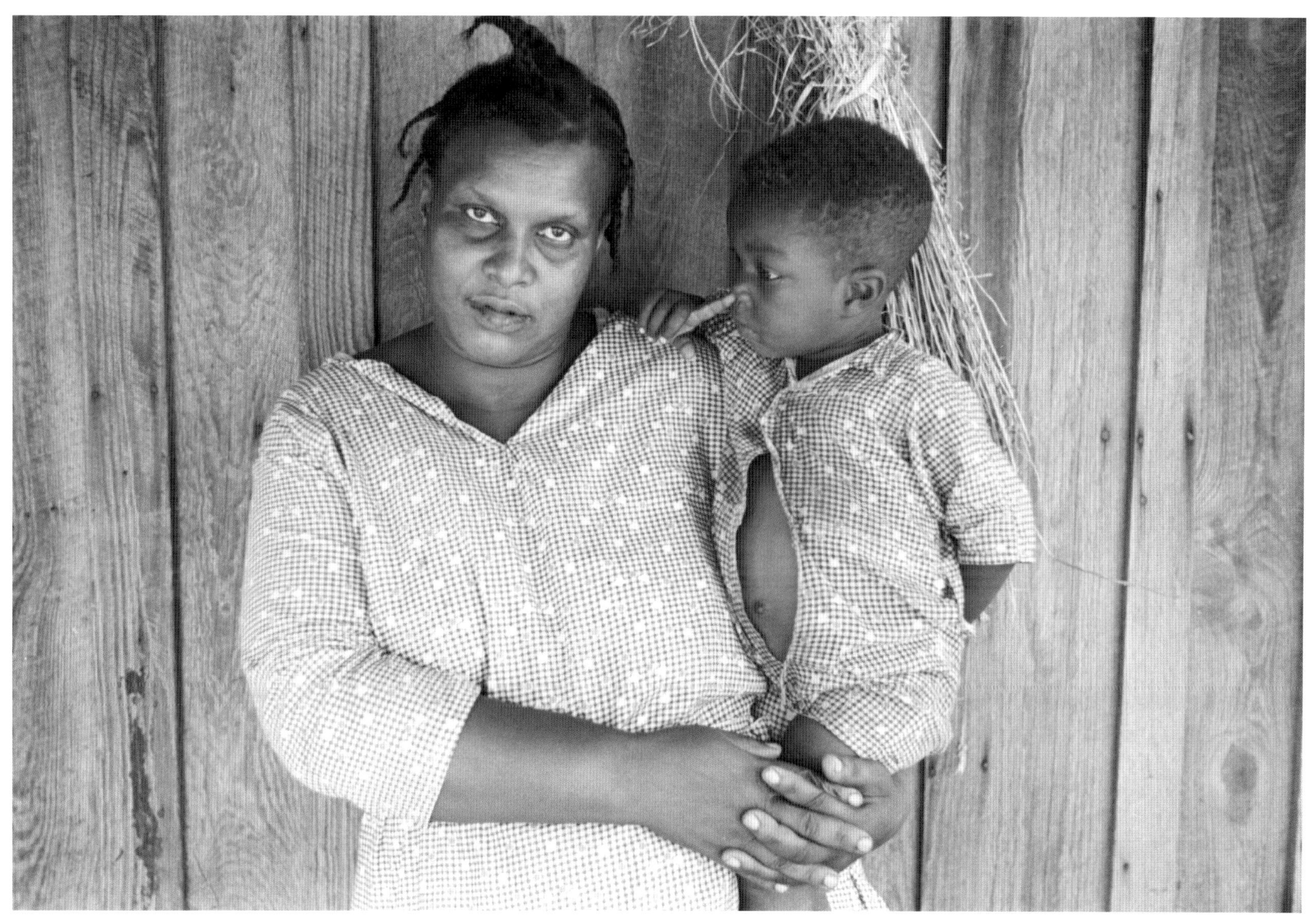

A woman rehabilitation client and her child dressed in clothing from the same fabric.

(Ben Shahn, October 1935) Farm Security Administration Photograph Collection, Prints & Photographs Division, Library of Congress, LC-USF33–006055–M2

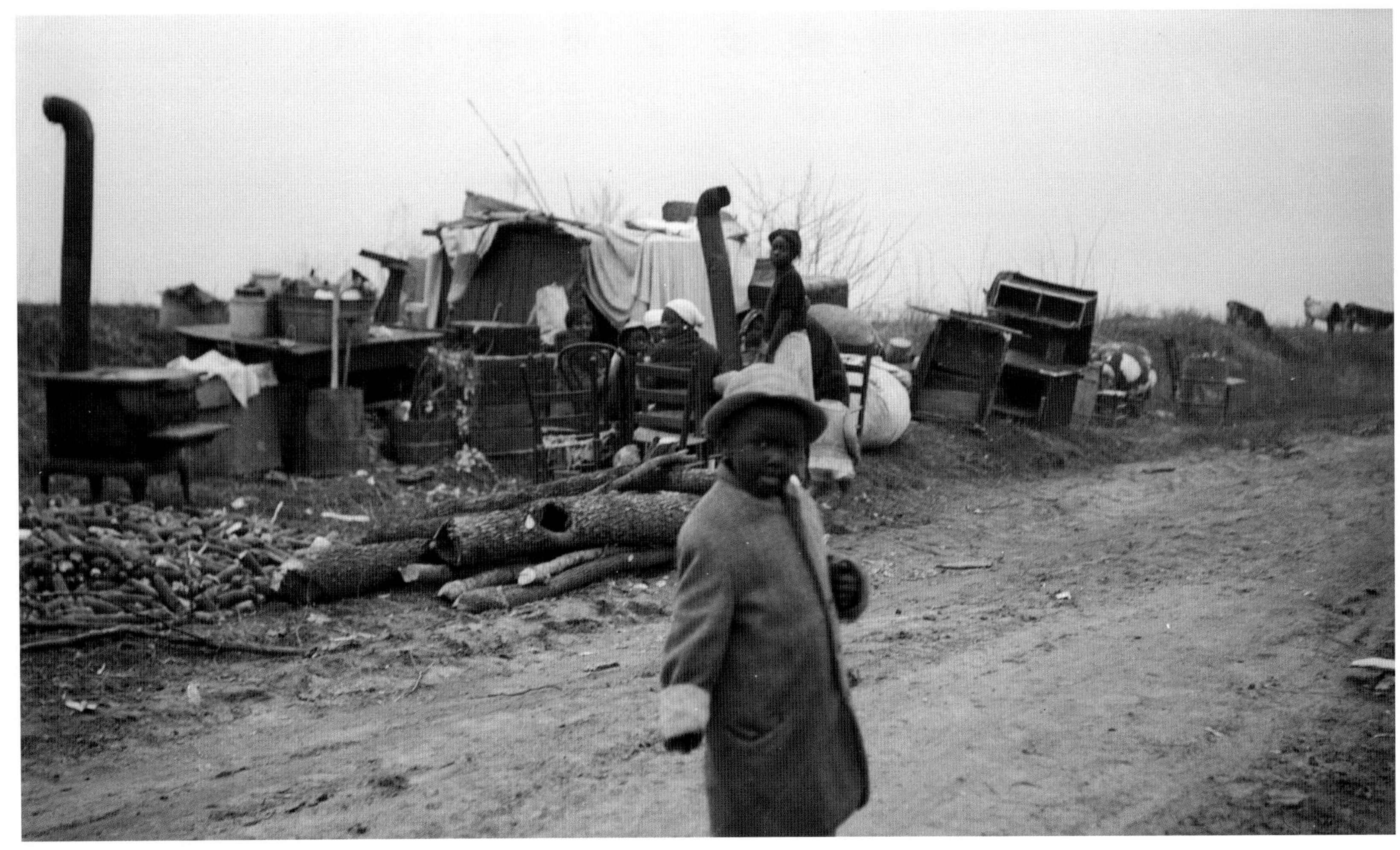

Sharecropper families evicted from the Dibble plantation near Parkin. John Vachon, the photographer, wrote, "They were . . . evicted the week of January 12, 1936, the plantation having charged that by membership in the Southern Tenant Farmers' Union they were engaging in a conspiracy to retain their homes; this contention granted by the court, the eviction, though at the point of a gun, was quite legal. The pictures were taken just after the evictions. . . . Eventually, evicted sharecropper families would be moved to a temporary tent colony."

(John Vachon, January 1936) Farm Security Administration Photograph Collection, Prints & Photographs Division, Library of Congress, LC-USF34–014008–E

FIVE | HOUSES

ACCORDING TO ONE 1930s observer poor southern farmers' shacks were so badly built that tenants could study astronomy through the roof and geology through the floor. Rupert Vance, a highly respected University of North Carolina sociologist, conducted an extensive examination of the South and "cotton culture" during the 1920s and 1930s and came to much the same conclusion. Vance, who was born in Conway, Arkansas, wrote that the worst housing in the nation was in the Cotton Belt and was directly linked to the poverty associated with the tenancy system. Arkansas, as a state with high rates of both tenancy and rural poverty, clearly had its share of farm families who were "miserably housed, miserably fed, miserably clothed," as described by US secretary of agriculture Henry A. Wallace, in an article for the *New York Times* in 1937.

Wallace visited Little Rock in November 1936 to speak to the Arkansas Farm Bureau Federation and toured eastern Arkansas, along with Mississippi, Alabama, and Georgia. Though the worst of the Great Depression seemingly had passed, Wallace wrote in the *Times*: "Any one [*sic*] who travels from Arkansas to Georgia by automobile as I did recently, cannot help realizing that the agricultural problem is far from solved. In this area, there are hundreds of thousands of miserable, unpainted shacks, constructed more than fifty years ago, some of them with holes in the roof and some without glass in the windows or doors in the door openings."

Wallace's drive through Arkansas took him through much of the same general region of the state visited by Ben Shahn the year before. Shahn took more pictures of "miserable, unpainted shacks" than did any other RA/FSA photographer traveling the state. Houses played a significant role in these photographs in Arkansas. As the outward, highly visible expression of a person's status, houses could imply much about one's financial condition, quality of life, and even character. As the tenants and sharecroppers in these early RA/FSA photos lived in houses provided by landlords, the condition and quality of those houses suggested more about the landlords and their attitudes toward their workers than about the workers themselves. This likely was a subtext of the message intended by the RA/FSA.

The cabins Shahn photographed were small, perhaps one to four rooms and constructed of rough, unpainted boards often haphazardly nailed together, or logs notched and fitted into one another. Their roofs sag, windows and doors are unscreened, and some cabins even lack doors. According to Donald Holley in *Uncle Sam's Farmers,* "Indoor plumbing was unknown," therefore, families had outdoor privies, and sometimes no facilities at all. Tenants and sharecroppers had no vegetable gardens; landlords didn't provide enough land for gardens, and laborers lacked the time and energy to tend them anyway. Such conditions were not only insecure and uncomfortable but unsanitary and unhealthy as well. As Holley writes, tenants and sharecroppers—including their children—suffered from malnutrition, pellagra, malaria, and hookworm and had poor dental health. Moreover, with no possibility of escaping the situation, children were destined to grow up into the same life.

There are few shots of interiors of tenants' and sharecroppers' homes. Shahn explained the cabins were too dark inside; he avoided using a flash because he wanted to capture a sense of the poor lighting. His pictures taken inside are dim and a little out of focus; they include an oil drum converted into a stove and another of an actual stove placed in the corner of a cabin with a dented pot, a bucket, and a coffee pot sitting on its top. Pages from newspapers and magazines are pasted on the nearby walls—poverty's stopgap to block drafts.

Rexford Tugwell's farm resettlement program focused specifically on the design and construction of houses built for settlers on each tract of land, anticipating they would be incentives for farmers to apply to the program. Holley reports that the houses were intended to be a demonstration of healthy farm living and, in their design for "utility and economy," support the work of the farm. Houses in Arkansas followed a standardized wood-frame design with variations to avoid the "government-housing" look, but had no costly decorative or unnecessary features. They had three to five bedrooms, a living room, and a kitchen with a built-in sink, pantry, and screened porch. Interior walls were pine and kitchens were painted white, with linoleum on the floor. Though some houses had running water, indoor bathrooms were generally eliminated in the South to save money, but each house had a clean water source and a sanitary privy.

Russell Lee's photos of houses at Lake Dick and Arthur Rothstein's from Plum Bayou document these descriptions. They both show the white-painted wood-frame houses, with similar but slightly different exteriors. All interiors are paneled in pine except the kitchens where the white walls suggest cleanliness. At Lake Dick, Lee seemed to pay more attention to the kitchens; his pictures clearly show electrical appliances and ceiling lighting as well as running water in the sink. Though most of the houses appear very sparely designed and furnished, many congressmen considered their costs to the government to be too high. At Plum Bayou and Lake Dick, for example, new four-room houses were valued respectively at $3,666 and $2,388, according to Marion Clawson, a government agricultural economist. Clawson pointed out, however, that the new houses led to an all-important sense of "pride of ownership, comfort, and satisfaction," and were significant to the resettled farm families who were successful.

Country music legend Johnny Cash was one of those who testified to the comfort and satisfaction families felt with the resettlement homes. The Cash family relocated to the Dyess Colony in March of 1935. Cash, who was only three years old at the time, states firmly that the house promised new life to the family. In his autobiography, Cash wrote of the house at Dyess: "And that's when I saw the Promised Land: a brand new house with two big bedrooms, a living room, a dining room, a kitchen, a front porch and a back porch, an outside toilet, a barn, a chicken house and a smokehouse. To me, luxuries untold. There was no running water, of course, and no electricity; none of us even dreamed of miracles like that."

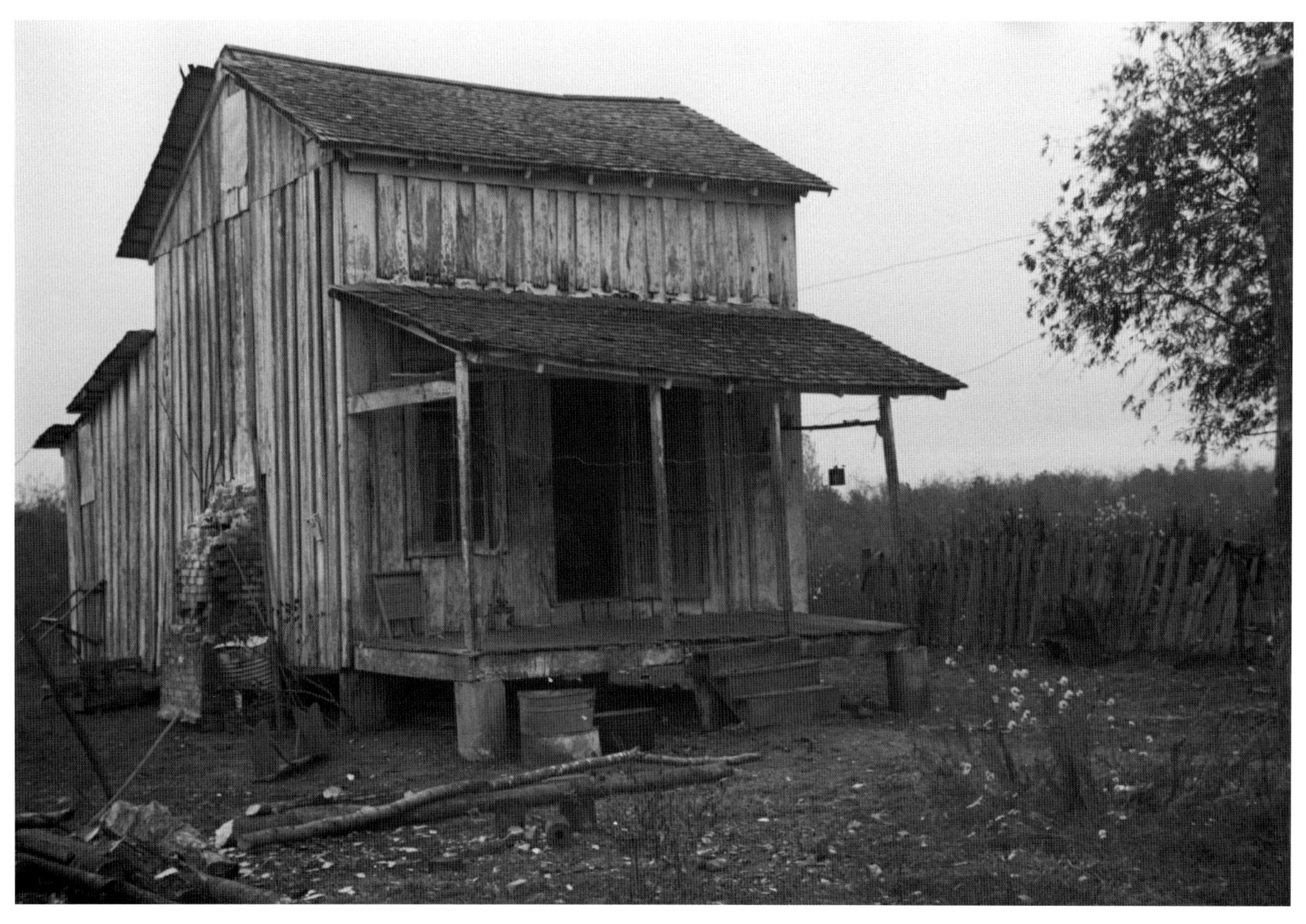

A sharecropper's cabin and yard.

(Ben Shahn, October 1935) Farm Security Administration Photograph Collection, Prints & Photographs Division, Library of Congress, LC-USF33–006162–M3

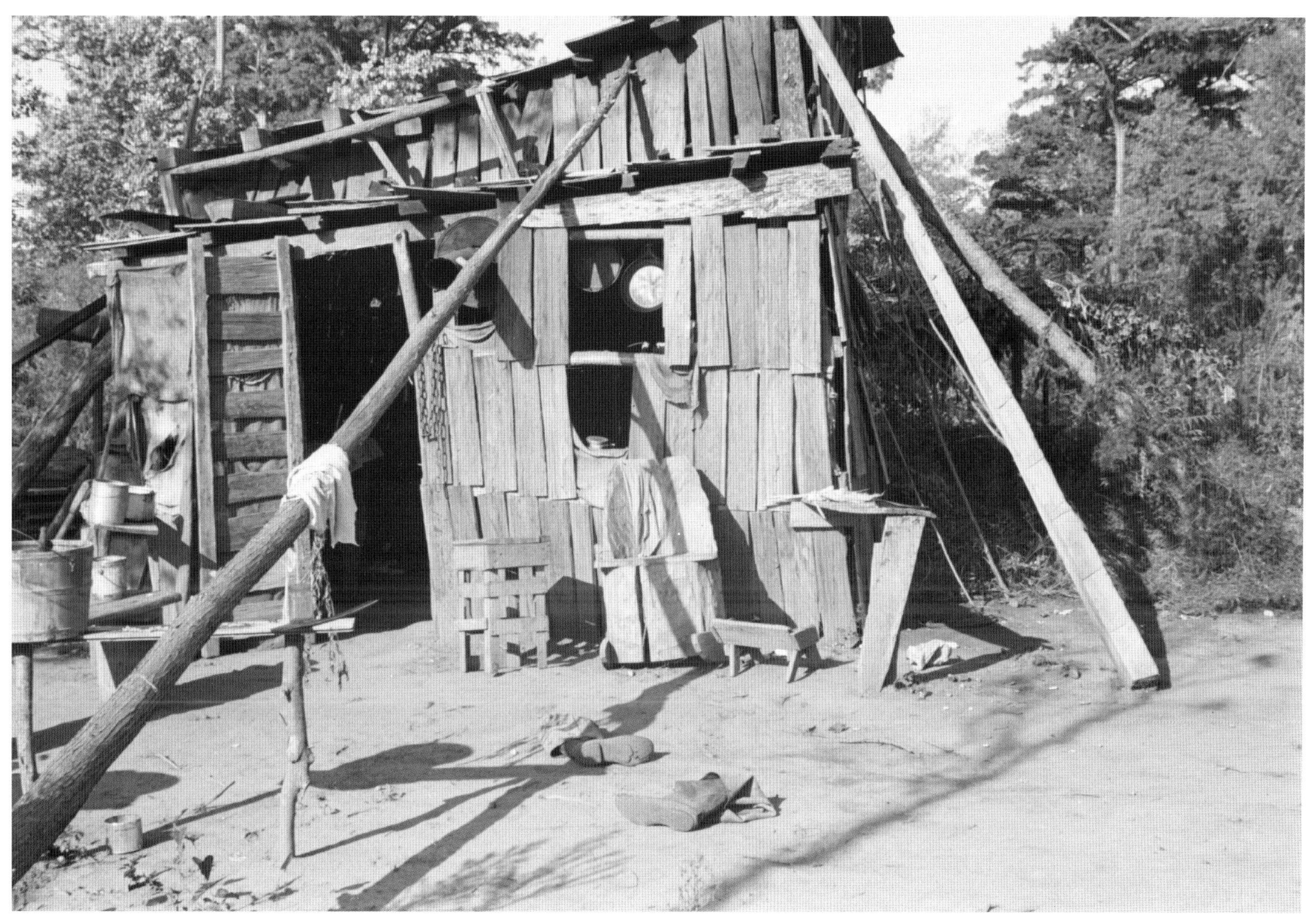

A squatter's home.

(Ben Shahn, October 1935) Farm Security Administration Photograph Collection, Prints & Photographs Division, Library of Congress, LC-USF33–006029–M1

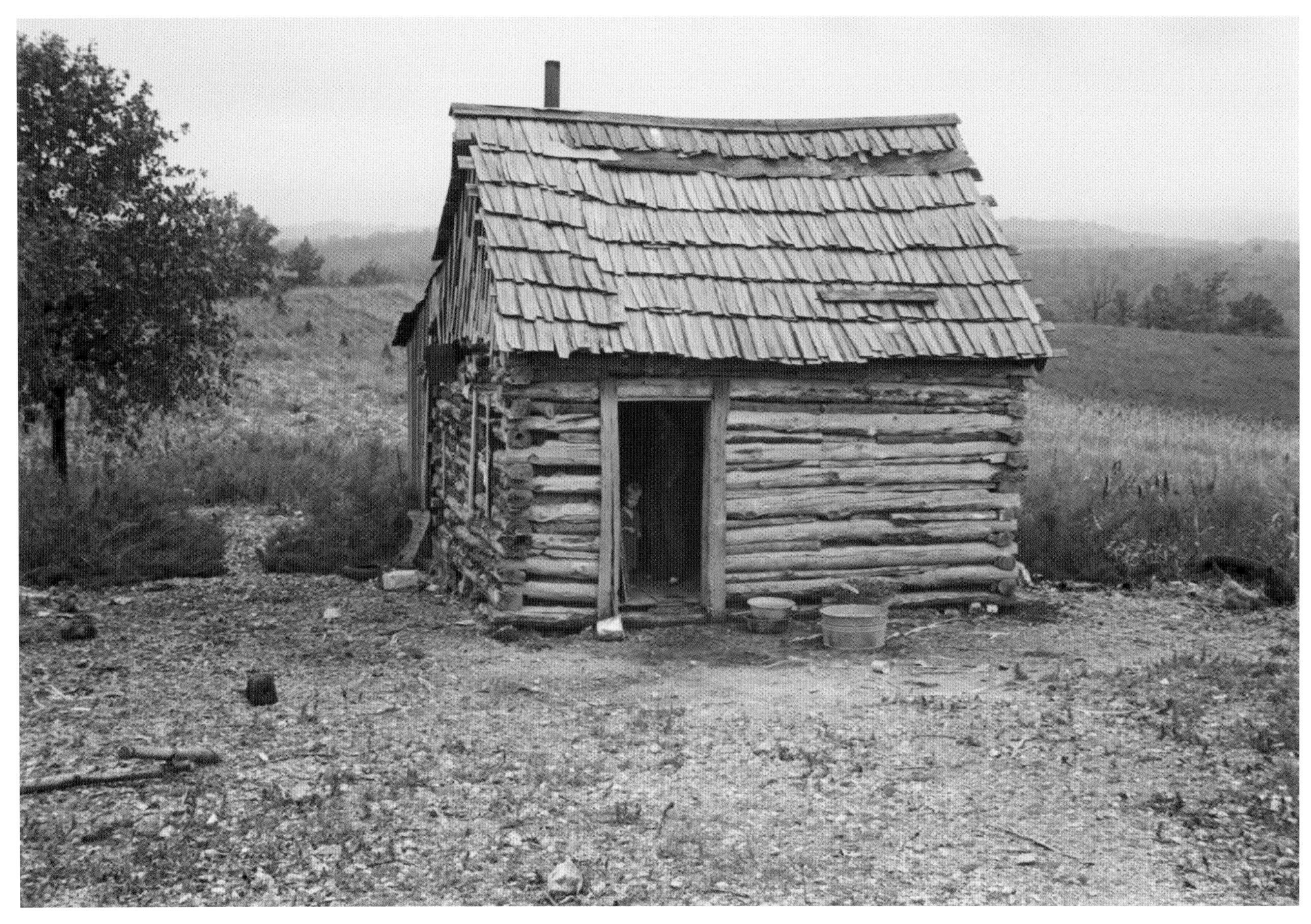

The home of a destitute Ozark family on the Case plantation in Pulaski County.

(Ben Shahn, October 1935) Farm Security Administration Photograph Collection, Prints & Photographs Division, Library of Congress, LC-USF33–006073–M3

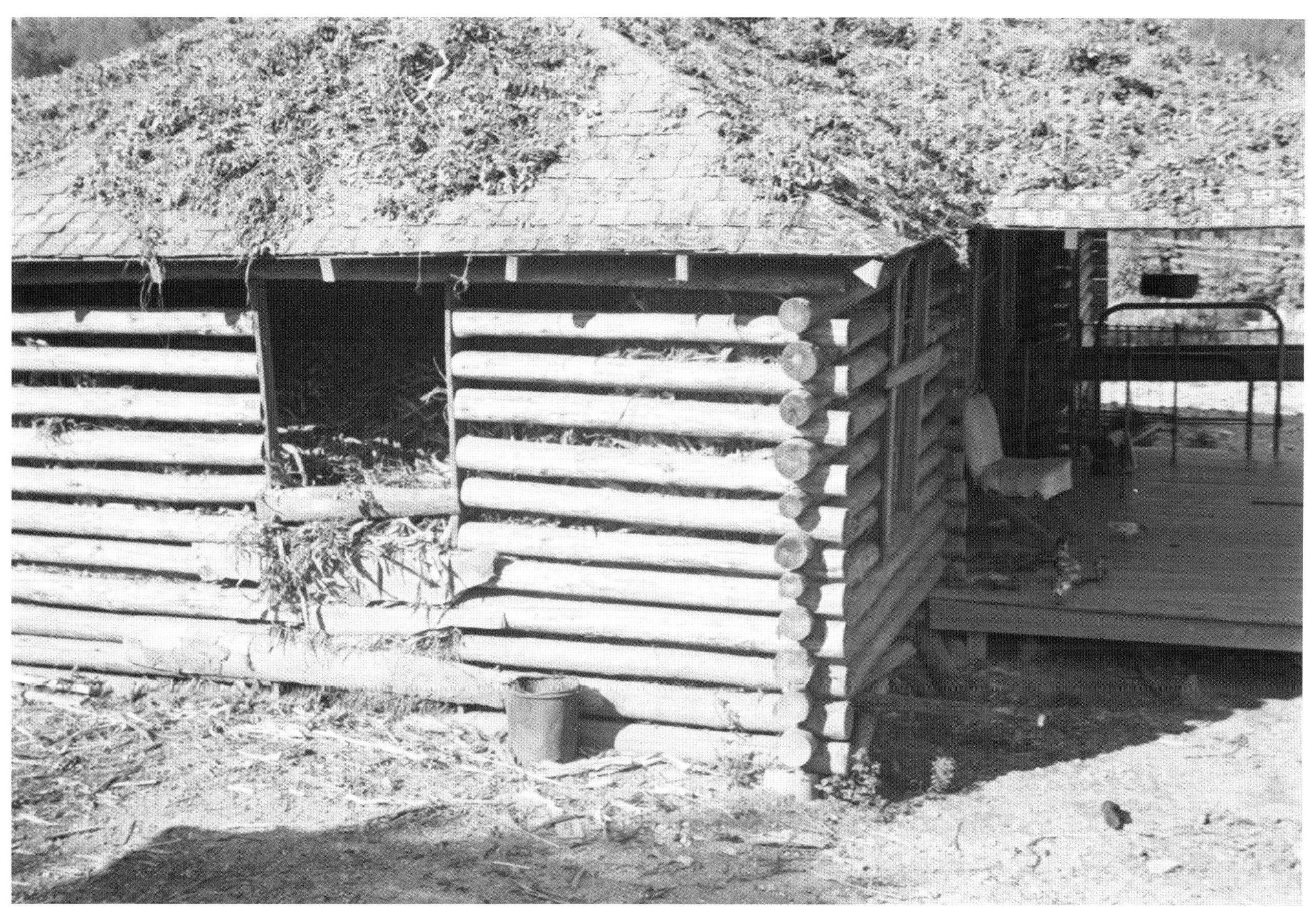

According to Shahn, a rehabilitation client used auto license plates for the roof of this house, though the photo does not show them clearly.

(Ben Shahn, October 1935) Farm Security Administration Photograph Collection, Prints & Photographs Division, Library of Congress, LC-USF33–006057–M1

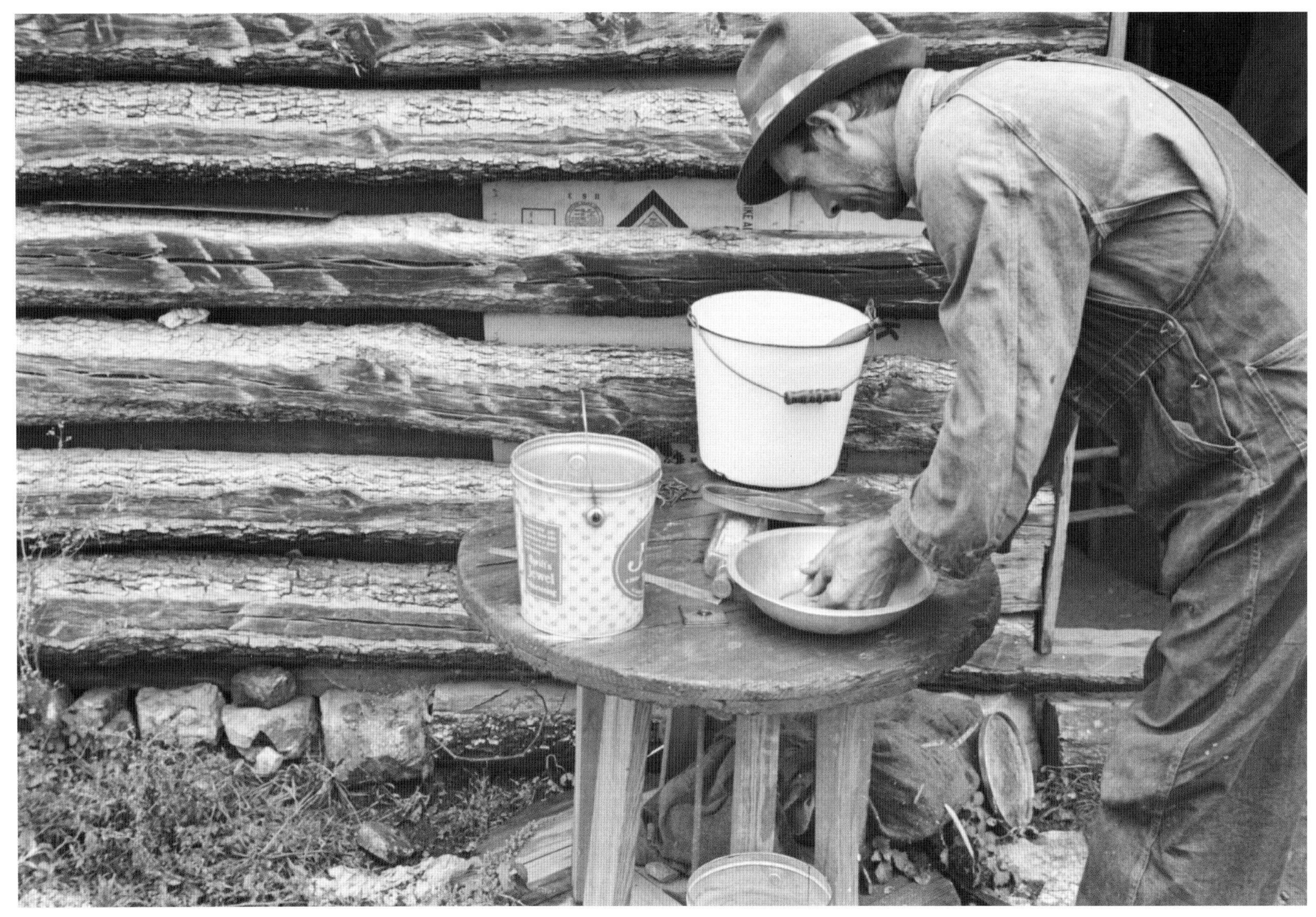

Shahn captioned this photo, "Washing facilities in the Ozarks."

(Ben Shahn, October 1935) Farm Security Administration Photograph Collection, Prints & Photographs Division, Library of Congress, LC-USF33–006034–M5

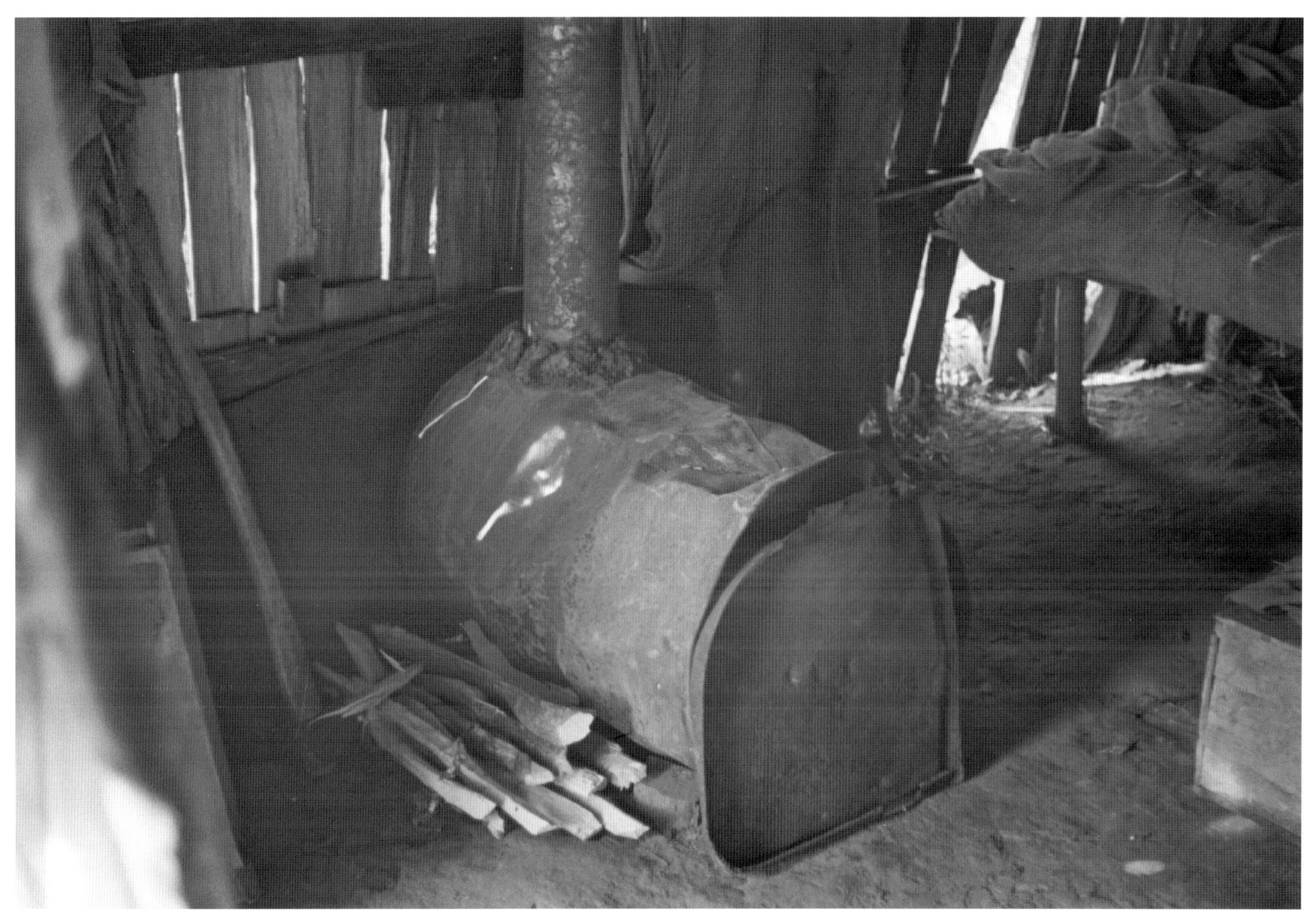

Old oil drum converted into a stove.

(Ben Shahn, October 1935) Farm Security Administration Photograph Collection, Prints & Photographs Division, Library of Congress, LC-USF33–006030–B-M3

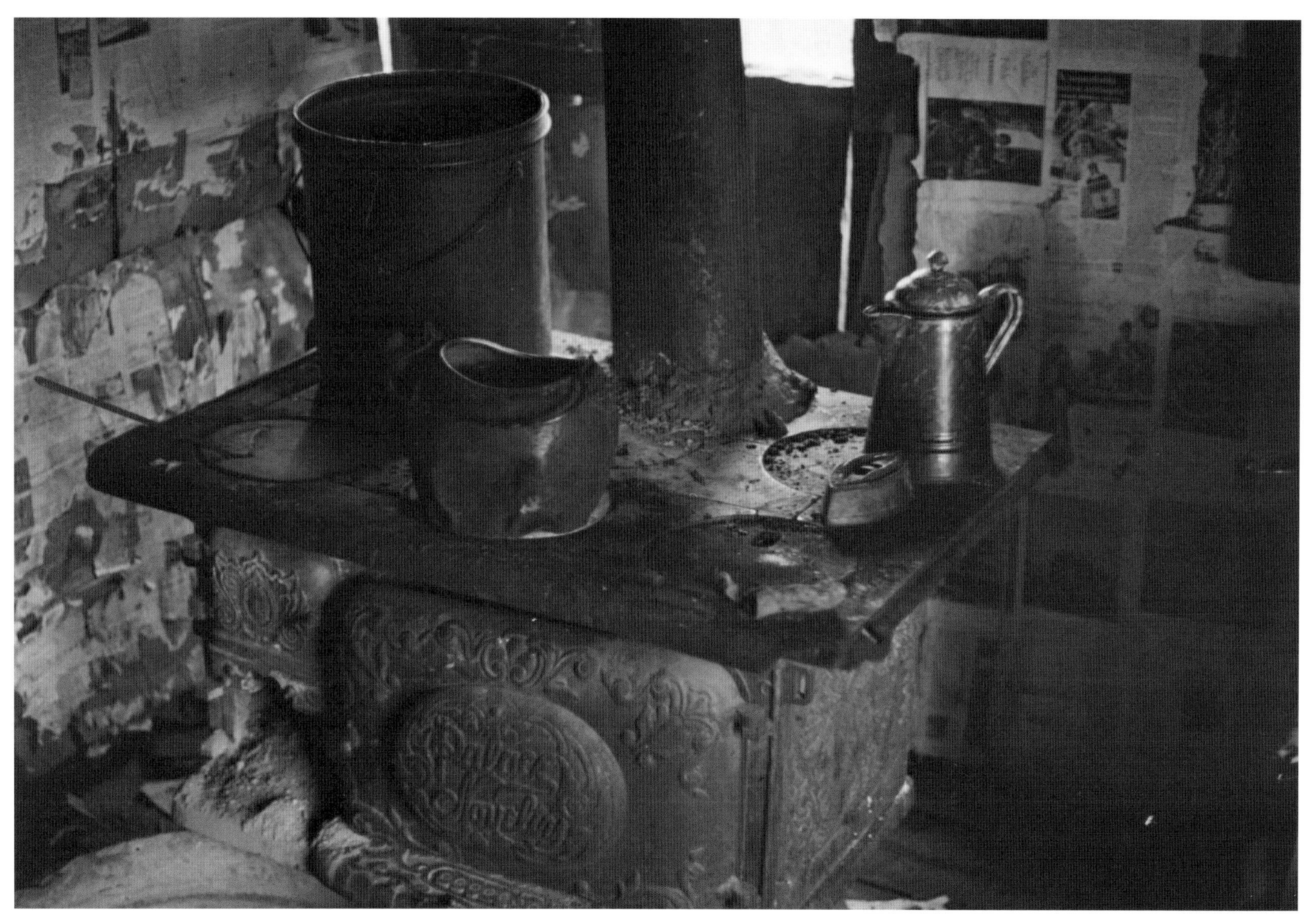

Old woodstove in a cabin's interior, with pages of newspapers and magazines pasted on the walls.

(Ben Shahn, October 1935) Farm Security Administration Photograph Collection, Prints & Photographs Division, Library of Congress, LC-USF33–006073–M5

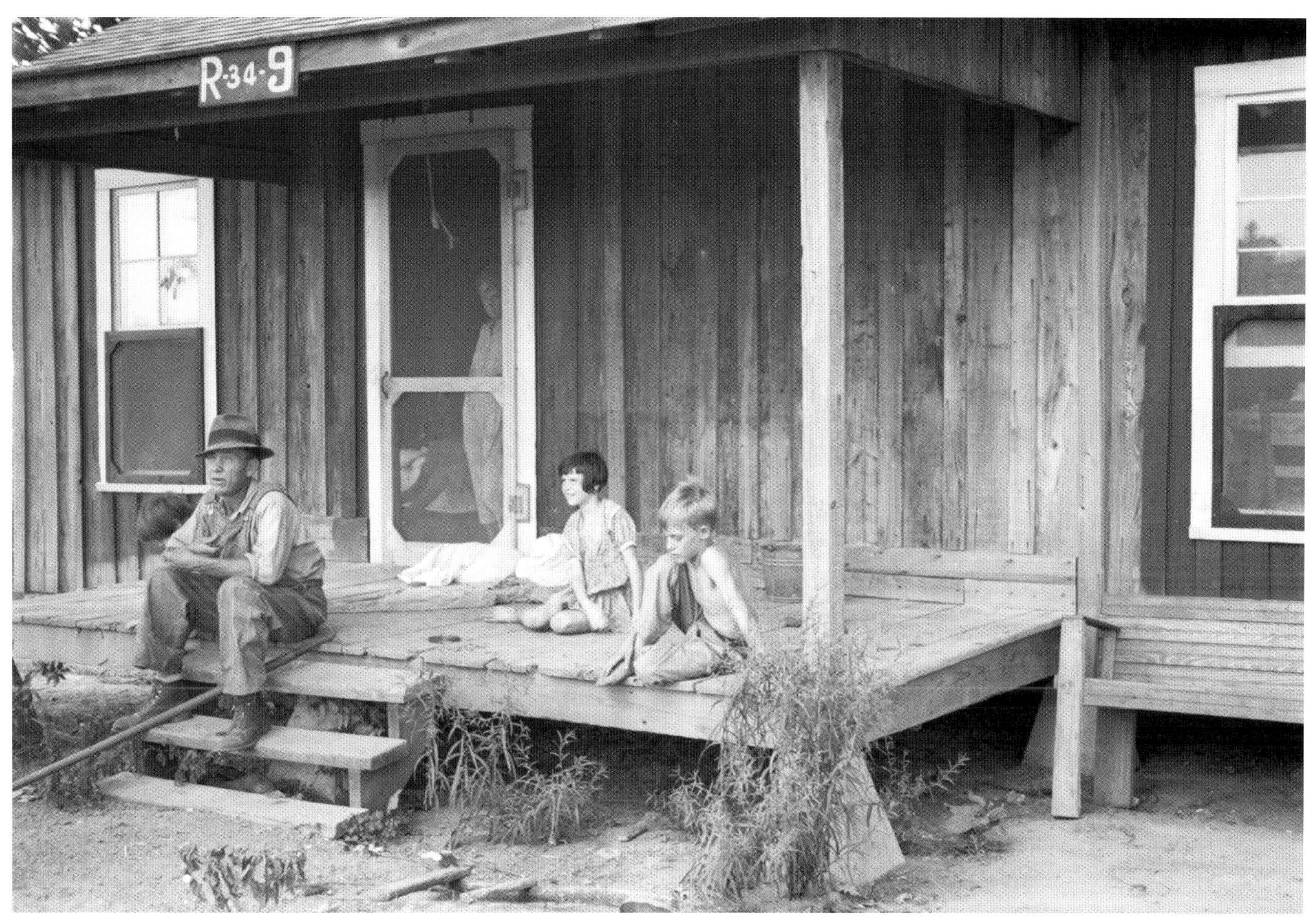

A sharecropper family on the front porch of their company house on the Wilson cotton plantation.

(Arthur Rothstein, August 1935) Farm Security Administration Photograph Collection, Prints & Photographs Division, Library of Congress, LC-USF33–002012–M2

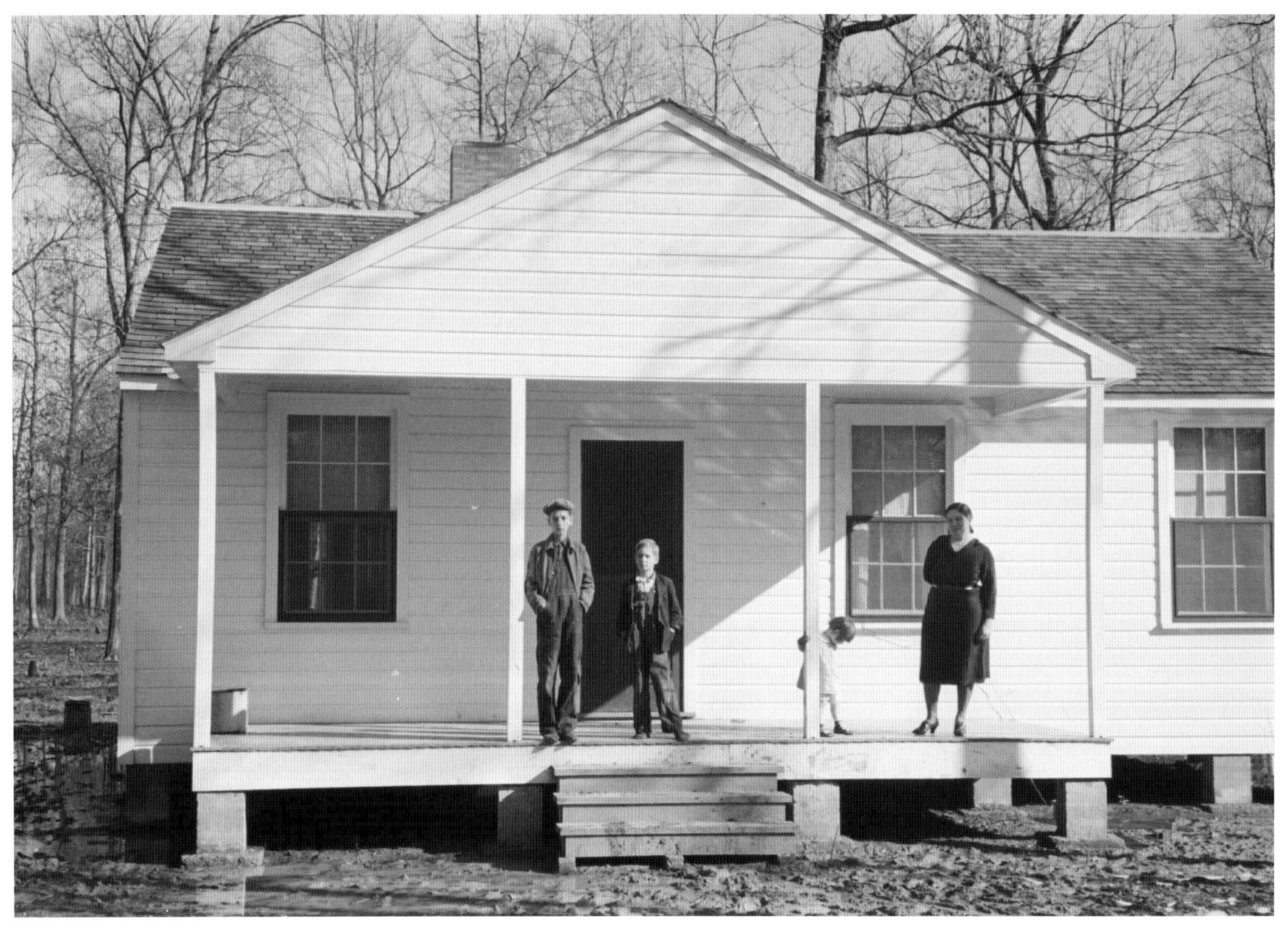

A house at the Chicot farm, typical of the white wood-frame structures on resettlement farms.

(Russell Lee, January 1939) Farm Security Administration Photograph Collection, Prints & Photographs Division, Library of Congress, LC-USF33–011921–M5

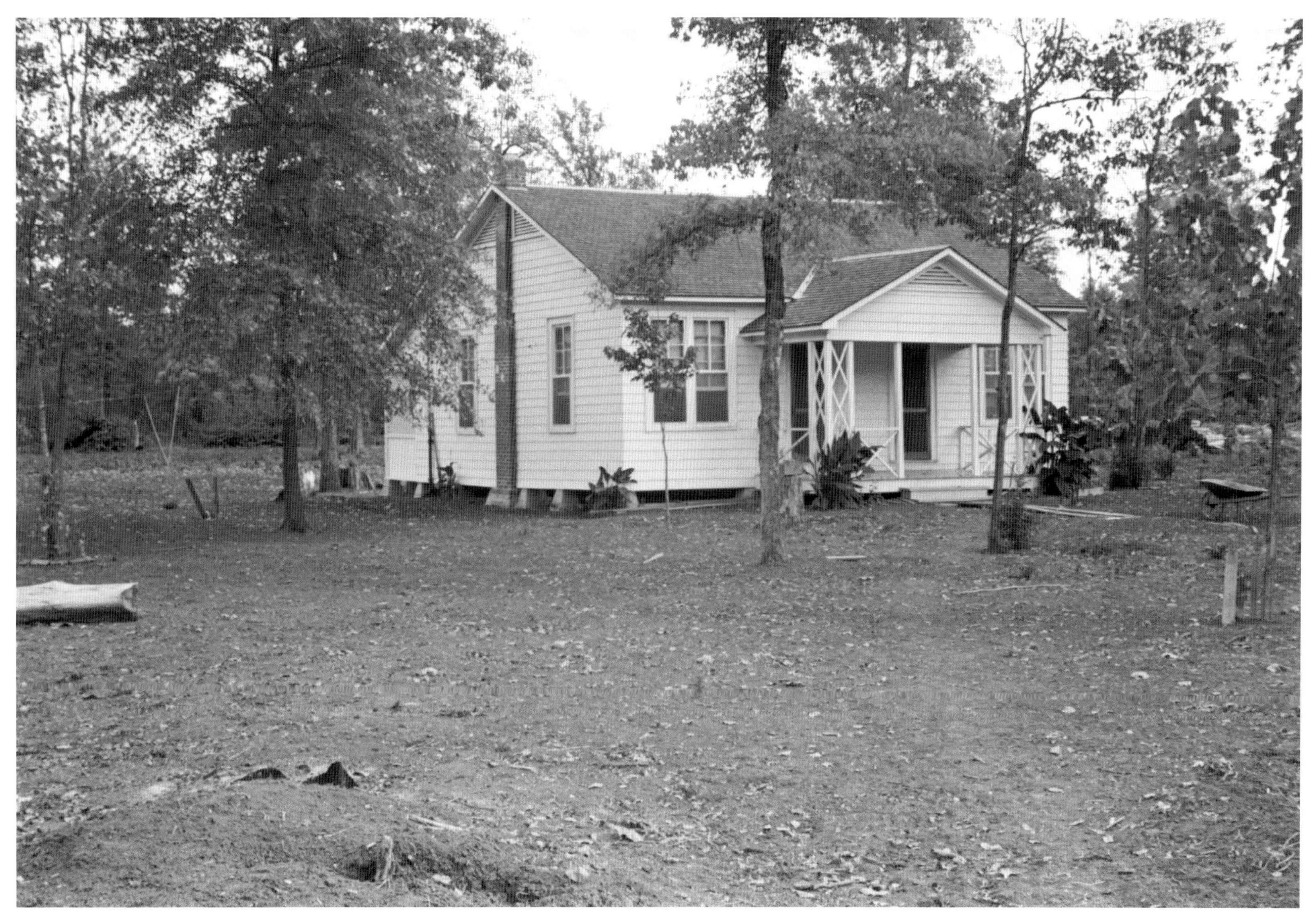

A farmhouse at the Dyess Colony.

(Ben Shahn, September 1935) Farm Security Administration Photograph Collection, Prints & Photographs Division, Library of Congress, LC-USF33–006046–M2

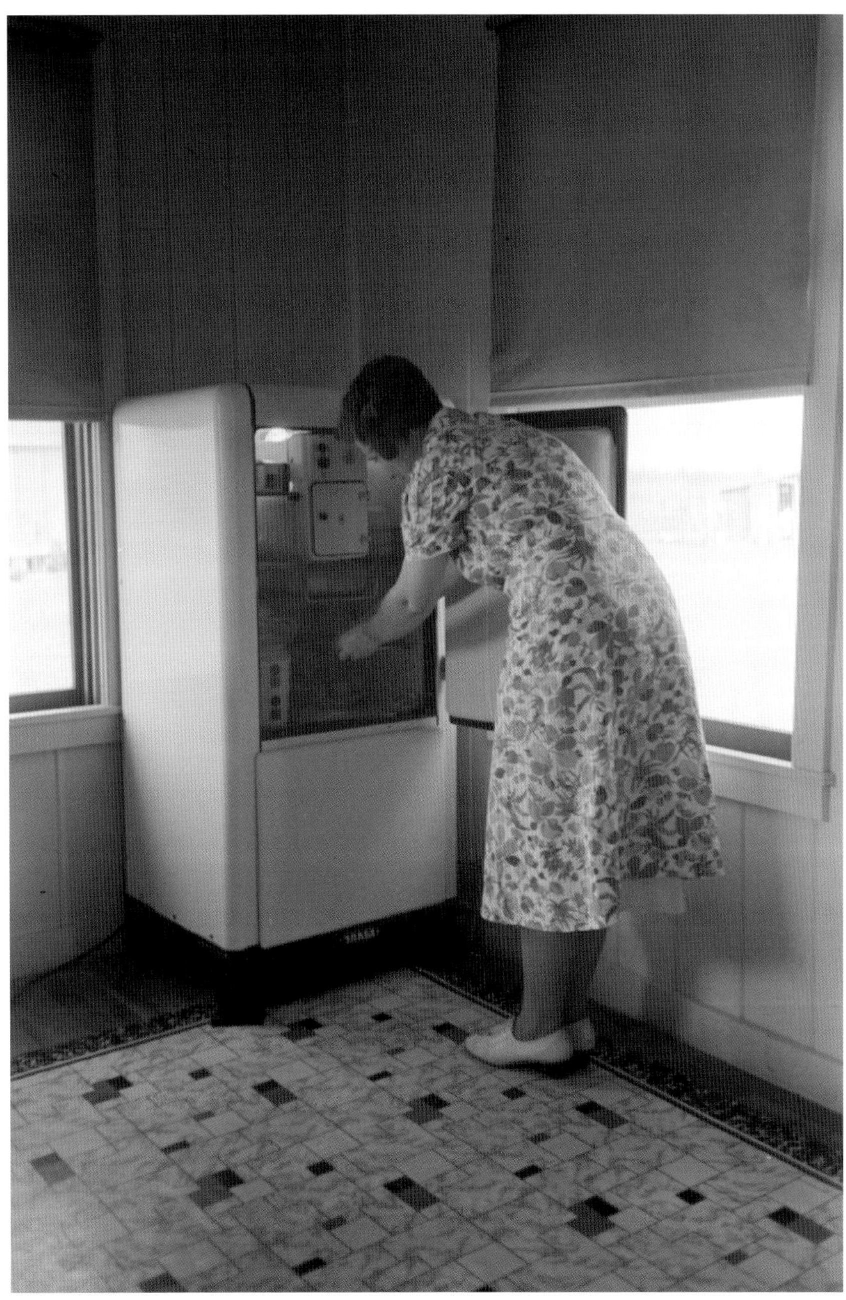

The kitchen in a Lake Dick farmhouse, equipped with an electric refrigerator.

(Russell Lee, October 1938) Farm Security Administration Photograph Collection, Prints & Photographs Division, Library of Congress, LC-USF33–011673–M5

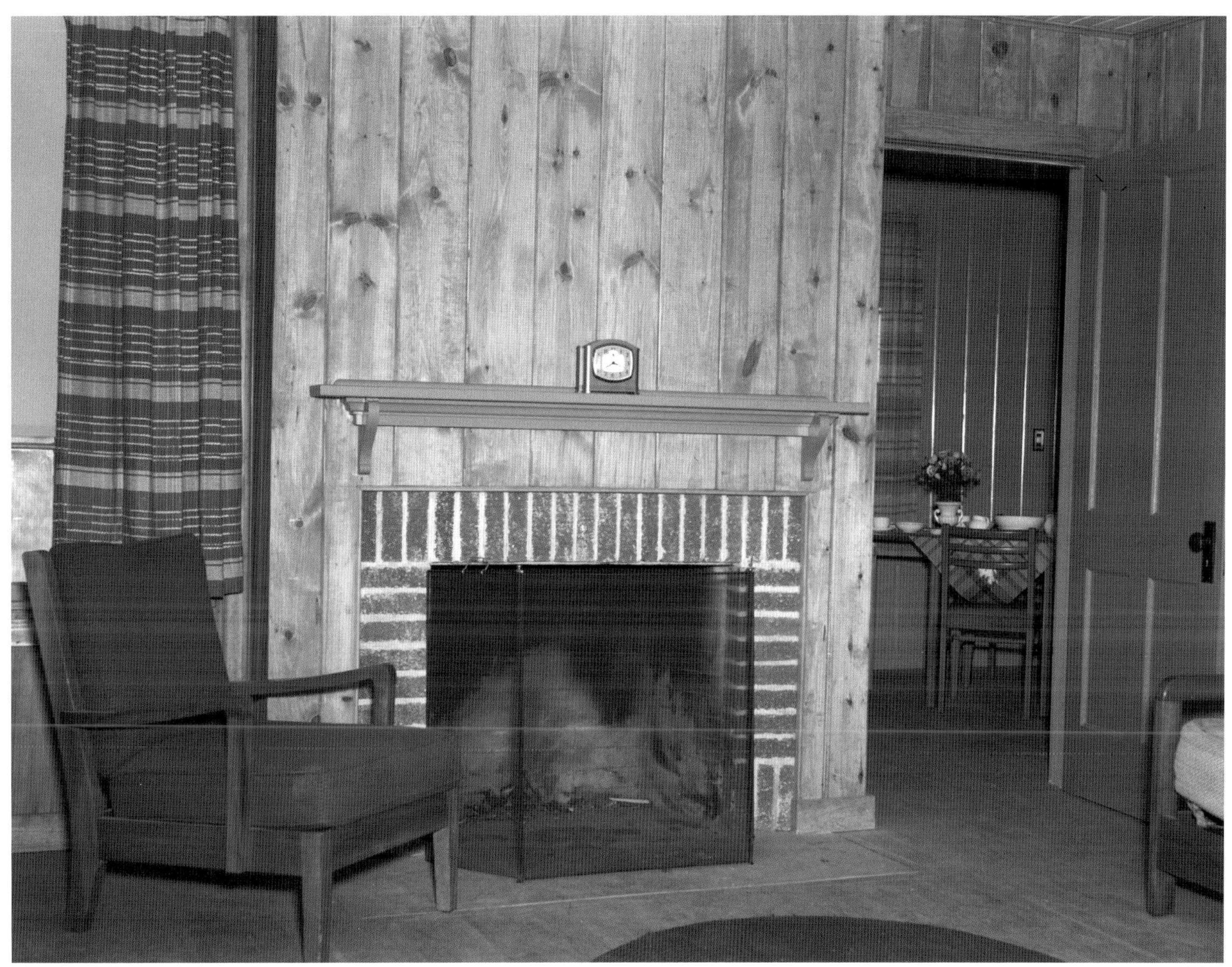

Living room in a Plum Bayou project house with decorative fireplace mantel and pine board walls.

(Arthur Rothstein, April 1937) Farm Security Administration Photograph Collection, Prints & Photographs Division, Library of Congress, LC-USF34–025306–D

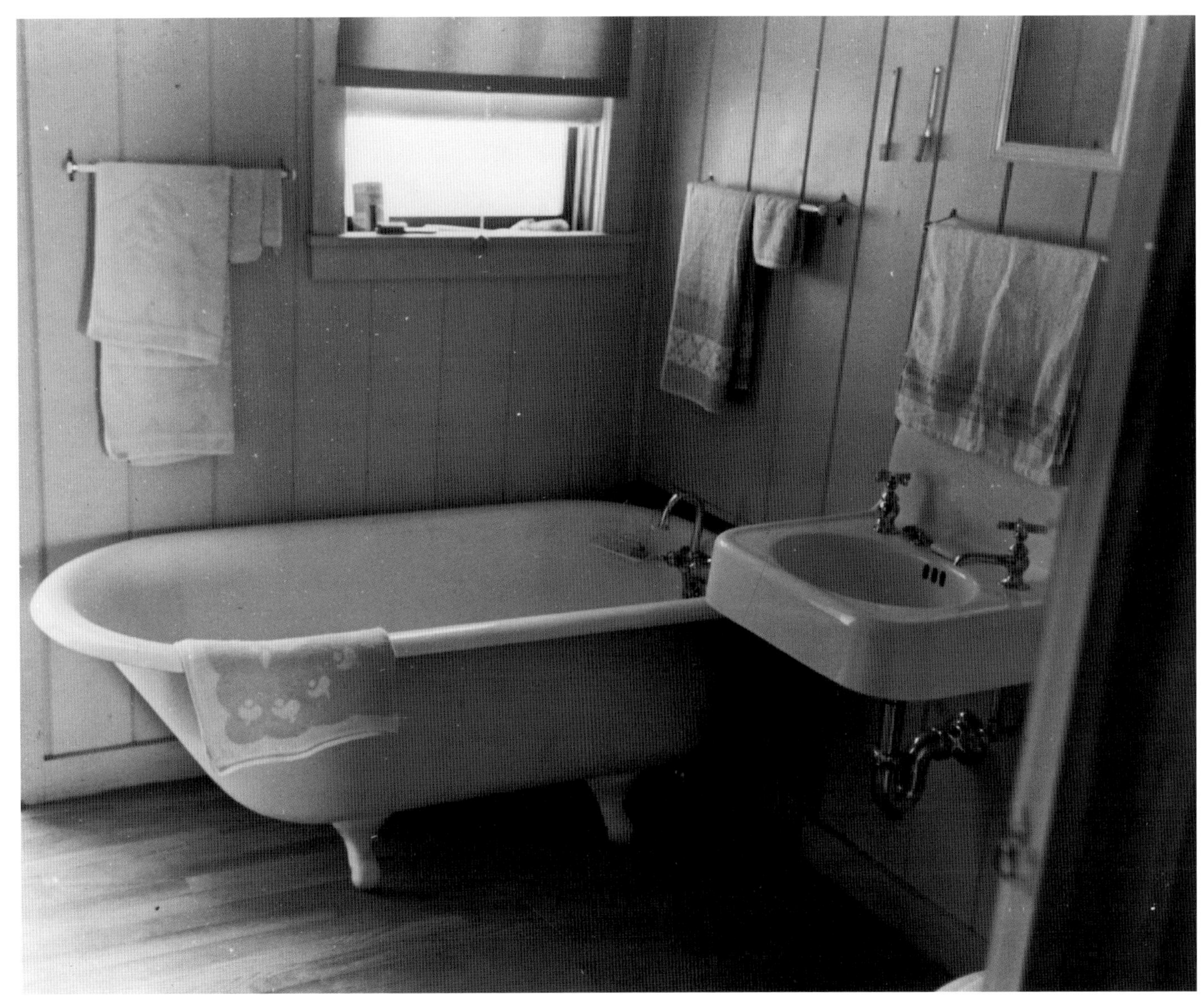

Lake Dick resettlement farmhouses were outfitted and plumbed for bathrooms.

(Russell Lee, September 1938) Farm Security Administration Photograph Collection, Prints & Photographs Division, Library of Congress, LC-USF33–011672–M5

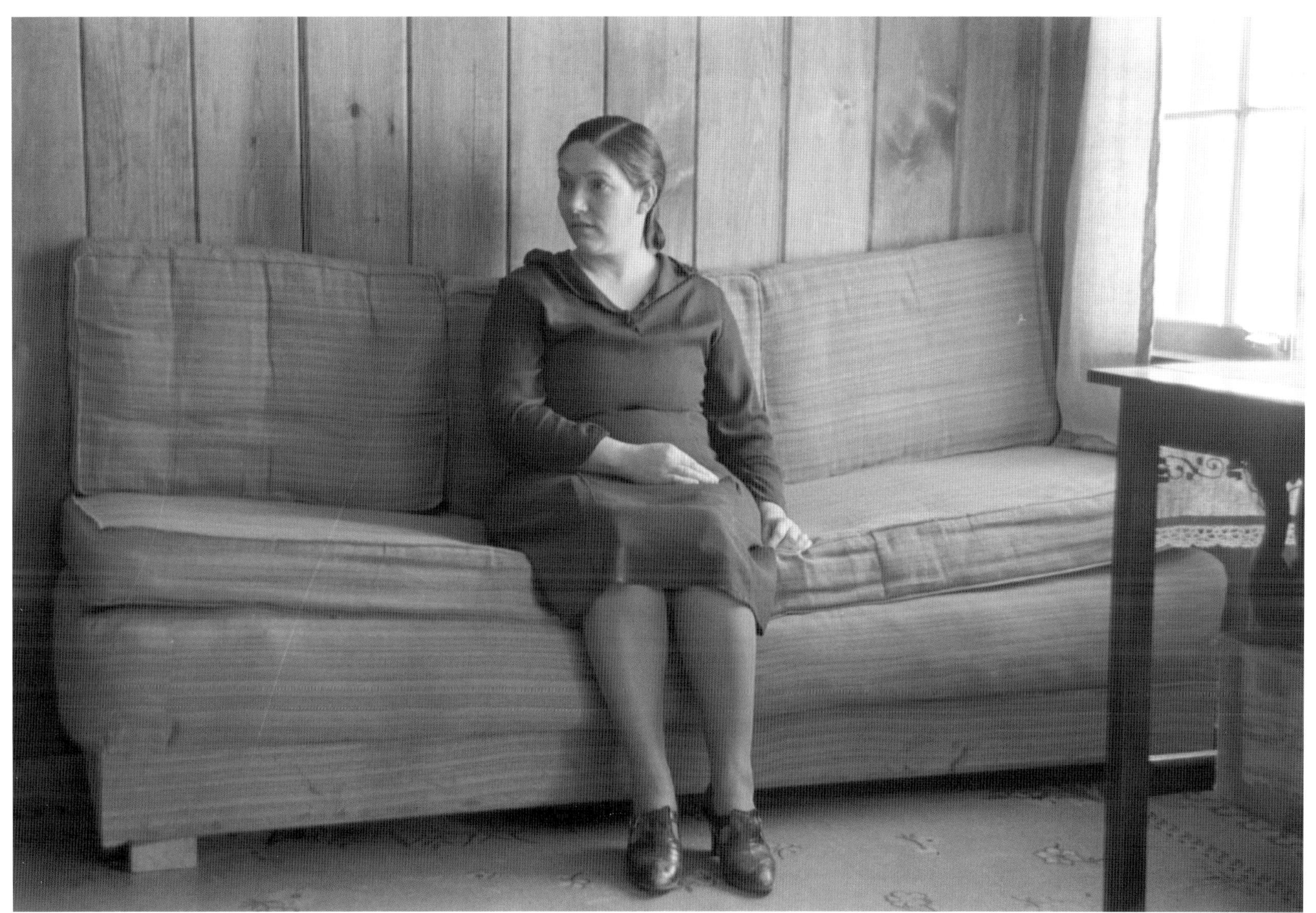

Homesteader farmwife at Chicot and her homemade sofa.

(Russell Lee, January 1939) Farm Security Administration Photograph Collection, Prints & Photographs Division, Library of Congress, LC-USF33–011918–M1

SIX | FOOD

FOOD SECURITY WAS a persistent and worrying issue during the Depression, beginning with a food shortage crisis in 1930–1931 and leading to government concern about southerners' inadequate diets, an emphasis on home gardens, and federal and state sponsorship of community canning centers. New pressure cookers were widely available, and agricultural extension agents and government brochures explained how to process food safely.

The food crisis that swept across much of the midsection of the country, including Arkansas, unnerved everyone. The US Department of Agriculture declared 1930 the "driest growing season on record," according to Roger Lambert in "Hoover and the Red Cross in Arkansas"(in the *Arkansas Historical Quarterly*). States were unable to handle the volume of demand for help, and congressional delegations appealed to the federal government for assistance. President Hoover, however, turned to the Red Cross, asking the organization to handle the distribution of surplus commodities to the needy. The volume of demand could at times strain Red Cross resources; one such event occurred in 1931 when a group of Lonoke County farmers converged on a distribution center in England. Though conflict was avoided, the story of Arkansas's "rioting farmers" made headlines around the country, according to Lambert.

Roosevelt, in taking office in 1933, did not hesitate to use the federal government to help and began a program of food relief assistance. According to Floyd Hicks and C. Robert Lambert, who described these programs in Arkansas, the Federal Surplus Relief Corporation (FSRC) determined that the state was among the neediest with its almost 38 percent unemployment rate and wages at about half what they had been in 1929. This opened the door to a slew of federal initiatives to relieve hunger, adding to the surplus commodity distribution, programs such as school lunches, relief gardens, canning projects, and food stamps.

The RA/FSA photographs of home gardens and canning document the results of these government programs, all intended to relieve the food crisis and to improve Arkansans' diet as well. Though every family was encouraged to have a garden, relief clients were specifically required to do so by the State Emergency Relief Commission, which was delegated by the federal government to oversee commodity distribution. Arkansas, through the commission, made a major push for home gardens. Hicks and Lambert report that by the winter of 1934 provisions had been made for about 100,000 subsistence gardens, and two dozen Arkansas cities had established community gardens.

Arkansans were encouraged to produce and then preserve as much of their own food as they could, enough to feed a family for a full year, if possible. Under this new state and federal pressure, the home canning done by Arkansas farm women for decades took on a special urgency. The Arkansas Agricultural Extension Service and the US Department of Agriculture launched programs to teach newer and safer methods of canning.

New pressure cooker equipment helped to shorten the canning process. Free community canning centers were set up in rural areas for those who couldn't afford their own pressure cookers or find one to borrow. By the mid-1930s there were twelve hundred canning centers across the state, according to Hicks and Lambert. Farm women could bring vegetables, fruit, meat, and even milk to a community center and do their family's canning. Sometimes during the peak of canning season, women would even move into tents near community canning centers to have better access to the equipment.

The canning movement was well established by 1935 when RA/FSA photographers came to Arkansas. They visited community canning centers and took pictures of their operation, as well as home demonstration supervisors and extension agents explaining how to prepare food for canning. Their photos also show women at work canning produce in their kitchens on government resettlement farms, where families were expected to produce much of their own food; the resettlement farmhouses were even built with large pantries to accommodate shelves of jars and tins of preserved food. RA/FSA photos show women proudly displaying quart jars filled with fruits and vegetables, pantry shelves full of quart and half-gallon jars and tins, and a man emerging from his storage cellar.

Through these various programs, the government was also promoting a more varied and healthier diet for southerners. Tenants, sharecroppers, small farmers, and other poor Arkansans were accustomed to the monotony of salt pork, molasses, and cornbread, a diet so poor in nutrition that many—especially children—suffered from pellagra, rickets, and poor dental health. Margaret Hagood, in her 1939 examination of southern tenant women (*Mothers of the South: Portraiture of the White Tenant Farm Woman*), found that, though mothers prepared three meals a day, there was little variety in food—milk, some fresh vegetables in the summer, a limited amount of canned vegetables in the winter, bread, and salt pork. She related conditions involving housing and diet to intestinal track diseases and typhoid in children.

The sociologist Rupert Vance in studying southern culture in the 1930s pointed out that people seemed firmly attached to their "meat, meal and molasses" even though the region offered abundant plant and wildlife to vary their diet. The reasons, he believed, were, first, that all three were cheap and easy to buy, and second, because of the strength of food traditions in the South, even though they resulted in weakening people and left them impoverished and sick. Vance concluded that "food likes and dislikes [were] matters of habit imposed by culture"; they demonstrated that region, class, race, and education impacted southerners' food choices.

For his book *Stories of Survival*, William Downs talked with Arkansans about their memories of growing up during the Depression, and asked them whether they recalled being hungry. Some responded with stories of large vegetable gardens, berry-picking in the woods, milking their family's cows, and feeding chickens. They remembered their families raising all of their own food and never going hungry. But others had a different experience, growing up in houses where cotton grew right up to the porch and there was no room for a garden; in fact, there wasn't even very much of the "meat, meal and molasses."

In an interview for the Ozark Oral History Project in November of 2003, a man recalled: "I've went to the breakfast table when all there was was sawgnun [*sic*] molasses and cornbread. That's not a very good combination, but you'd eat it. That's all there was." A woman quoted in Downs's book remembered being told, "Well, you lived in the country, so you had plenty to eat." To which the woman responded, "Then, why was I so hungry all the time?"

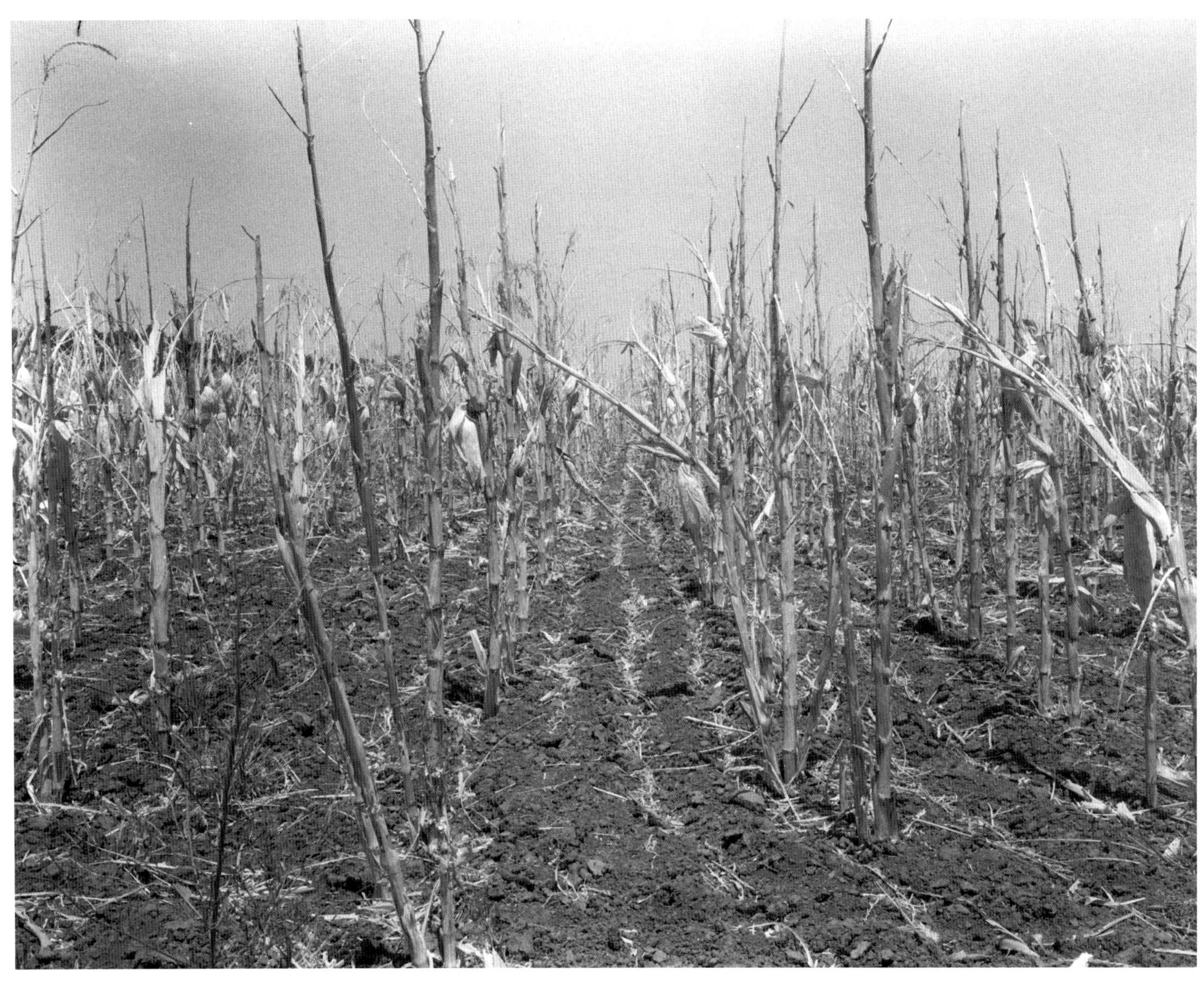

A cornfield near Russellville ravaged by drought and grasshoppers.

(Dorothea Lange, August 1936) Farm Security Administration Photograph Collection, Prints & Photographs Division, Library of Congress, LC-USF34–009658–C

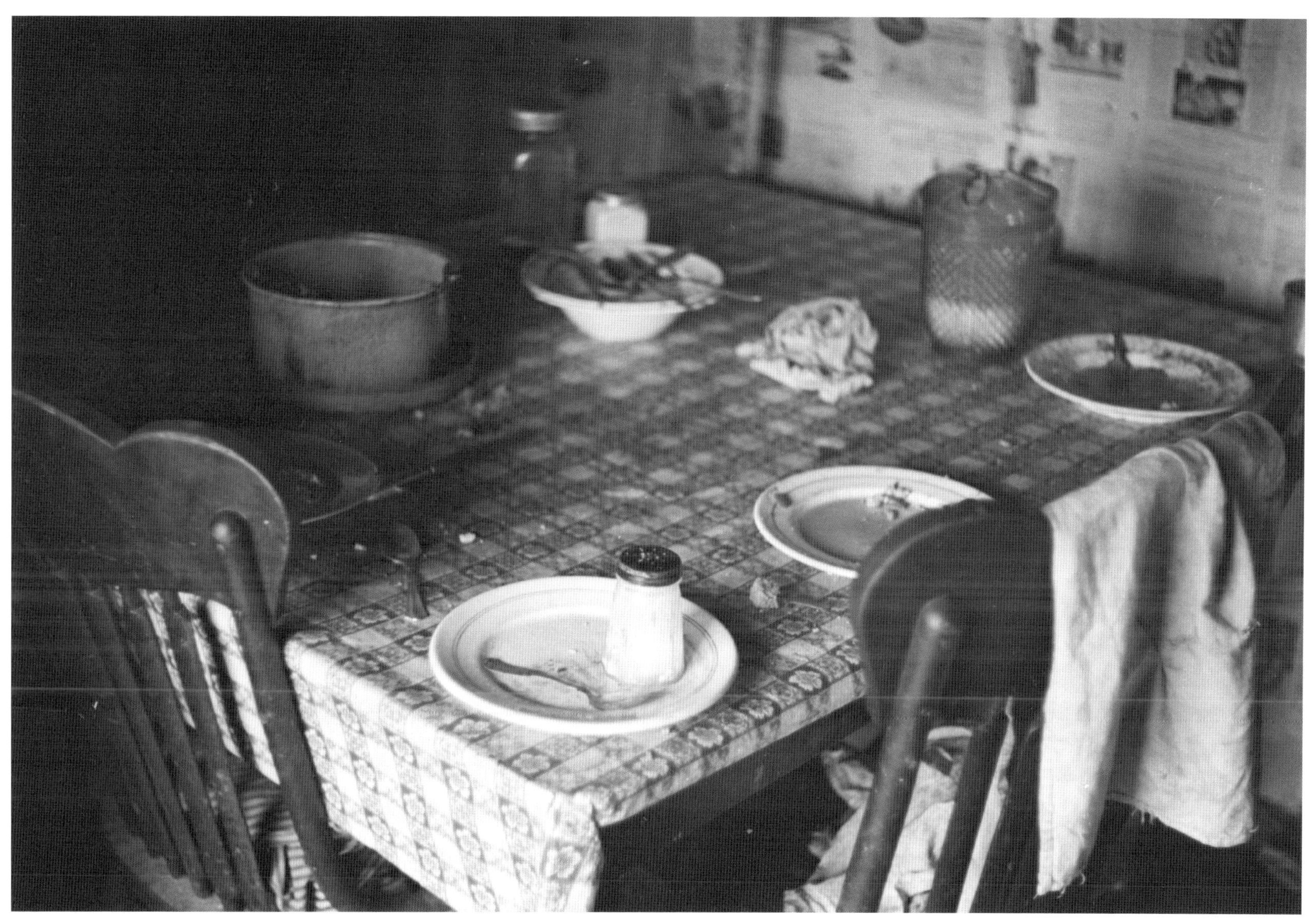

A kitchen table set for a meal in the home of a destitute Ozark family.

(Ben Shahn, October 1935) Farm Security Administration Photograph Collection, Prints & Photographs Division, Library of Congress, LC-USF33–006072–M1

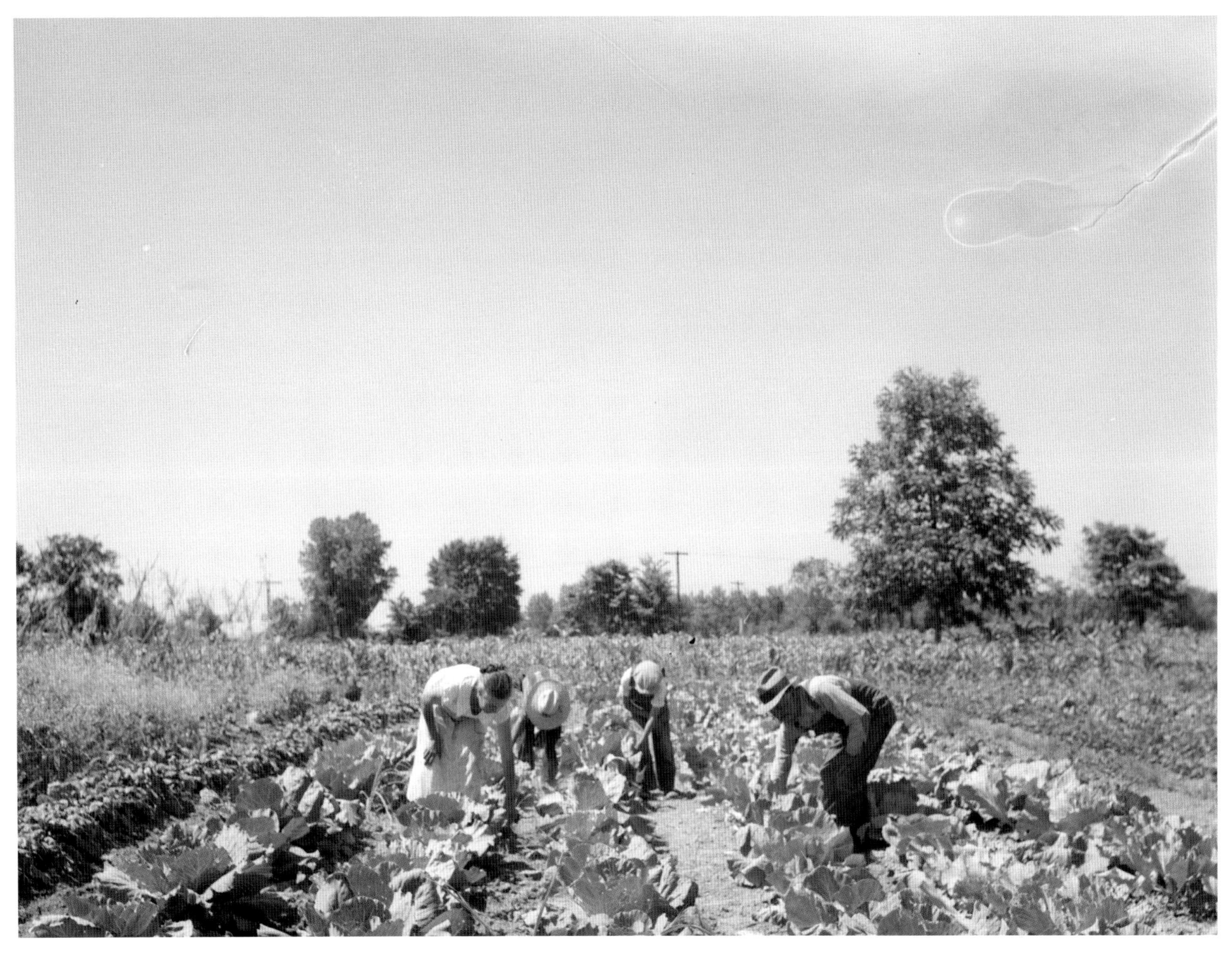

Rehabilitation clients tending cabbages in their garden near Batesville.

(Carl Mydans, June 1936) Farm Security Administration Photograph Collection, Prints & Photographs Division, Library of Congress, LC-USF34–006369–D

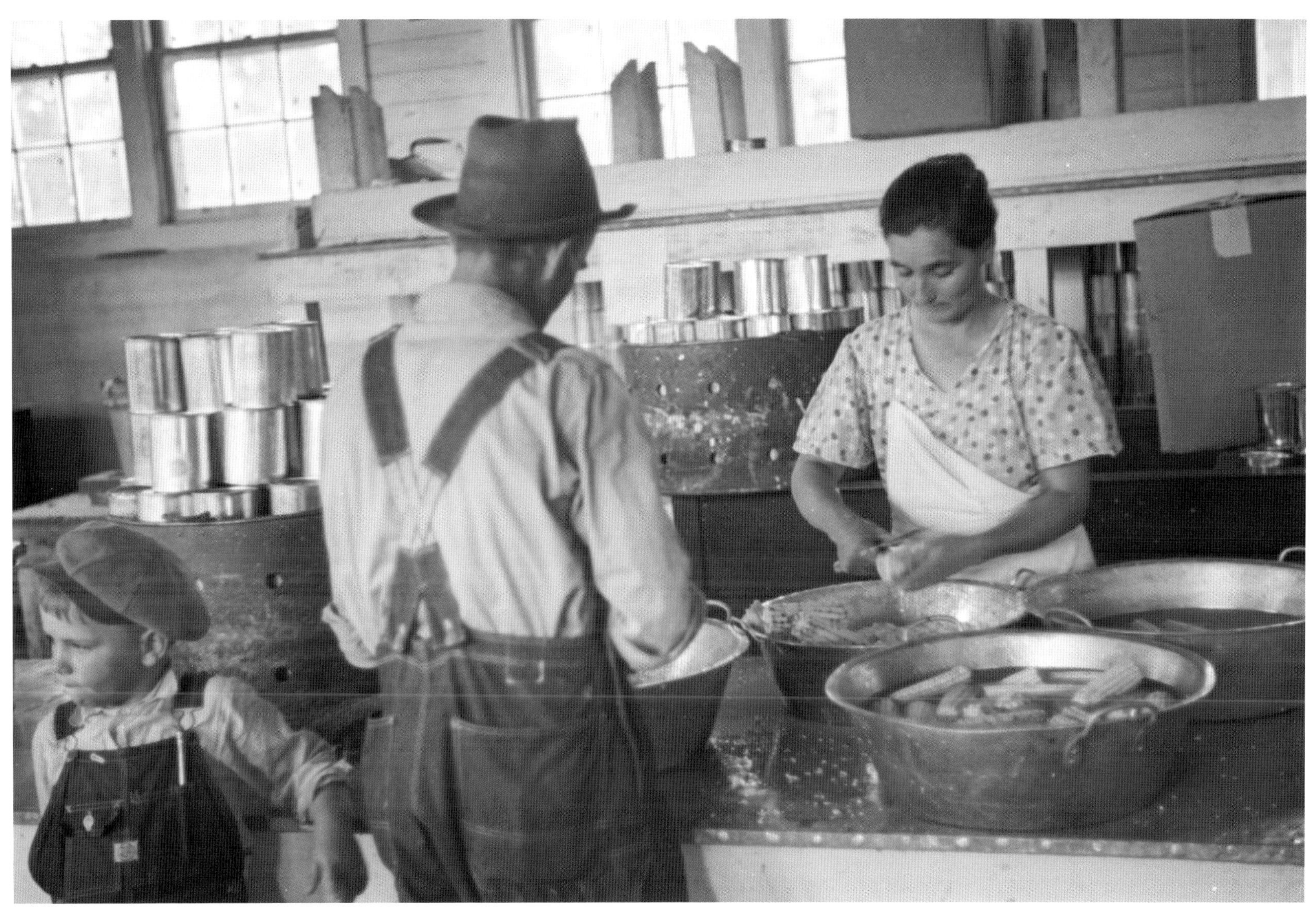

Community canning kitchen at Dyess Colony where families without a pressure cooker could can their own produce.

(Ben Shahn, September 1935) Farm Security Administration Photograph Collection, Prints & Photographs Division, Library of Congress, LC-USF33–006047–M3

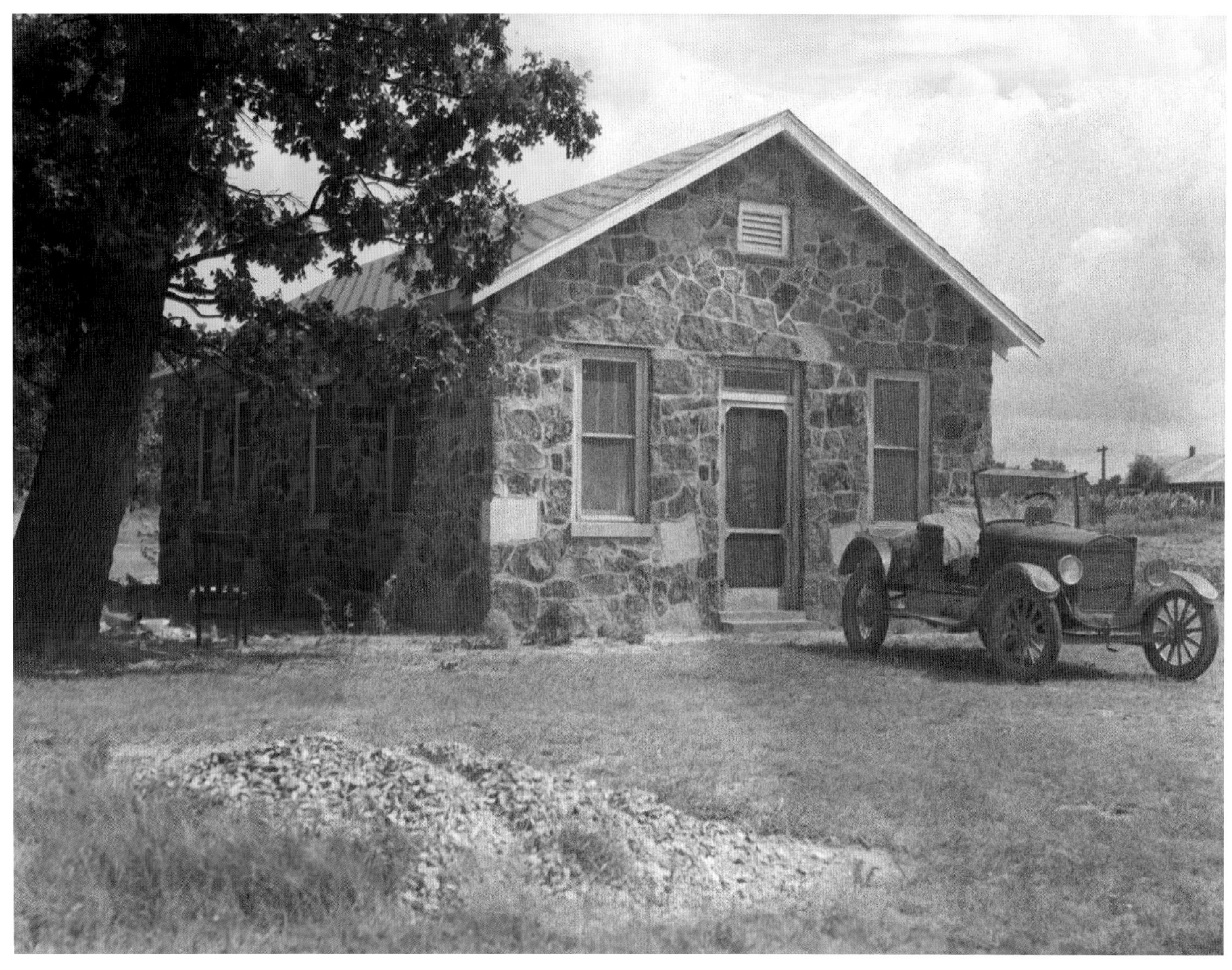

A community canning kitchen in Pope County.

(Arthur Rothstein, August 1935) Farm Security Administration Photograph Collection, Prints & Photographs Division, Library of Congress, LC-USF34–000428–D

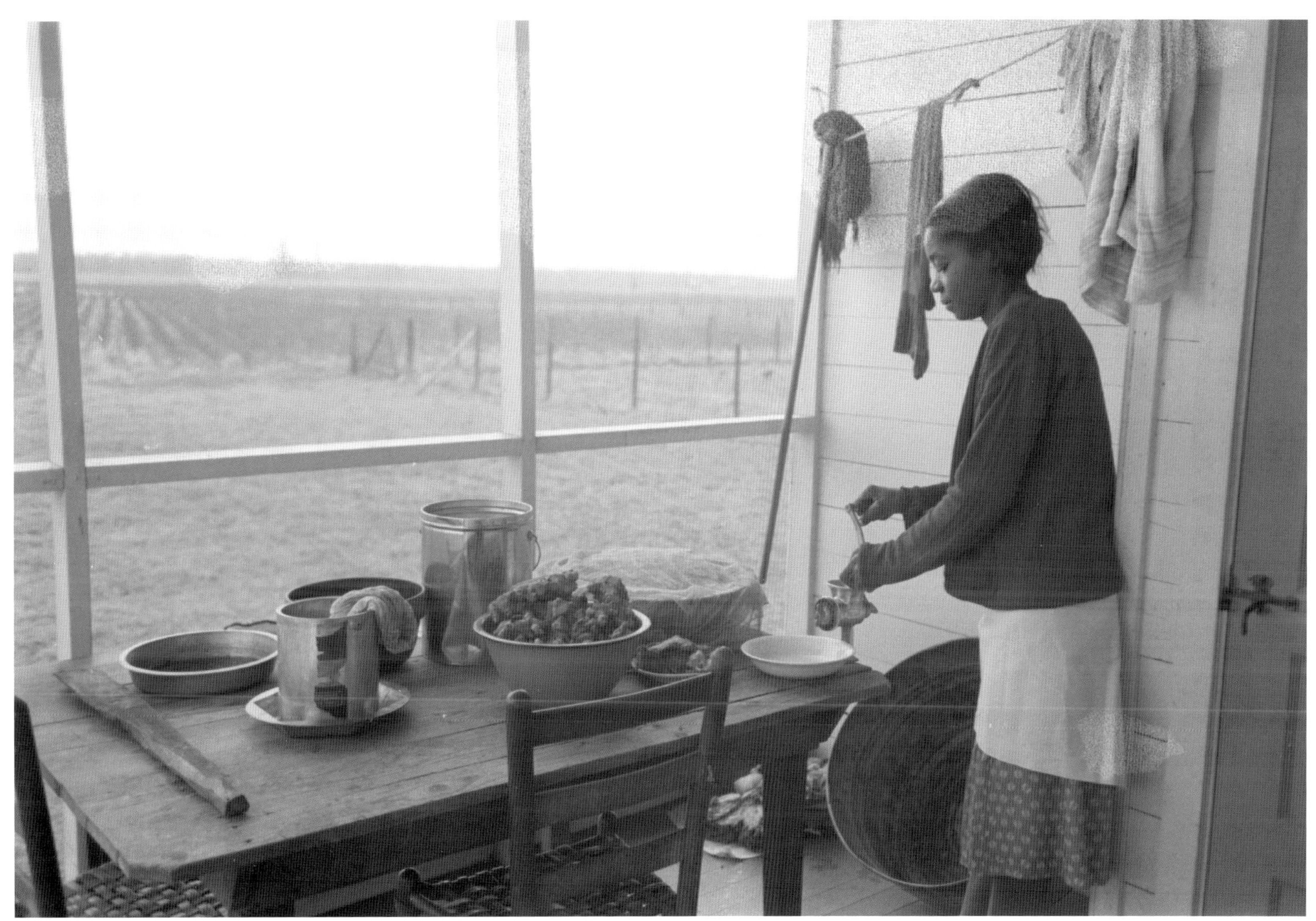

A Lakeview resettlement project farmwife grinds meat to make sausage on her back porch.

(Russell Lee, December 1938) Farm Security Administration Photograph Collection, Prints & Photographs Division, Library of Congress, LC-USF33–011916–M2

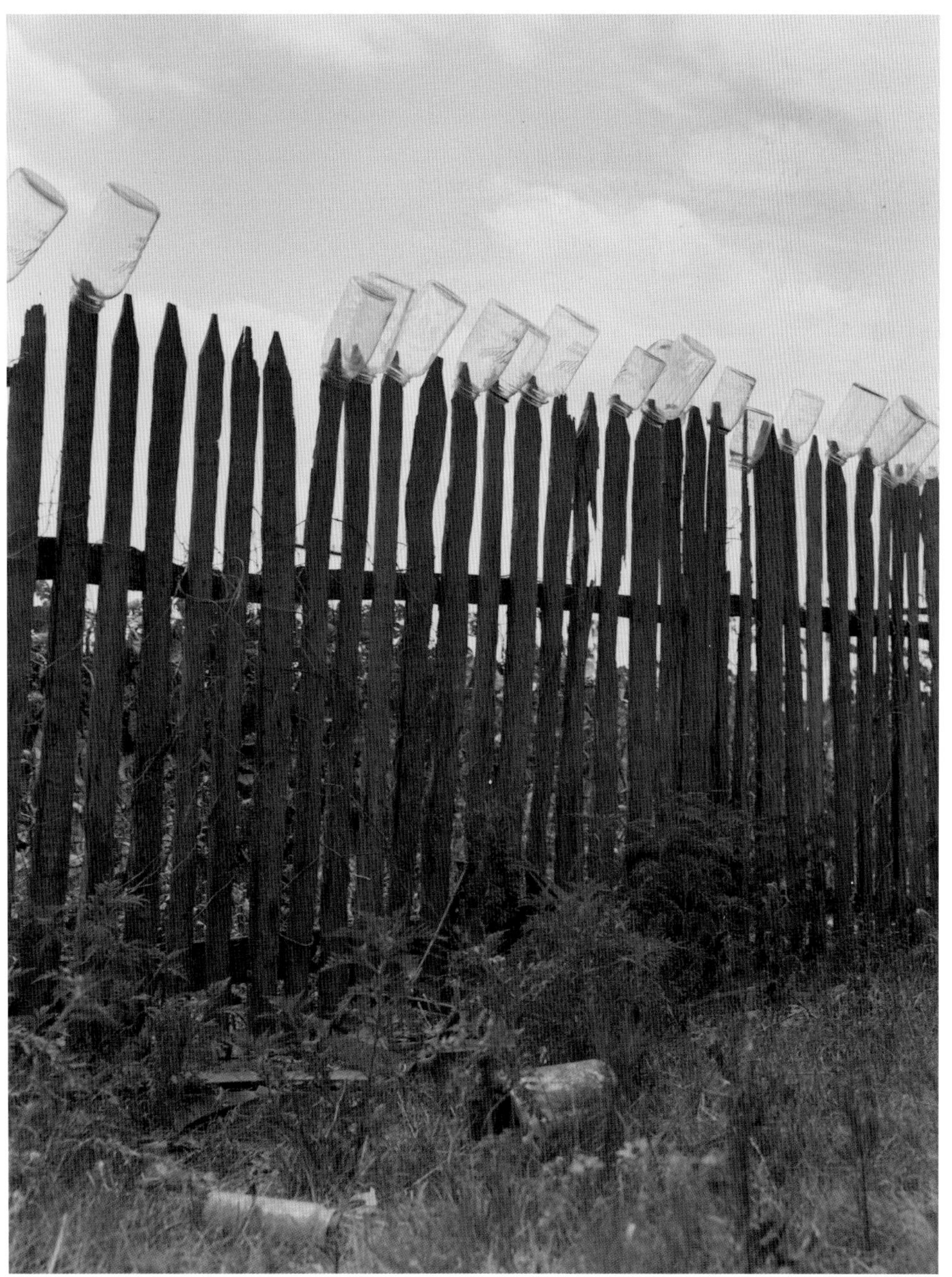

Dorothea Lange wrote: "Fruit jars being sterilized on old lady Graham's back fence in berry season. Near Conway, Arkansas. 'We just gather and can peas, beans, berries, and sausage when we butcher the hogs in the winter. We put up seventy-five quarts of berries, sixty of beans, sixty of kraut, thirty of grapes and twenty of peaches. I swapped two bushels of grapes and got two bushels of peaches and I swapped one bushel of grapes for one bushel of apples.'"

(Dorothea Lange, June 1938) Farm Security Administration Photograph Collection, Prints & Photographs Division, Library of Congress, LC-USF34–018287–C

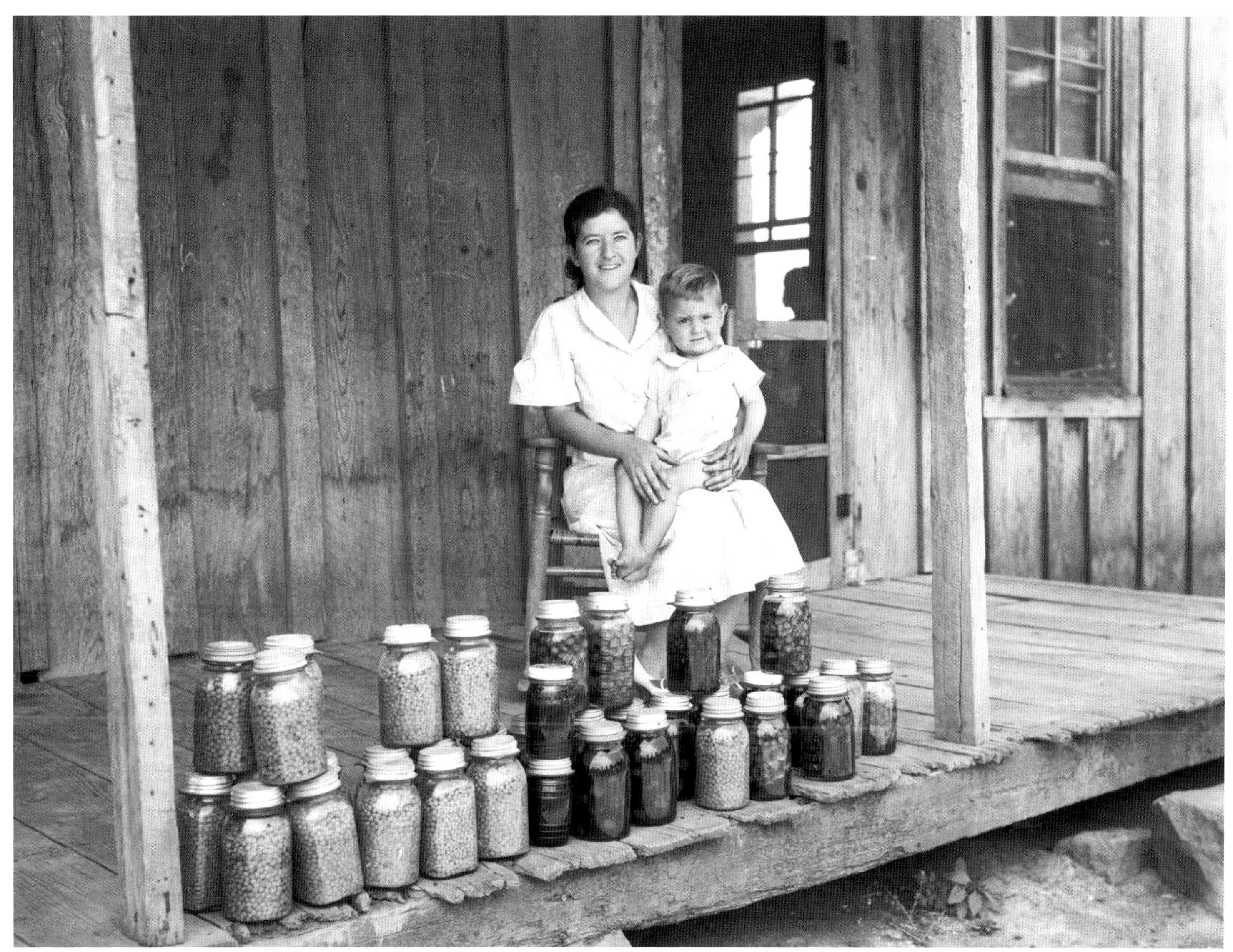

A farmwife and her jars of canned food, near Batesville.

(Carl Mydans, June 1936) Farm Security Administration Photograph Collection, Prints & Photographs Division, Library of Congress, LC-USF34–006366–D

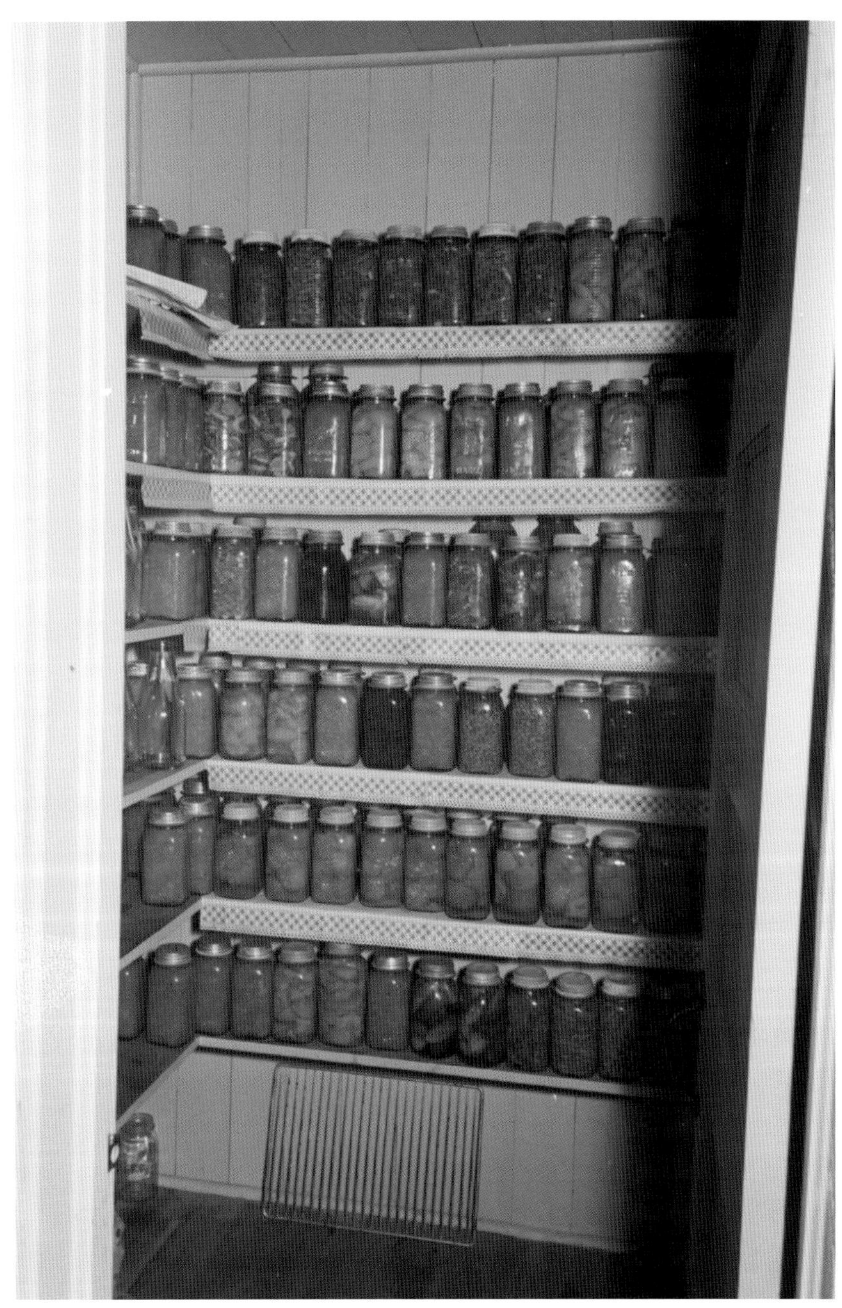

Pantry stocked with canned produce in a Lake Dick farmhouse.

(Russell Lee, September 1938) Farm Security Administration Photograph Collection, Prints & Photographs Division, Library of Congress, LC-USF33–011666–M5

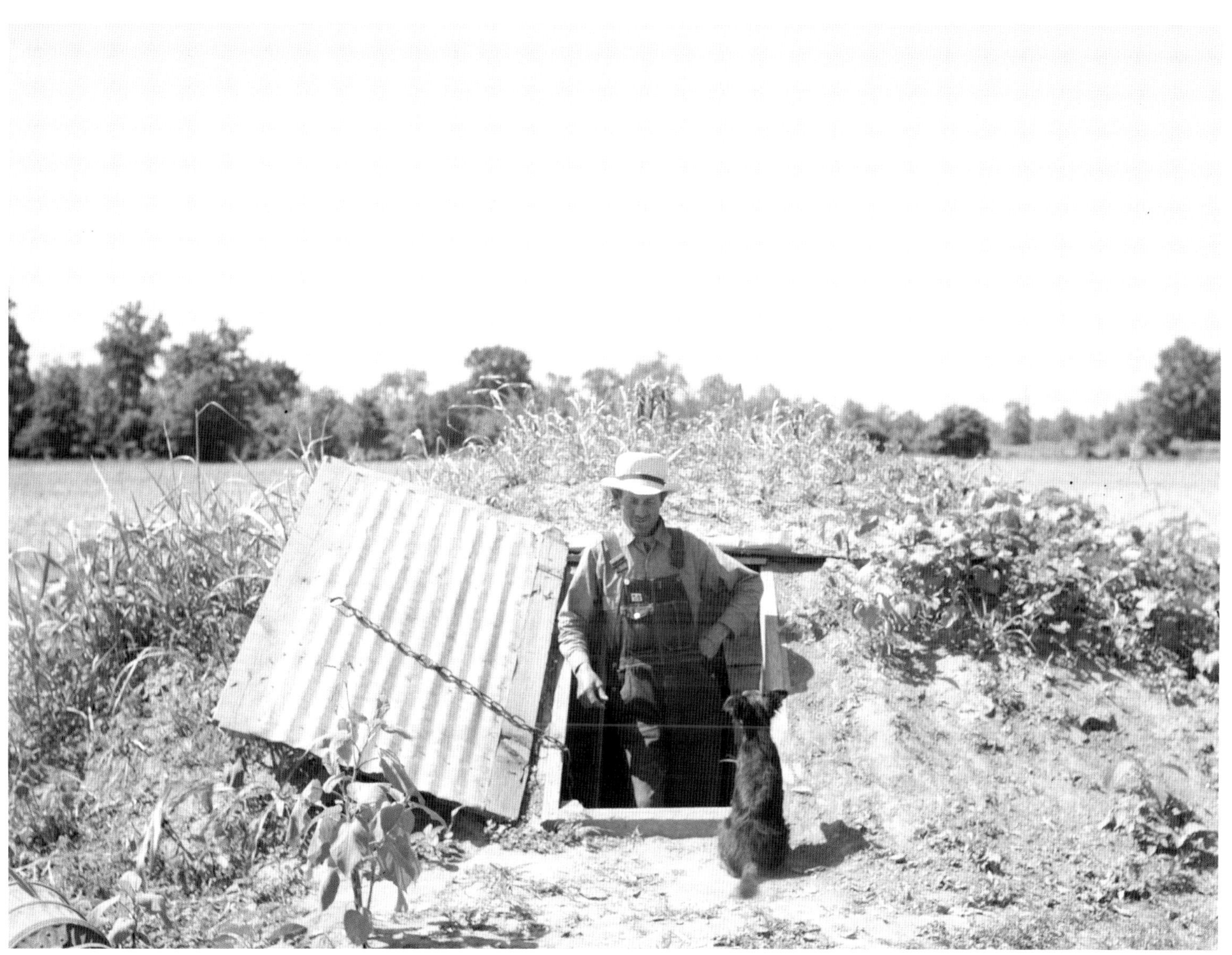

Storm cellar where hundreds of jars of canned food could be stored; near Batesville.

(Carl Mydans, June 1936) Farm Security Administration Photograph Collection, Prints & Photographs Division, Library of Congress, LC-USF34–006461–D

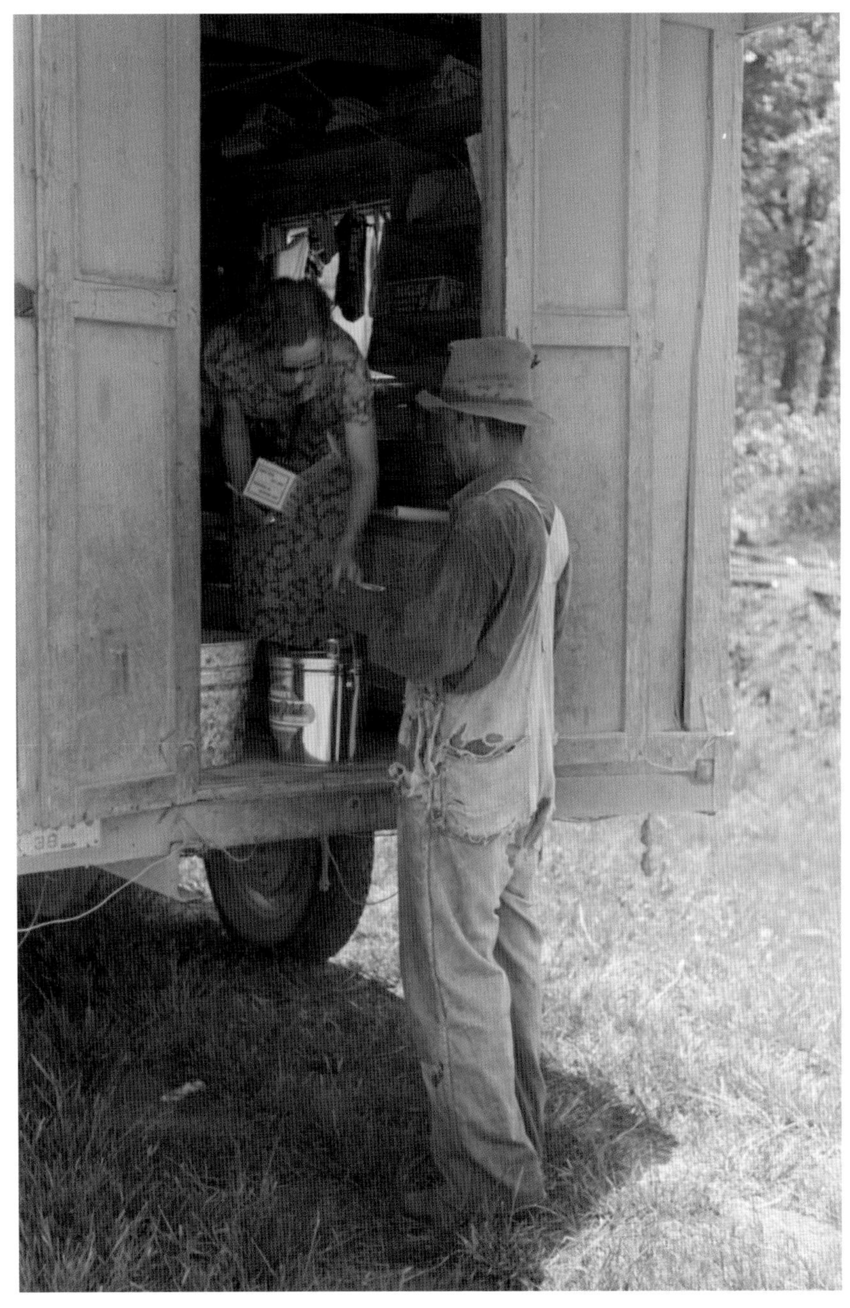

A farmer makes a purchase at a traveling grocery store near Forrest City. In rural areas of the South some enterprising small-town grocers sent out wagons to more remote areas, usually carrying canned goods and prepared foods.

(Russell Lee, September–October 1938) Farm Security Administration Photograph Collection, Prints & Photographs Division, Library of Congress, LC-USF33–011621–M5

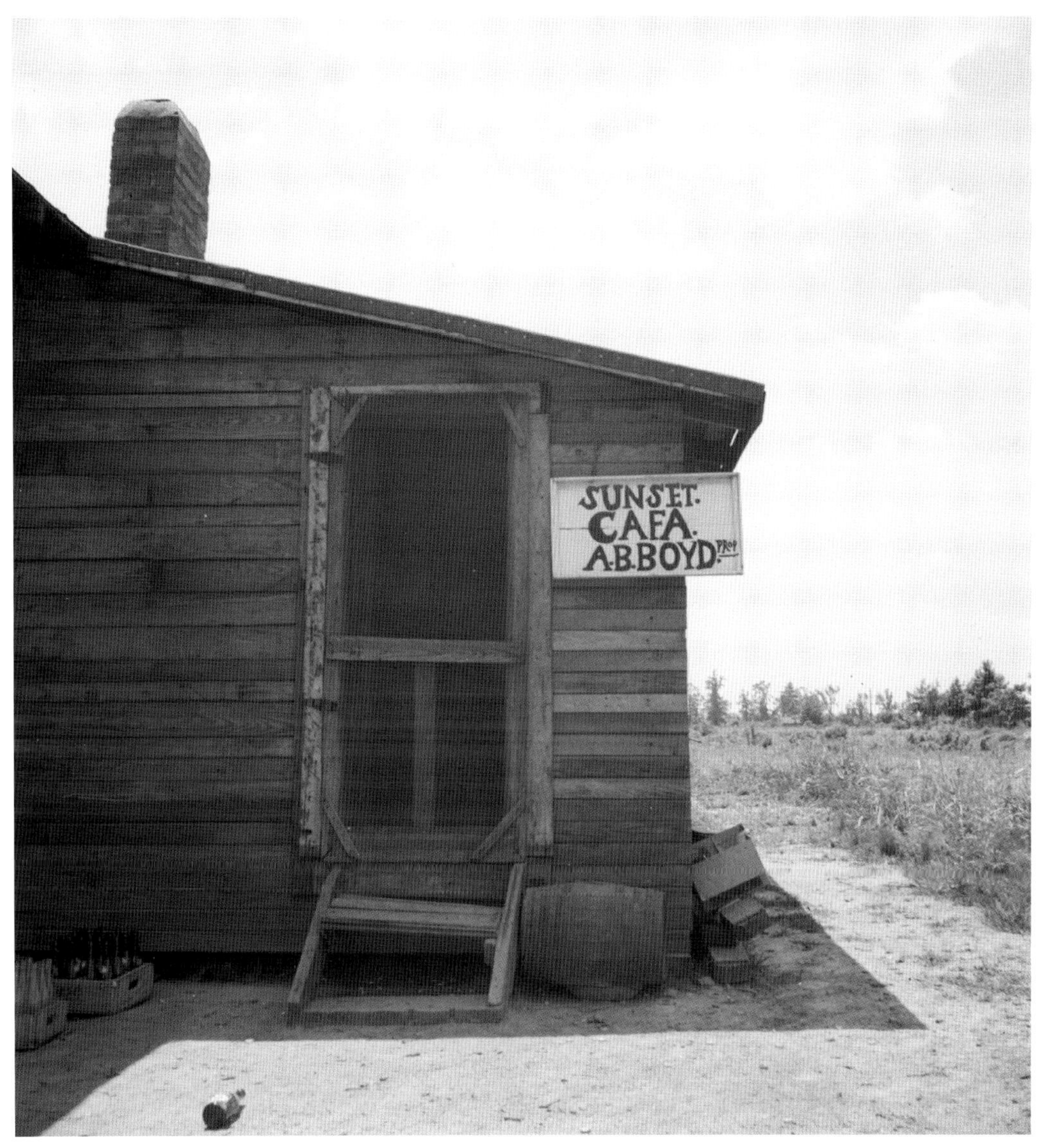

"The Sunset Cafa [*sic*], A.B. Boyd, Prop."

(Dorothea Lange, May 1940) Farm Security Administration Photograph Collection, Prints & Photographs Division, Library of Congress, LC-USF34–017580–E

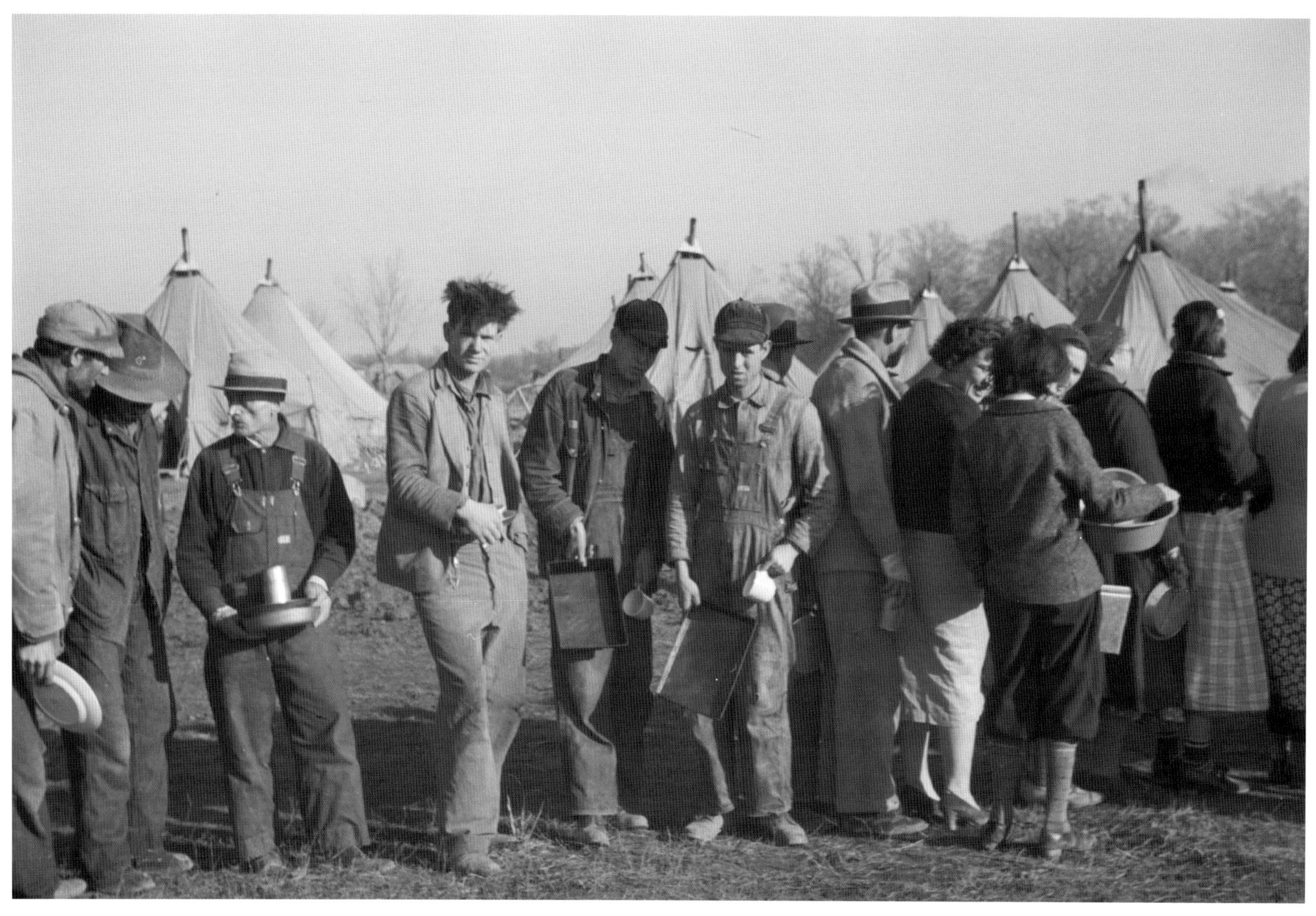

Refugees in a food line at an American Red Cross camp in east Arkansas, after the 1937 Mississippi River flood.

(Walker Evans, February 1937) Farm Security Administration Photograph Collection, Prints & Photographs Division, Library of Congress, LC-USF33–009220–M2

SEVEN | CHILDREN

PHOTOGRAPHS OF CHILDREN are among the most poignant in the Arkansas collection. In most pictures, they stand still and solemnly face the photographer, with none of the camera savvy of twenty-first-century children. In most of the pictures they are at home, usually with siblings or a parent, in school, or in the cotton fields where they are working—some as young as eight or ten years old.

The photographs therefore show the conditions in which children of tenants and sharecroppers live—the houses, their clothing, and their health; their families, their schoolrooms, their role as laborers, and their play. Children in their vulnerability can arouse compassion and protectiveness in viewers, which was Ben Shahn's point when, in his discussion with Roy Stryker about the effectiveness of RA/FSA photos, he told Stryker that in order to engage people's emotions with a photo of soil erosion, it would be helpful to add a starving child. Shahn was trained as an artist and had been a social activist; he was clearly aware of how to utilize images to frame a message.

Critics, keeping Shahn's comment in mind, might dismiss the RA/FSA photos of children as deliberately created to manipulate viewers' emotions in promoting government relief programs. However, the hard facts of their lives were undeniable, no matter how photographers chose to present these children. The photos raised questions about the morality underlying landlords' treatment of tenants and sharecroppers and could make a powerful argument in support of the RA/FSA relief programs for poor farmers. In contrast to the pictures of tenants and sharecroppers, those of children on resettlement farms show life as more secure and comfortable; houses are cleaner, there is good food, schools are better equipped, and children are healthier.

Roughly 360,000 children fourteen and under lived in rural Arkansas in the 1930s, many of them members of the families of tenants, sharecroppers, or rehabilitation clients. According to state and national government reports on the health, education, and housing of children in Arkansas and the rest of the South, their living conditions were inadequate, deprived, insecure, and lacking in creature comforts. In the book *Stories of Survival,* William Downs recounts Arkansans' memories about growing up during the Depression; their stories flesh out the statistics in government reports and corroborate what the RA/FSA photos show.

The Arkansans in Downs's book remember how much they had to work, doing house chores by ages four and five. By age ten they could clean, straighten up, and make beds; by twelve or thirteen, they could cook a meal if necessary. One man told Downs that at six years old, he was responsible for milking fifteen cows by hand every morning. Margaret Hagood, who studied farmwives in the Depression in *Mothers of the South,* confirmed these stories. She found that children helped wash canning jars, churn milk to make butter, hand-wash and dry dishes after meals, hang clothes out to dry in the sun, feed farm animals, cut wood and make fires, gather eggs, and even help clean up the "two-holer" outdoor toilets.

The RA/FSA photos show children in cotton fields, as young as eight and ten, chopping and picking. According to one report, a ten-year-old could pull a cotton sack seven feet long and pick eighteen pounds a day, about one-third of what an adult male pulling a nine-foot sack could pick. A woman recalled for Downs how hot it could get working in the cotton field, especially barefoot. She would use a hoe to dig down below the topsoil to find a cooler place to stand as she moved down the rows.

In rural areas, the school year was scheduled around the cotton season so that children would be available to work—to chop cotton in the spring and pick in the fall. Children might go barefoot most of the year, according to Downs's interviewees, and even get frostbite walking to school during the winter; RA/FSA photos show children without shoes at home and at school. Arkansas had a system of one-room schools to serve rural areas where one teacher had to handle all grades at once, as well as arrive at school early enough in the winter to start up a fire in the stove and warm the building. Shahn photographed a one-room school in the Ozarks where there was a mix of ages and facilities appeared to be barely adequate.

Arkansas public schools were poorly funded in the 1930s. Paralysis of the state's agricultural economy had dried up the property taxes that supported schools, seriously straining local school budgets. Of the available funding, Arkansas Department of Education reports show that nonrural white schools received the most support, followed by rural white schools and then schools for African Americans. Not only were per-student expenditures lower in African American schools, but salaries for teachers were worse and students often had to buy their own books. Arkansas's poor support for African American schools was addressed at least partially by nearly four hundred Rosenwald schools built in the state during the 1920s and 1930s. With primary funding by the Julius Rosenwald Foundation supplemented by local contributions, more than five thousand of these schools were built to improve African American education in the South. Though 75 percent of Arkansas children five through fourteen years old attended school, few went on to high school. Not only were they needed at home to work, but seventeen counties in the state didn't even have a high school; continuing on in school meant a child would have to leave home, which stressed a family emotionally as well as financially.

The early RA/FSA photographs implied the hopelessness of a child's breaking the chain of poverty in such a system, especially a child who who could scarcely imagine a different kind of life. In contrast, however, the later RA/FSA photographs of life on resettlement farms suggest that government programs could change that future through the clean and comfortable new houses and schools that were well equipped, provided a hot meal, and offered a variety of learning experiences. Russell Lee took a series of photographs at resettlement farm schools on the Lake Dick and Lakeview projects. Brief descriptions of the pictures follow, as unfortunately, their technical quality interferes with reproduction.

At Lake Dick in November 1938 Lee spent his time in an elementary school, photographing children engaged in their classes, writing on the blackboard and working at their desks. The schoolrooms, like the farmhouses, are paneled in pine boards, and the facilities—the blackboard, the furniture—all appear to be in good condition. In one picture children are shown praying before sitting down to lunch. The photos taken at Lakeview in December 1938 are more extensive, showing children from nursery school through the twelfth grade. The school, built by the federal government, was in the Lakeview School District and operated by the State Department of Vocational Education, according to a government document about the resettlement project.

Lee's pictures track nursery school children through the day as they willingly accept doses of cod liver oil, wash up before lunch, eat lunch, and then take afternoon naps. He photographed older students in class writing on the blackboard, but he also took pictures of boys in shop learning to make furniture, and girls in home economics where they practice sewing in a sewing room and cooking in a model kitchen. In one picture a group of students works on typewriters to write and edit the school newspaper.

The message in these pictures must have been a reassuring one about socializing children into an acceptable value system for whites concerned about the government's investment in a resettlement project for African Americans. Young black children were learning good hygiene, and older ones were being trained in useful vocational skills, as they were not expected to seek higher education. In effect, they were being instructed in how to be responsible, respectful citizens with limited ambition. The message, however, might not have been so reassuring for large farm operators who would likely prefer a labor force with less education.

Though the resettlement farm projects promised a better life for the children of poor farmers, it's not likely they rescued many from the kinds of families shown in the early RA/FSA photos. Farmers selected for resettlement had to meet qualifications beyond the reach of most of those at the very bottom—the poorest sharecroppers whose children were left with little chance of escaping their background of poverty.

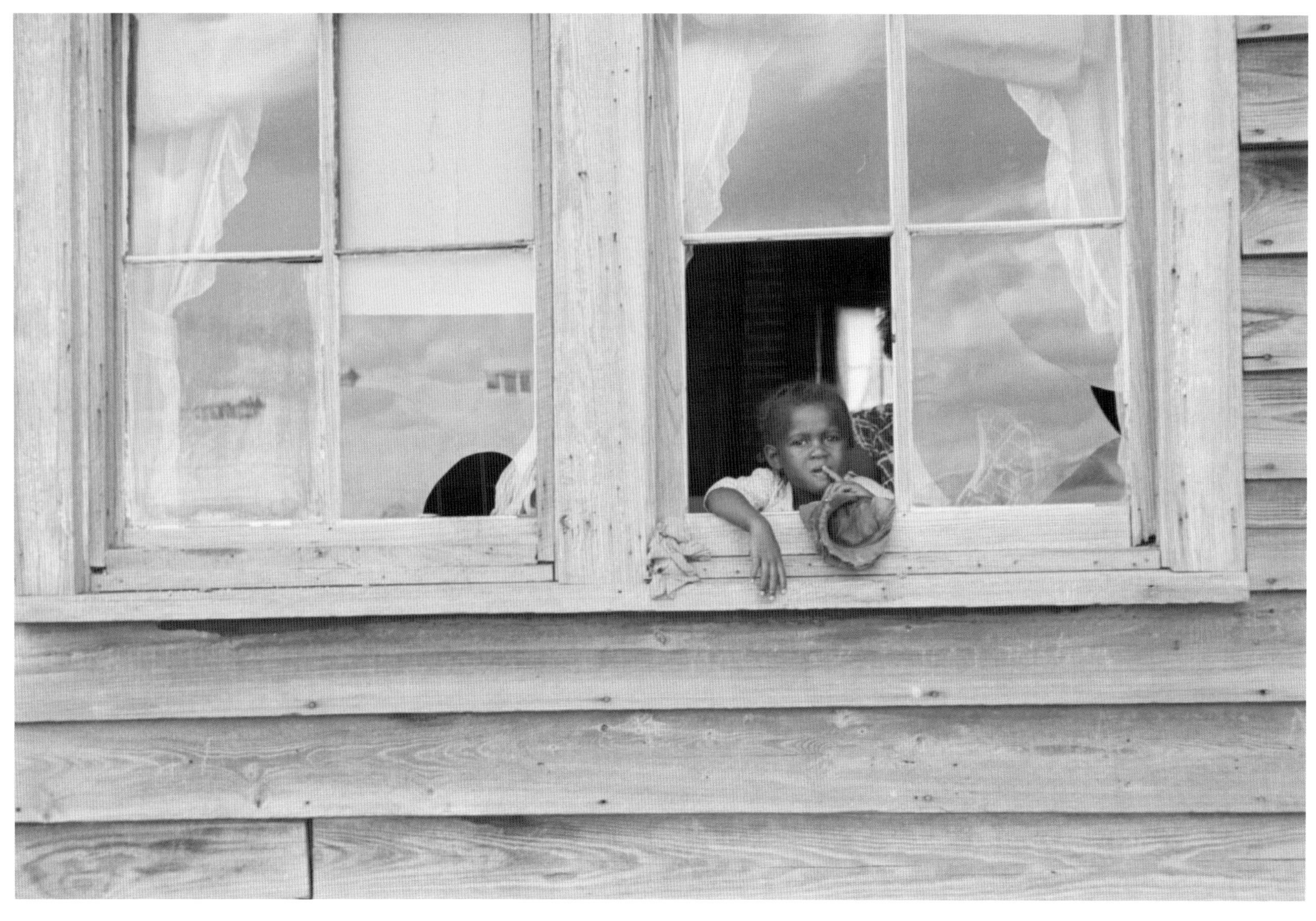

Child of a sharecropper family, near Little Rock.

(Ben Shahn, October 1935) Farm Security Administration Photograph Collection, Prints & Photographs Division, Library of Congress, LC-USF33–006026–M3

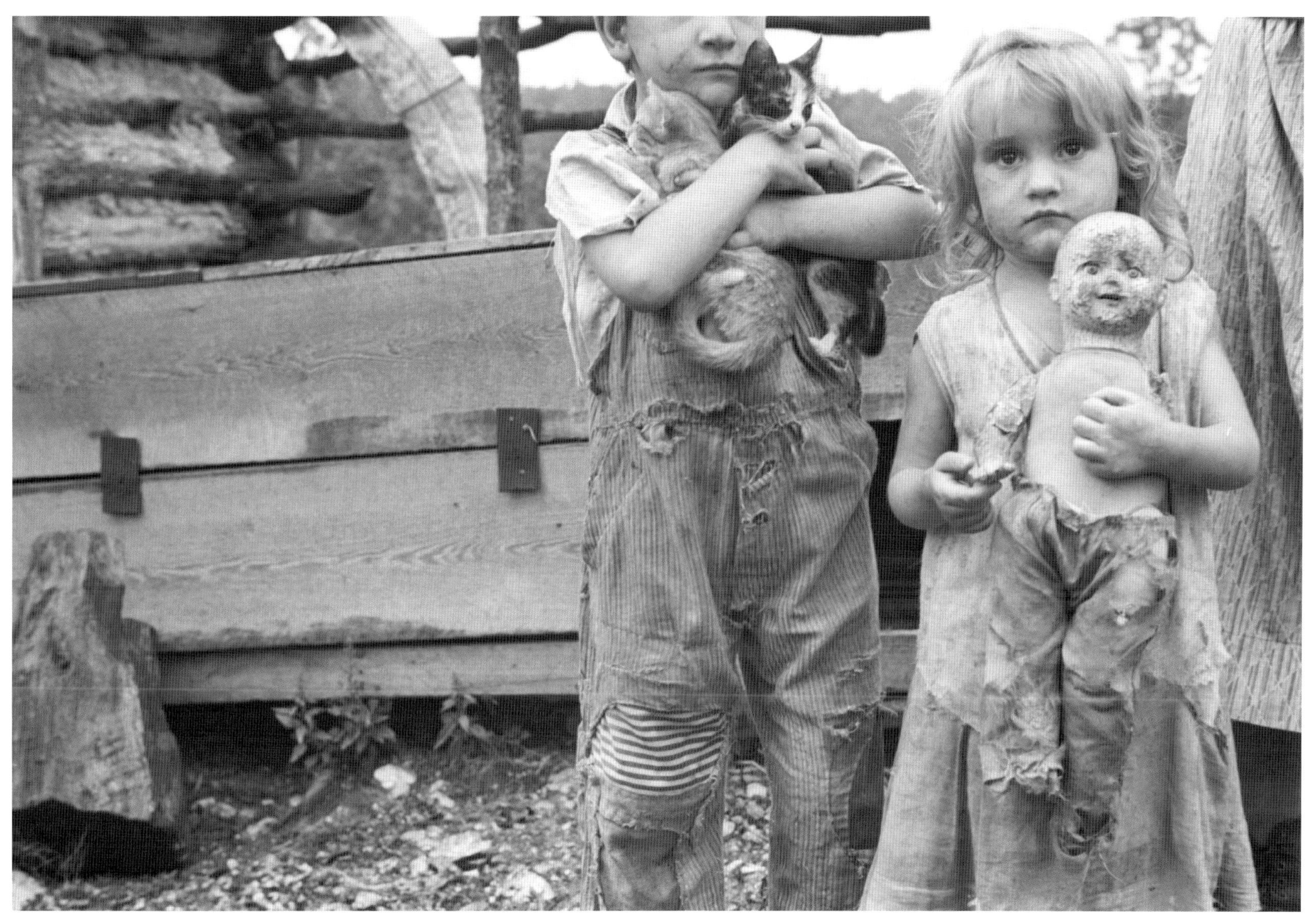

Children of a destitute Ozark mountaineer with kittens and a bedraggled doll.

(Ben Shahn, October 1935) Farm Security Administration Photograph Collection, Prints & Photographs Division, Library of Congress, LC-USF33–006032–M3

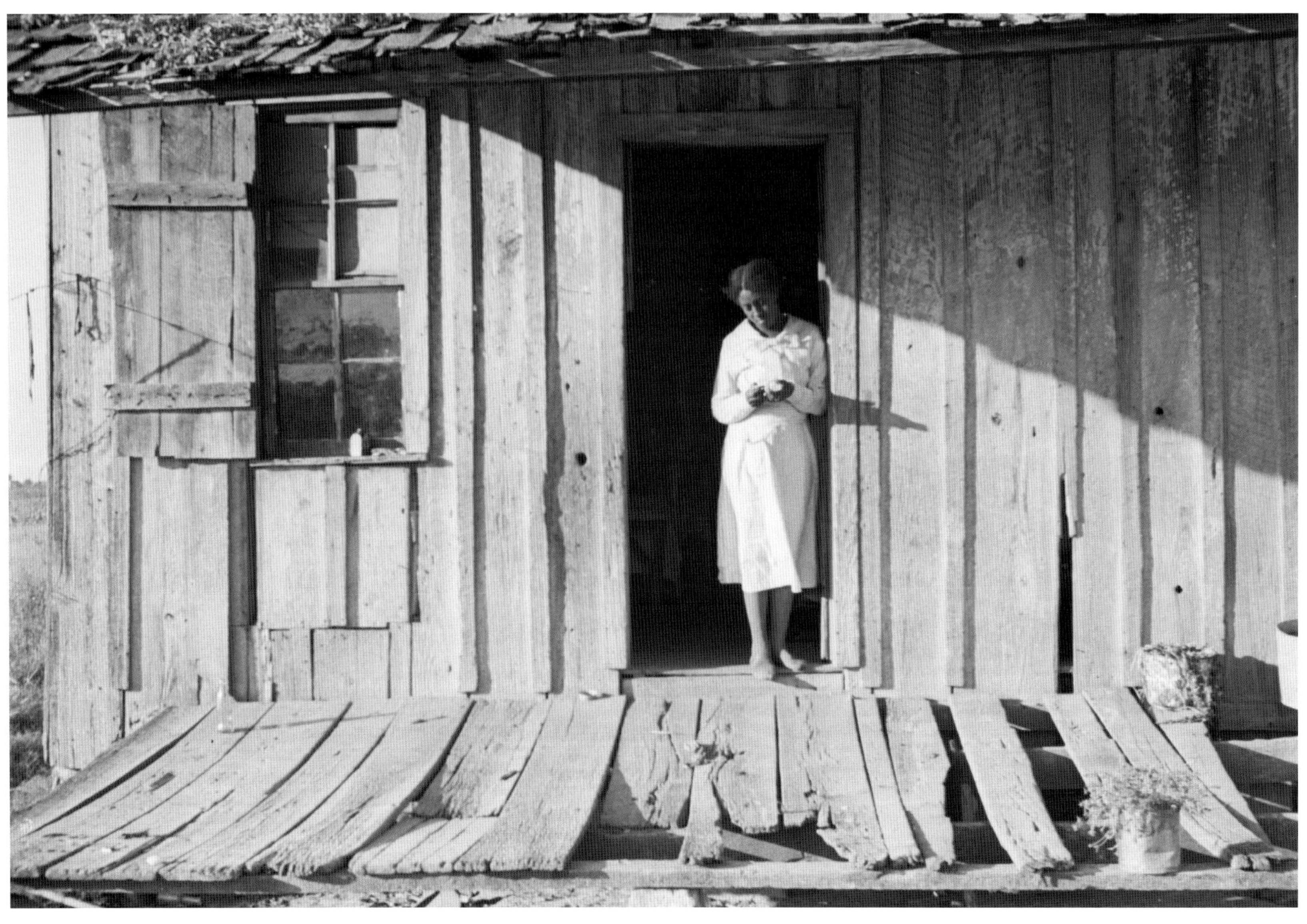

The daughter of a sharecropper in the doorway of her family's home.

(Ben Shahn, October 1935) Farm Security Administration Photograph Collection, Prints & Photographs Division, Library of Congress, LC-USF33–006106–M5

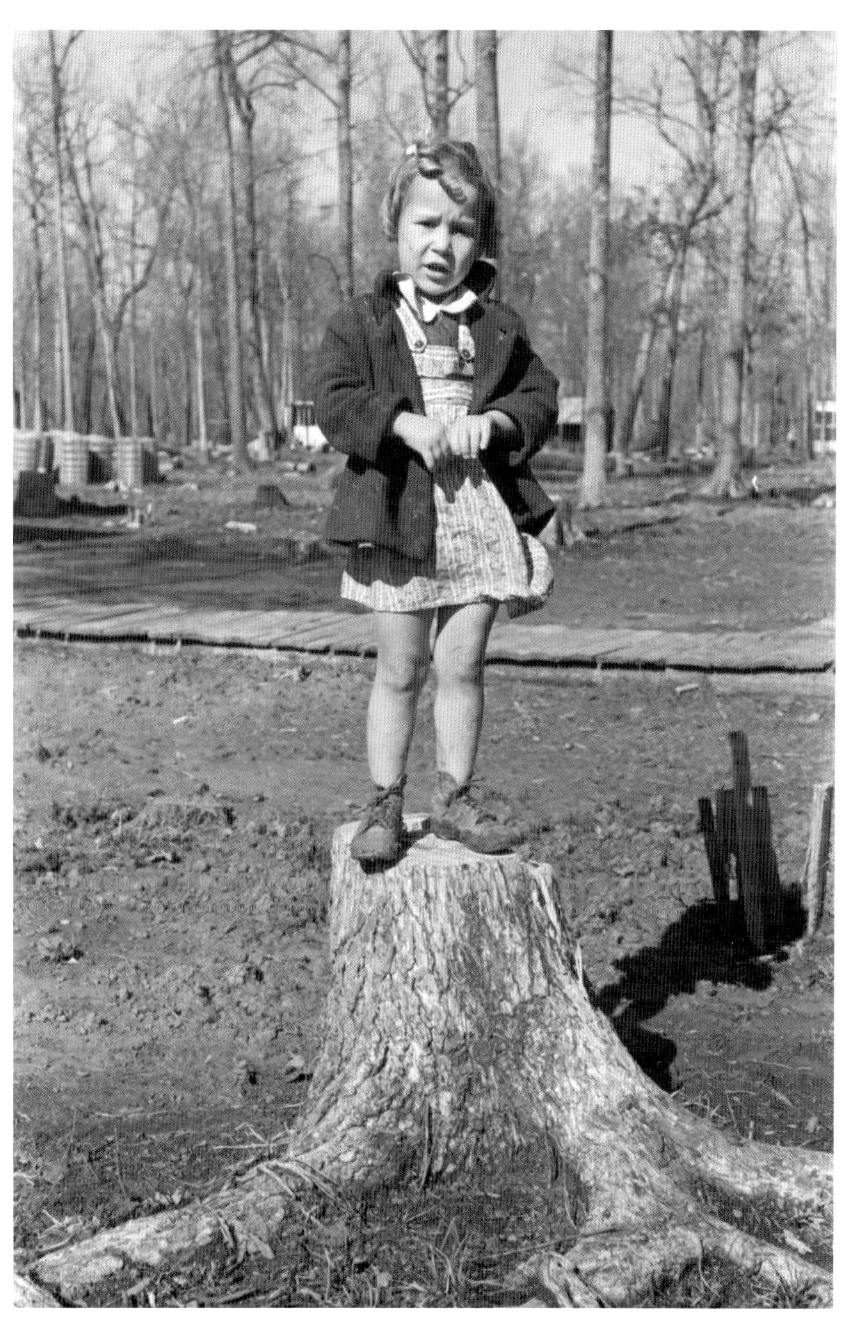

Daughter of farmer at the Chicot resettlement farm.

(Russell Lee, September 1939) Farm Security Administration Photograph Collection, Prints & Photographs Division, Library of Congress, LC-USF33–011936–M4

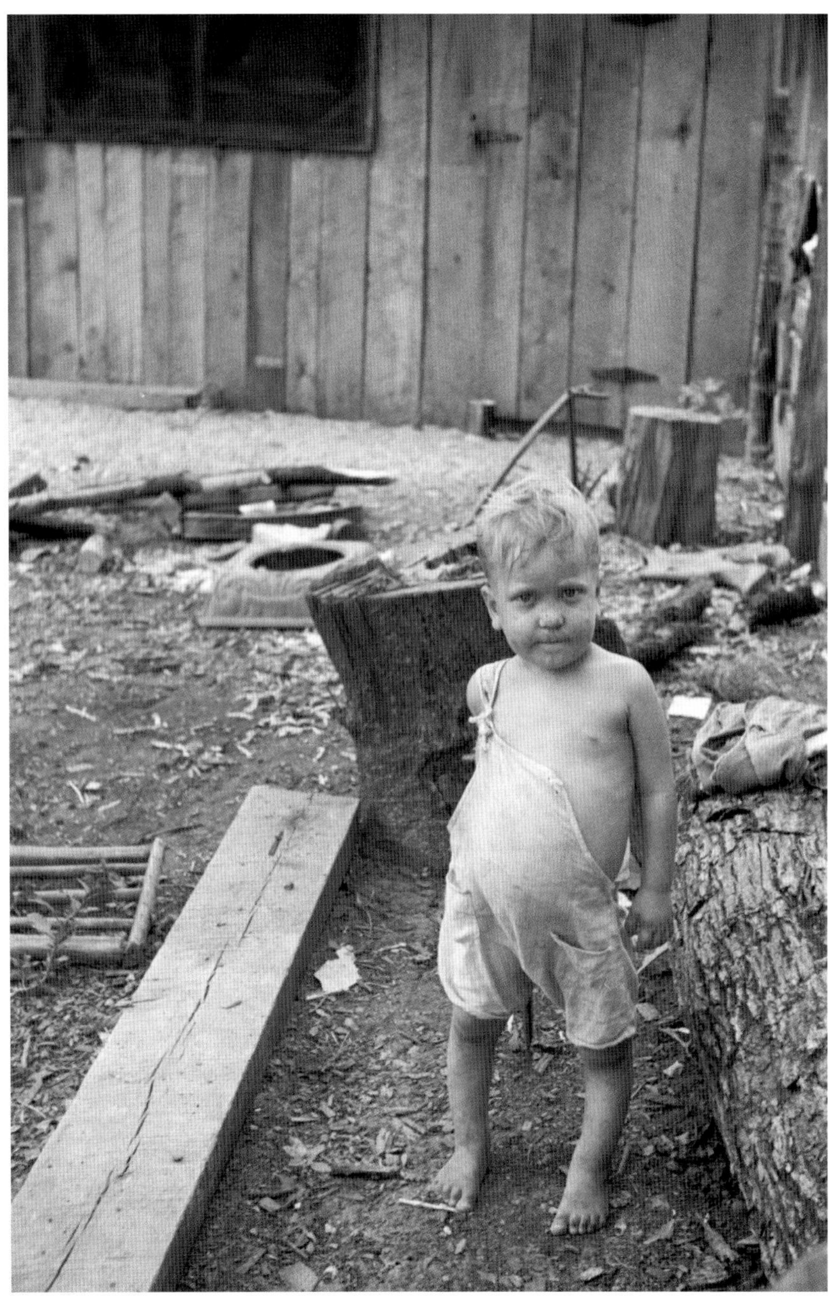

Sharecropper's child possibly suffering from rickets and malnutrition, the Wilson cotton plantation in Mississippi County.

(Arthur Rothstein, August 1935) Farm Security Administration Photograph Collection, Prints & Photographs Division, Library of Congress, LC-USF33–002002–M2

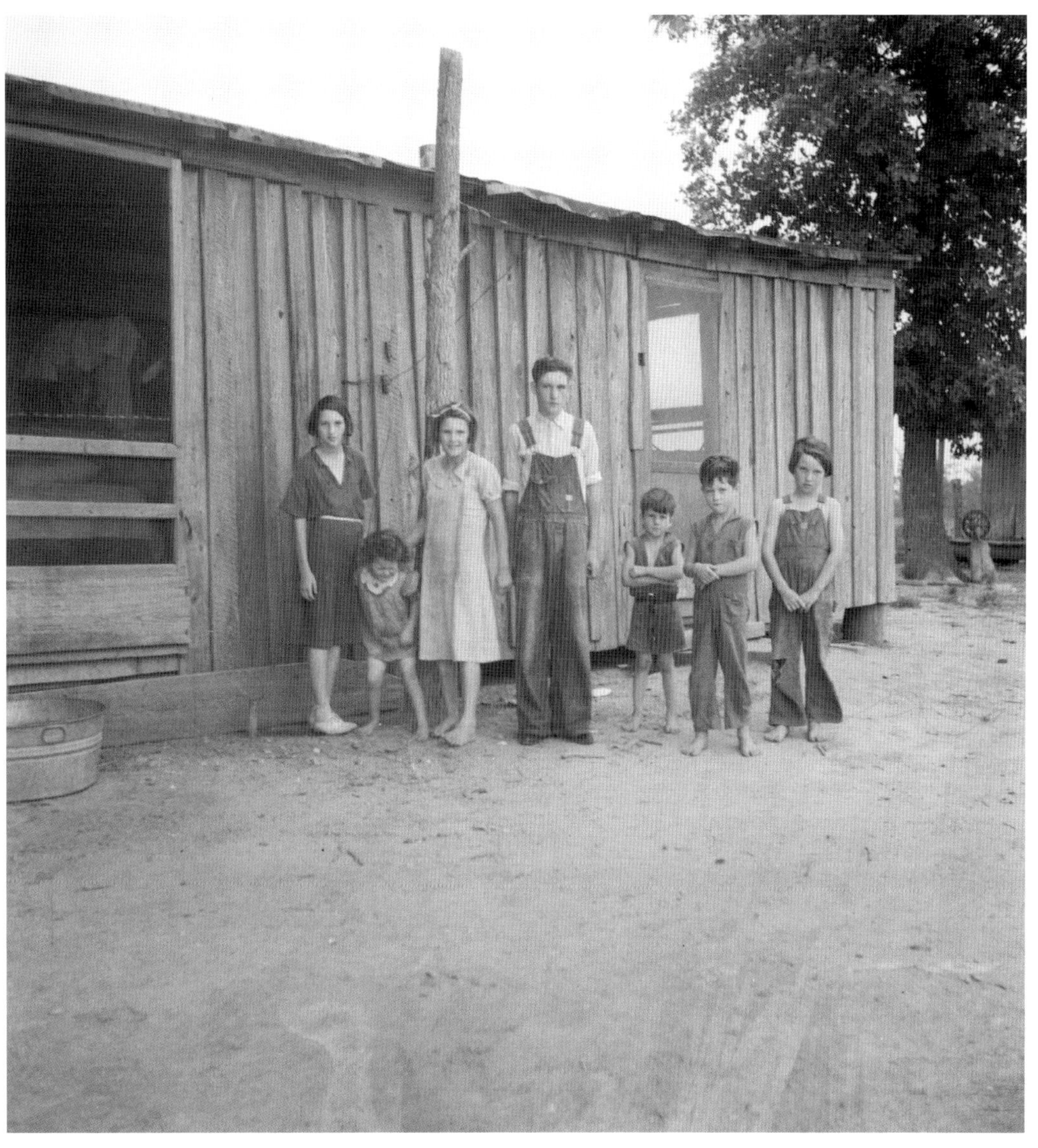

Seven from a family of ten children who escaped the spring 1937 Mississippi River Valley flood in a boat.

(Dorothea Lange, June–July 1937) Farm Security Administration Photograph Collection, Prints & Photographs Division, Library of Congress, LC-USF34–017576–E

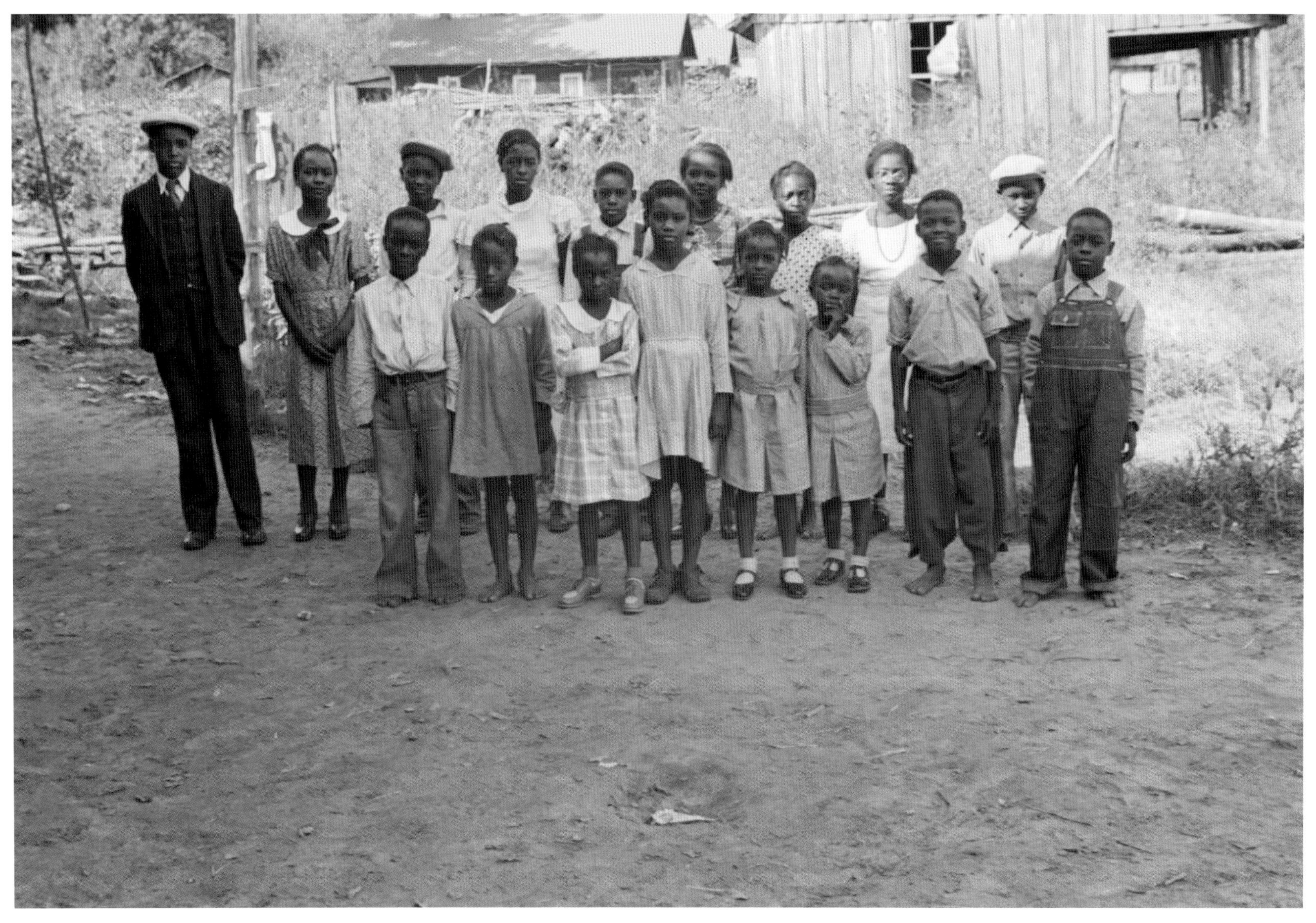

Children from sharecropper families around Little Rock.

(Ben Shahn, October 1935) Farm Security Administration Photograph Collection, Prints & Photographs Division, Library of Congress, LC-USF33–006026–M4

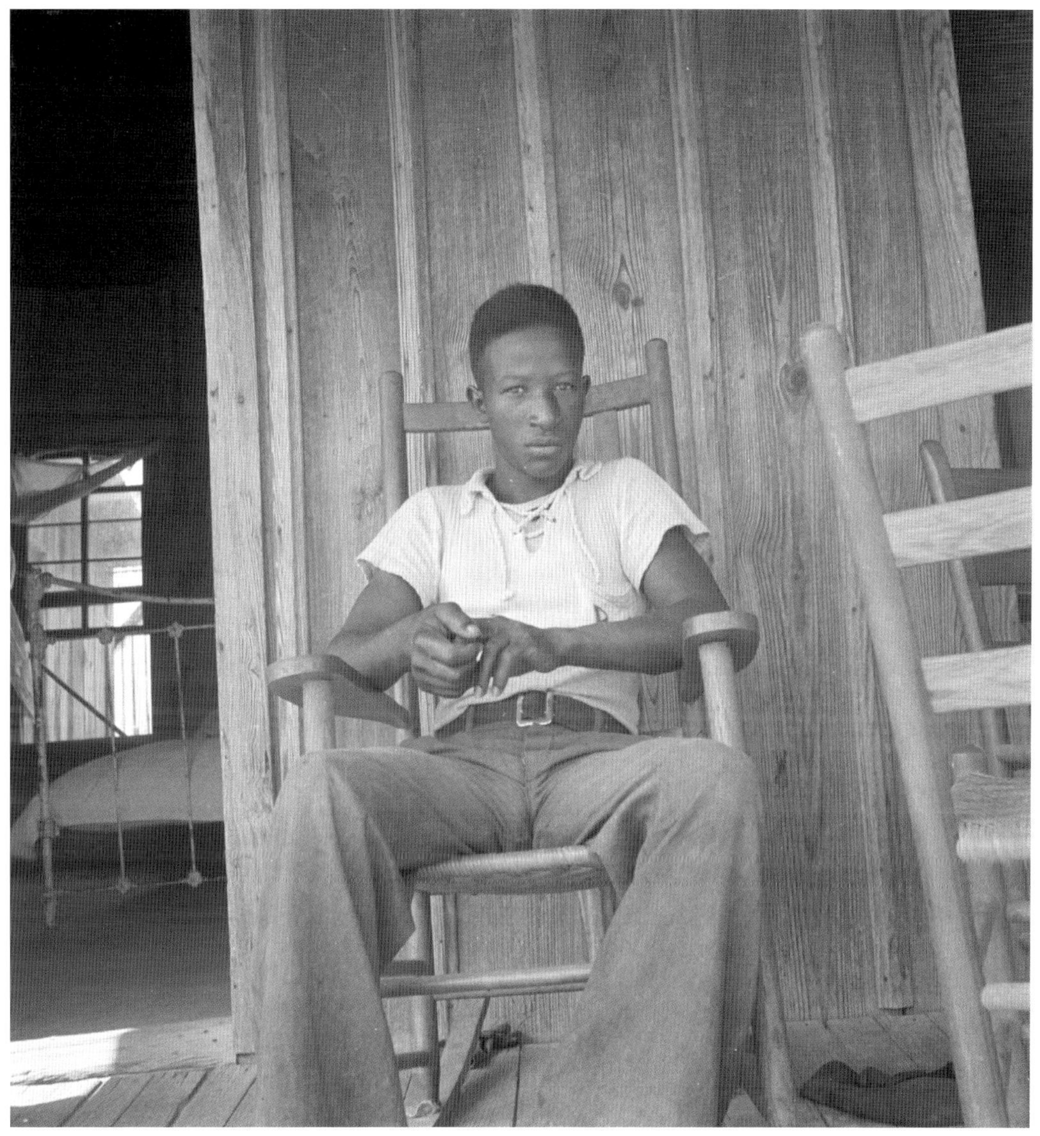

The son of an illiterate sharecropper near Earle who "wants a high school education," according to Dorothea Lange.

(Dorothea Lange, July 1936) Farm Security Administration Photograph Collection, Prints & Photographs Division, Library of Congress, LC-USF34–009766–E

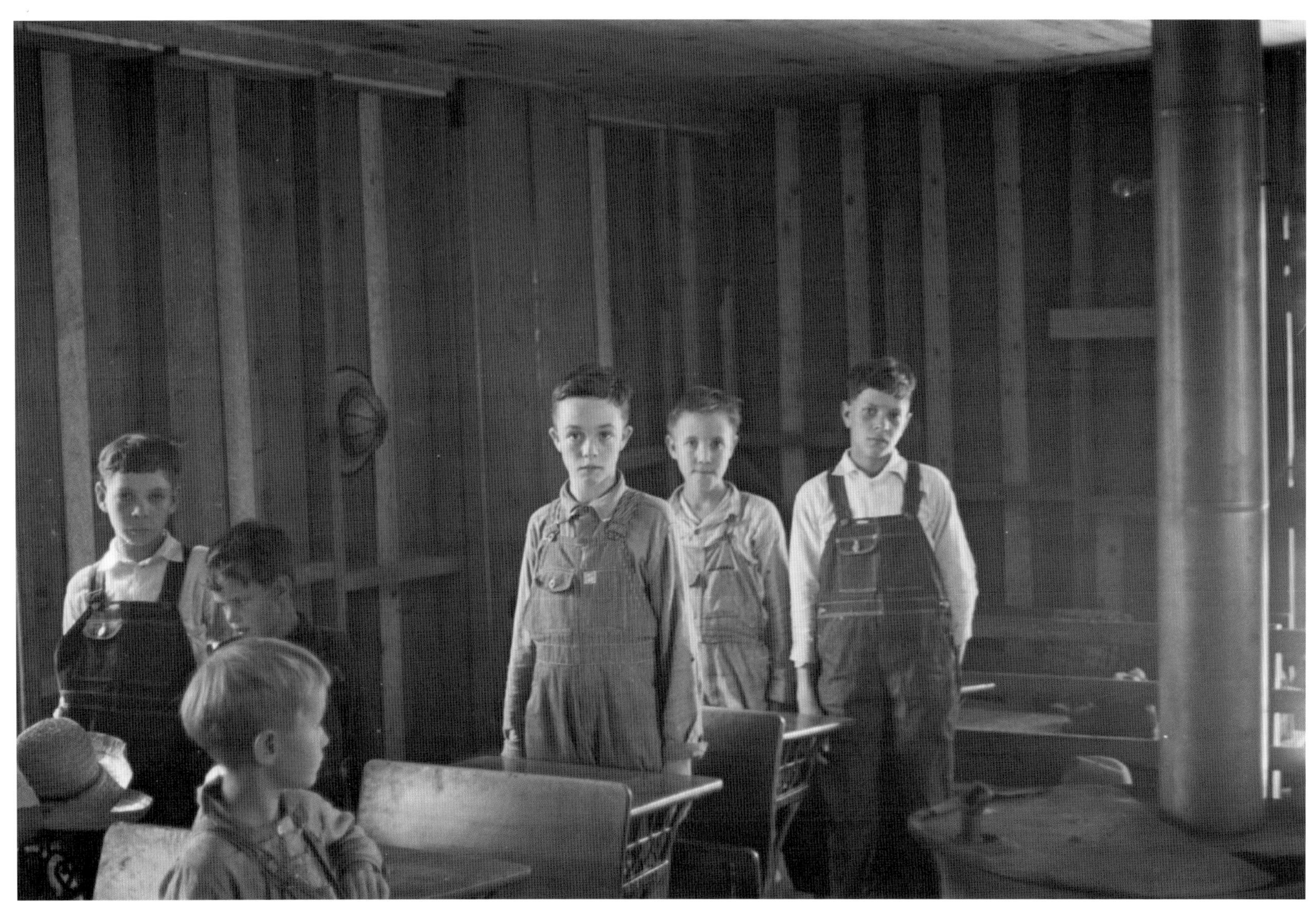

Children in a small rural school in the Ozarks.

(Ben Shahn, September 1935) Farm Security Administration Photograph Collection, Prints & Photographs Division, Library of Congress, LC-USF33–006090–M5

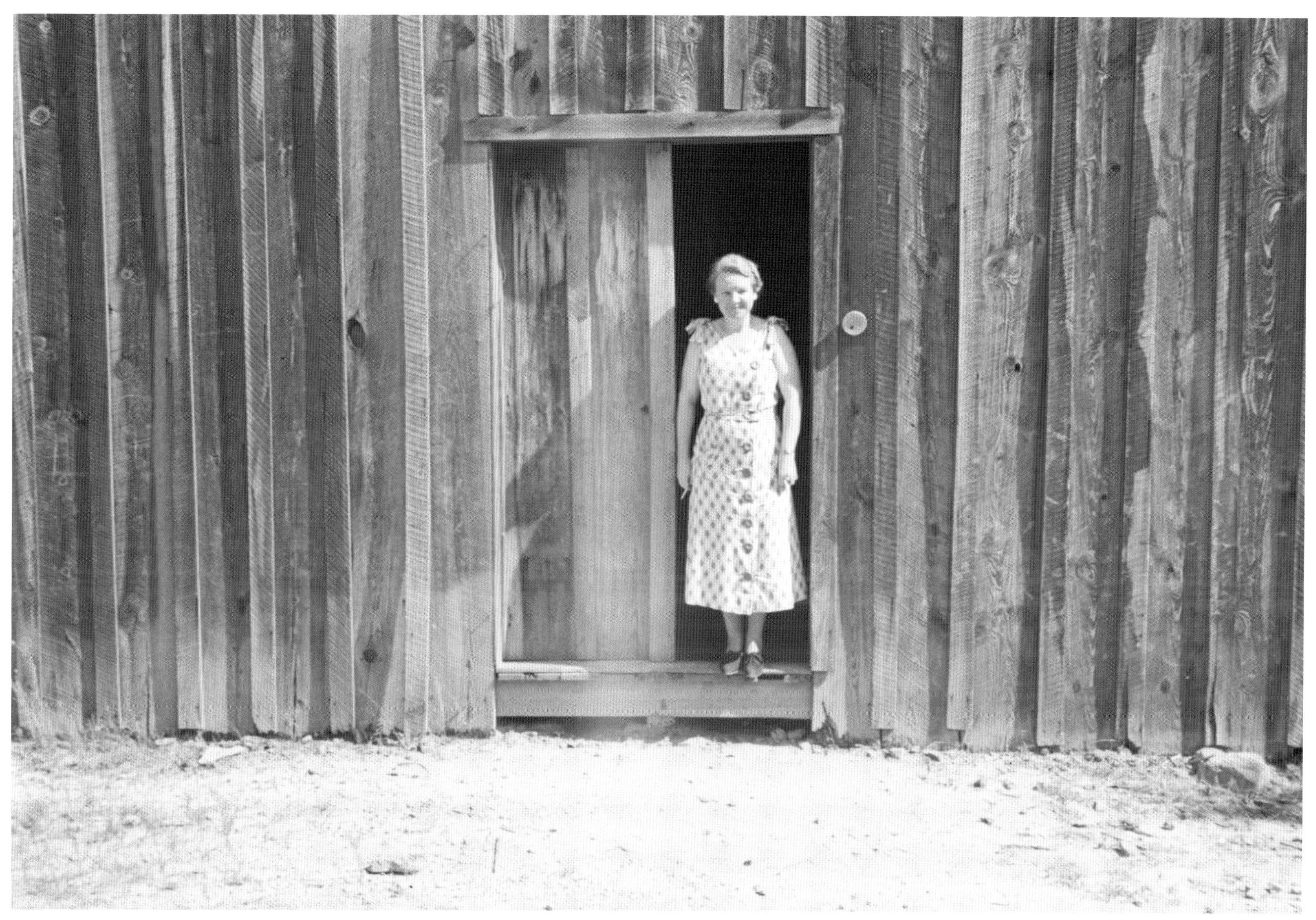

Schoolteacher for a small rural school in the Ozarks.

(Ben Shahn, September 1935) Farm Security Administration Photograph Collection, Prints & Photographs Division, Library of Congress, LC-USF33–006062–M5

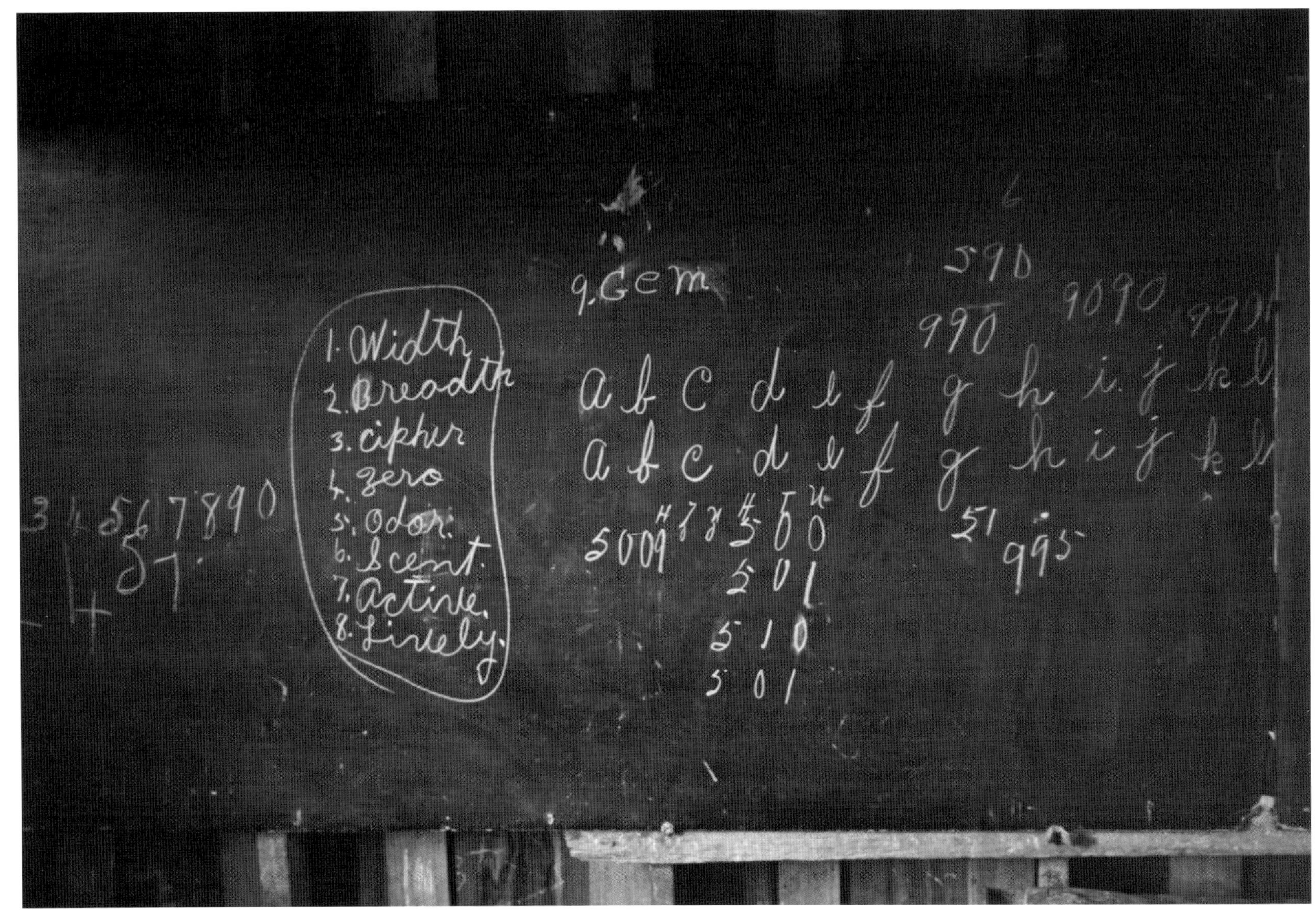

Lessons written on the scratched and damaged blackboard at a small Ozarks school.

(Ben Shahn, September 1935) Farm Security Administration Photograph Collection, Prints & Photographs Division, Library of Congress, LC-USF33–006090–M1

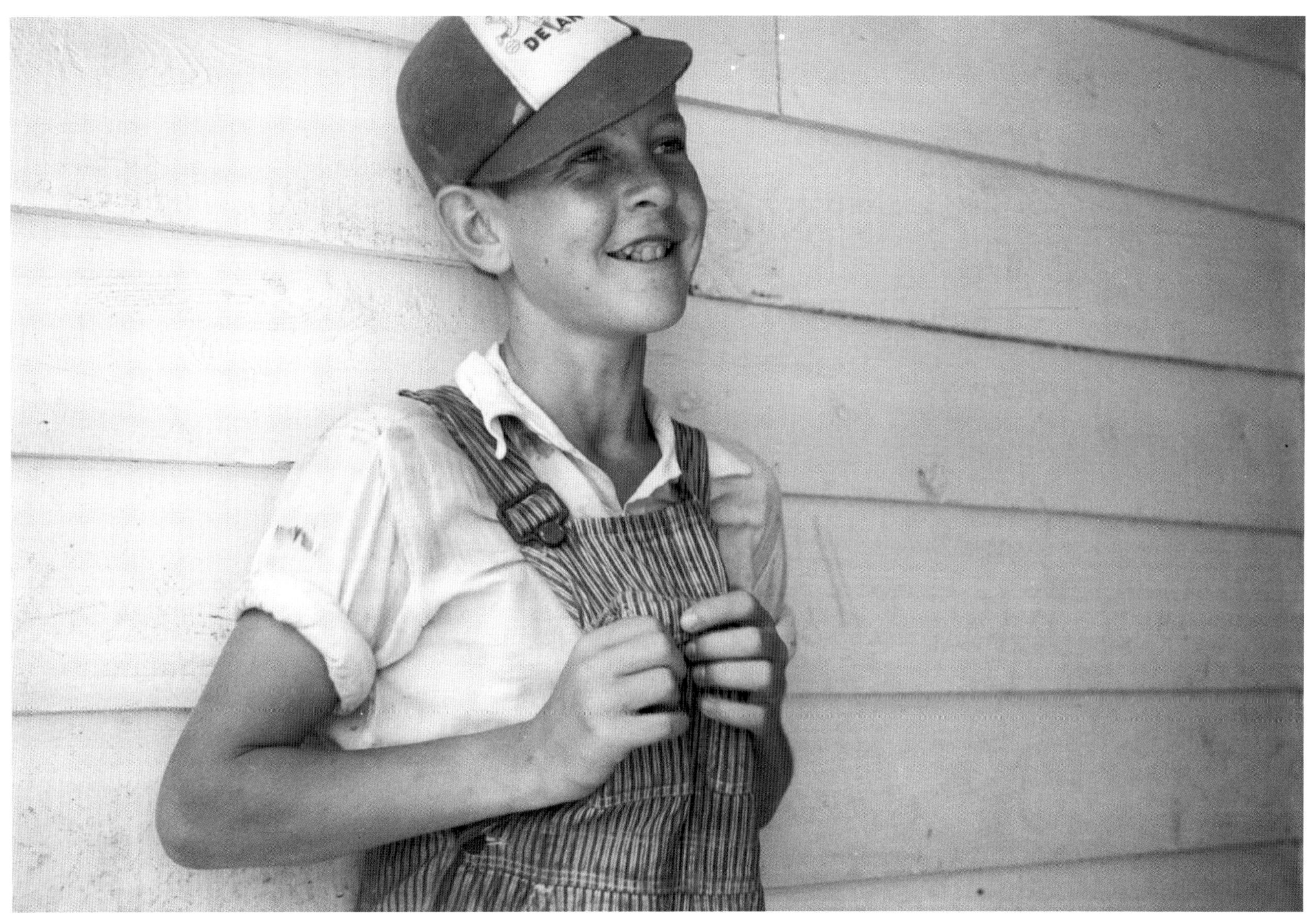

A member of the 4-H Club and son of a Dyess Colony resettlement family.

(Arthur Rothstein, August 1935) Farm Security Administration Photograph Collection, Prints & Photographs Division, Library of Congress, LC-USF33–002004–M1

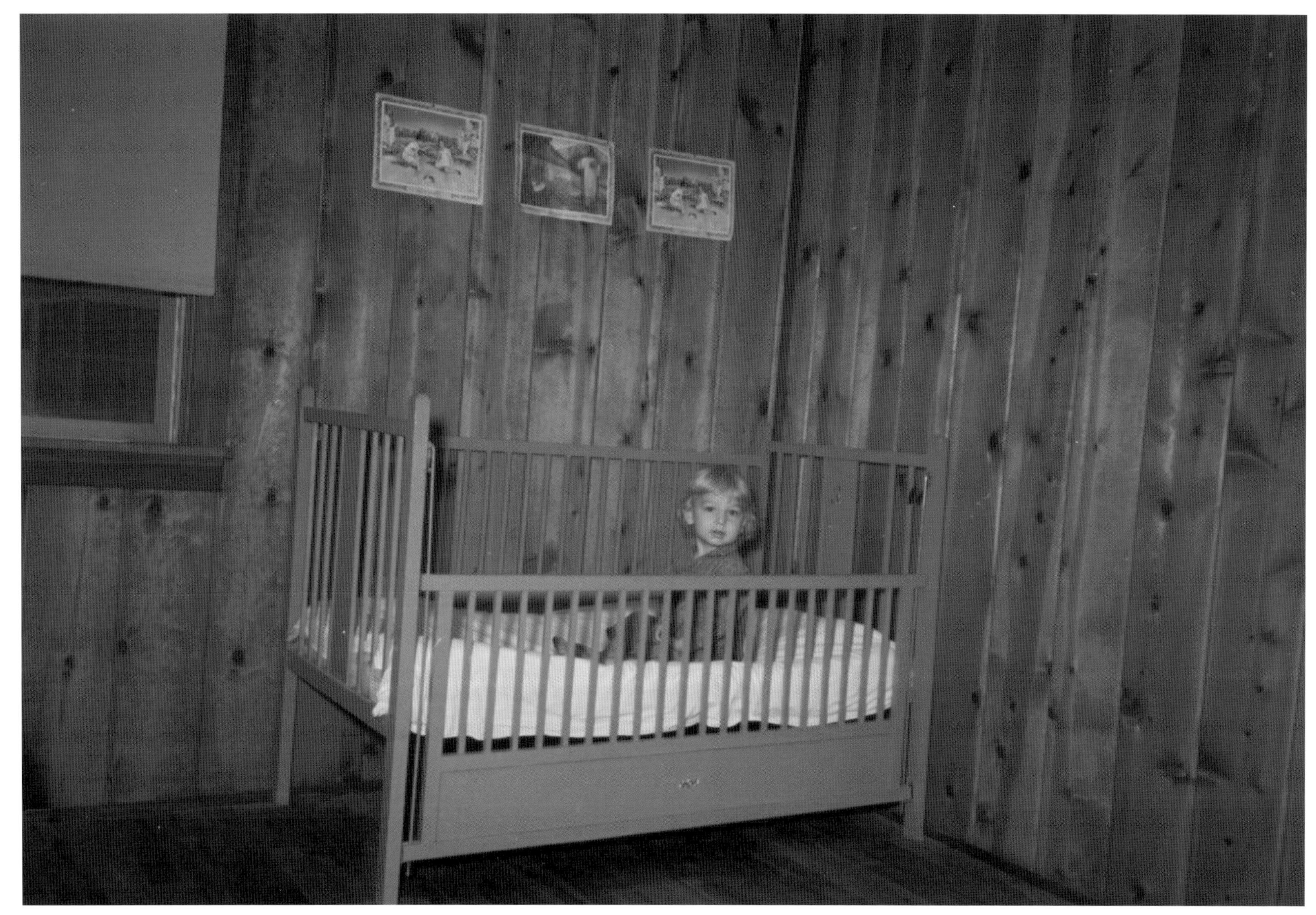

Child of a Lake Dick resettlement family.

(Russell Lee, September 1938) Farm Security Administration Photograph Collection, Prints & Photographs Division, Library of Congress, LC-USF33–011666–M3

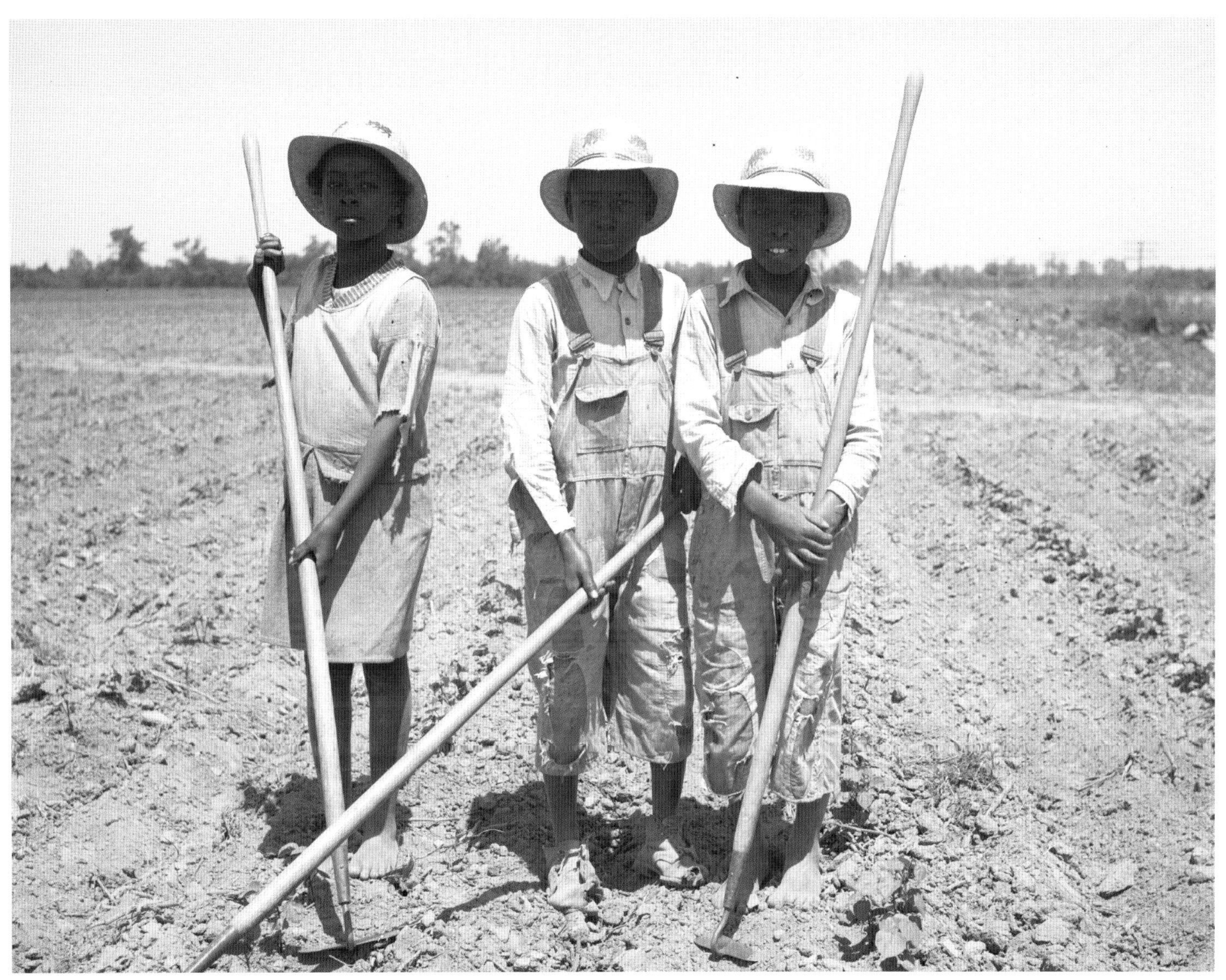

Children chopping cotton near Marked Tree; ages (*left to right*) are ten years, thirteen years, and eight years.

(Carl Mydans, June 1936) Farm Security Administration Photograph Collection, Prints & Photographs Division, Library of Congress, LC-USF34–006345–D

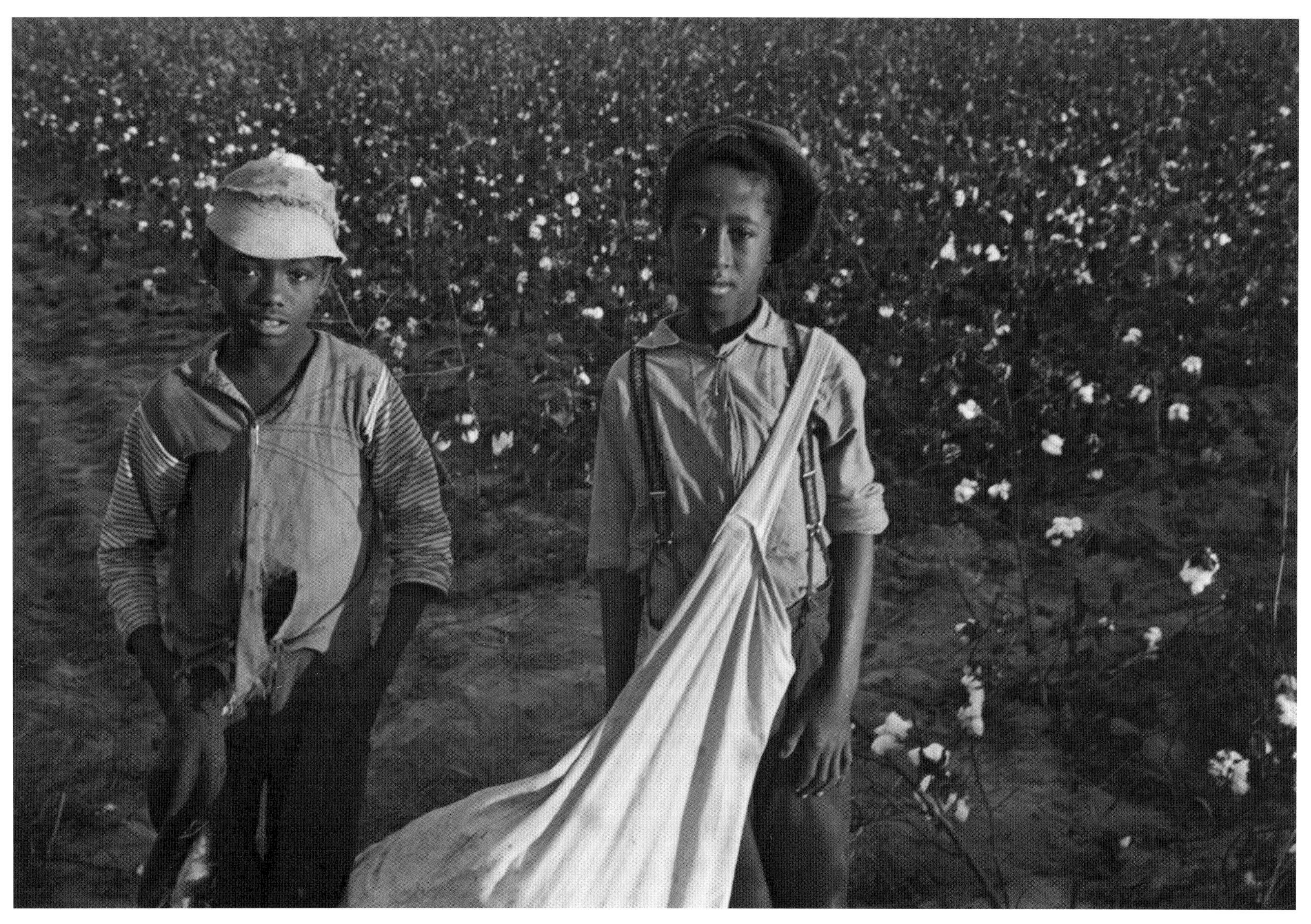

Children picking cotton, Pulaski County.

(Ben Shahn, October 1935) Farm Security Administration Photograph Collection, Prints & Photographs Division, Library of Congress, LC-USF33–006021–M1

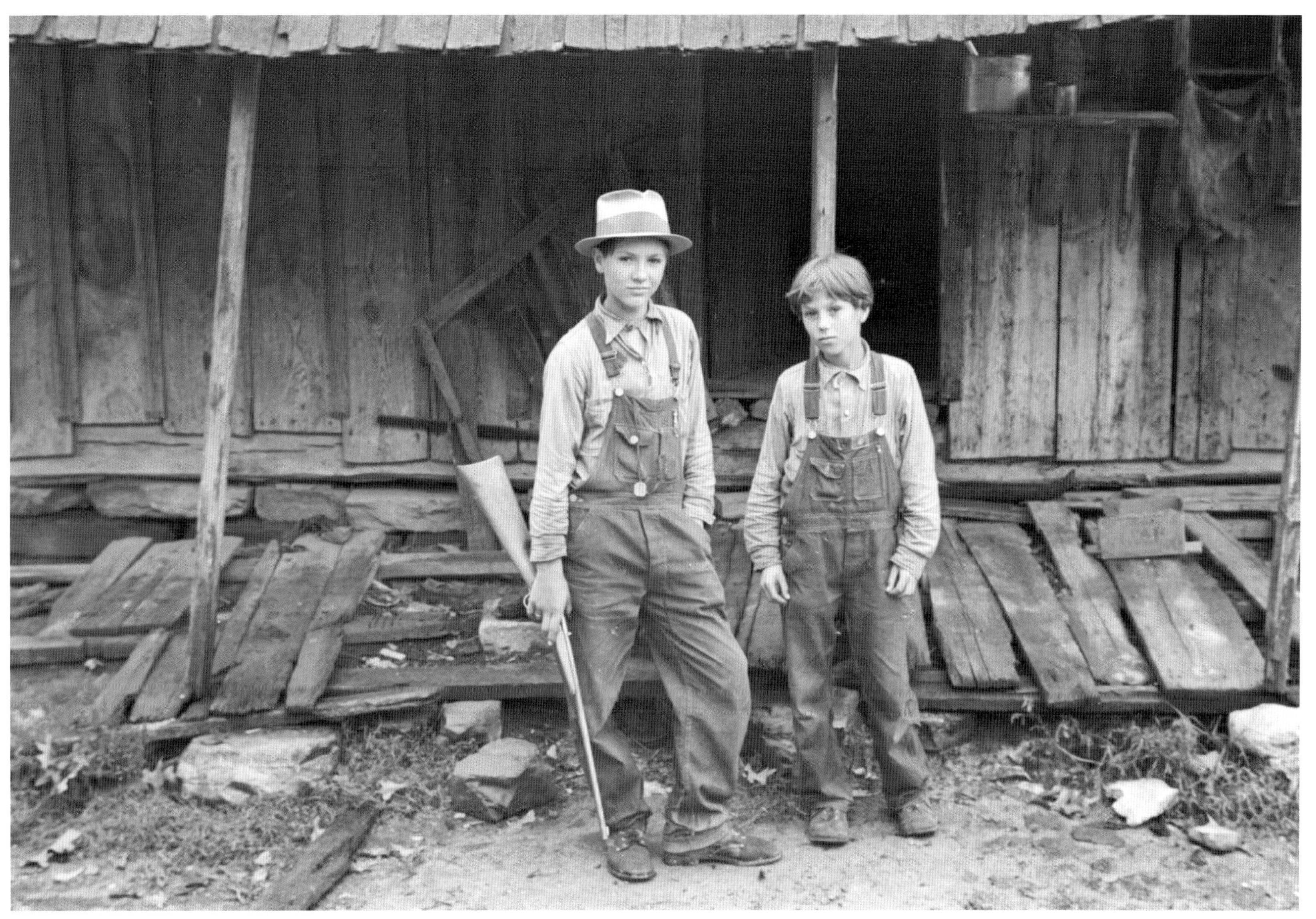

Children of tenant farmer Sam Nichols in front of their family's house. One holds a rifle.

(Ben Shahn, October 1935) Farm Security Administration Photograph Collection, Prints & Photographs Division, Library of Congress, LC-USF33–006038–M1

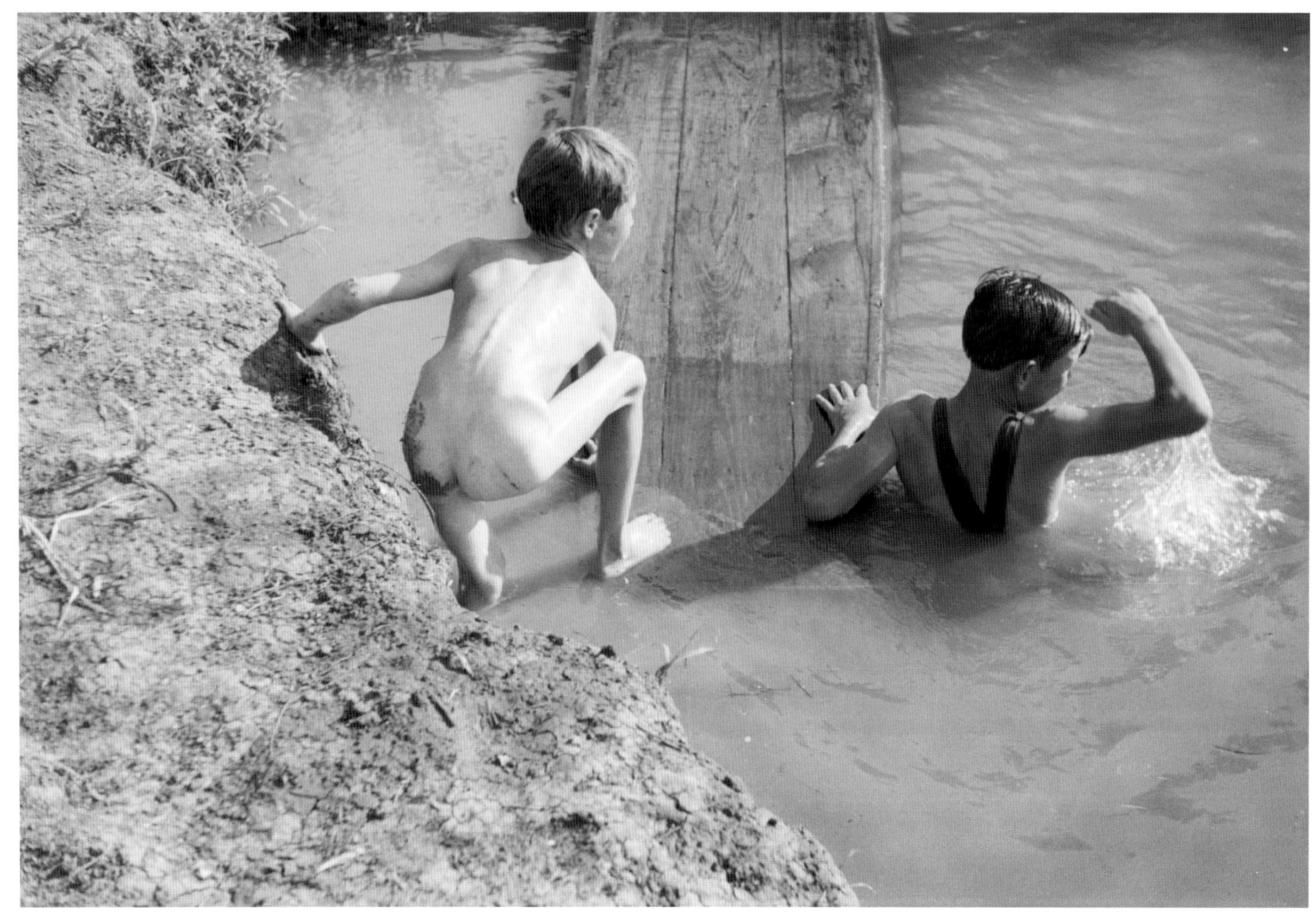

Children at the Dyess resettlement farm.

(Arthur Rothstein, August 1935) Farm Security Administration Photograph Collection, Prints & Photographs Division, Library of Congress, LC-USF33–002005–M2

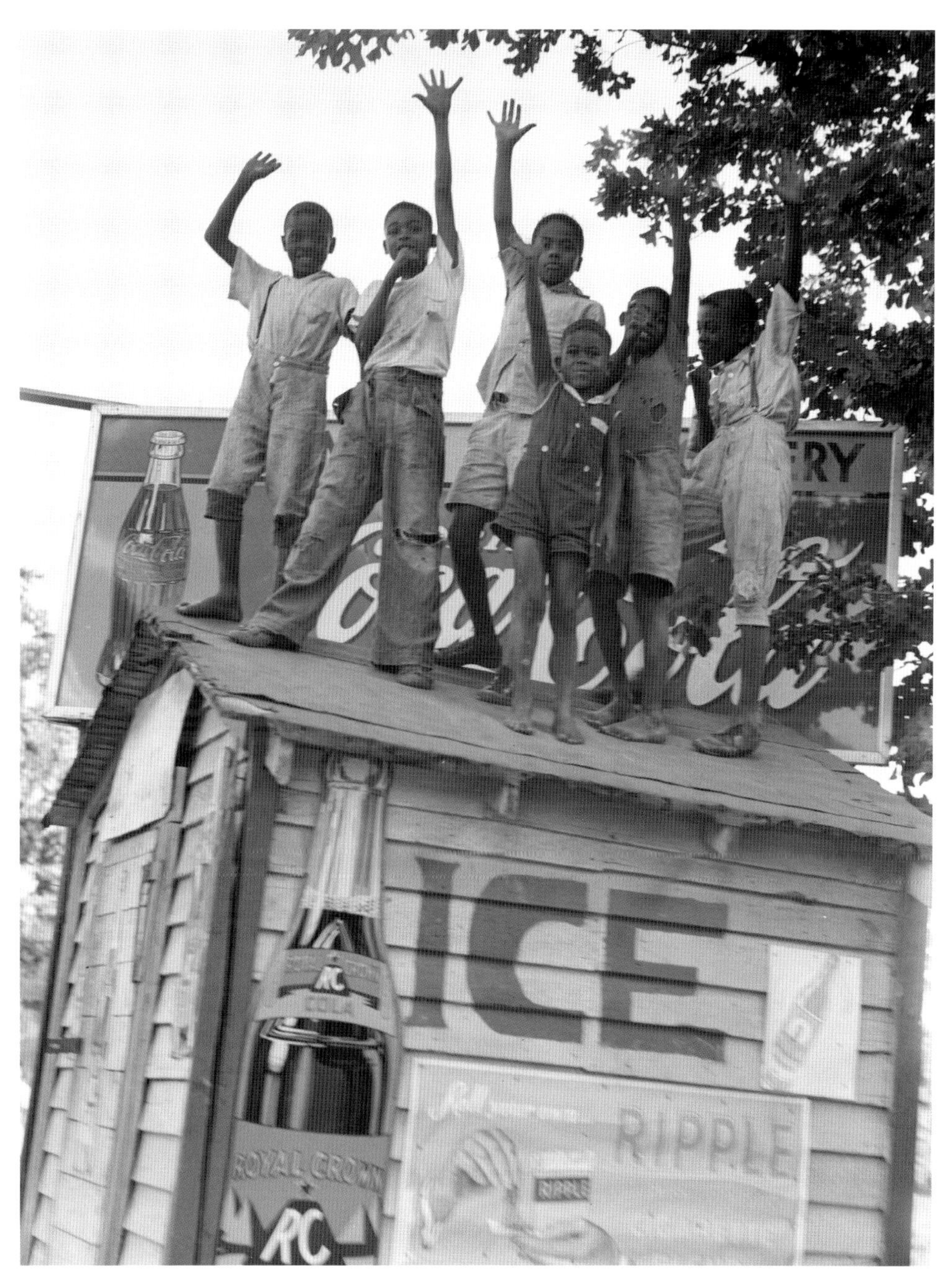

Children on top of a soft drink stand in Little Rock.

(Dorothea Lange, June 1938) Farm Security Administration Photograph Collection, Prints & Photographs Division, Library of Congress, LC-USF34–018259–C

EIGHT | THE FLOOD OF 1937

THE 1937 FLOOD has been described as "the 1,000-year flood" and possibly the worst ever in Arkansas history. In January, the Mississippi River and its tributaries broke through old levees and overflowed into nearly 2 million acres (roughly 7 percent of the state) of low-lying land in counties across the Arkansas Delta. Hit hardest in the area were the indigent sharecroppers who accounted for most of the region's 140,000 inhabitants; as floodwaters rose and ran into their cabins, they fled for higher ground, with 50,000 ending up in Red Cross camps that had been hurriedly built in places like Marianna and Forrest City. Others found their way to Memphis or to homes of relatives, or to other refugee centers around the state.

The Red Cross in its annual report estimated that about 44,000 Arkansas families were affected by the flood and that it damaged or destroyed more than four hundred dwellings. Altogether, the Red Cross provided $1.17 million (approximately $20 million in 2015 dollars) to the state in shelter, food, loans, and other assistance. Still, the brunt of the flood was borne by urban areas up the Mississippi and in the Ohio River Valley where damage to industry and housing was far costlier. Among the eleven states affected by the flood, though, Arkansas suffered the highest number of deaths with thirty-seven, most from disease rather than drowning.

The 1937 flood was caused by an unusual weather pattern that produced heavy rainfall early in January along the Ohio and Mississippi river valleys, according to David Welky in *The Thousand-Year Flood: The Ohio-Mississippi Disaster of 1937*. The US Weather Bureau put the floodwater total at 165 billion tons throughout the eleven affected states, enough to cover 204,000 square miles (an area roughly the size of Colorado and Oregon together) to a depth of 11.2 inches. Areas where normally around 4 inches of rain fell in January got nearly three times that amount. Conditions were even more miserable for people living in drafty and leaky sharecropper cabins when freezing temperatures left a skin of ice on floodwaters and severely complicated evacuation.

The rain had started in eastern Arkansas early in January, but the situation quickly turned critical around January 20 when the Arkansas River tributaries backed up, unable to empty into the cresting Mississippi River. A report from the resident manager at the Dyess Colony in Mississippi County told the story of the nearby Tyronza River overflowing its banks for a second time that month on January 20, but "covering a greater area than the first rise." The Dyess manager began to evacuate families from their homes into the colony's community center, and by January 22 approximately fifteen hundred people were sheltered there. He wrote that the ice and freezing rain made the operation of trucks and tractors in the evacuation very difficult. By January 24, a Sunday, with electricity gone, no fresh water and floodwaters still rising, the colony was completely evacuated by truck to Memphis and Bassett.

To the northwest, a businessman in Greene County began keeping detailed notes on broadcasts from radio station KBTM in Jonesboro on January 22, as it reported emergency messages calling for help with supplies and rescues of families stranded by the flood. For two days, a Lake City woman about to give birth was marooned on her roof—"Must have help at ONCE!" read the writer's notes. KBTM announced that people at Monette and Black Oak were stuck and needed help; Walnut Ridge and Otwell Clubhouse were sending boats to Caraway and Lake City; a young boy was reported to have frozen to death on a levee after his family near Monette sent him out to get help. Very quickly people began to offer cash rewards to anyone who could assist rescues.

The Arkansas Red Cross had started relief efforts by mid-January, with the national office becoming more involved as the crisis worsened, as recorded in the national organization's annual report. Throughout the region, the Red Cross set up seventy-five tent cities and other facilities for flood refugees where they were provided shelter, food, clothing, and medical care. Several towns on Crowley's Ridge, which was about two hundred feet above the lowlands, became campsites. One thousand refugees were sent to Jonesboro; the small town of Marianna had 3,500. The slightly larger town of Forrest City, which had a population of only 5,500 but was conveniently located on a railway line, received 12,000 refugees.

Two RA/FSA photographers, Walker Evans and Edwin Locke, were sent to Arkansas to take pictures of camps at Marianna and Forrest City in February. They took only a few photos of the flood itself, shooting from the train that carried them into Arkansas. Instead, they focused on conditions in camps, visiting both the black and white sections of the segregated facilities; they photographed lines of refugees waiting for food, heaps of belongings people had managed to bring with them, rows of pyramid-shaped tents, and refugees looking shocked and despondent.

"Flooders" were housed in cotton compresses, which could also accommodate medical facilities. In the big open building, they had to stake out a place on the floor to pile their things, and then make sure to keep an eye on them; in the close quarters, there was scant privacy. Others were assigned to tents that measured 16 by 16 feet; though the tents allowed some hint of solitude, they were vulnerable to rain and sleet, had rough board flooring and were heated by smoky woodstoves. Because of crowded conditions in the camps there was fear of epidemics of influenza, pneumonia, and typhoid fever; however, perhaps because the US Public Health Service took measures to immunize refugees, those diseases were blocked, although an outbreak of meningitis in Jonesboro did result in twelve deaths.

Two meals a day were prepared and served by the US Army, the Arkansas National Guard, and volunteers. Locke and Evans, in particular, focused many of their pictures on refugees standing in long lines, holding pans and plates. One of Evans's most famous photographs is his shot of five African American refugees pressed together in a line, with two of them—a man and a woman—grasping a bowl and a pie plate in their hands (see figure Intro.15). He also photographed a stack of slabs of cornbread that looked more like pieces of thick cardboard.

The people in Evans's and Locke's photos from Marianna and Forrest City may have been mostly sharecroppers from nearby counties such as Phillips, Lee, St. Francis, Cross, or Crittenden, all crisscrossed by rivers and creeks that likely flooded them out of their homes. As the floodwaters receded through February and March, issues arose with refugees in the Red Cross camps. The federal government, anticipating a major humanitarian crisis as people returned to damaged or even missing homes, preferred the refugees remain in the camps longer; however, the local planters—who often were serving as local administrators of relief efforts—were in favor of sharecroppers getting back to work as soon as the plowing and planting season began. The sharecropper refugees, planters feared, would find the camps and life off the farm offered better conditions and they would never return to the fields.

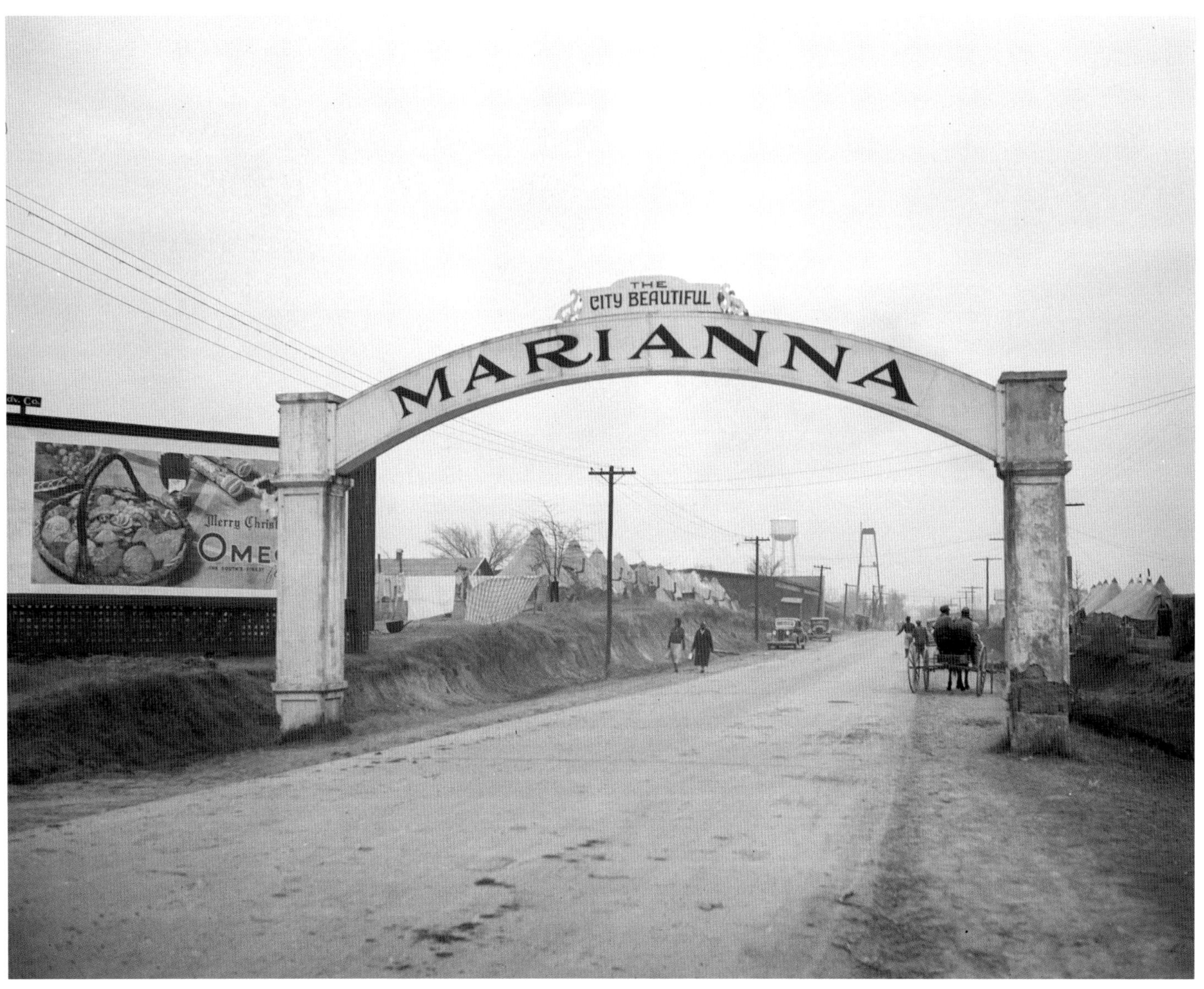

The entrance to Marianna in Lee County during the 1937 flood.

(Walker Evans, February 1937) Farm Security Administration Photograph Collection, Prints & Photographs Division, Library of Congress, LC-USF34–008213–C

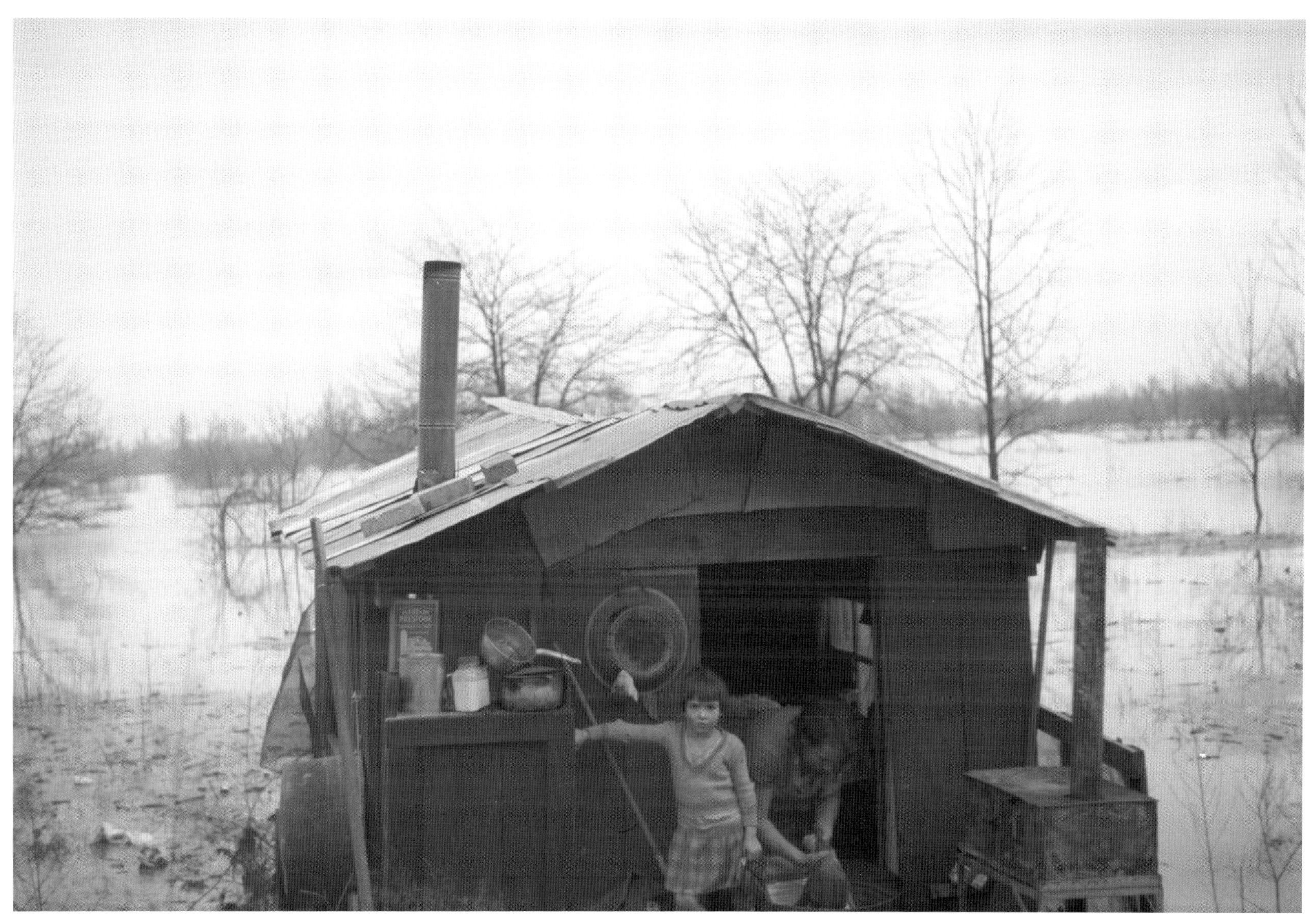

A family caught in the flood built an ark.

(Edwin Locke, February 1937) Farm Security Administration Photograph Collection, Prints & Photographs Division, Library of Congress, LC-USF33–004234–M5

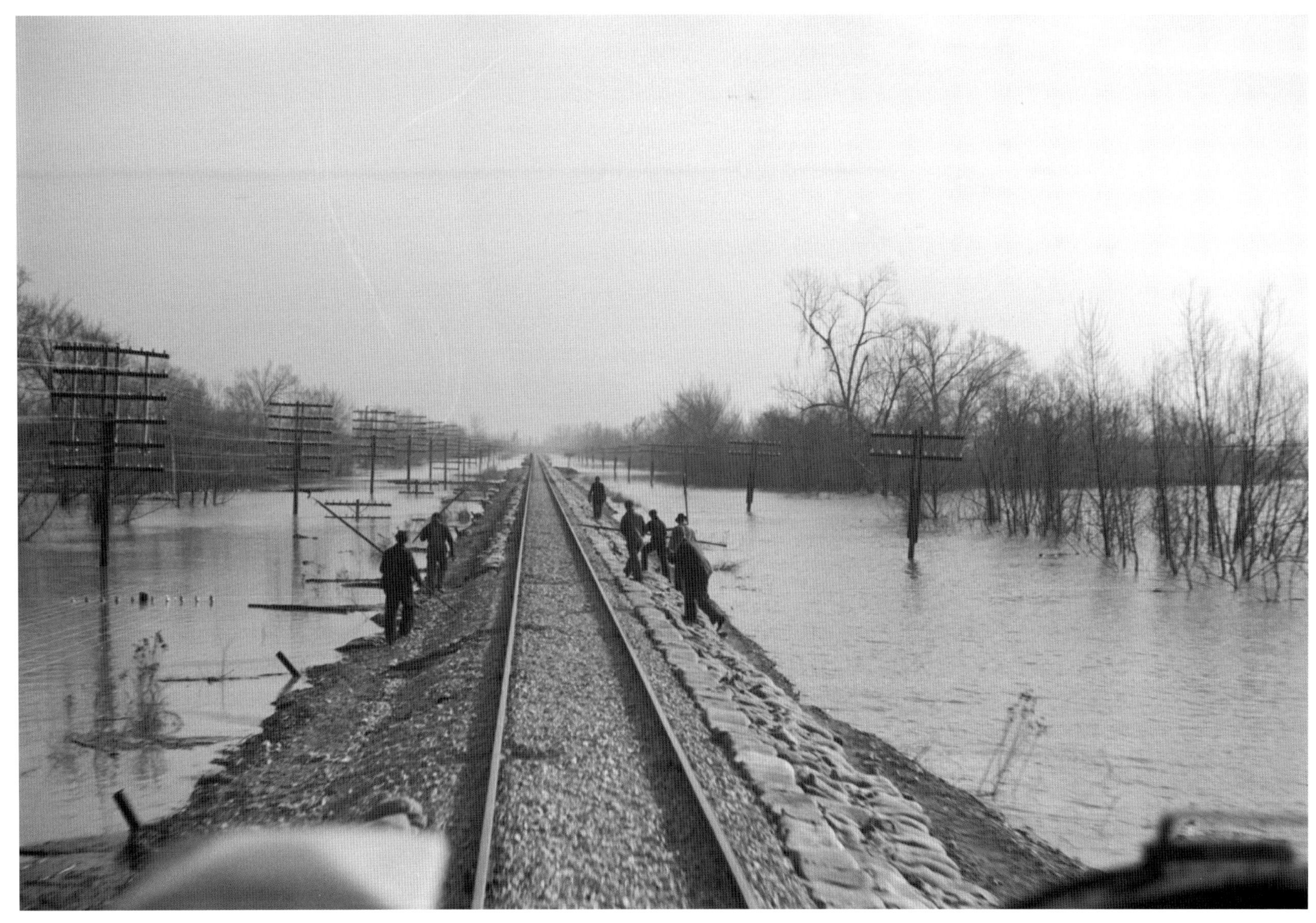

A view from the train en route from Tennessee to Arkansas showing the depth of the water near the tracks.

(Edwin Locke, February 1937) Farm Security Administration Photograph Collection, Prints & Photographs Division, Library of Congress, LC-USF33–004179–M2

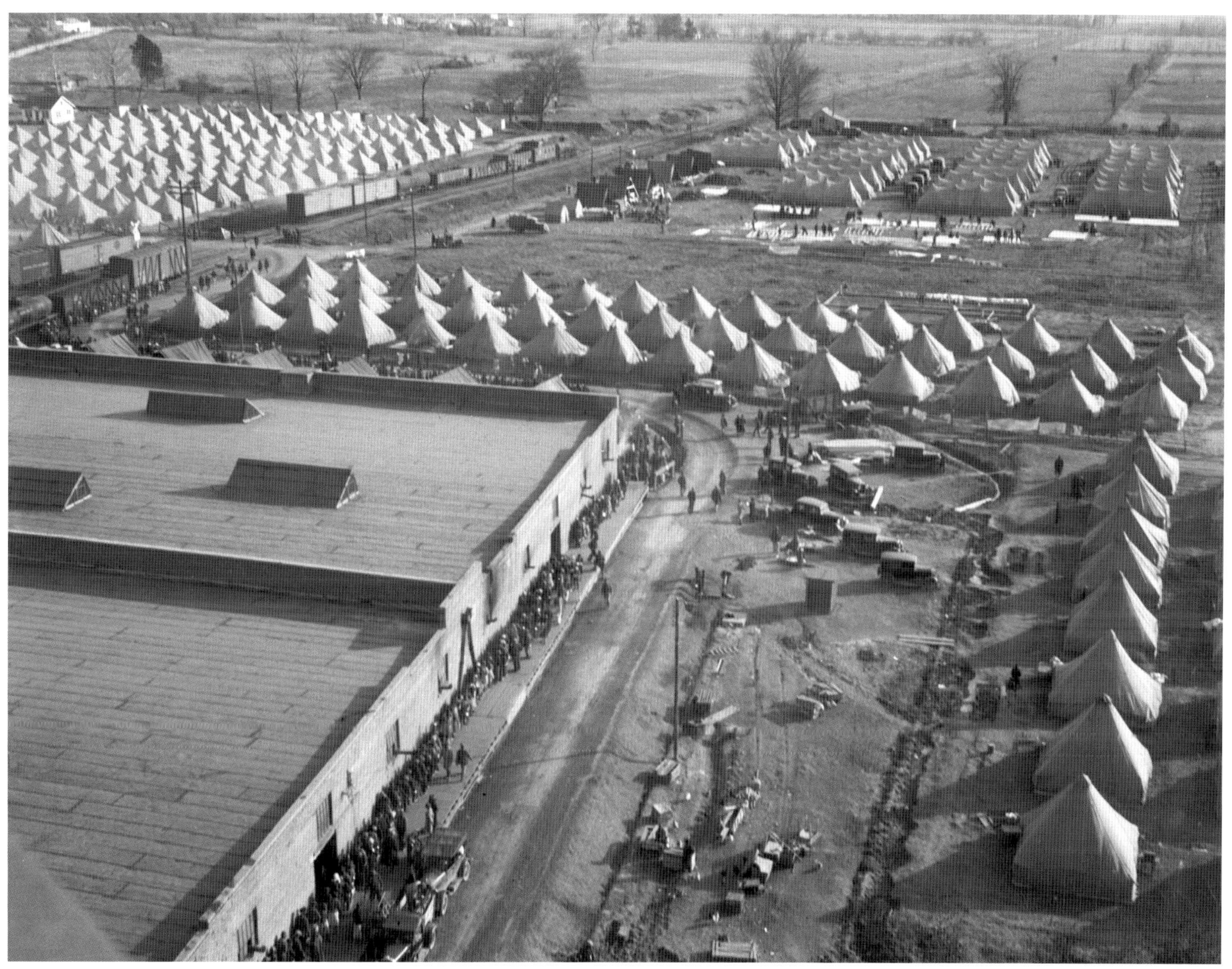

An aerial overview of the layout of the refugee camp at Forrest City.

(Edwin Locke, February 1937) Farm Security Administration Photograph Collection, Prints & Photographs Division, Library of Congress, LC-USF34–013048–D

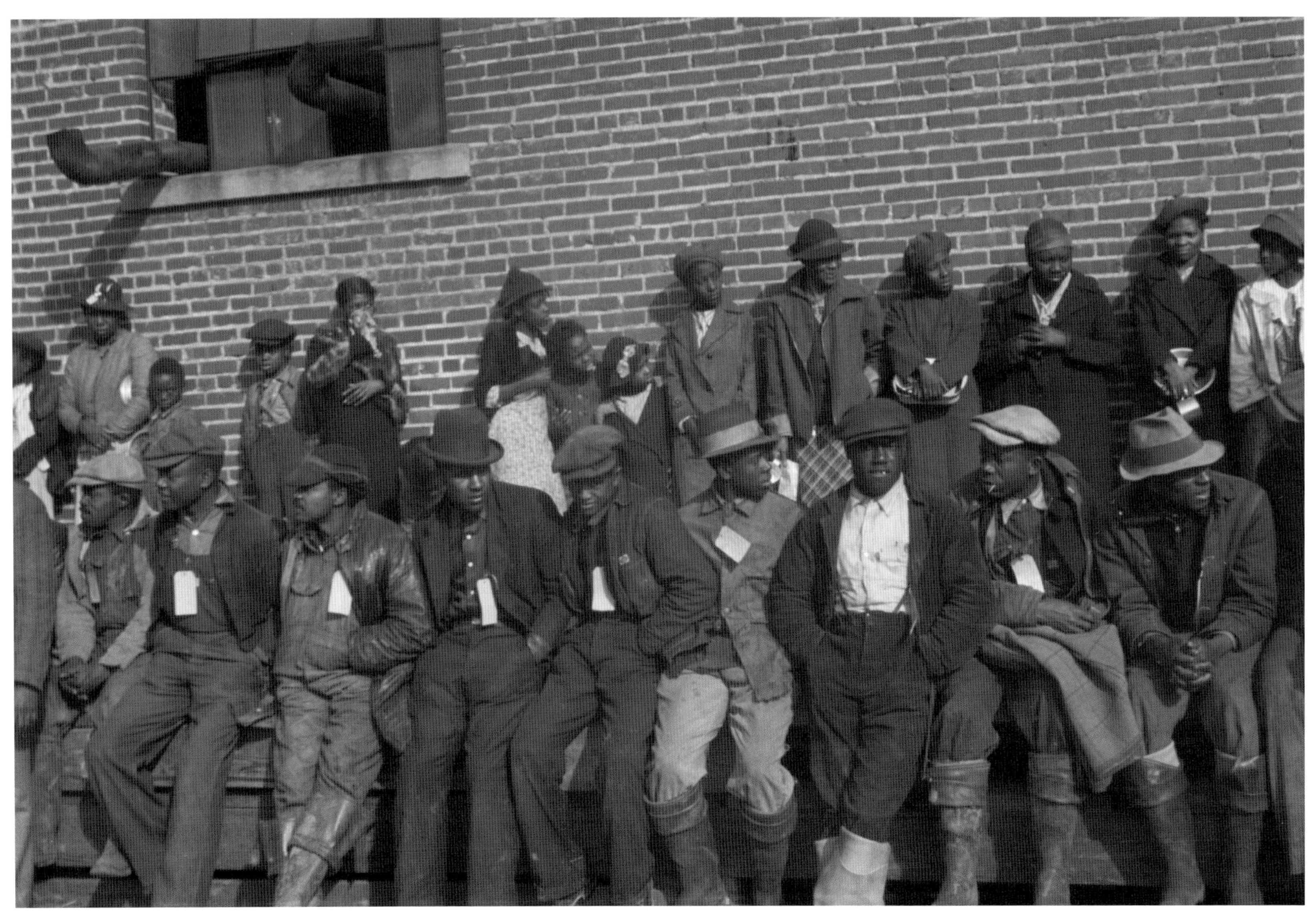

Flood refugees with identification tags after registering in the camp at Forrest City.

(Edwin Locke, February 1937) Farm Security Administration Photograph Collection, Prints & Photographs Division, Library of Congress, LC-USF33–003196–M4

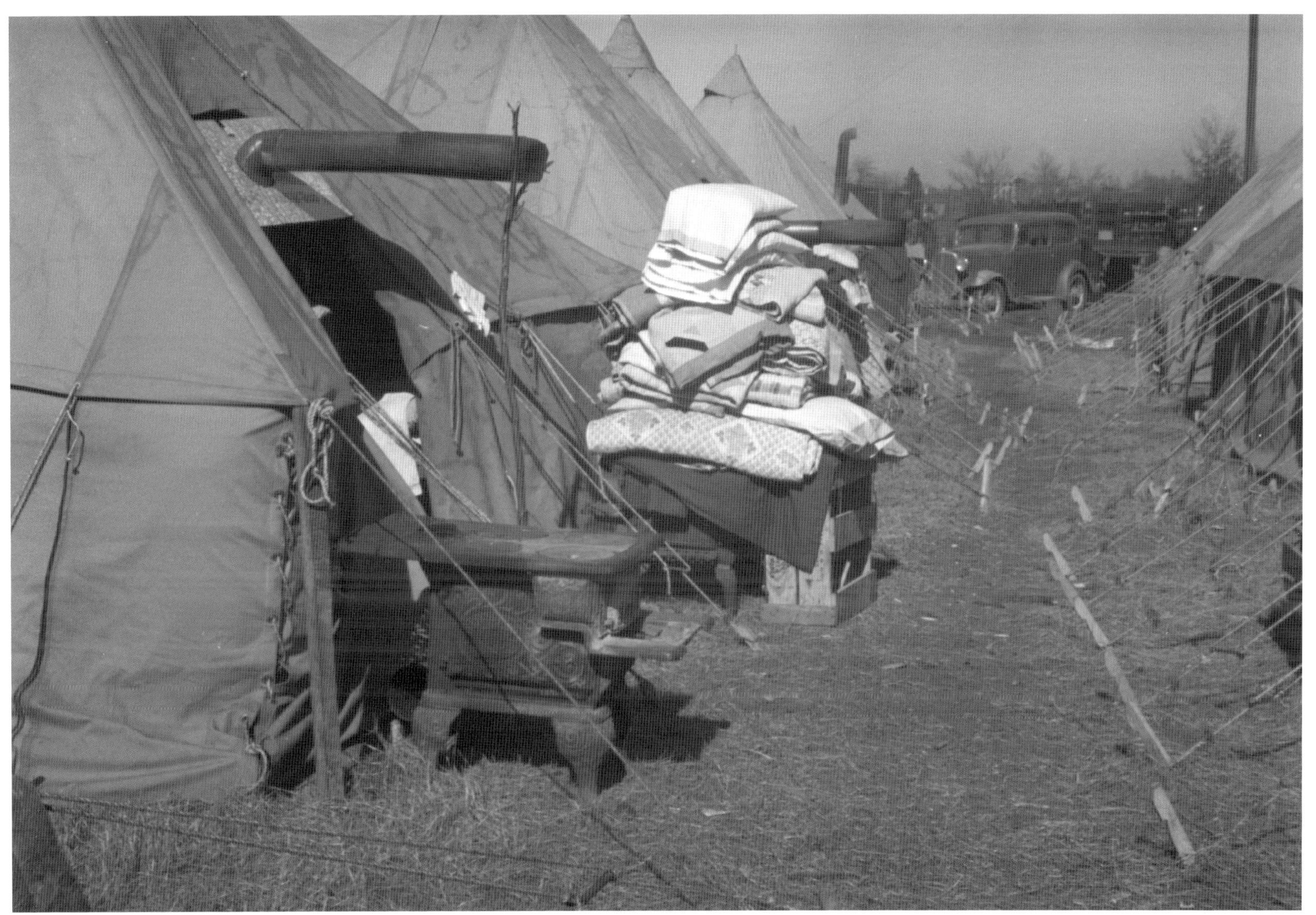

Refugees' belongings stacked outside a tent in the Forrest City refugee camp.

(Walker Evans or Edwin Locke, February 1937)
Farm Security Administration Photograph Collection, Prints & Photographs Division, Library of Congress, LC-USF33–031347–M1

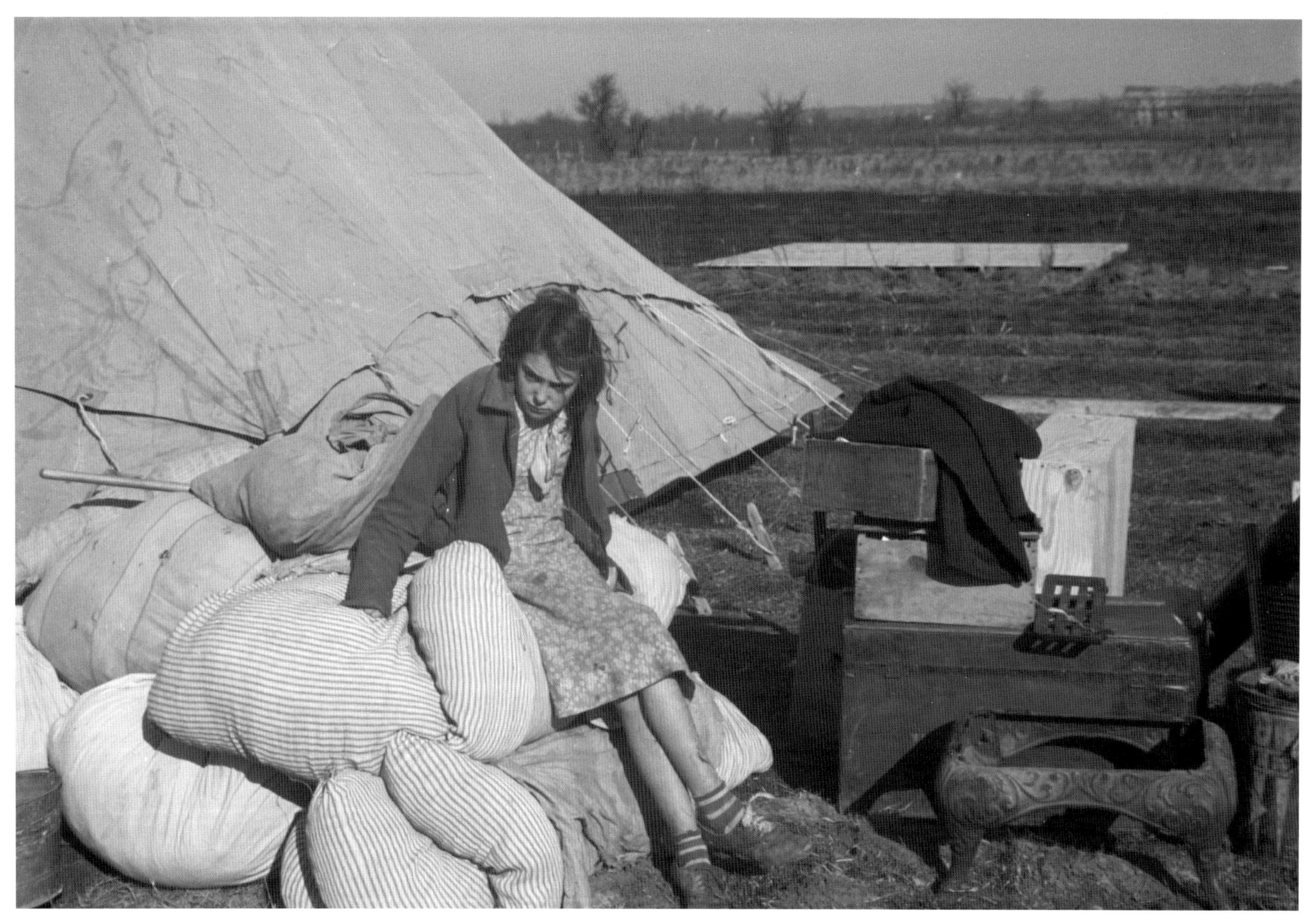

A young girl with her family's possessions near a tent in a refugee camp.

(Walker Evans, February 1937) Farm Security Administration Photograph Collection, Prints & Photographs Division, Library of Congress, LC-USF33–009240–M3

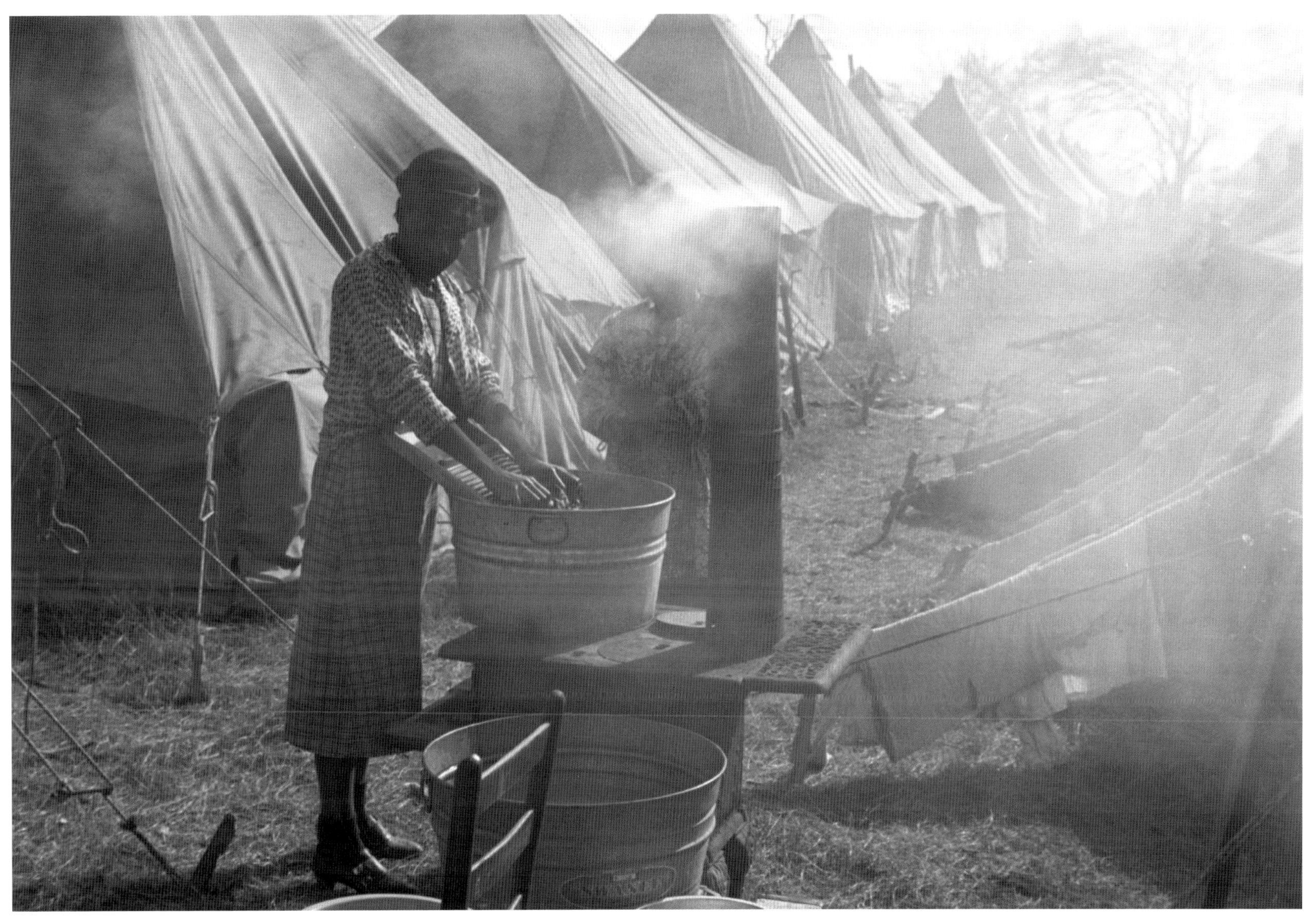

A flood refugee washes clothes in the camp at Forrest City.

(Edwin Locke, February 1937) Farm Security Administration Photograph Collection, Prints & Photographs Division, Library of Congress, LC-USF33–004194–M3

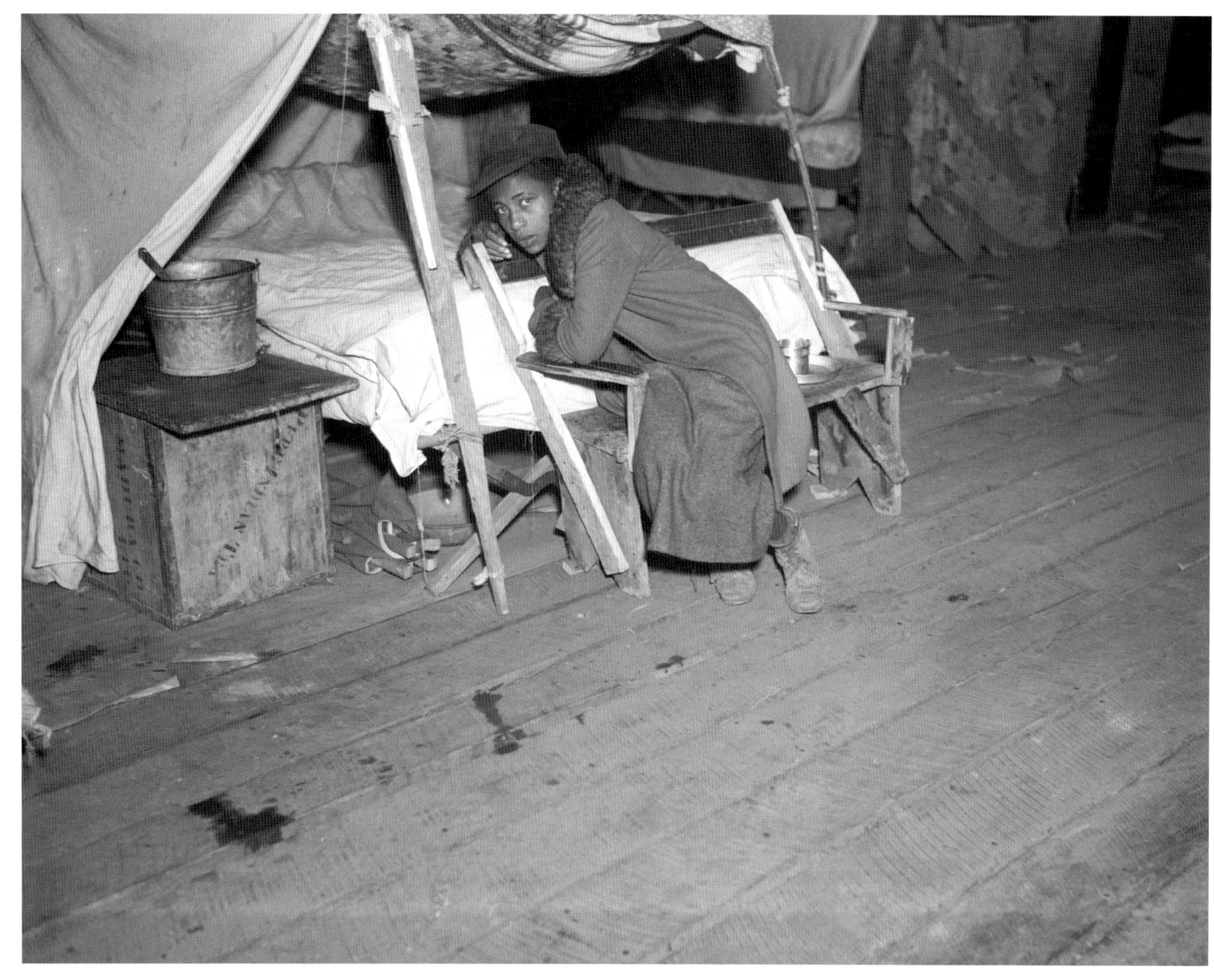

A woman keeps watch over her family's belongings in the temporary infirmary at a refugee camp.

(Walker Evans, February 1937) Farm Security Administration Photograph Collection, Prints & Photographs Division, Library of Congress, LC-USF34–008206–C

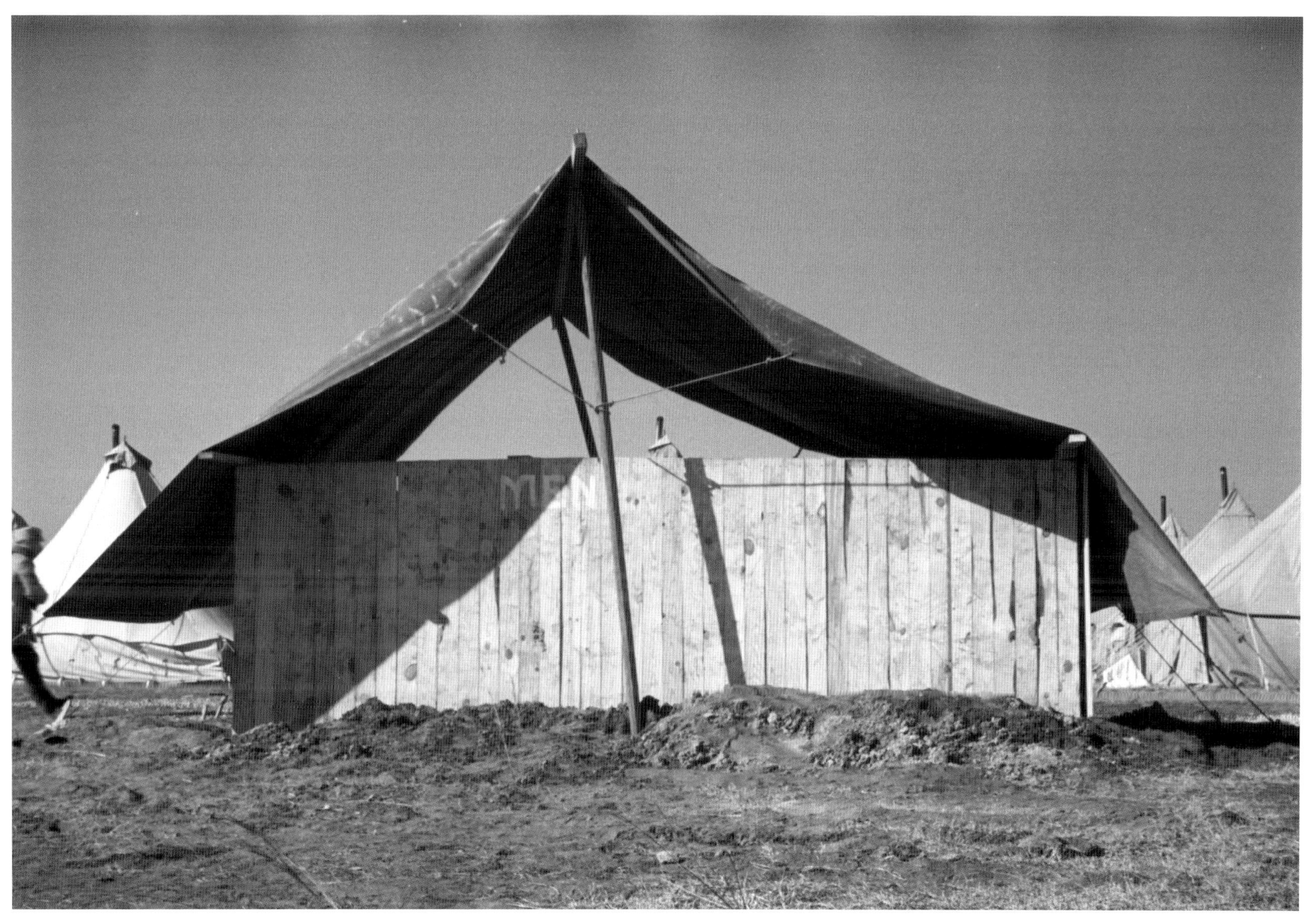

Facilities designated for men at the Forrest City camp.

(Edwin Locke, February 1937) Farm Security Administration Photograph Collection, Prints & Photographs Division, Library of Congress, LC-USF33–004202–M2

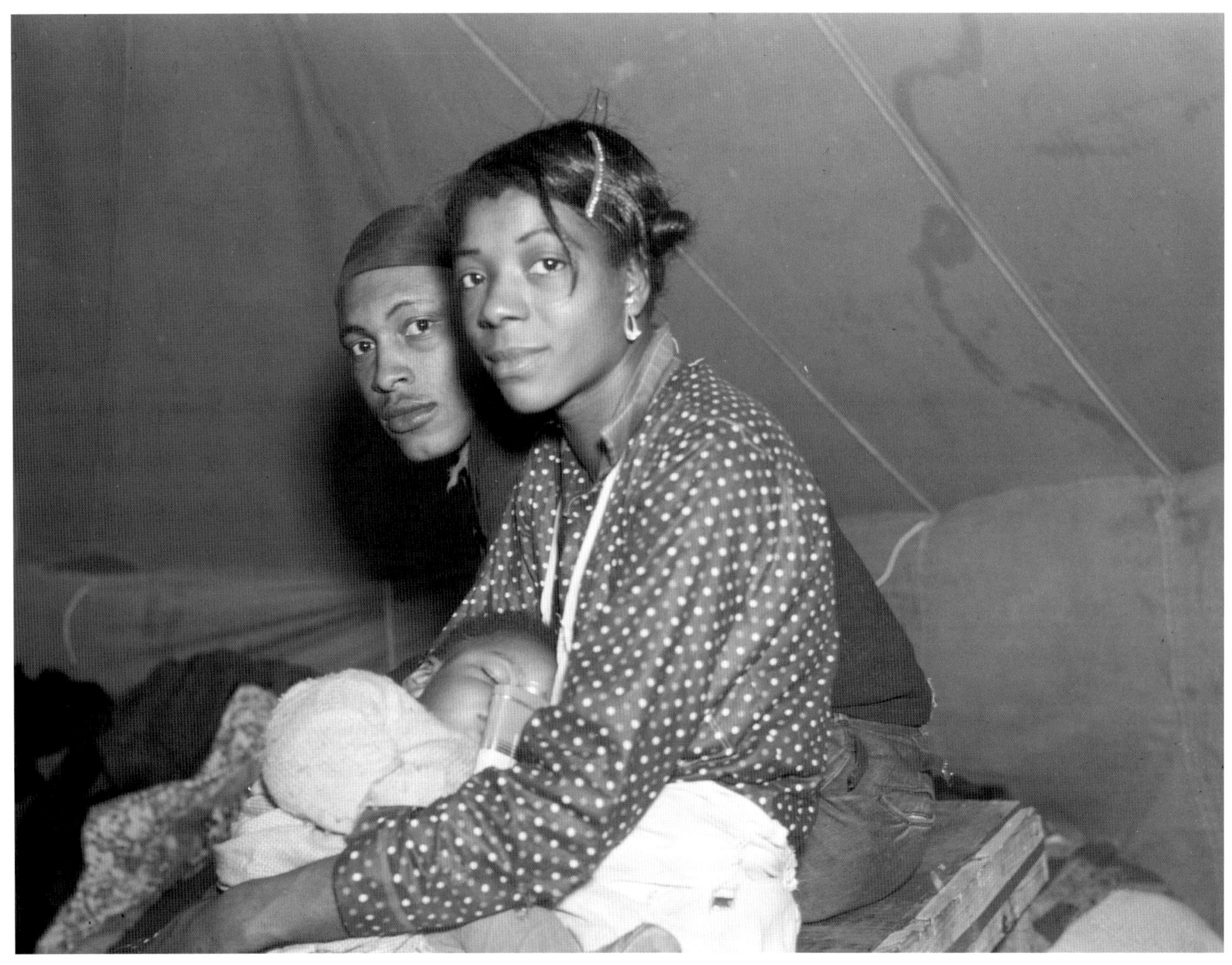

Flood refugees in their tent at the Marianna camp.

(Edwin Locke, February 1937) Farm Security Administration Photograph Collection, Prints & Photographs Division, Library of Congress, LC-USF34–013163–D

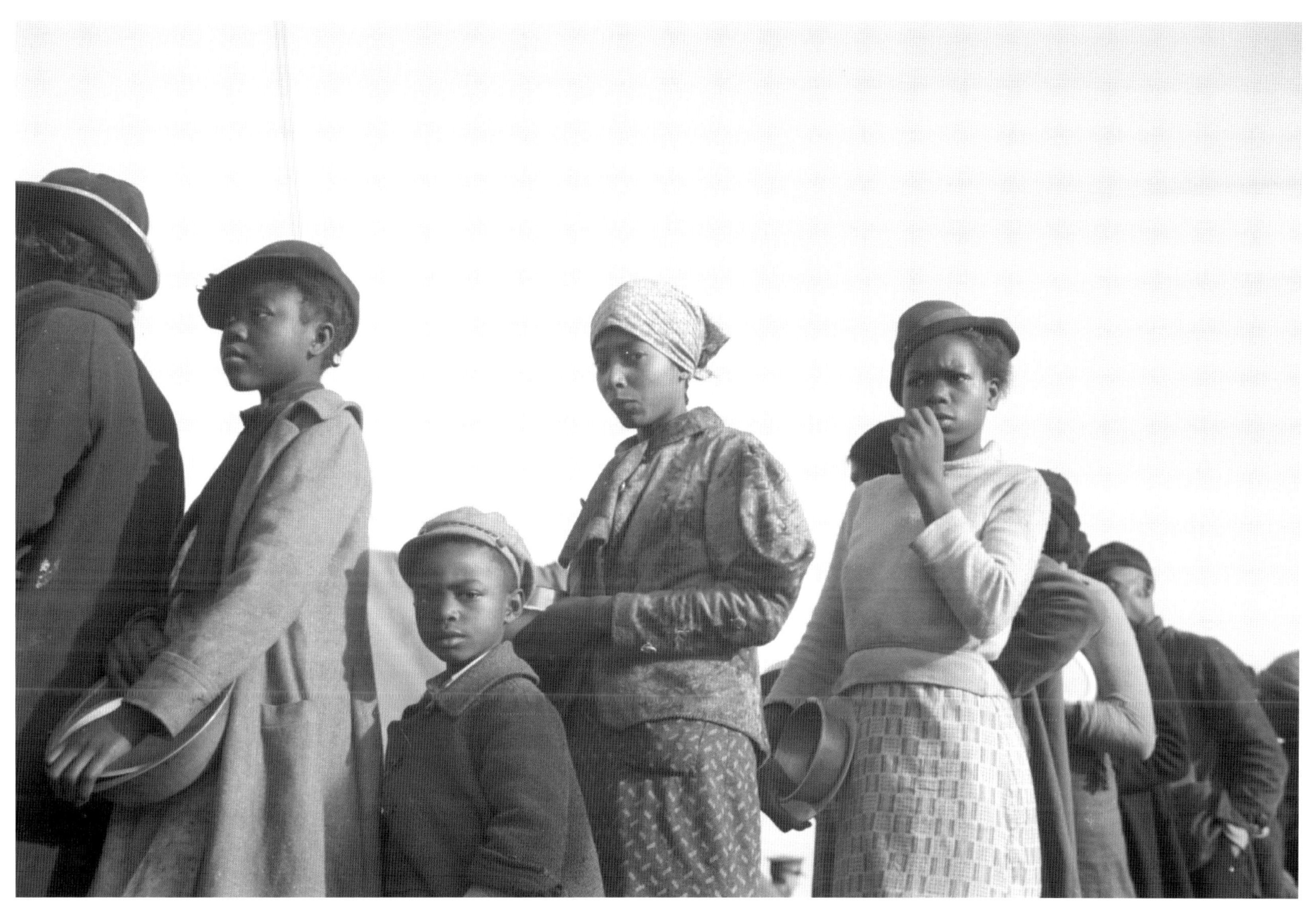

Flood refugees in the food line at the Forrest City camp.

(Walker Evans, February 1937) Farm Security Administration Photograph Collection, Prints & Photographs Division, Library of Congress, LC-USF33–009211–M4

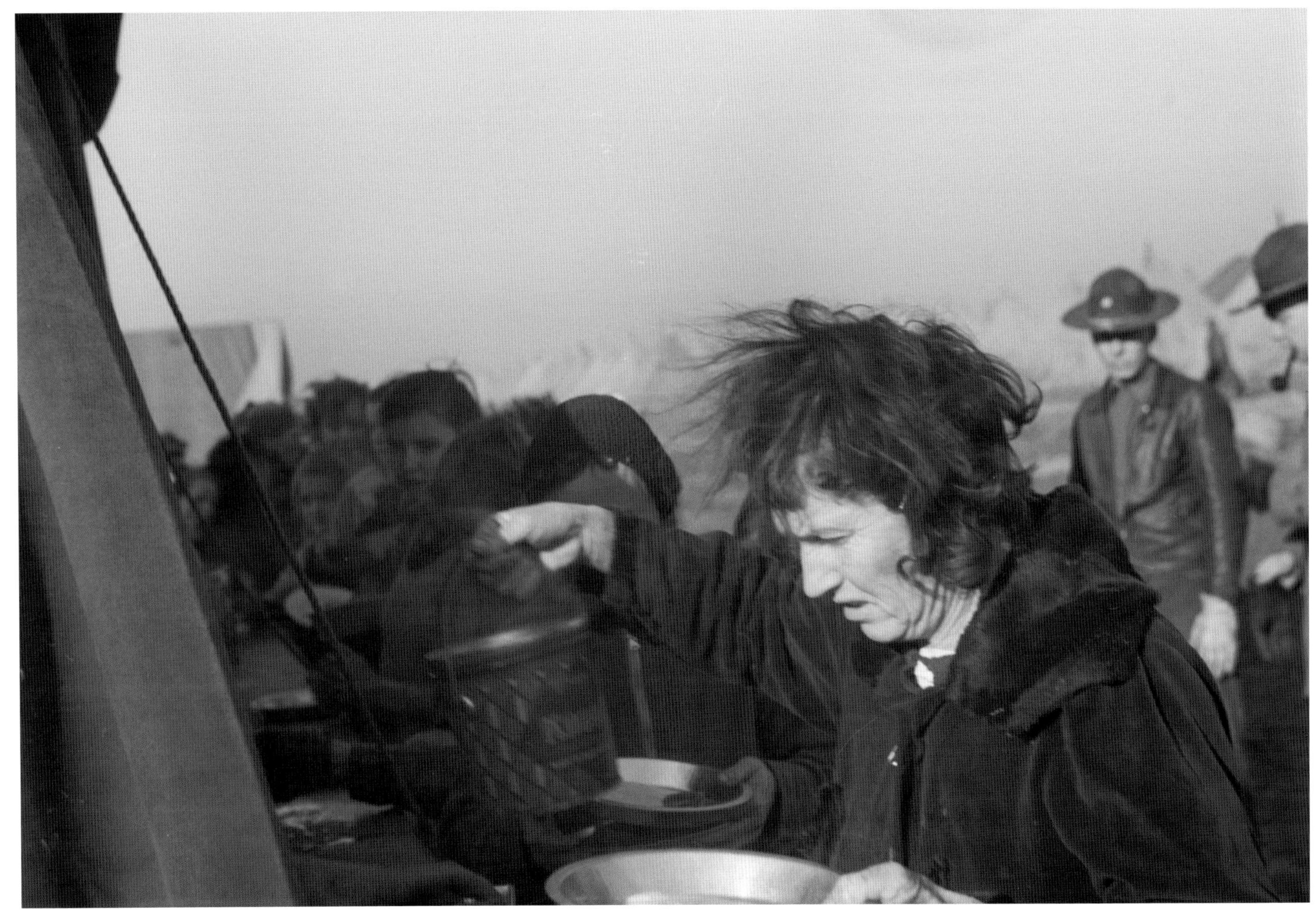

A woman serving herself in the food line.

(Edwin Locke, February 1937) Farm Security Administration Photograph Collection, Prints & Photographs Division, Library of Congress, LC-USF33–004216–M1

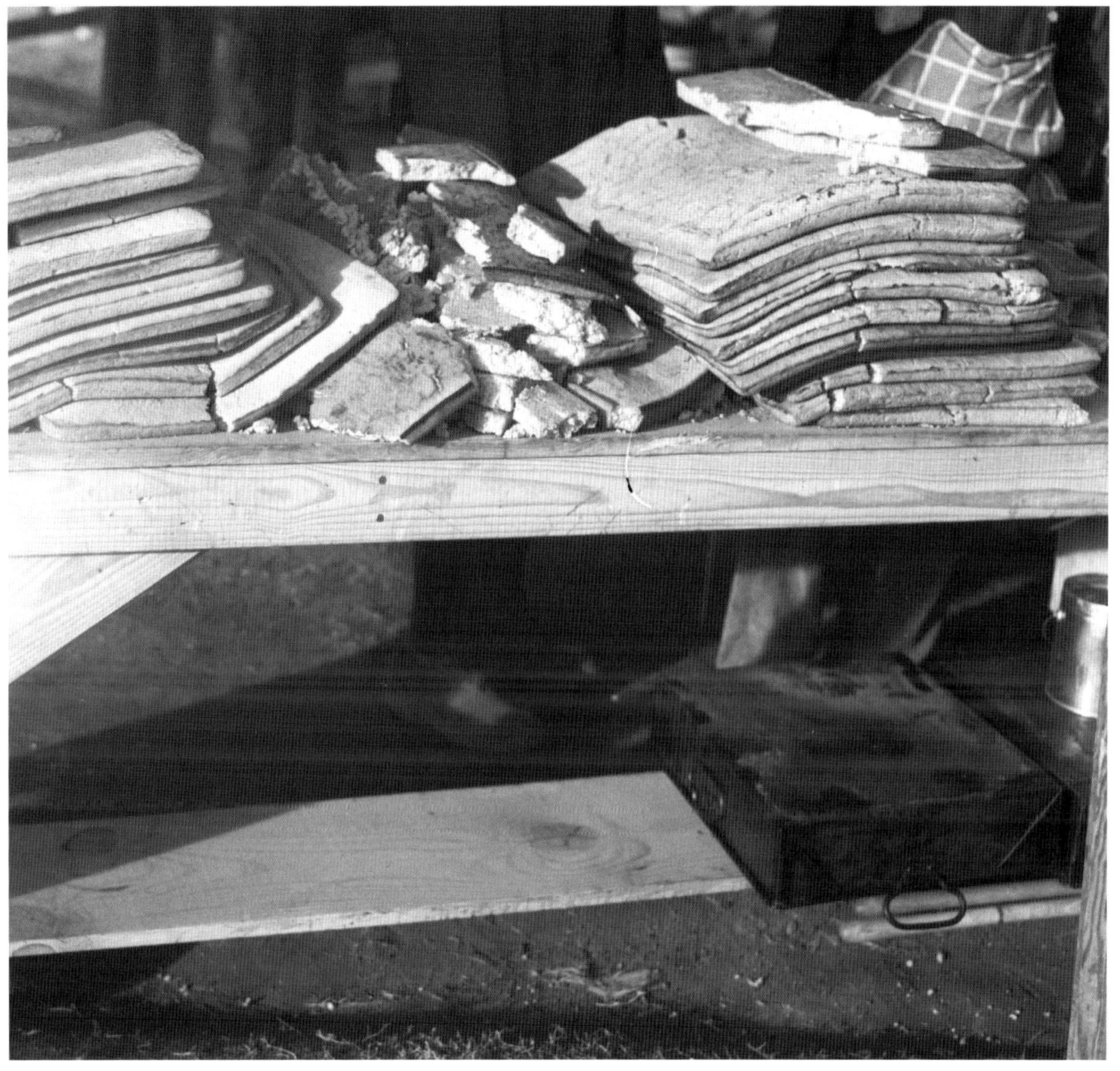

Stacks of cornbread prepared for refugees' meal in a camp.

(Walker Evans, February 1937) Farm Security Administration Photograph Collection, Prints & Photographs Division, Library of Congress, LC-USF34–008192–E

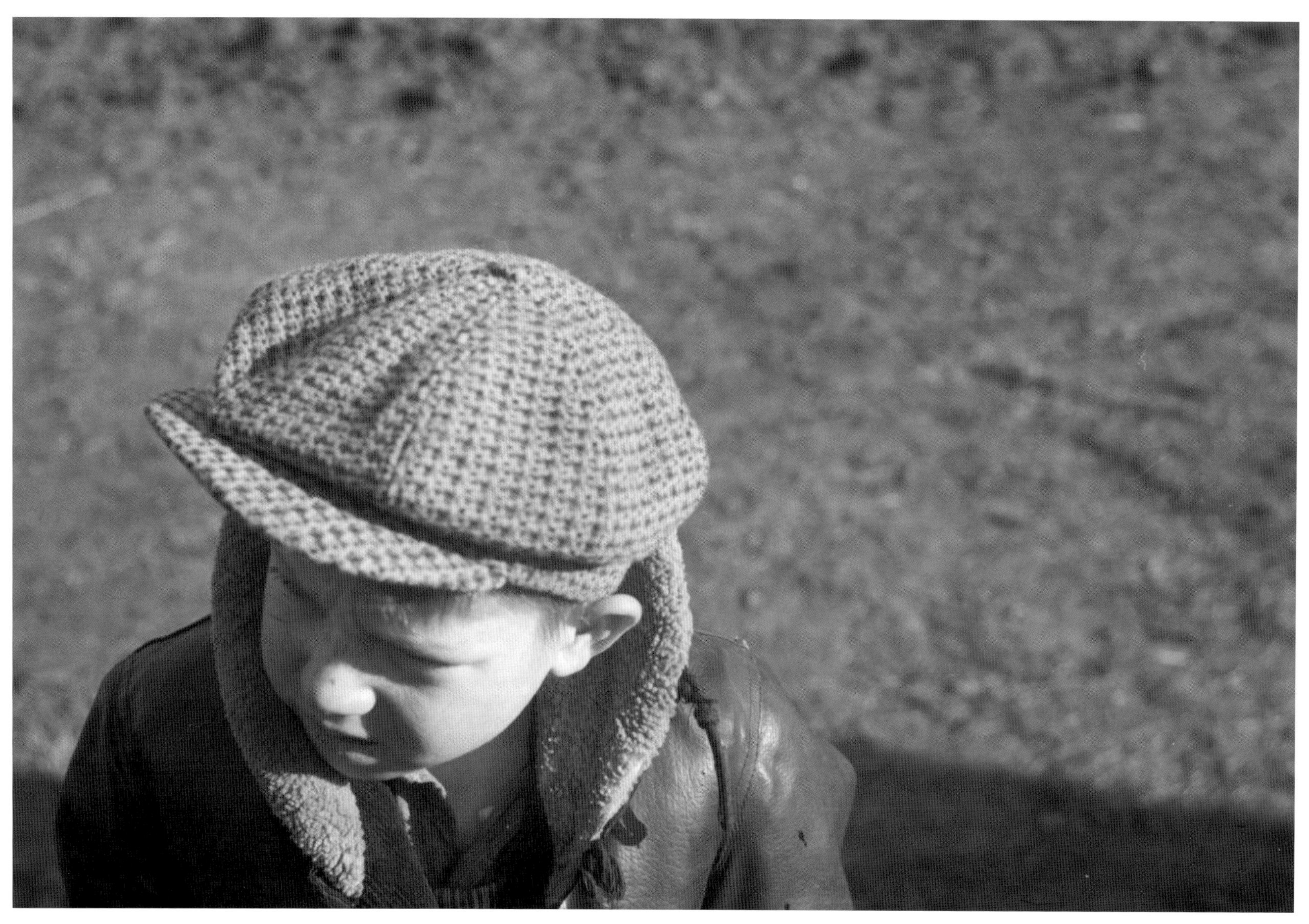

A young boy in the refugee camp at Forrest City waiting for food.

(Edwin Locke, February 1937) Farm Security Administration Photograph Collection, Prints & Photographs Division, Library of Congress, LC-USF33–004218–M4

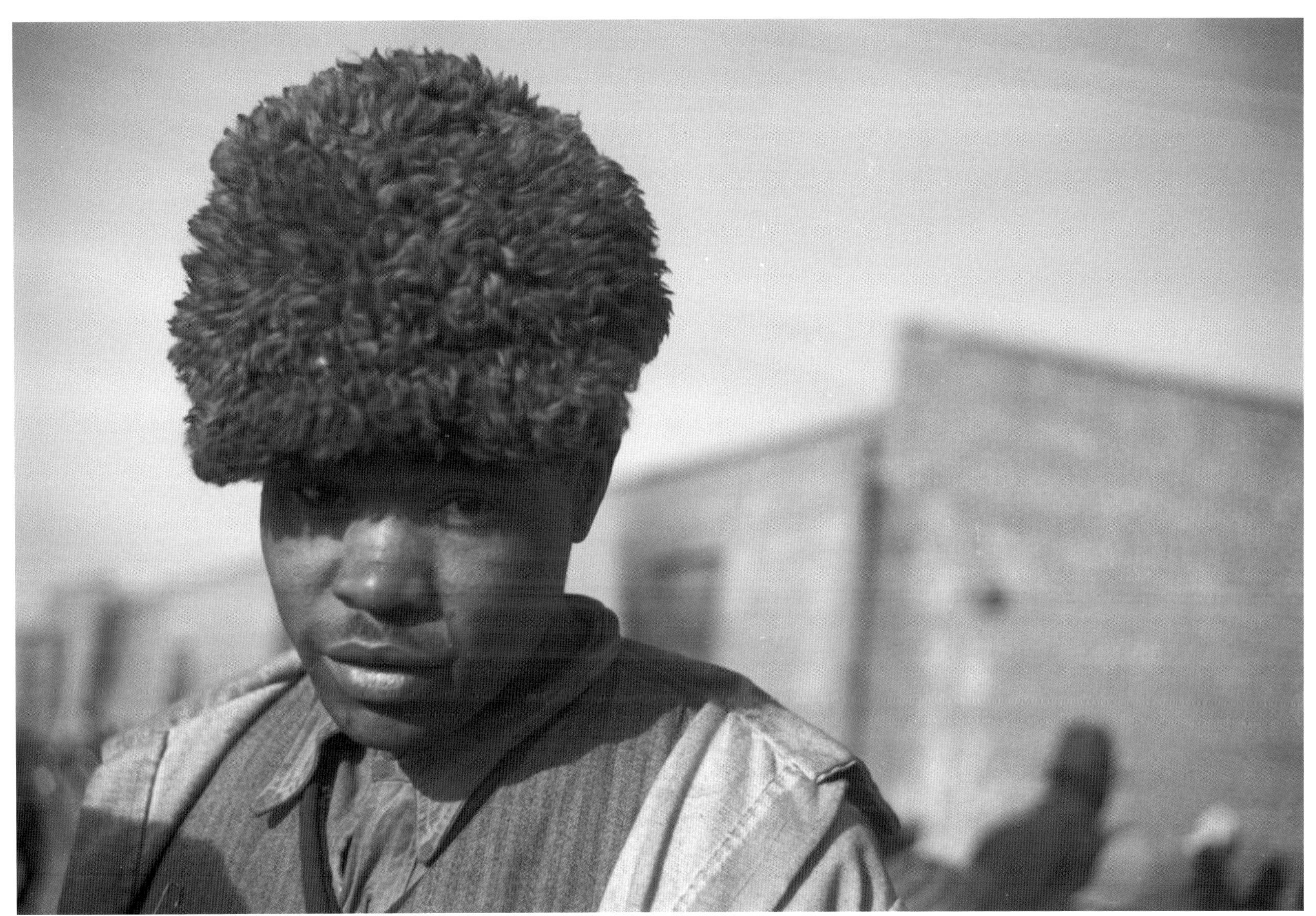

A young flood refugee and his hat.

(Walker Evans, February 1937) Farm Security Administration Photograph Collection, Prints & Photographs Division, Library of Congress, LC-USF33–009222–M4

NINE | SMALL TOWNS

ARKANSAS WAS NEARLY 80 percent rural in the 1930s, a state of small towns and farms linked by narrow blacktop and gravel roads. RA/FSA photographers spent a lot of time on these roads as their assignments often took them to government agricultural relief projects out in the country. "As they travel from project to project and from state to state, the Small Town is their daily environment: they drive through it, eat in it, sleep in it," wrote Edwin Rosskam, an RA/FSA photographer and editor, in his introduction to the Sherwood Anderson book *Home Town*. They also took photos of these small towns; "pictures of anything from gas stations to town meetings, from cattle auctions to church services."

As early as the fall of 1935 Roy Stryker had begun to think of the RA/FSA photography project as serving a purpose potentially more significant than as a publicity resource for the Resettlement Administration and other agencies. By enlarging their focus of the photos, the project could develop into a valuable historical archive of images documenting American life during the Depression. One of the ideas that expanded this reach arose from Stryker's meeting with an old friend, the sociologist Robert Lynd, who had coauthored *Middletown,* an important 1920s study on life in a small midwestern city. Jack Hurley (*Portrait of a Decade*) writes that Lynd convinced Stryker of a direct relationship between the way of life in small towns and the agency's emphasis on the problems of rural poverty. Stryker responded immediately by brainstorming ideas for photos of small towns.

The result was an extensive shooting script he circulated to photographers early in 1936, which broadened the dimensions of the photo project to a larger vision of American life in the 1930s. He asked photographers to look for "small-town" pictures when they were on assignments that more directly served the purposes of the agency. Samples of the shooting scripts, including the 1936 script and an updated one on small towns from 1939, are available in *The Likes of Us: America in the Eyes of the Farm Security Administration* by Stu Cohen and Peter Bacon Hales, and on the Library of Congress website.

Stryker's 1935 script was a lengthy list of ideas and images he associated with small-town life, including stores, inside and outside views and display windows, especially farming feed and seed stores; churches on Sunday; "court day" and the courthouse square; men loafing under trees; local baseball games; fences of all types; signs, on trees, barns, and in towns and villages; the country and the nature of the land with hills, mountains, and valleys; how people look; main street; ice cream parlors; railroad stations and watching the trains "go through"; sitting on the front porch.

The pictures of Arkansas small towns follow much of Stryker's script. They include nearly three dozen towns from Altheimer to Zinc, and primarily show downtown business areas in cities like Clarksville, Fayetteville, Rogers, and Fort Smith where people shop and pause to visit. In Jerome and Batesville, men gather in front of stores or the courthouse and "loaf." There are storefront signs and window displays in Marianna, Marked Tree, West Memphis, Pine Bluff, and Altheimer, and a few pictures of a church in Little Rock and small railroad stations. Most of the people in the photos probably considered themselves poor, but not as poor as Arkansans shown in the photos of tenants and sharecroppers and certainly of a better class.

The photos of towns suggest a similar pattern and rhythm of activity typical of their role as gathering places for carrying out the rituals of community, for trading information, and for commerce. But each town is unique in its details—idiosyncratic hand-painted signs, the shape of buildings around a square, and faces of people recognizable to anyone familiar with a certain town. Overall, the images capture some of the texture of small-town life at a certain time and place, documenting a social and physical environment and its values that Stryker sensed was fading away as America transformed from its traditional agrarian roots into an urbanized, mechanized, faster-paced, more worldly nation.

In 1973 when Stryker was in his eighties, he looked back on the small-town photographs and mused about their meaning for him. He told Nancy Wood, his collaborator on *In This Proud Land*, that through the photos, small towns appeared to "[possess] emotional and esthetic advantages: kinship with nature and the seasons, neighborliness, kindliness, spaciousness." That is, the photos implied towns were wholesome, pleasant places to live, based on traditional American values and where people took care of one another. However, Stryker emphasized that was only part of the story. Small towns also had disadvantages that were not easily visible: "laziness, pompousness, narrowness, lack of economic and cultural freedom." They could be mean, focused on class and caste, unwelcoming to those who were from the wrong racial, social, or economic group.

Despite those weaknesses, Stryker was nostalgic about the 1930s small towns—or rather, what they represented. To him they were symbols of a certain period in American history "when the world was safer and more peaceful. . . . [W]hen all there was to do was go down to the tracks and watch the [train] go through"—markers in time for measuring the changes in the nation that followed World War II. Though small towns and rural areas had been critical to the nation's food supply during the war, afterward they were not so important, and in losing their purpose they lost character. "A lot of people died and a lot of people moved away," Stryker said. "There settled over those little towns a permanent wistfulness." Or perhaps it was a melancholy for the myth of what small towns of the 1930s represented in the postwar years of transformation in the United States.

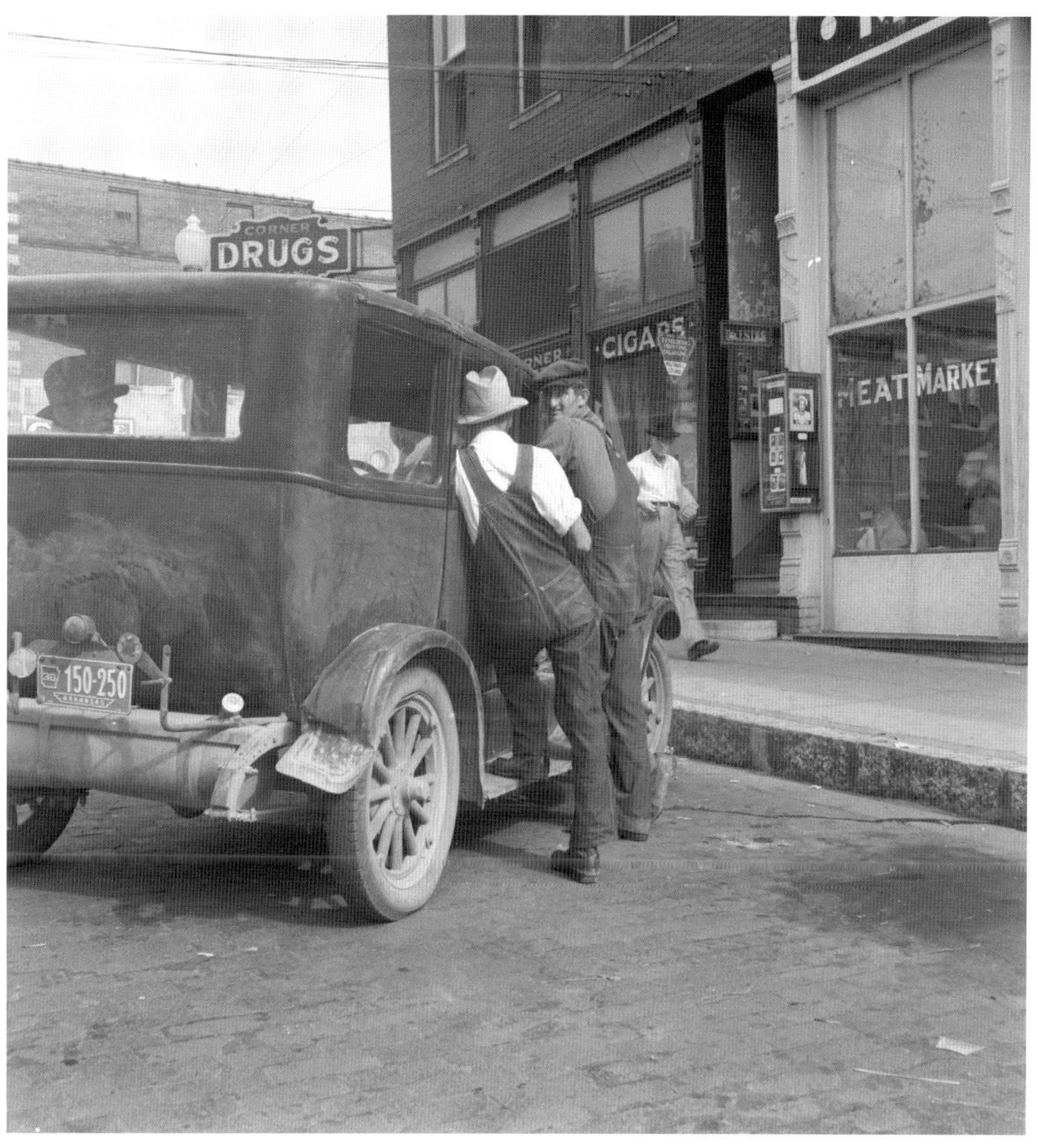

Downtown Rogers, 1938.

(Dorothea Lange, August 1938) Farm Security Administration Photograph Collection, Prints & Photographs Division, Library of Congress, LC-USF34–018972–E

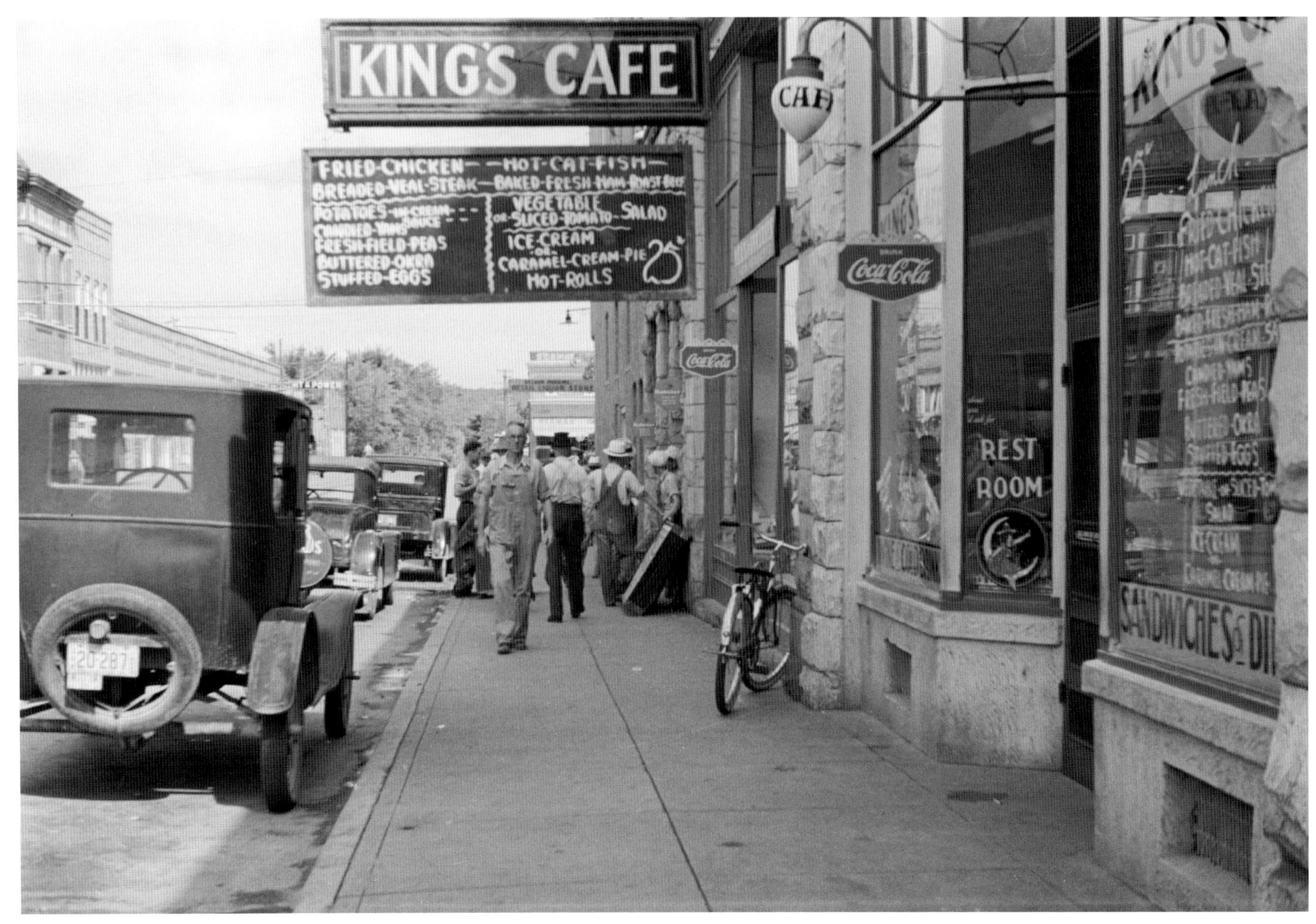

Signs on businesses at Clarksville, 1935.

(Arthur Rothstein, August 1935) Farm Security Administration Photograph Collection, Prints & Photographs Division, Library of Congress, LC-USF33–002016–M2

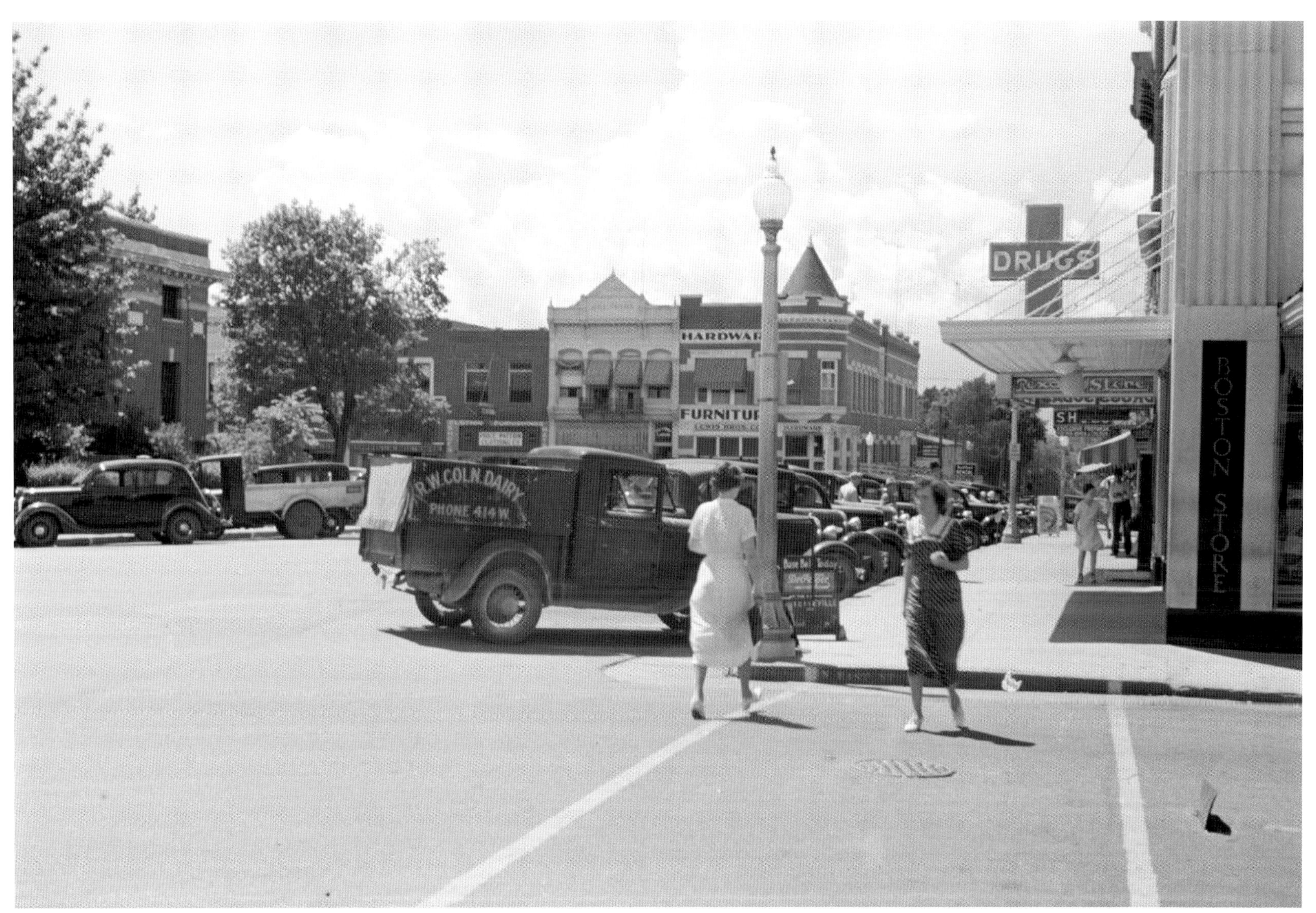

The square in Fayetteville, 1935.

(Arthur Rothstein, August 1935) Farm Security Administration Photograph Collection, Prints & Photographs Division, Library of Congress, LC-USF33–002017–M1

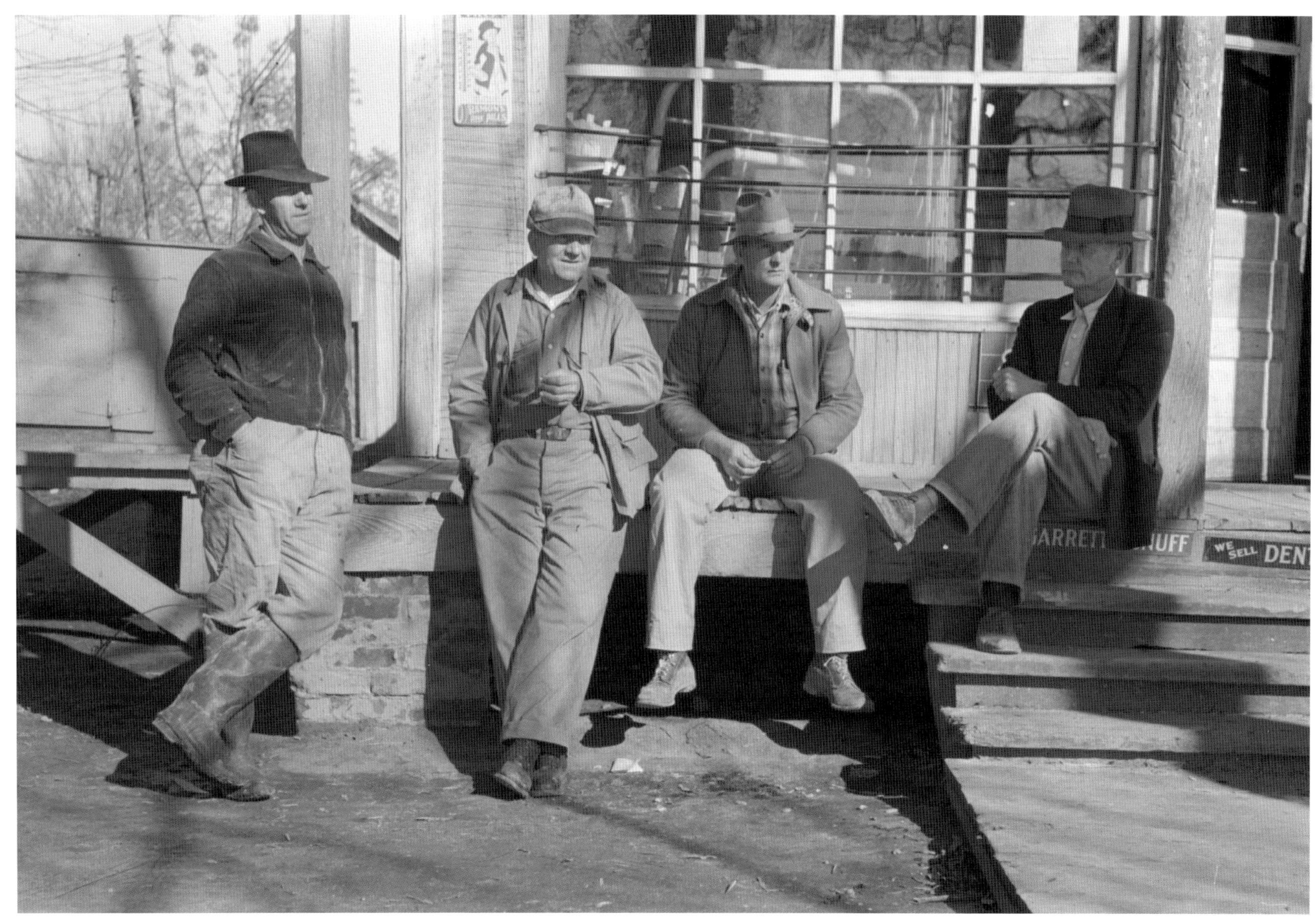

Men in front of the general store in Jerome, 1939.

(Russell Lee, January 1939) Farm Security Administration Photograph Collection, Prints & Photographs Division, Library of Congress, LC-USF33–011930–M1

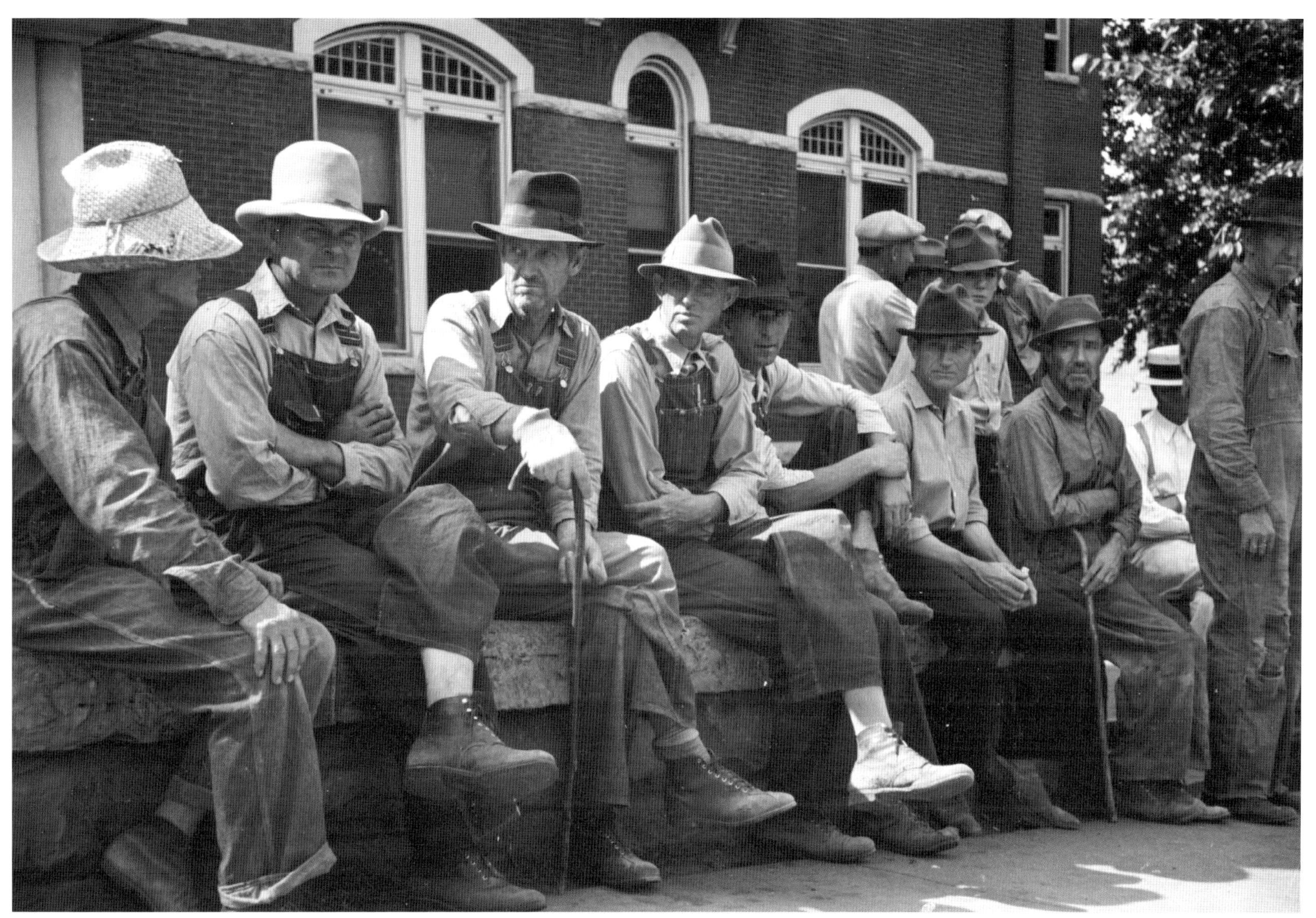

"Loafers' wall" near the courthouse in Batesville, county seat of Independence County. Carl Mydans wrote, "Once a few years ago a political situation was created when an attempt was made to remove the wall. It stays. When asked what they do there all day, one old fellow replied: 'W-all we all just a "set"; sometimes a few of 'em get up and move about to 'tother side when the sun gets too strong, the rest just "sets".'"

(Carl Mydans, June 1936) Farm Security Administration Photograph Collection, Prints & Photographs Division, Library of Congress, LC-USF33–000598–M4

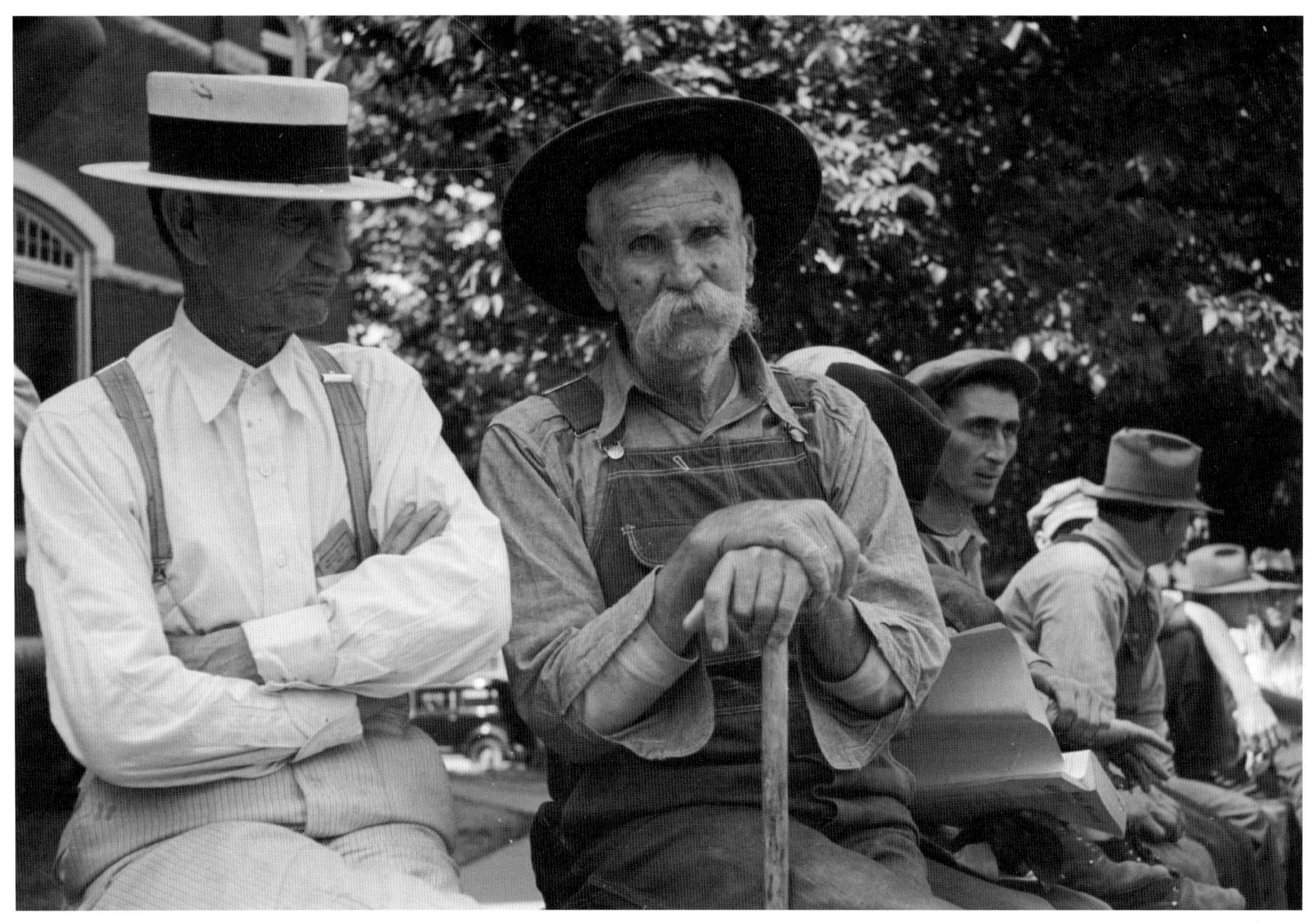

Men sat "from sun up until well into the night" on loafers' wall in Batesville.

(Carl Mydans, June 1936) Farm Security Administration Photograph Collection, Prints & Photographs Division, Library of Congress, LC-USF33–000598–M1

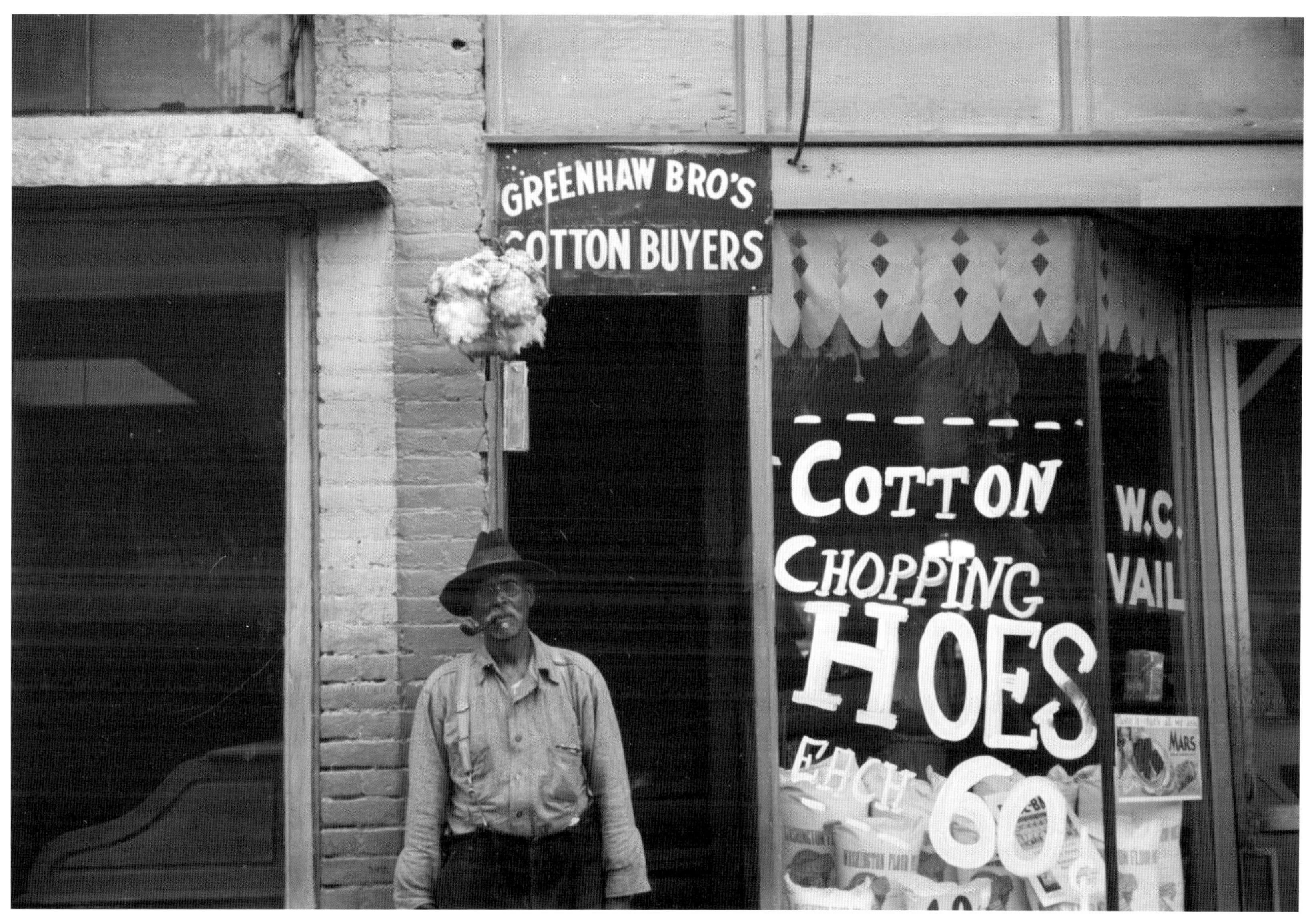

Hand-painted signs in Marianna, 1936.

(Carl Mydans, June 1936) Farm Security Administration Photograph Collection, Prints & Photographs Division, Library of Congress, LC-USF33–000596–M3

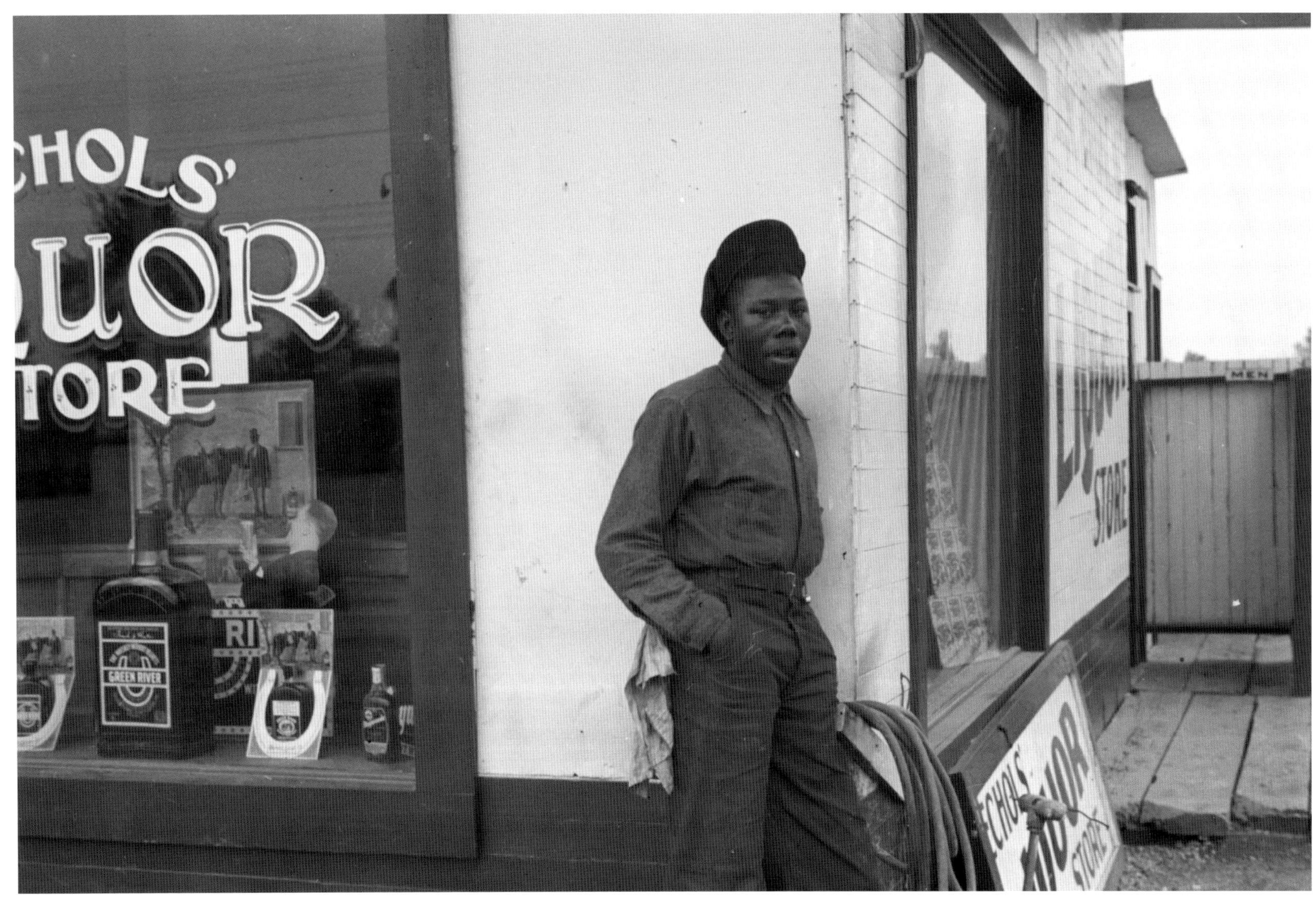

West Memphis, 1935.

(Ben Shahn, October 1935) Farm Security Administration Photograph Collection, Prints & Photographs Division, Library of Congress, LC-USF33–006084–M1

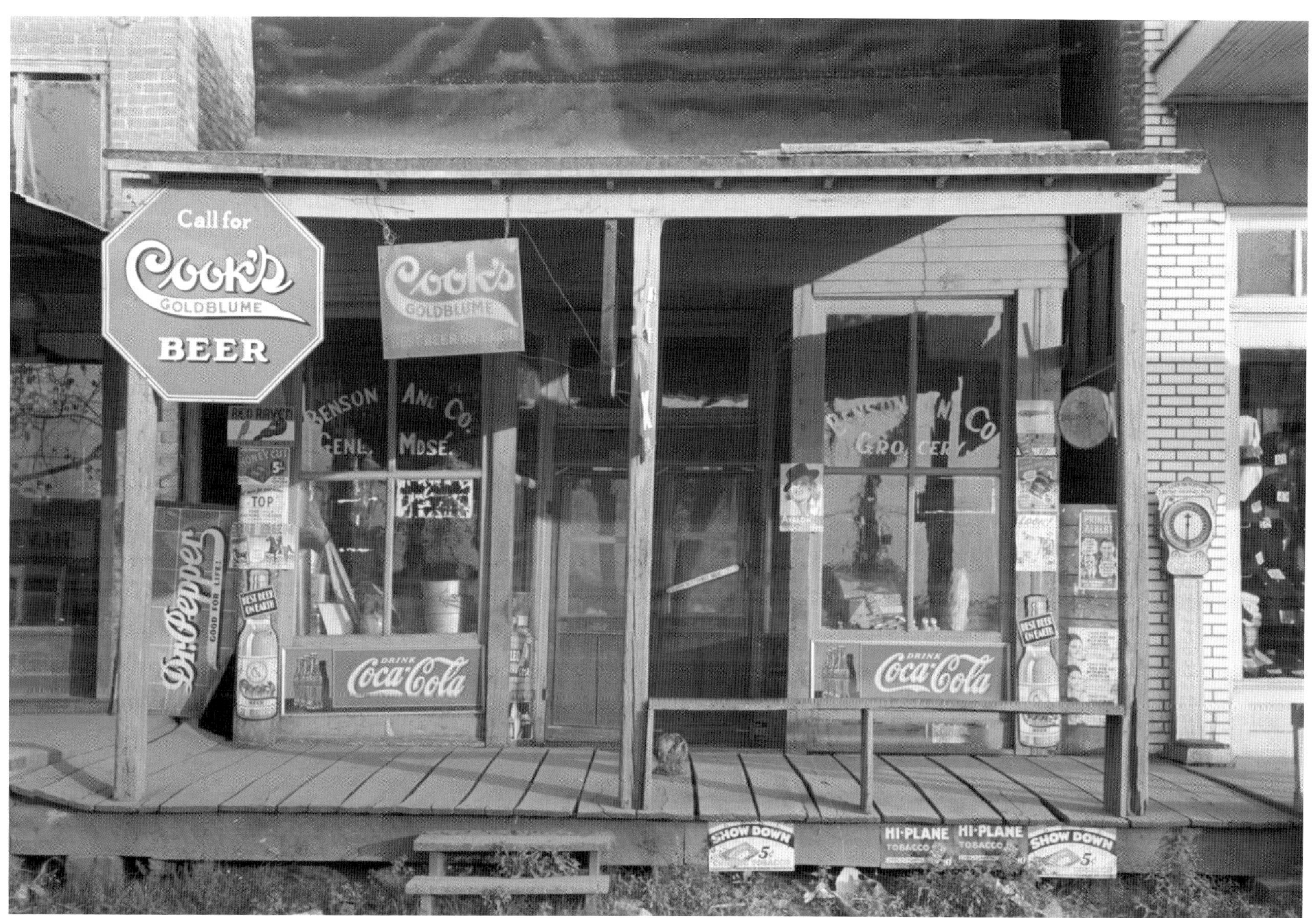

Storefront in Altheimer, 1938.

(Russell Lee, September–October 1938) Farm Security Administration Photograph Collection, Prints & Photographs Division, Library of Congress, LC-USF33–011695–M2

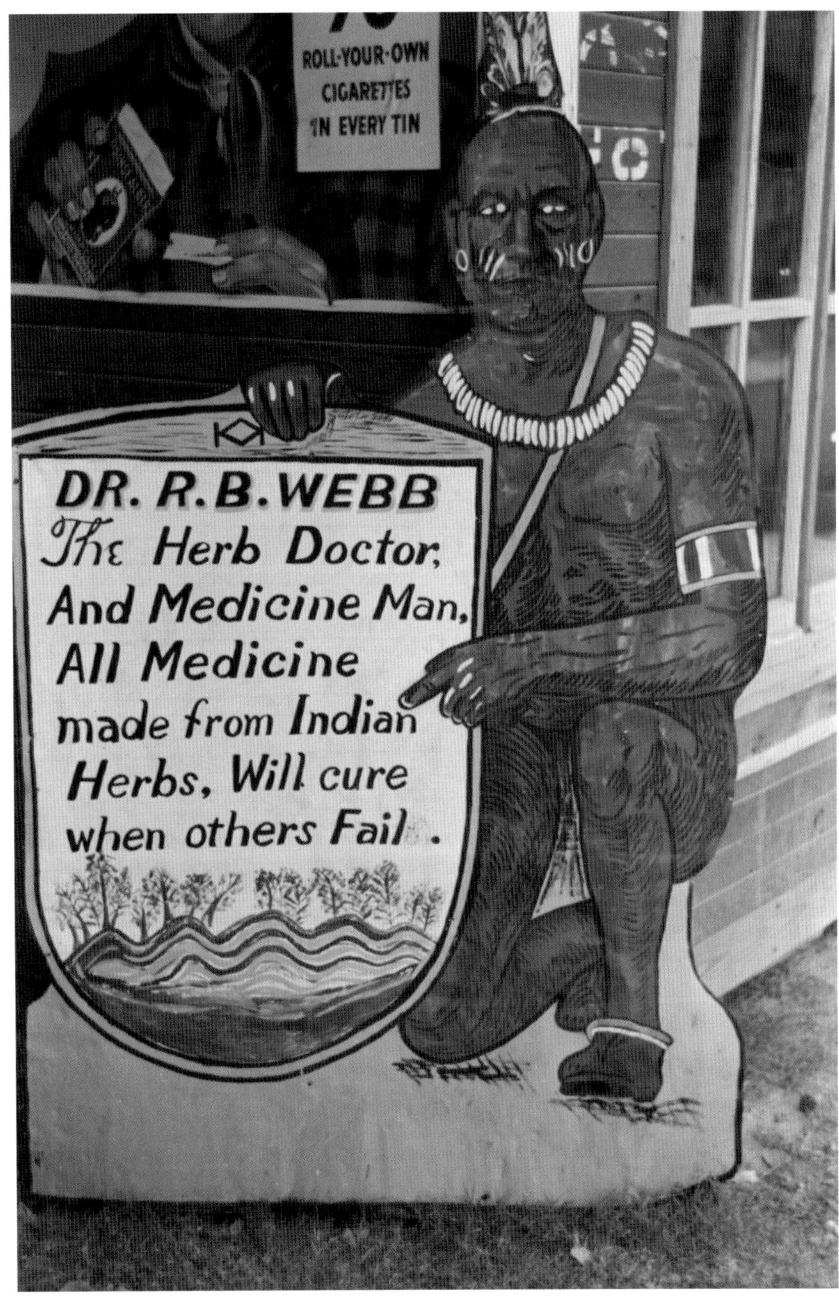

Sign for an herb doctor in Pine Bluff, 1938.

(Russell Lee, September–October 1938) Farm Security Administration Photograph Collection, Prints & Photographs Division, Library of Congress, LC-USF33–011697–M2

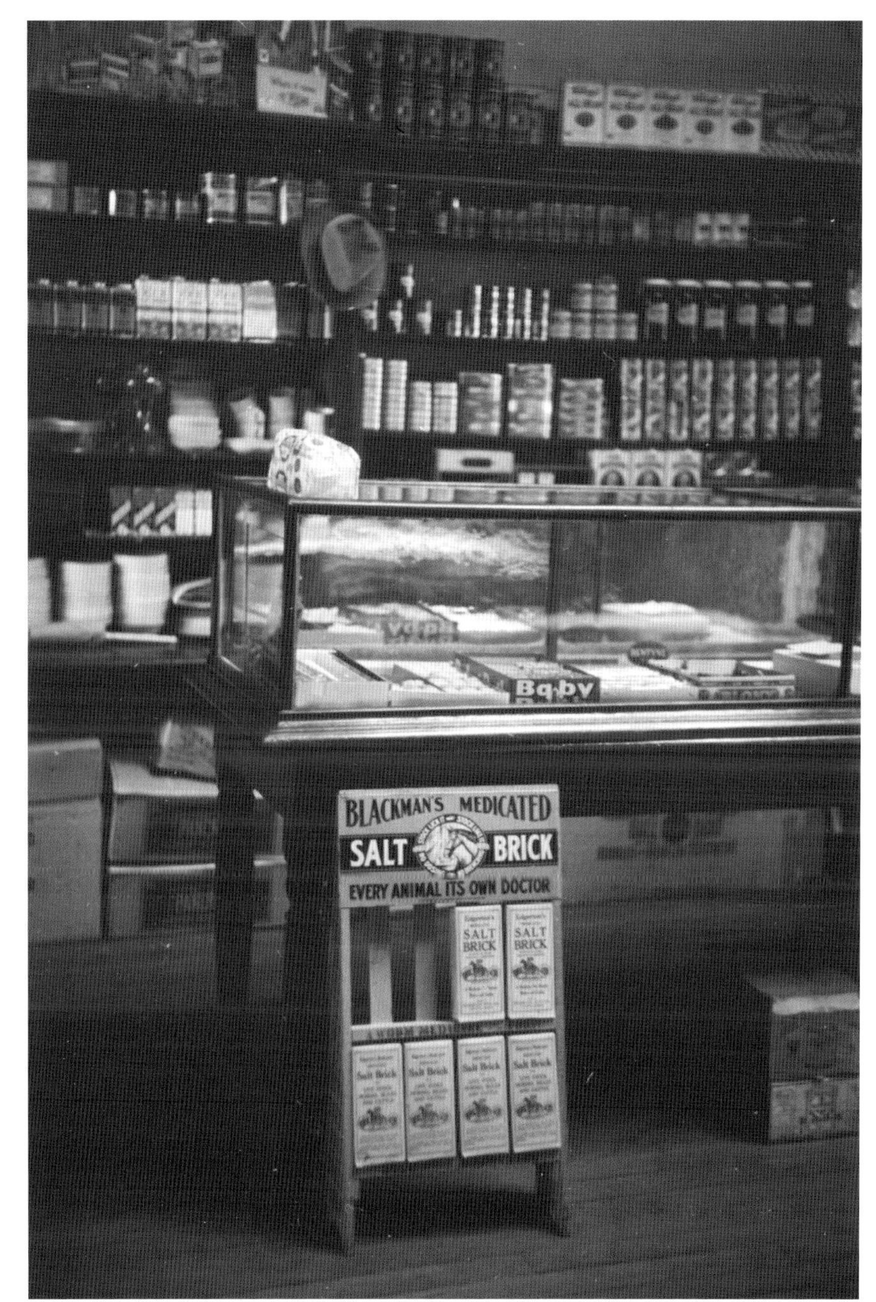

Goods in a Parkdale general store, 1936.

(Carl Mydans, June 1936) Farm Security Administration Photograph Collection, Prints & Photographs Division, Library of Congress, LC-USF33–000670–M1

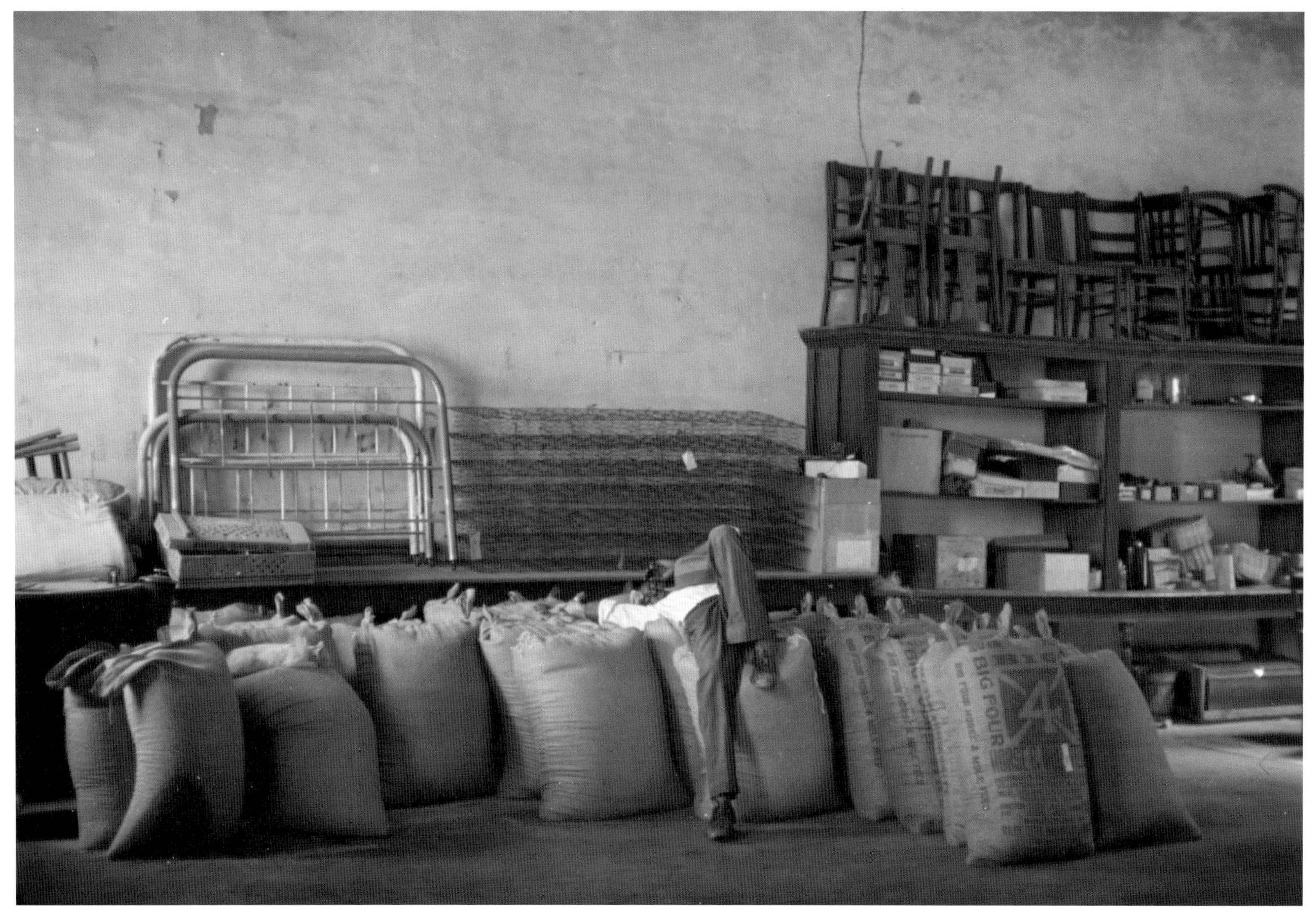

Man relaxing on sacks of horse and mule feed in a Parkdale store, 1936.

(Carl Mydans, June 1936) Farm Security Administration Photograph Collection, Prints & Photographs Division, Library of Congress, LC-USF33–000670–M3

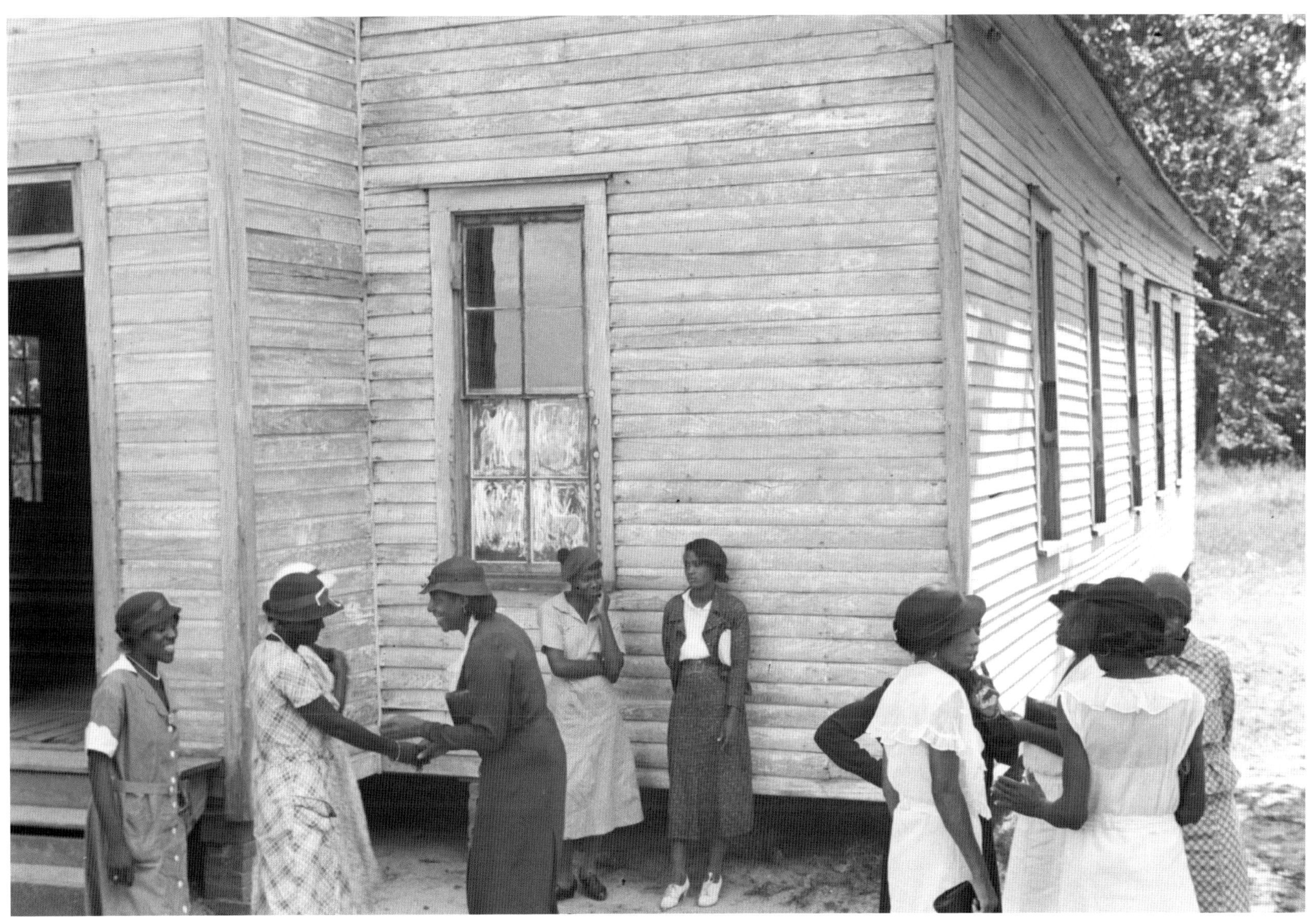

People visiting outside a church on a Sunday in Little Rock.

(Ben Shahn, October 1935) Farm Security Administration Photograph Collection, Prints & Photographs Division, Library of Congress, LC-USF33–006023–M1

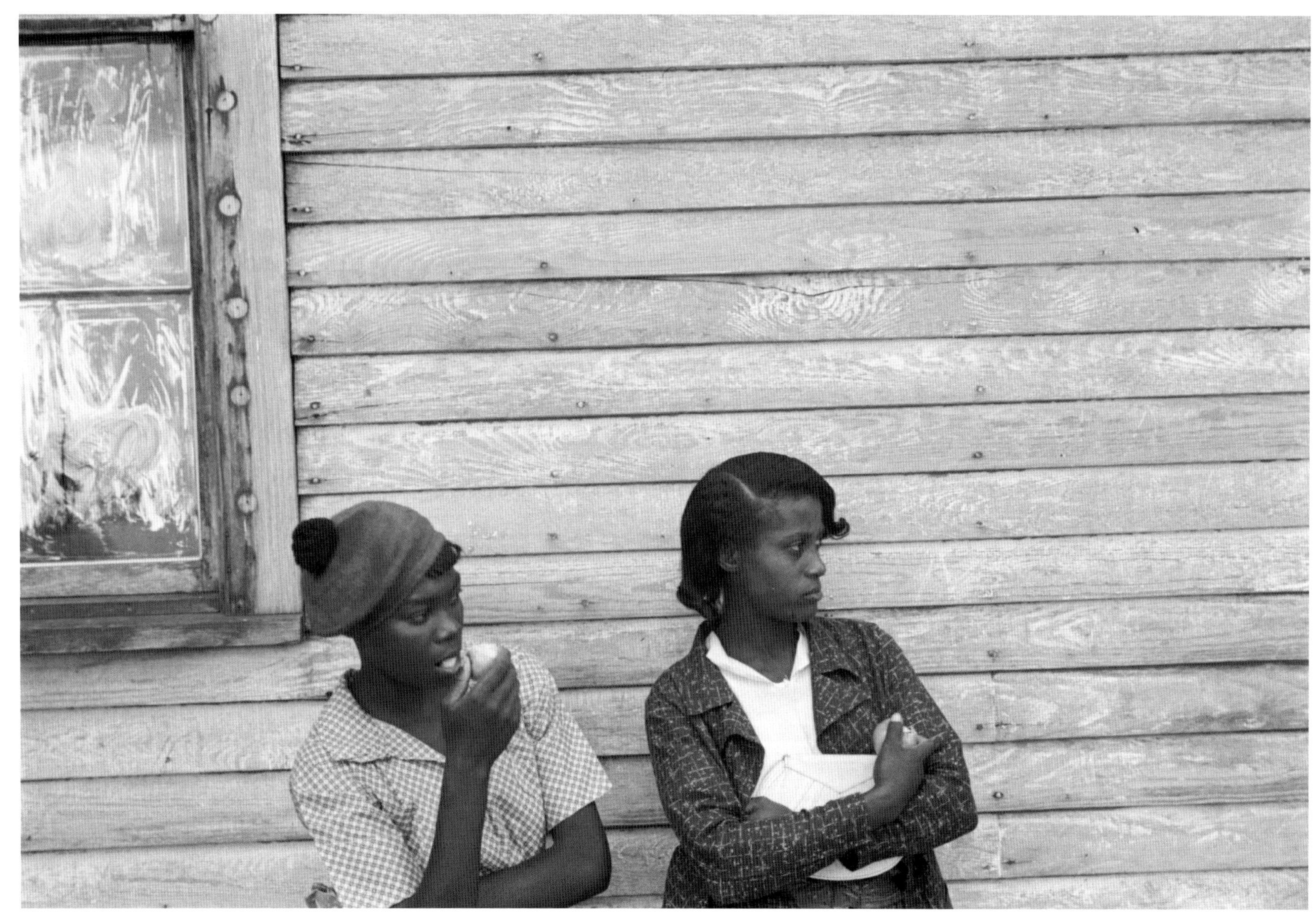

Outside church on Sunday in Little Rock.

(Ben Shahn, October 1935) Farm Security Administration Photograph Collection, Prints & Photographs Division, Library of Congress, LC-USF33–006024–M1

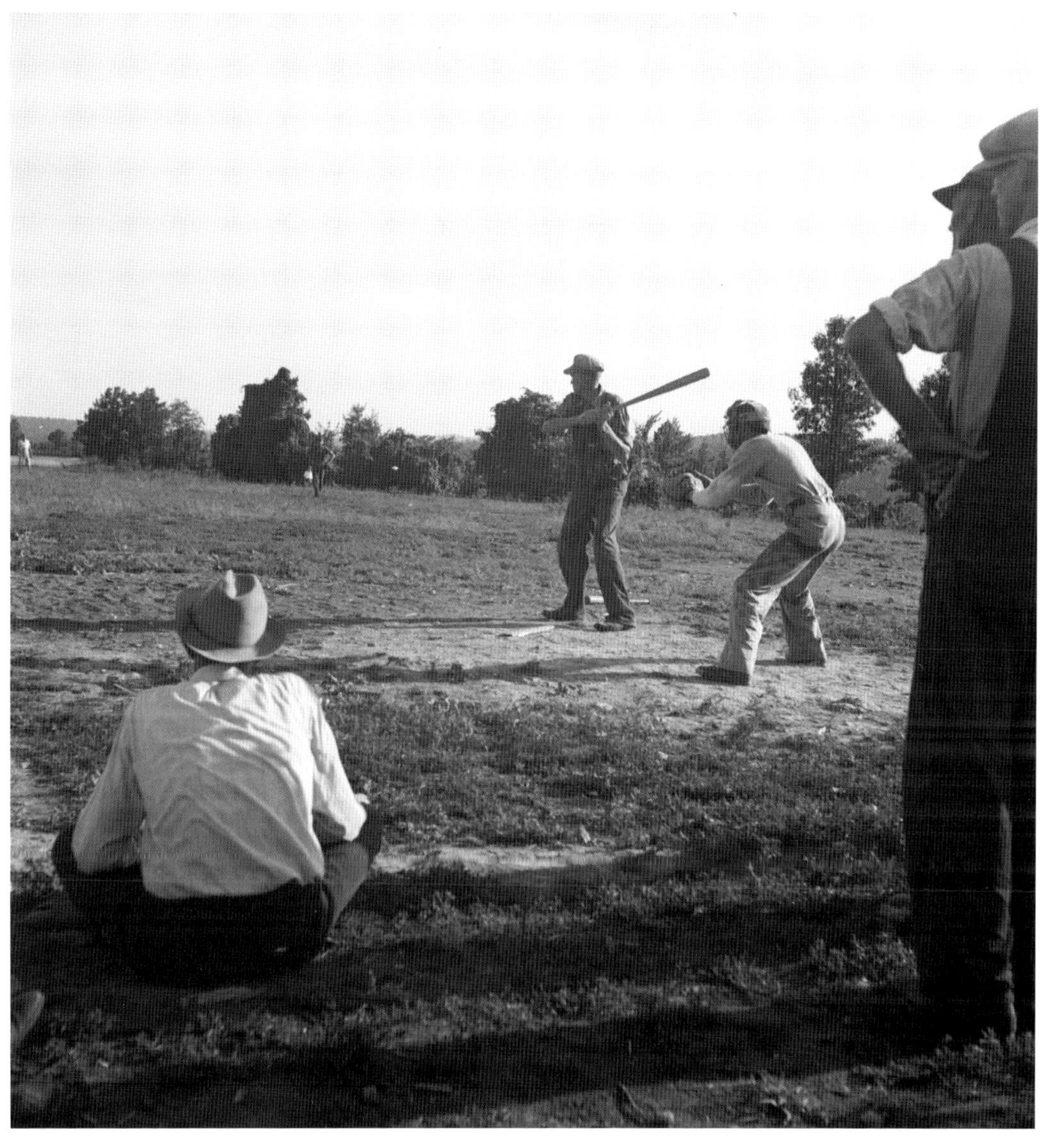

Farmers playing baseball near Mountain Home on US 62 in northern Arkansas. Dorothea Lange wrote that many from the area had gone to California to work in agriculture.

(Dorothea Lange, August 1938) Farm Security Administration Photograph Collection, Prints & Photographs Division, Library of Congress, LC-USF34–018962–E

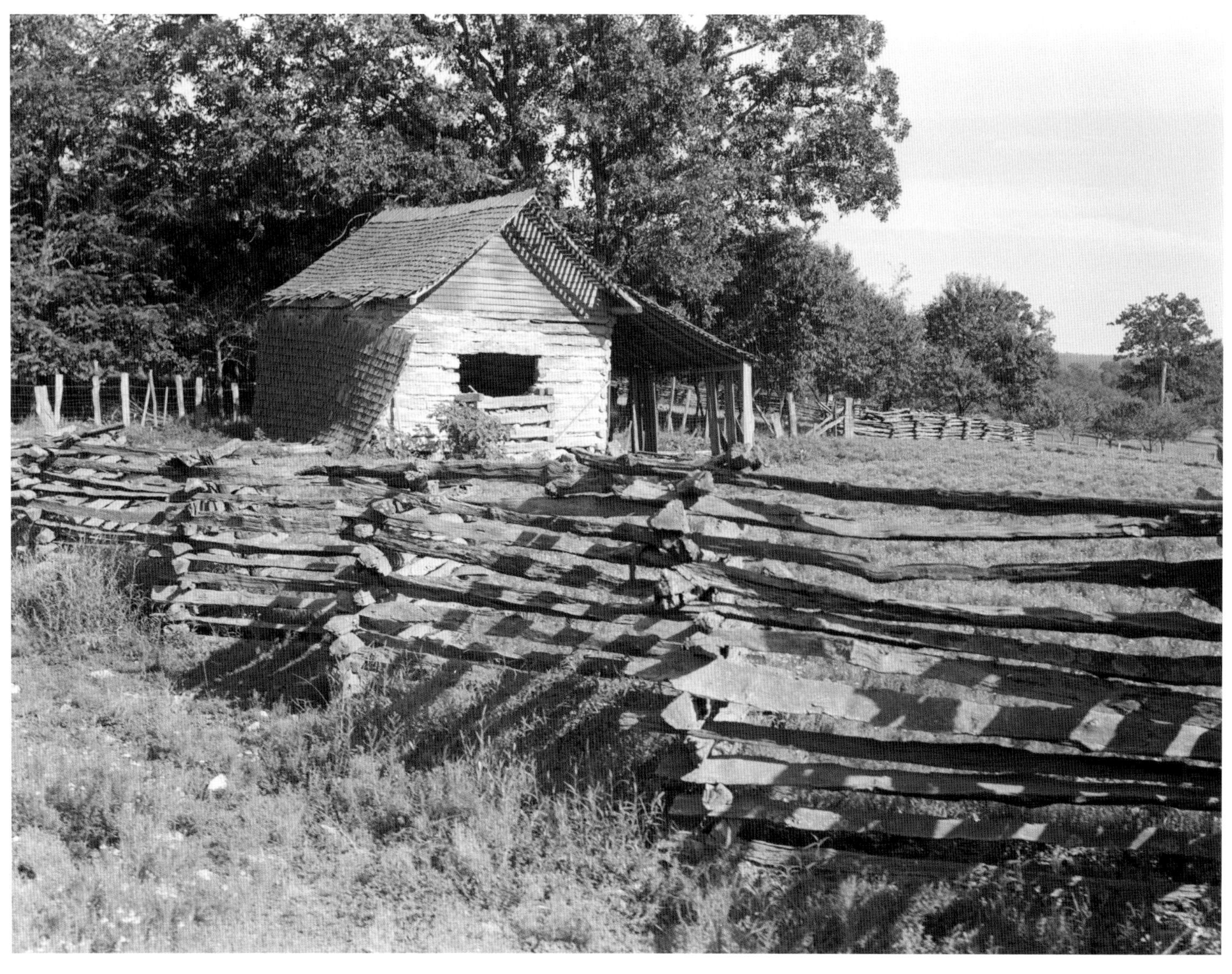

Split-log fence on US 62, 1938.

(Dorothea Lange, August 1938) Farm Security Administration Photograph Collection, Prints & Photographs Division, Library of Congress, LC-USF34–018968–E

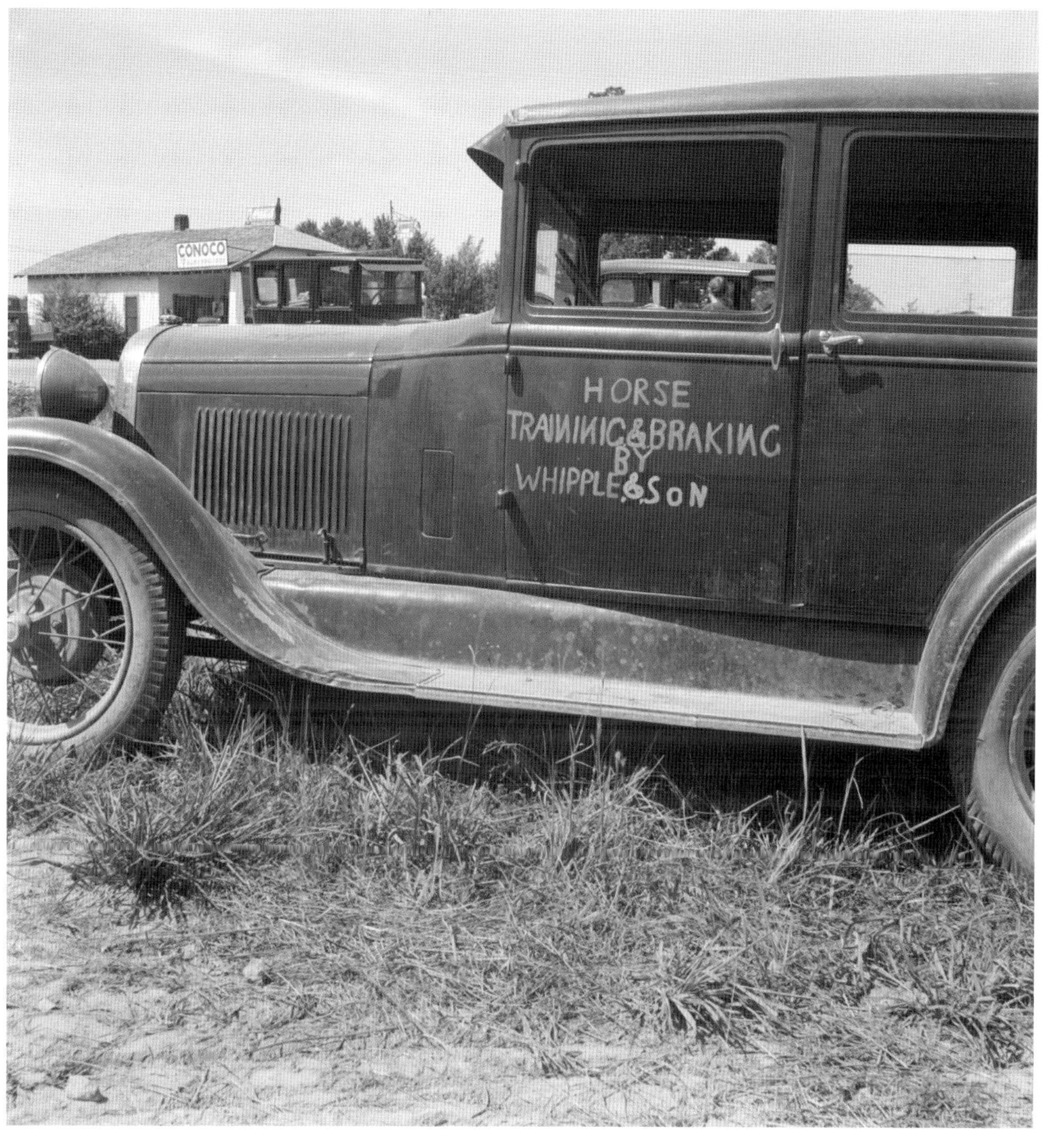

Handmade mobile advertising in north-central Arkansas, 1938.

(Dorothea Lange, August 1938) Farm Security Administration Photograph Collection, Prints & Photographs Division, Library of Congress, LC-USF34–018973–E

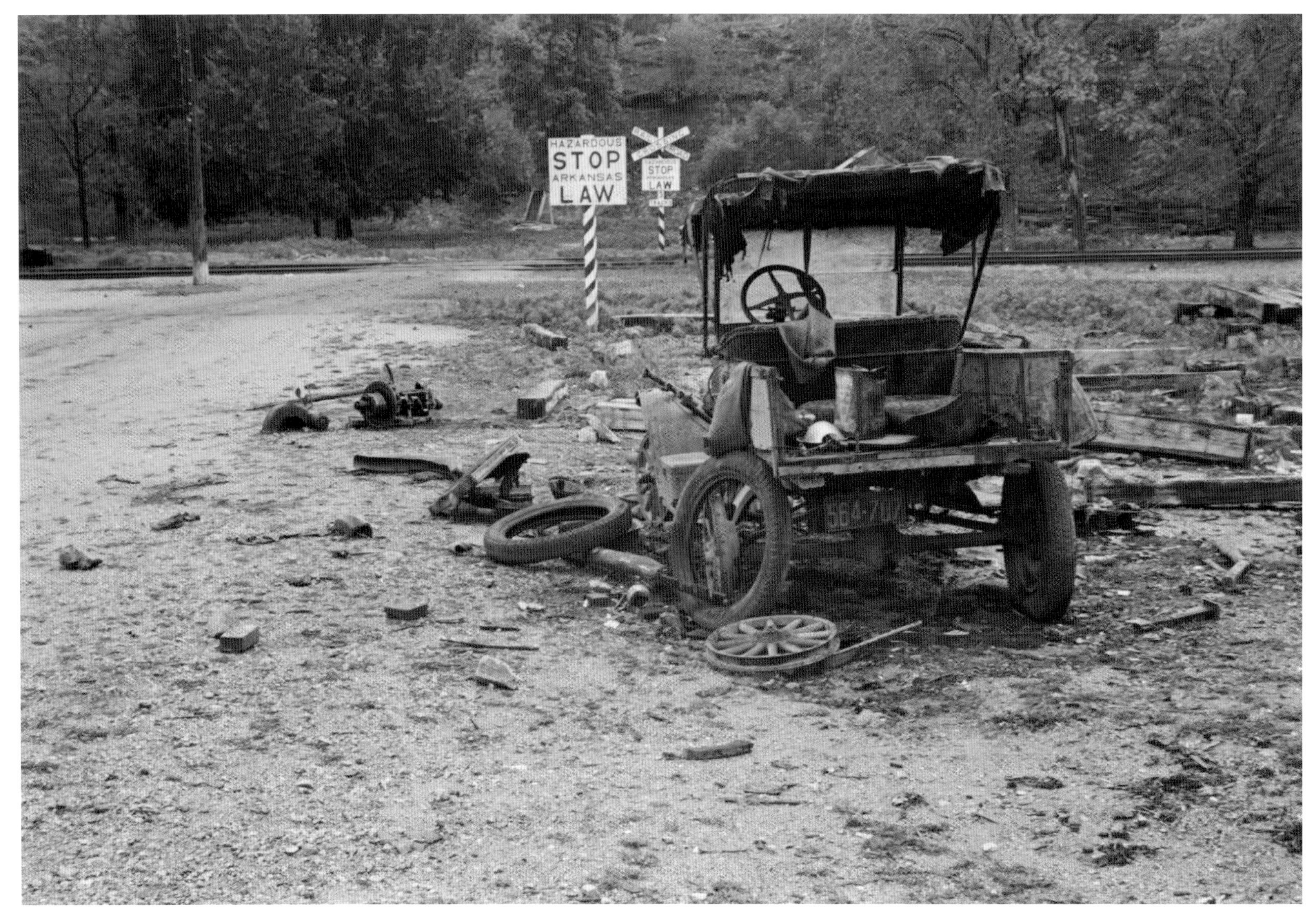

Outside Zinc in Boone County, 1935.

(Ben Shahn, October 1935) Farm Security Administration Photograph Collection, Prints & Photographs Division, Library of Congress, LC-USF33–006036–M3

TEN | PORTRAITS

IF ONE PERSON could speak knowledgeably about the quarter of a million images in the RA/FSA photography collection, it was Roy Stryker. In the 1973 book, *In This Proud Land,* he mused over the meaning and significance of the project with Nancy Wood:

> But the faces to me were the most significant part of the file. When a man is down and they have taken from him his job and his land and his home—everything he spent his life working for—he's going to have the expression of tragedy permanently on his face. But I have always believed that the American people have the ability to endure. And that is in those faces, too.

These faces are seen in the portraits throughout the collection, many of them among the "immortal pictures," as Richard Doud characterized them in his 1960s interviews with Stryker. Or as Stryker put it, the photos that "give your heart a tug." Most of the pictures in the file were the routine assignments demonstrating the good work done by New Deal agencies; they were straightforward records of activities, something like the photojournalism that Stryker called the "nouns and verbs" of photography. The portraits, however, were the best of the "adjectives and adverbs" that he said were "our kind of photography"; that is, the particular RA/FSA style. They were among the images that Stryker thought would prove to be of greatest value in the end, though they might have been overlooked in the 1930s. "You can't have perspective when history is your bedfellow," he told Wood.

The portraits are indeed among those most appealing to us now, the ones that offer a path to a deeper understanding of the lives of ordinary Arkansans in the 1930s. Ben Shahn knew this and told Doud in their 1962 interview that statistics alone couldn't convey the impact of the Depression to Americans as effectively as telling the story of one individual's experience. This chapter is a selection of those photos taken in Arkansas, the ones that may help us connect with those individual experiences. Some are among the better-known pictures associated with the Great Depression and have become a part of the record dedicated to the suffering and resilience of rural America. They are principally the work of Shahn, Dorothea Lange, and Russell Lee.

Shahn came to Arkansas in 1935 prepared to take pictures of cotton farming, bringing along a pile of books on cotton he had been studying. But overall, he was much more interested in the people he found and in their humanity rather than in their role in cotton cultivation. Shahn's skill at taking a photograph at just the right moment, catching a revealing gesture or the fleeting look in a person's eyes, reflected his admiration for the French photographer Henri Cartier-Bresson, who was known for his ability to anticipate the "peak moment of action" for pressing the shutter. Shahn's mastery of this technique can be seen in his Arkansas photographs, particularly among those of his most familiar images—the Boone County rehabilitation client, the few remaining residents of Zinc, and his share-croppers and cotton pickers.

Lange's portraits have a different quality from those of other RA/FSA photographers, but she of course had a different way of approaching her subjects, according to Anne Whiston Spirn, in *Daring to Look*. Whereas others sought an "honest image" by catching people off-guard through the use of right-angle camera devices or distractions, Lange's honest image meant having a direct connection with her subject. She told her apprentice Rondal [*sic*] Partridge, "I never steal a photograph. Never. All photographs are made in collaboration, as part of their thinking as well as mine." Her strongest Arkansas portrait was taken in Conway of an older woman sitting on her front porch; Lange called her "Arkansas Hoosier." Lesser known but yet intriguing is the photo of three women who are being transported from Memphis to an Arkansas plantation to do fieldwork. Lange's connection to these women and their response is the fulcrum of the photo that defines them as individuals.

Lee took only the occasional portrait in his many photos of resettlement farms, including a few of individual farmers. Though those pictures have Lee's particular touch of humanity, his more fascinating portraits don't even show faces. He told Jack Hurley in a 1973 interview, "I was interested in how people lived. . . . I felt that the inside of a house was a very important part of showing how people lived. Of course, the outside was important too. You could tell about people by how the flowers were placed and how things were kept up. I became concerned with details." Lee's portraits without faces included here show his search for comprehending the lives of two people in the details he captured in the photographs of a bedroom and of the bonnet, hands, and posture of a cotton picker.

In *Portrait of a Decade* Hurley relates a story about John Steinbeck visiting the RA/FSA offices in 1938 and stating he wanted to do a book on migrant labor. According to C. B. Baldwin, FSA assistant administrator at the time, Steinbeck was referred to Stryker, who spent several days with him going through the photo file. An FSA official then took him into the field, dressed as a migrant worker. From these experiences, Steinbeck produced *The Grapes of Wrath*, which was published in 1939. Baldwin considered the book and subsequent movie as terrific promotion for the FSA.

Stryker also recalled the incident and talked about it with Wood in *In This Proud Land*:

> I remember when Steinbeck came in and looked at the pictures for a couple of days. Those tragic, beautiful faces were what inspired him to write *The Grapes of Wrath*. He caught in words everything the photographers were trying to say in pictures. Dignity versus despair. Maybe I'm a fool, but I believe that dignity wins out. When it doesn't, then we as a people will become extinct.

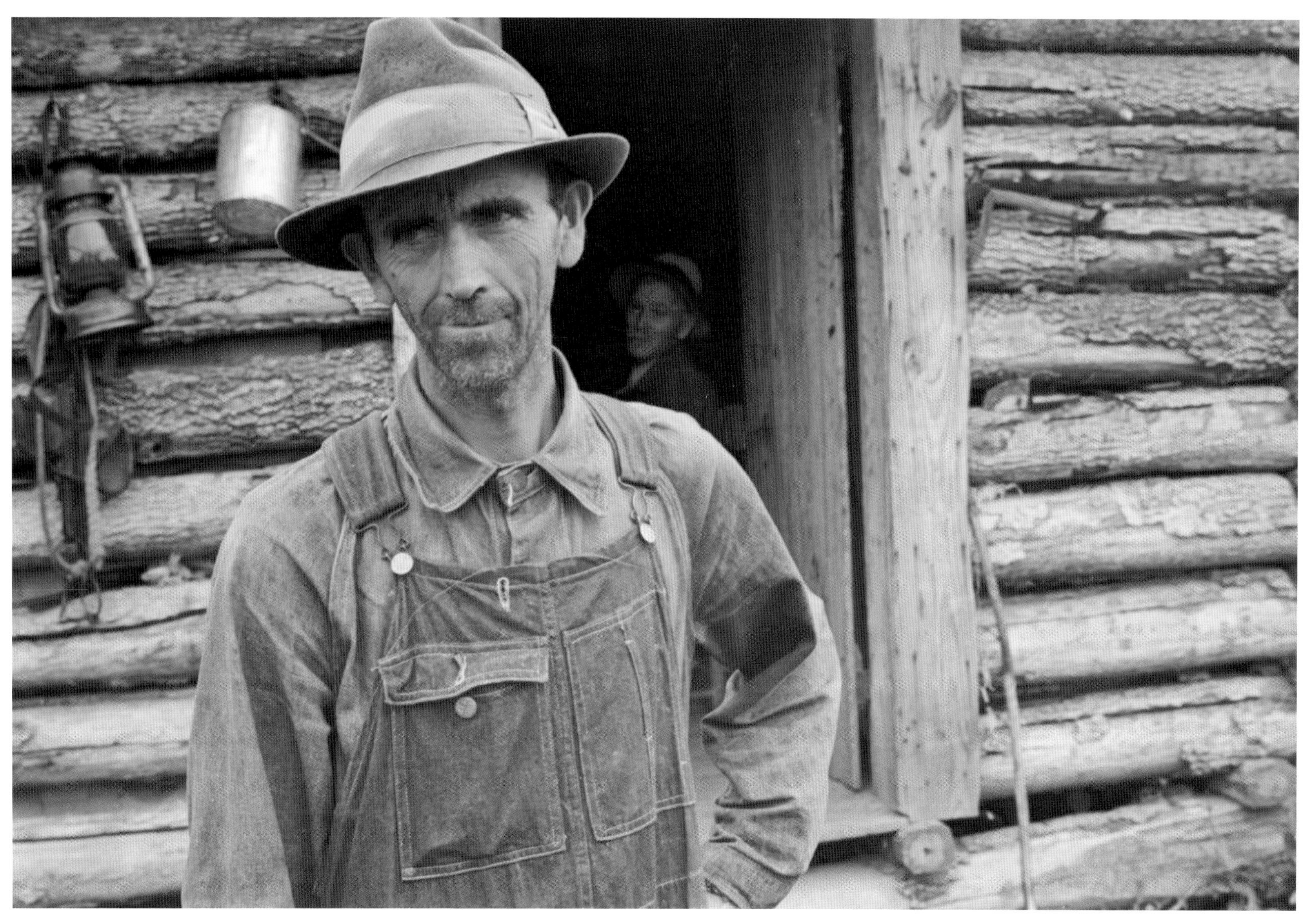

Boone County rehabilitation client.

(Ben Shahn, October 1935) Farm Security Administration Photograph Collection, Prints & Photographs Division, Library of Congress, LC-USF33–006033–M3

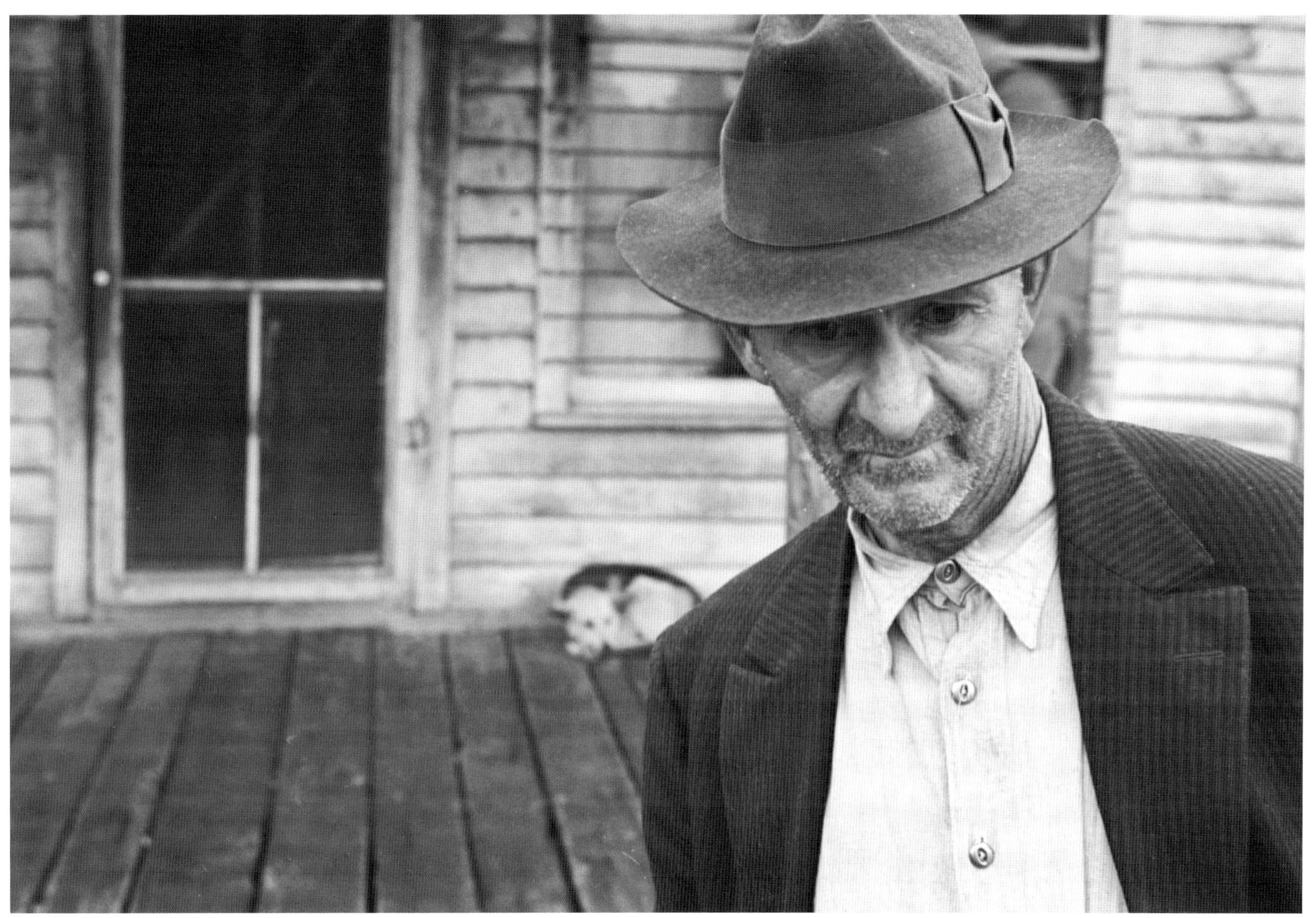

Two of the few remaining residents of Zinc.

(Ben Shahn, October 1935) Farm Security Administration Photograph Collection, Prints & Photographs Division, Library of Congress, LC-USF33–006036–M4

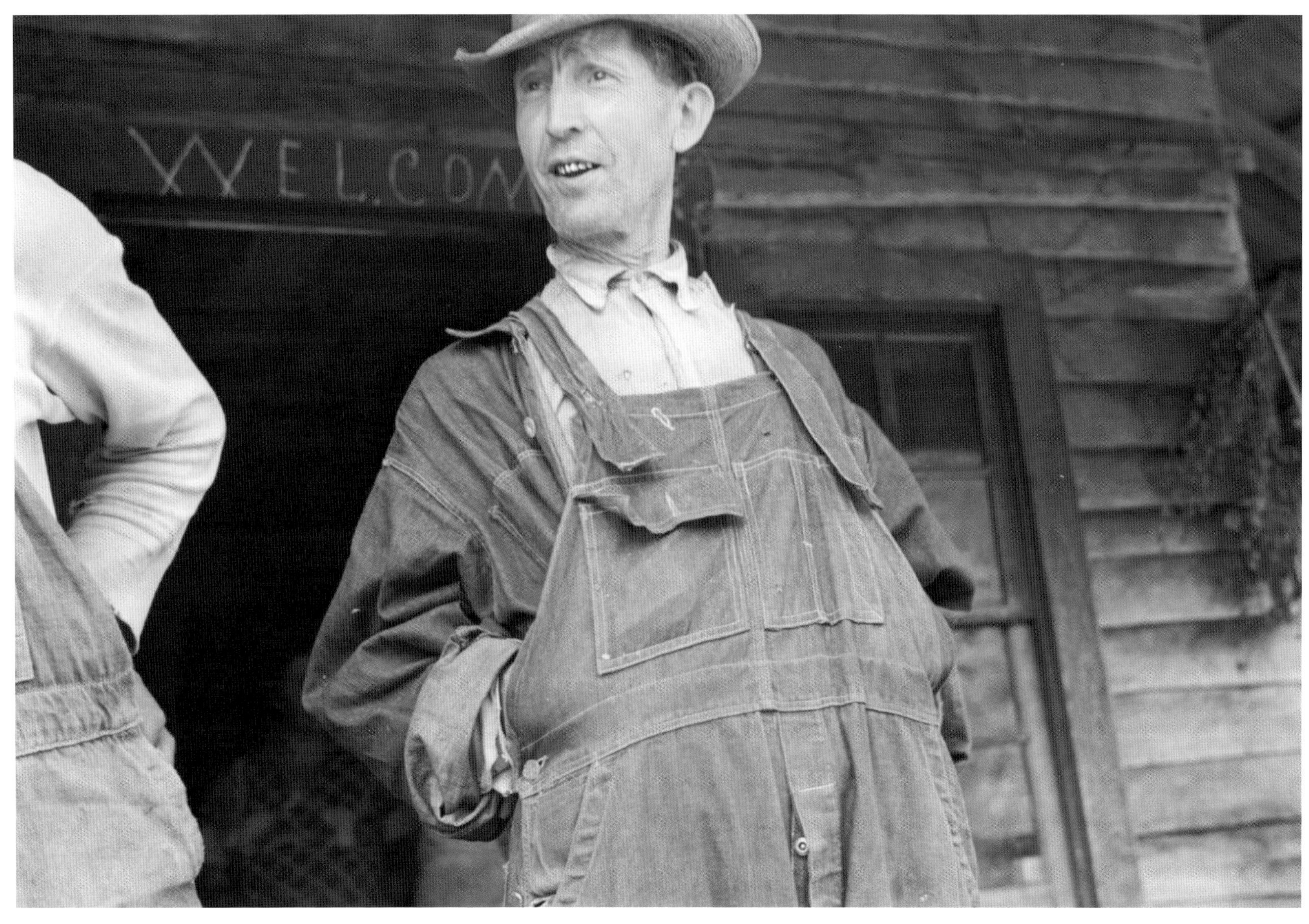

An "Ozark mountaineer."

(Ben Shahn, October 1935) Farm Security Administration Photograph Collection, Prints & Photographs Division, Library of Congress, LC-USF33–006063–M2

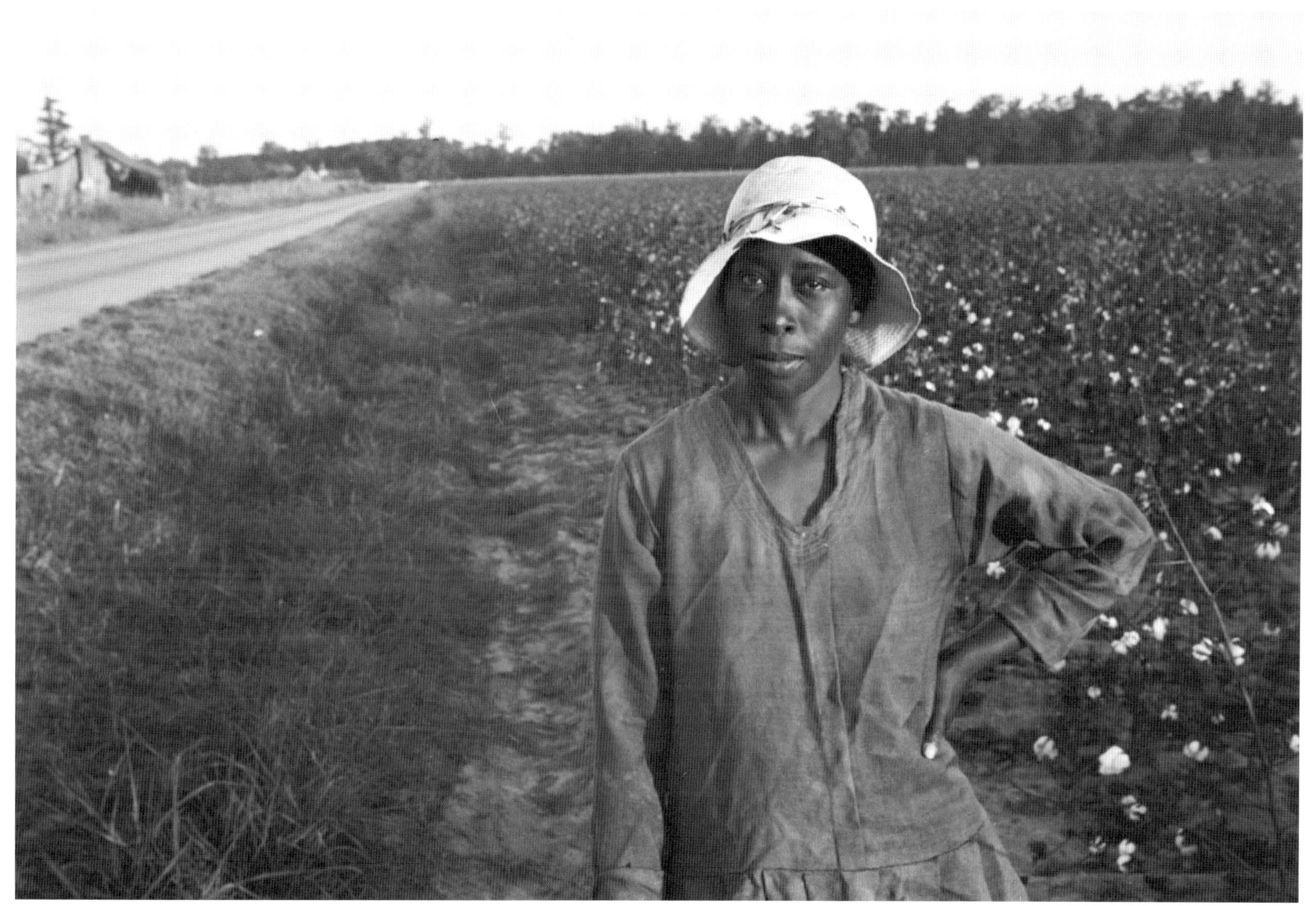

A cotton picker on the Alexander plantation.

(Ben Shahn, October 1935) Farm Security Administration Photograph Collection, Prints & Photographs Division, Library of Congress, LC-USF33–006022–M2

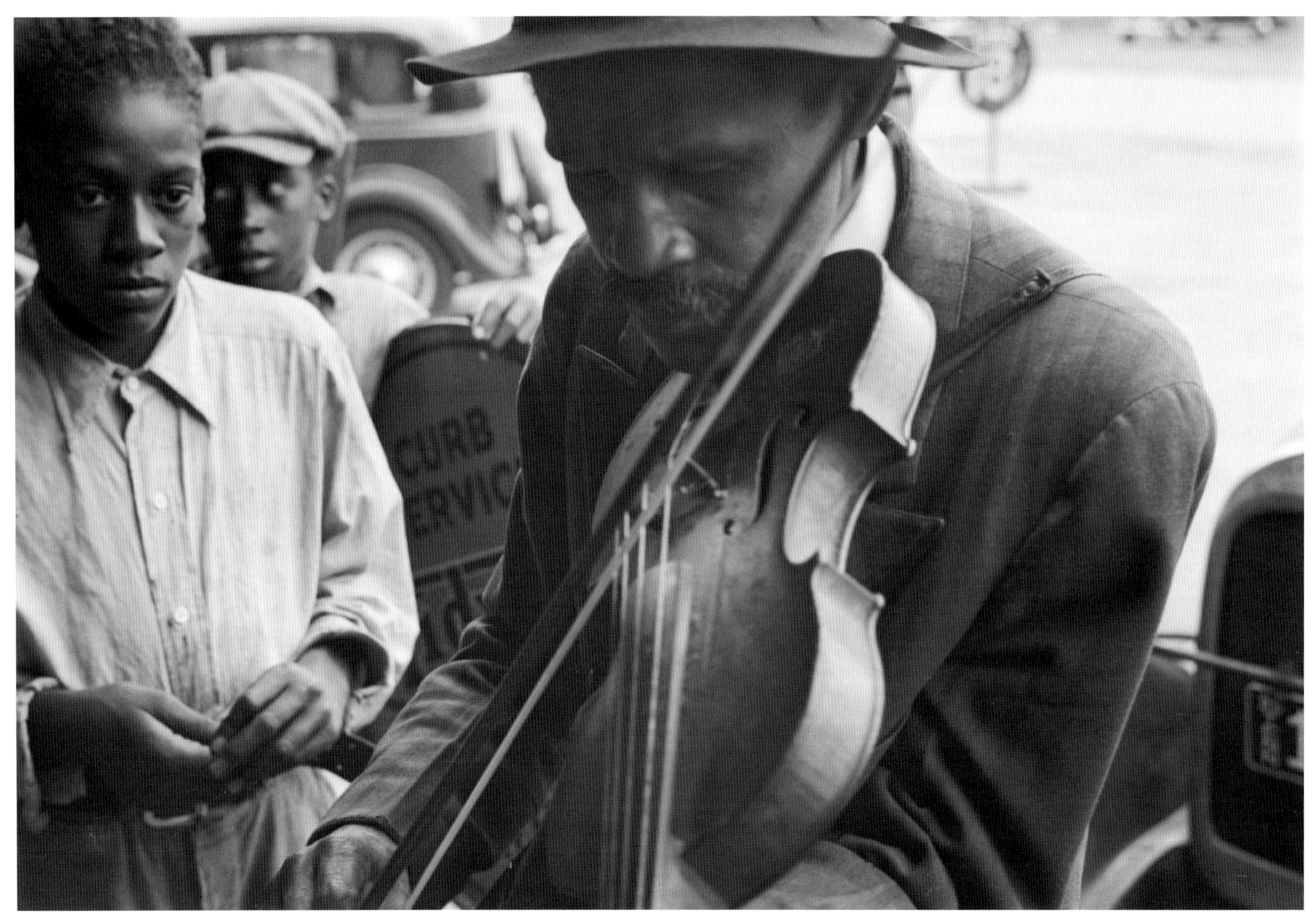

A blind street musician in West Memphis.

(Ben Shahn, October 1935) Farm Security Administration Photograph Collection, Prints & Photographs Division, Library of Congress, LC-USF33–006017–M2

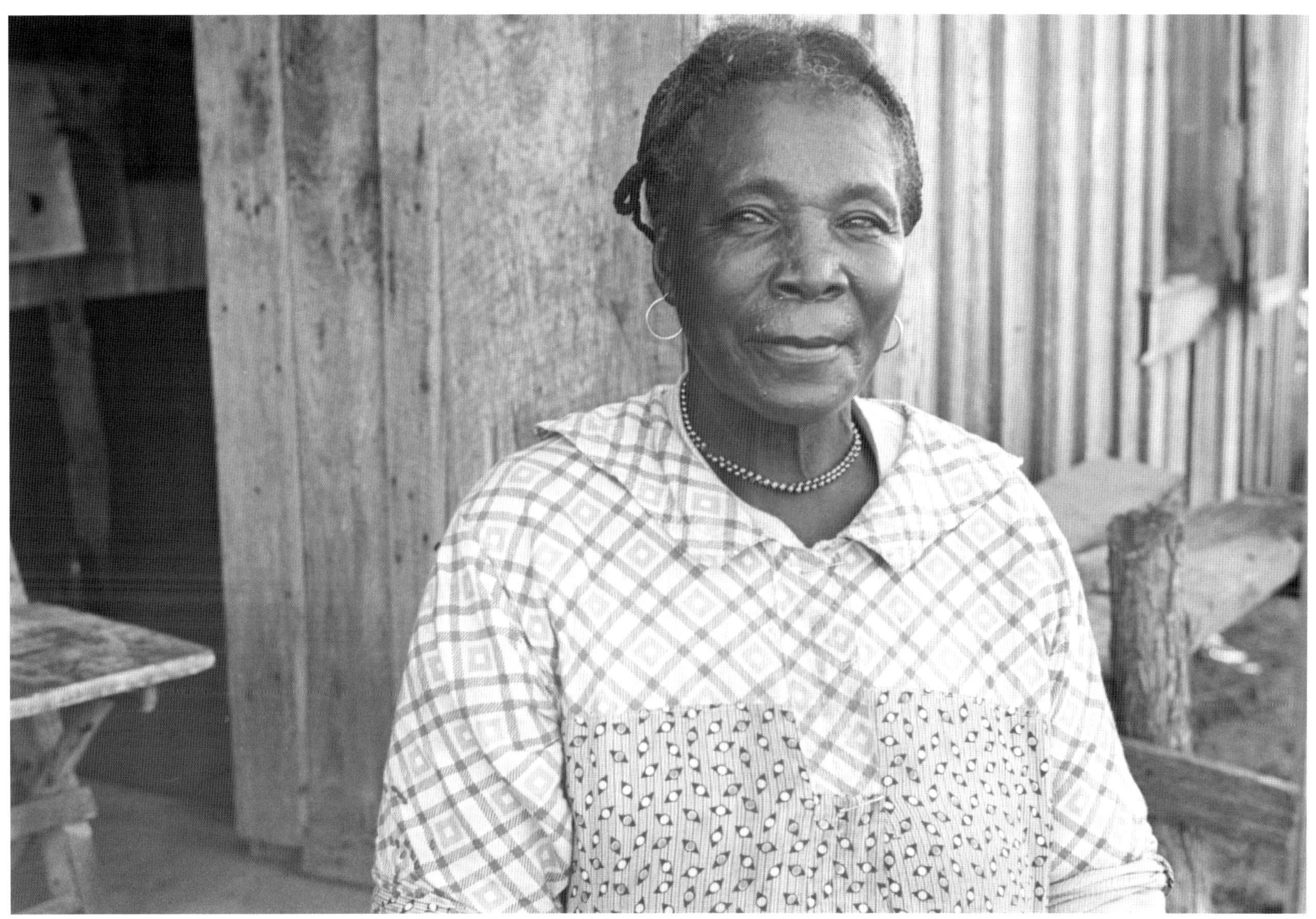

Wife of a sharecropper in Pulaski County.

(Ben Shahn, October 1935) Farm Security Administration Photograph Collection, Prints & Photographs Division, Library of Congress, LC-USF33–006020–M5

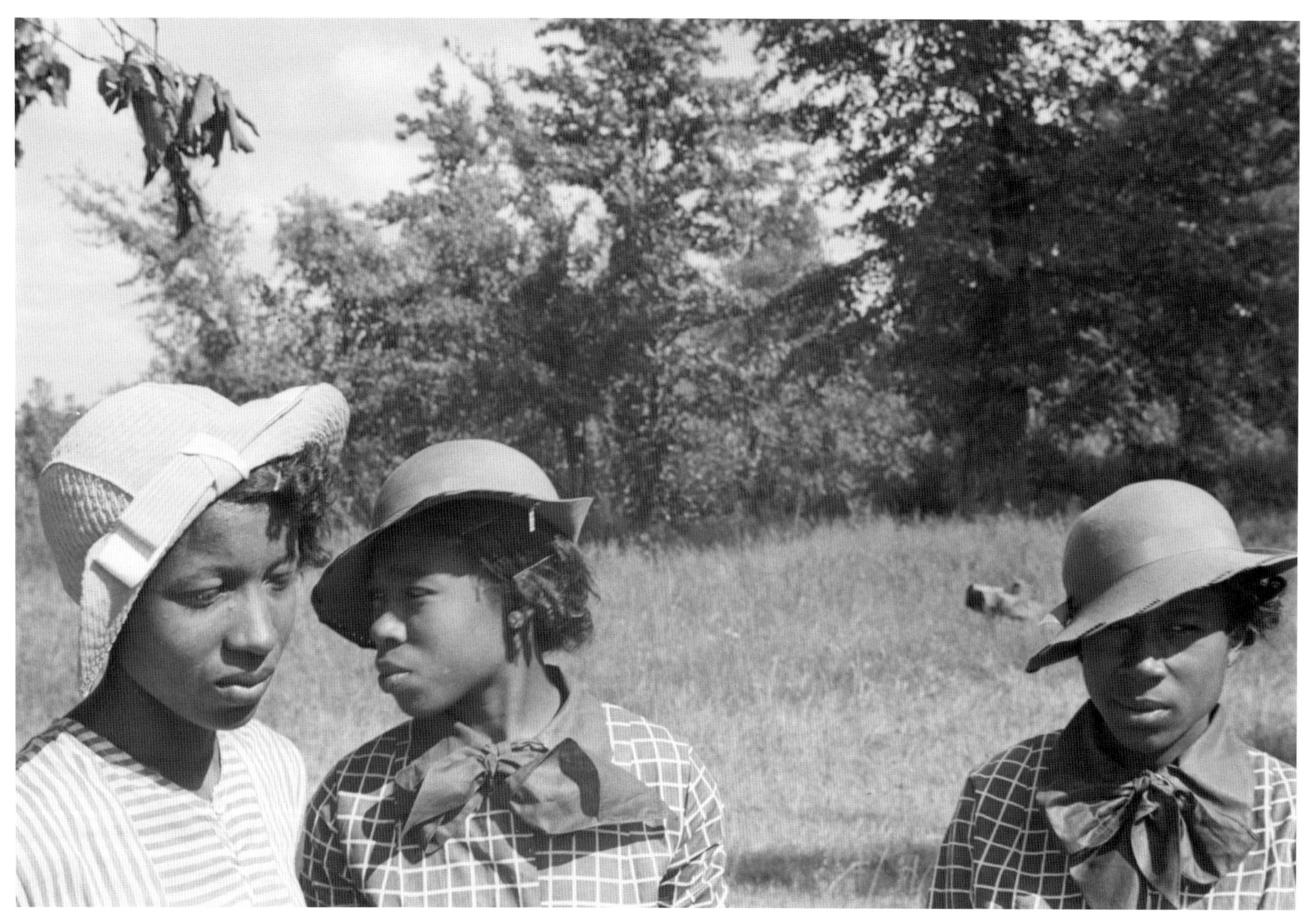

Young women outside church on Sunday.

(Ben Shahn, October 1935) Farm Security Administration Photograph Collection, Prints & Photographs Division, Library of Congress, LC-USF33–006025–M4

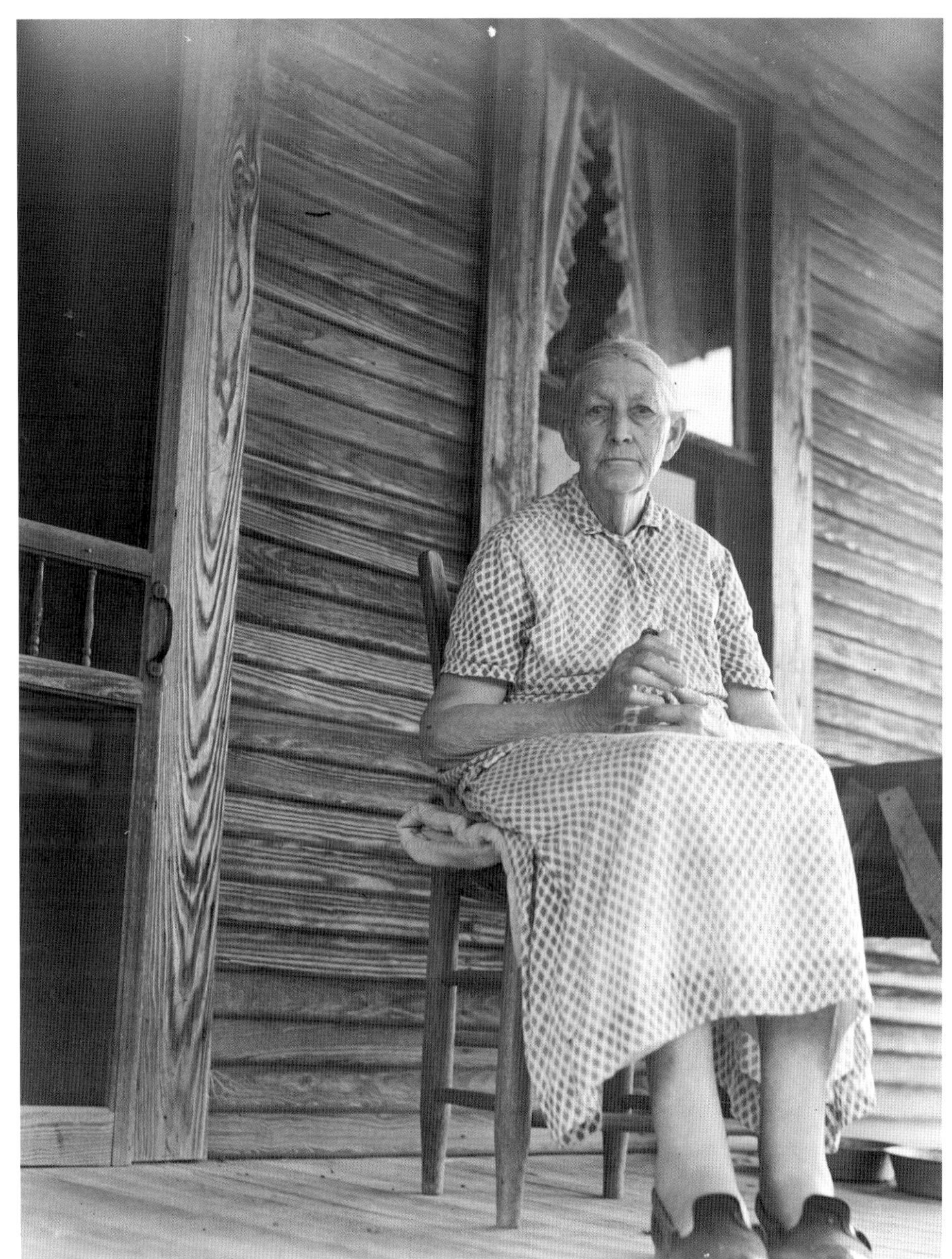

Dorothea Lange called this photo from Conway, "Arkansas Hoosier." She quoted this woman at length, noting that she was born in 1855: "My father was a Confederate soldier. He give his age a year older than it was to get into the army. After the war he bought 280 acres from the railroad and cleared it. We never had a mortgage on it. In 1920 the land was sold, the money divided. Now, none of my children own their land. It's all done gone, but it raised my family. I've done my duty—I feel like I have. I've raised twelve children."

(Dorothea Lange, June 1938) Farm Security Administration Photograph Collection, Prints & Photographs Division, Library of Congress, LC-USF34–018289–C

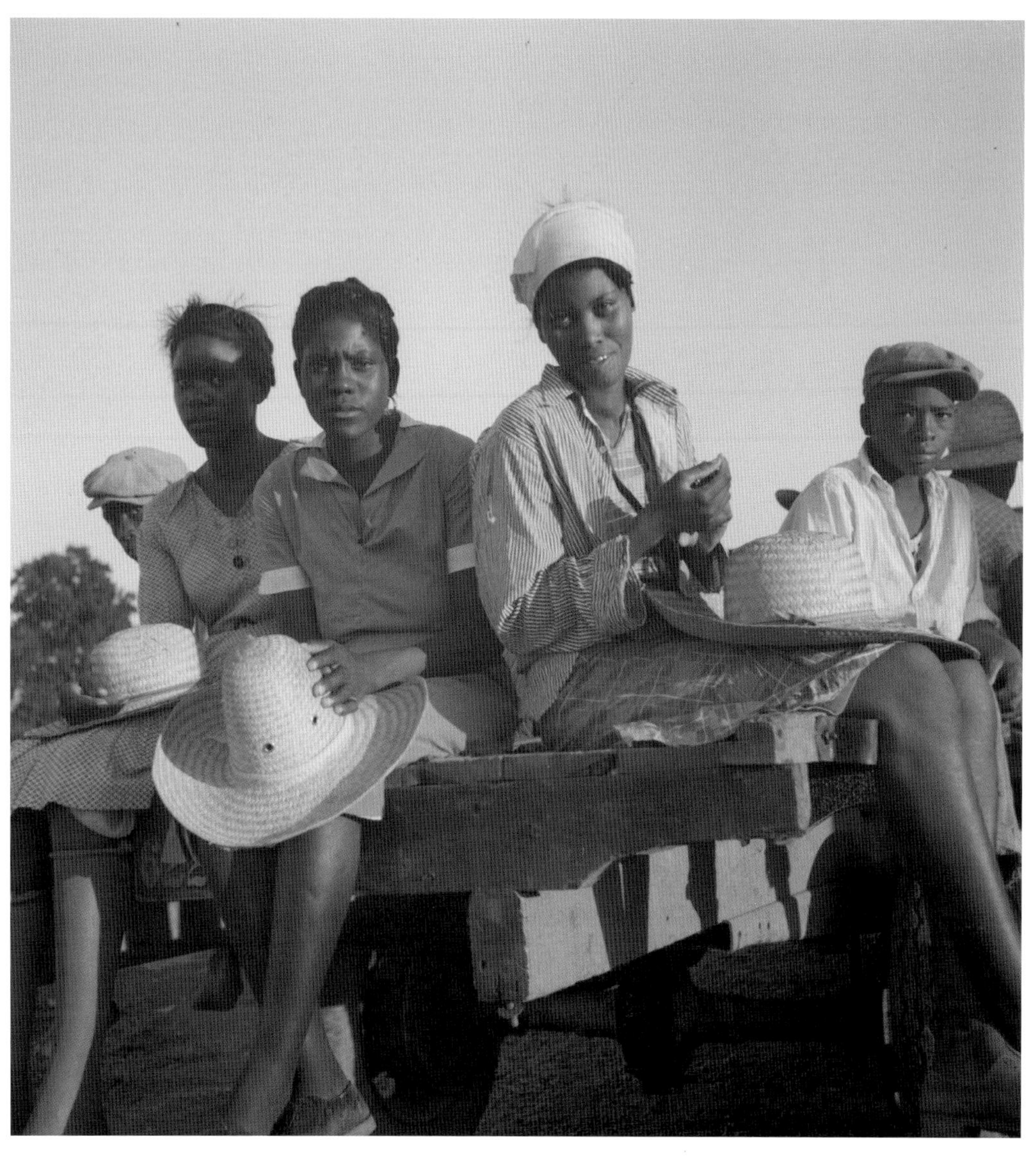

Day laborers loaded on a truck to be driven to the field.

(Dorothea Lange, July 1937) Farm Security Administration Photograph Collection, Prints & Photographs Division, Library of Congress, LC-USF34–017908–E

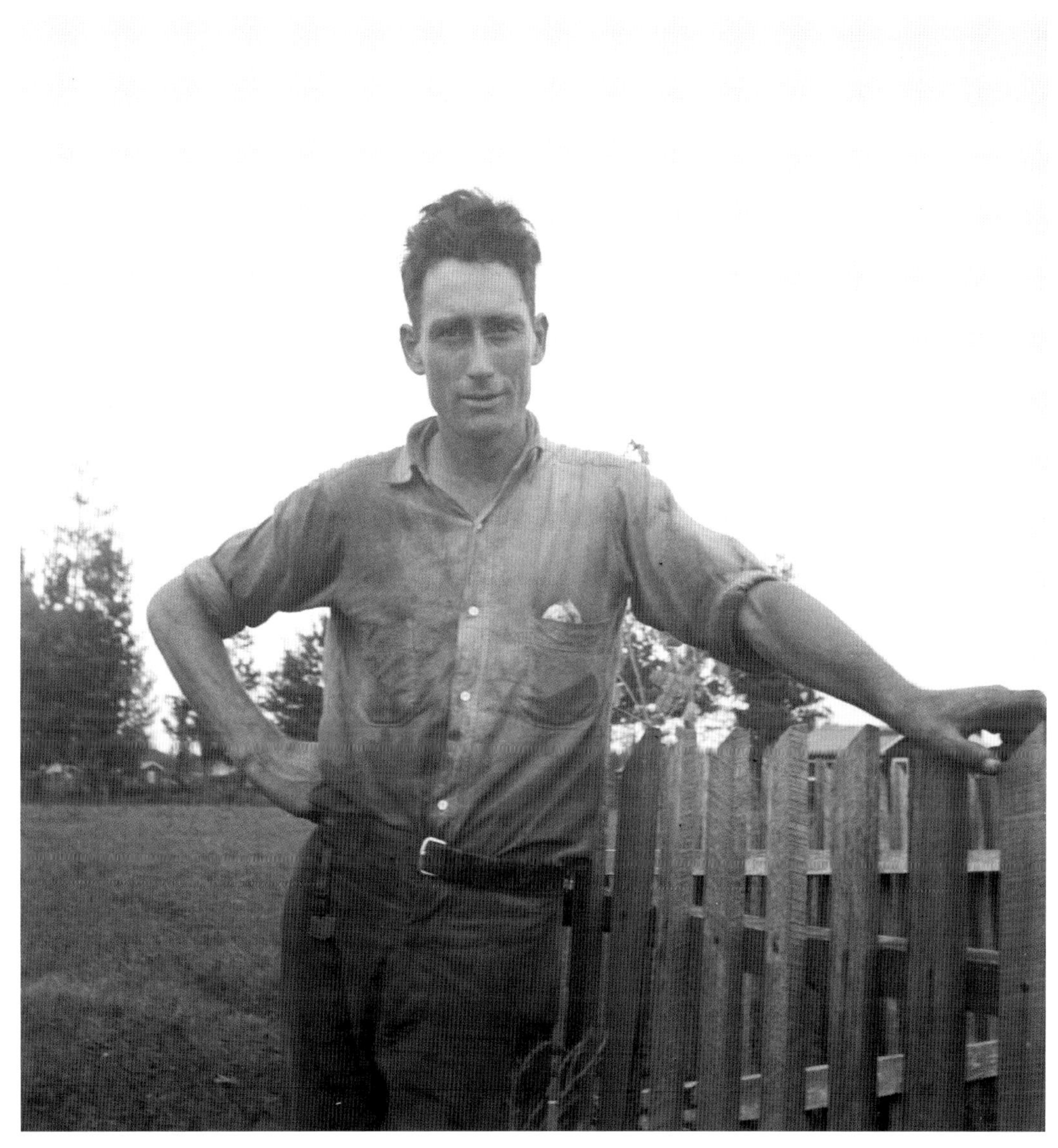

Farmer at the Lake Dick resettlement project.

(Dorothea Lange, August 1939) Farm Security Administration Photograph Collection, Prints & Photographs Division, Library of Congress, LC-USF34–018944–E

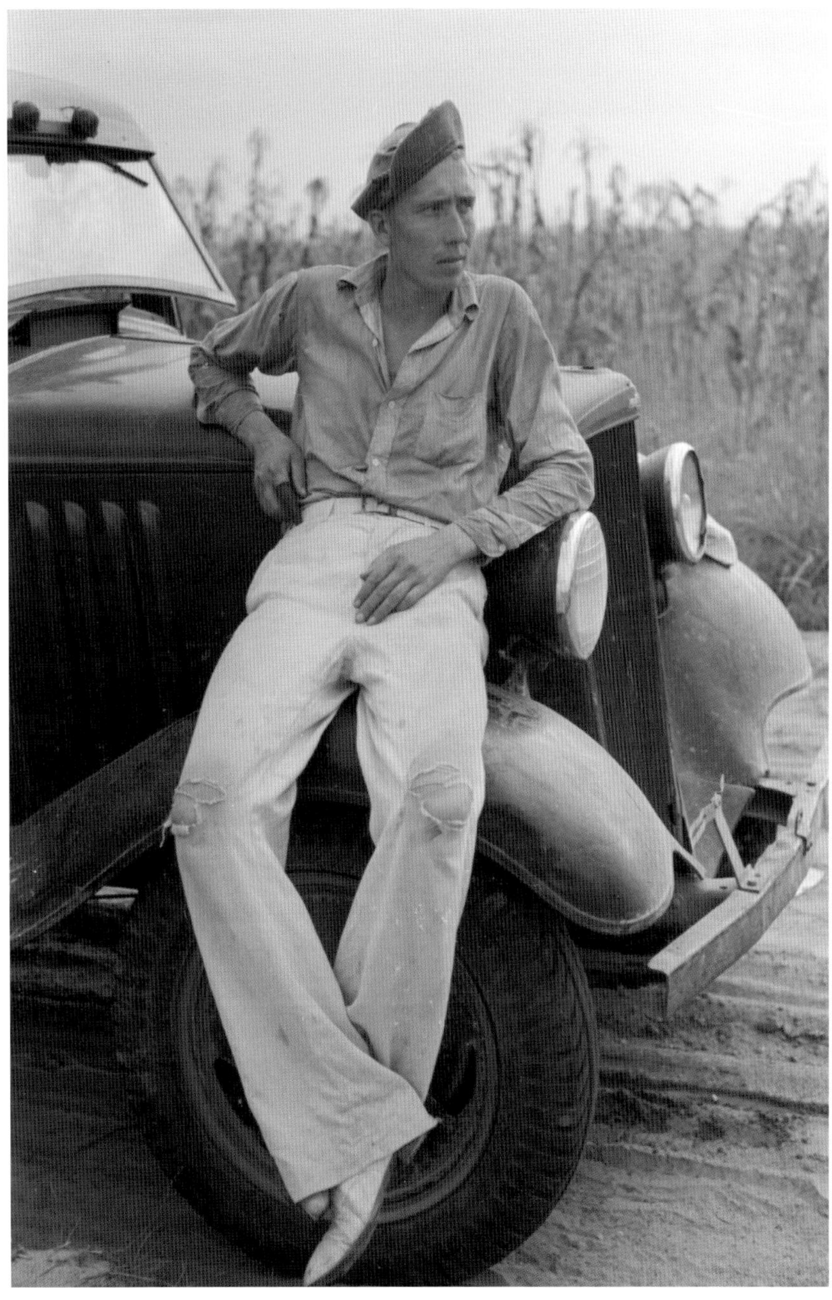

A Lake Dick farmer in light-colored trousers and white shoes.

(Russell Lee, September 1938) Farm Security Administration Photograph Collection, Prints & Photographs Division, Library of Congress, LC-USF33–011681–M1

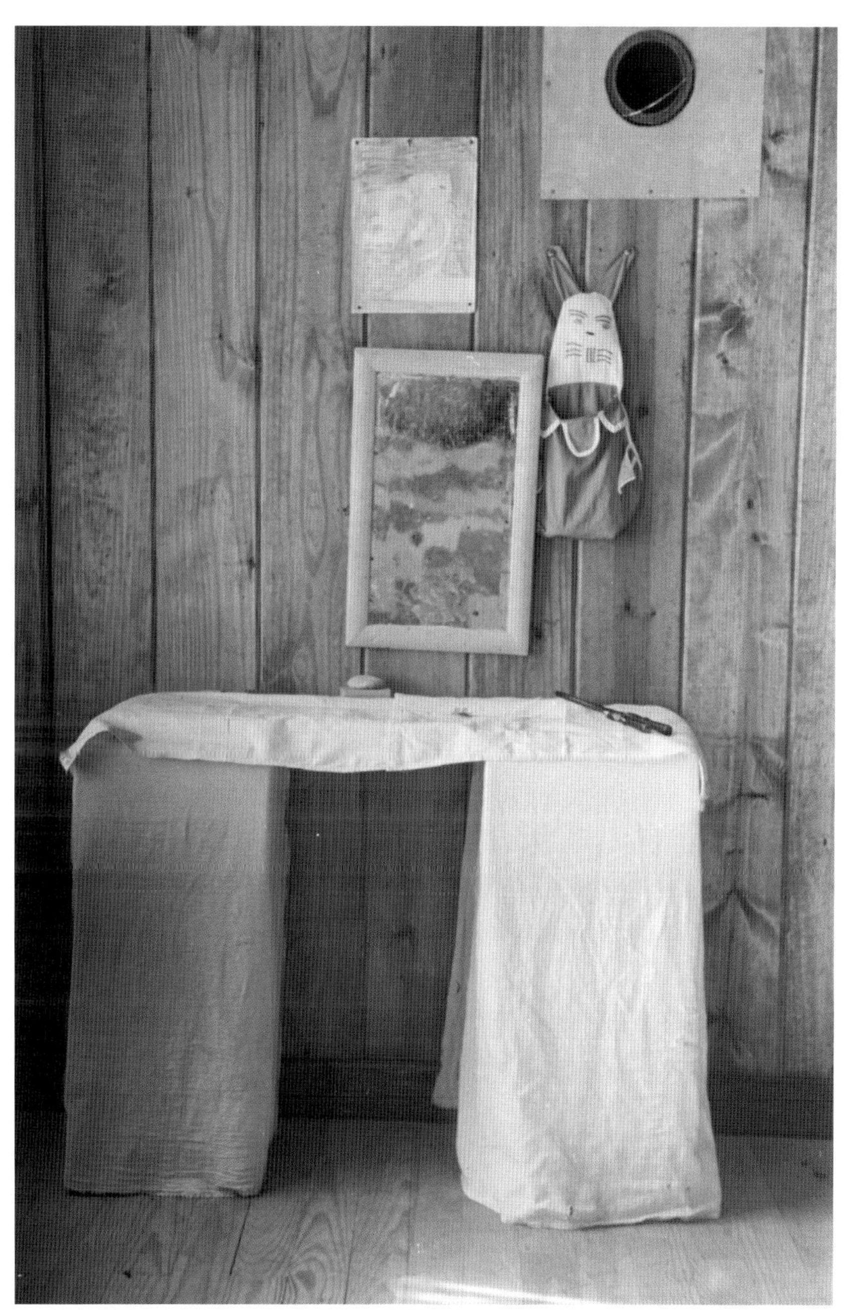

A child's bedroom at the Chicot resettlement farm.

(Russell Lee, January 1939) Farm Security Administration Photograph Collection, Prints & Photographs Division, Library of Congress, LC-USF33–011935–M1

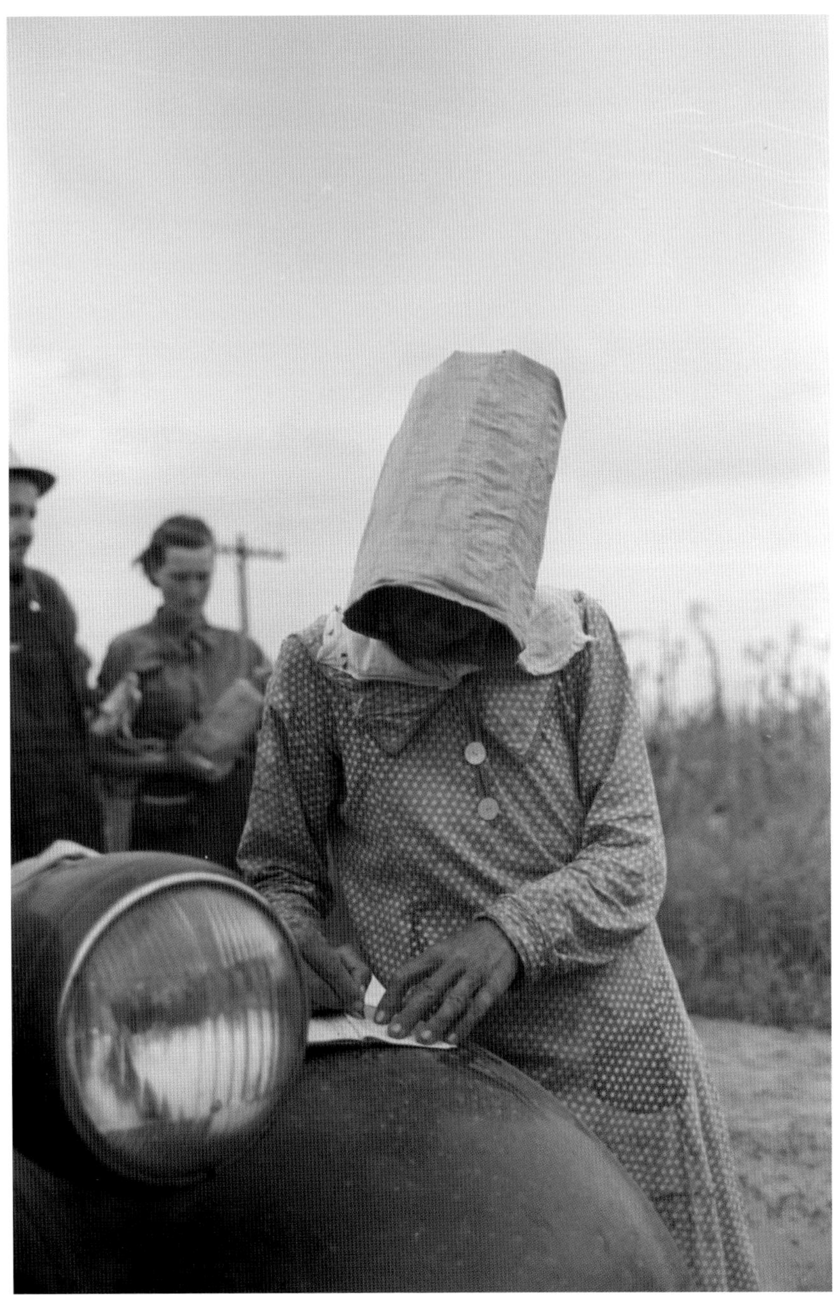

Woman cotton picker at Lake Dick.

(Russell Lee, September 1938) Farm Security Administration Photograph Collection, Prints & Photographs Division, Library of Congress, LC-USF33–011688–M1

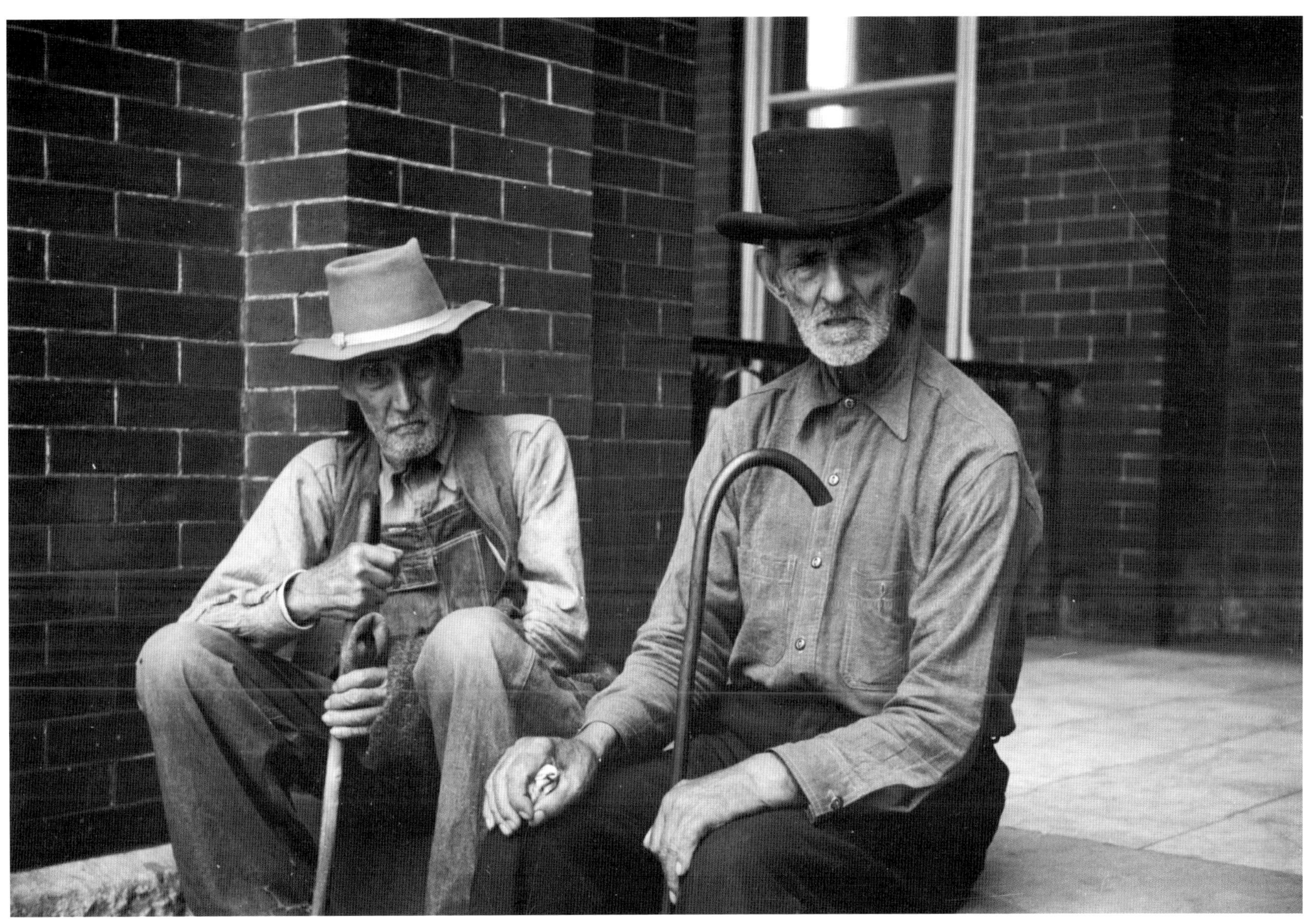

Men at the Batesville courthouse.

(Carl Mydans, June 1936) Farm Security Administration Photograph Collection, Prints & Photographs Division, Library of Congress, LC-USF33–000599–M1

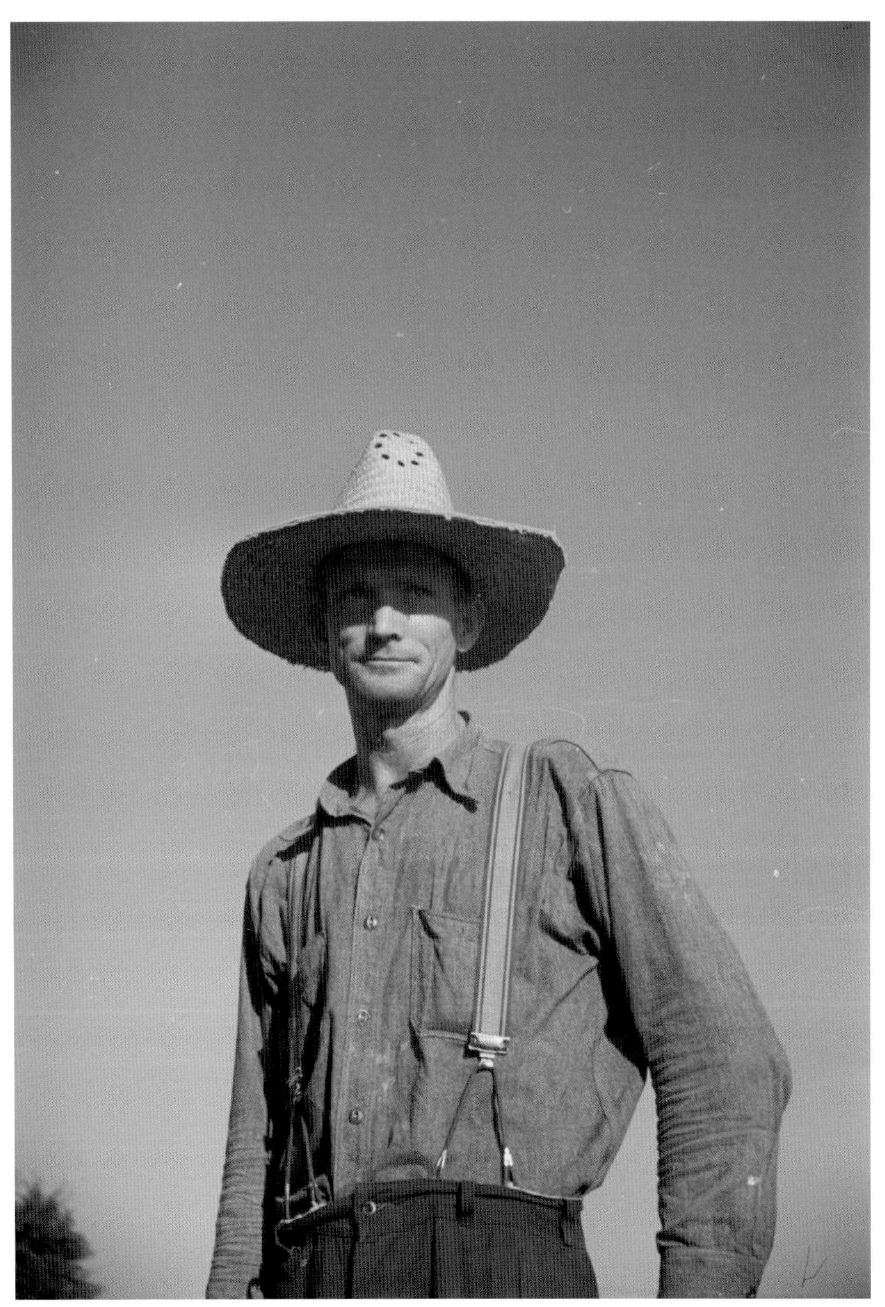

A farmer from Lake Dick.

(Carl Mydans, June 1936) Farm Security Administration Photograph Collection, Prints & Photographs Division, Library of Congress, LC-USF33–000632–M1

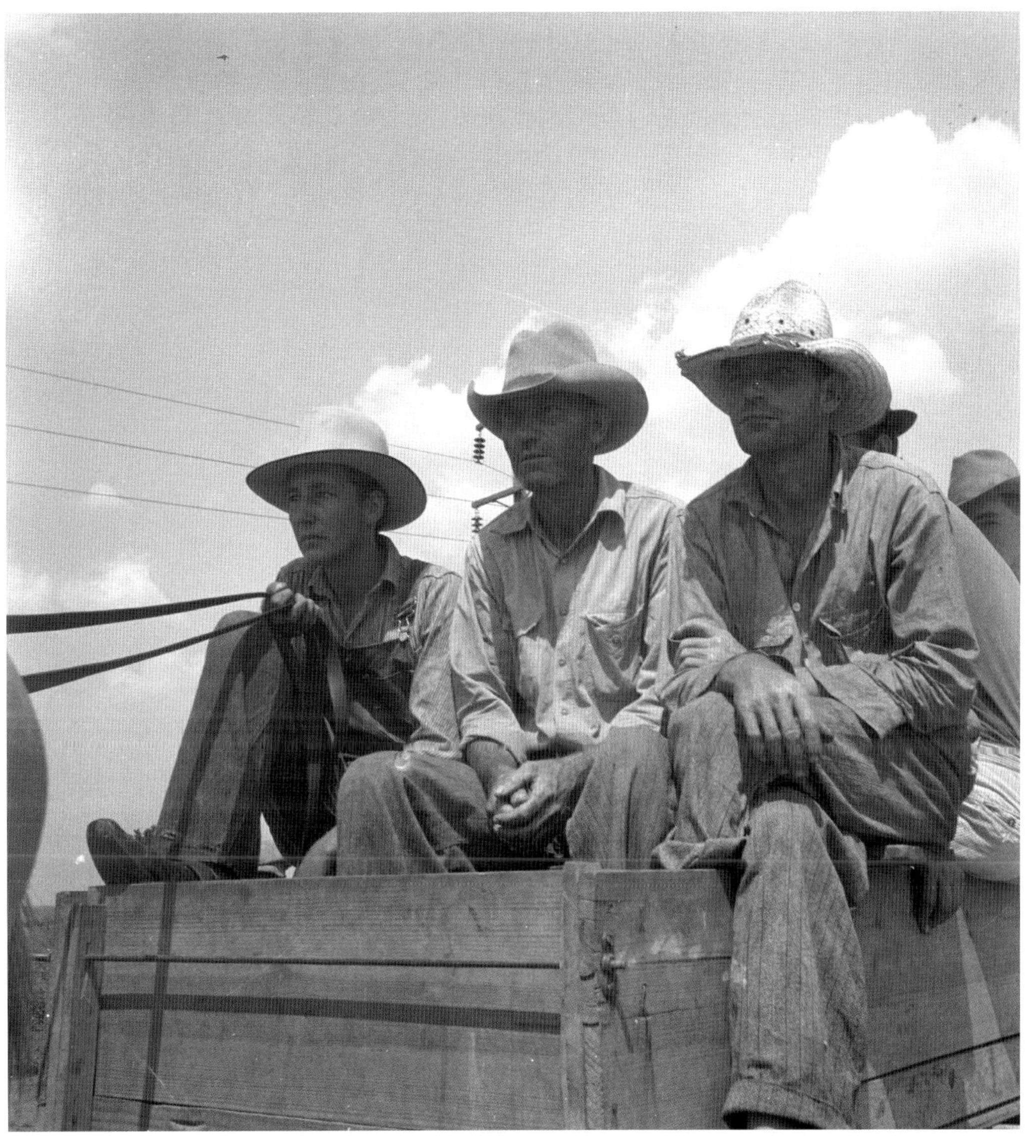

Arkansas sharecroppers going home, near Blytheville. Archibald MacLeish chose this picture to open his book-length poem *Land of the Free*, published in 1938. The caption he used with the photograph was, "We don't know."

(Dorothea Lange, August 1936) Farm Security Administration Photograph Collection, Prints & Photographs Division, Library of Congress, LC-USF34–009735–E

ELEVEN | DARING TO LOOK AT OURSELVES

BY 1940 RA/FSA photographers were spending less time and taking fewer pictures in Arkansas; in fact, only fifty-one photos were taken in 1940 though the usual number was two hundred to three hundred a year. In 1941, there were just two pictures from Arkansas, one of an administrator in Little Rock and the other of an auto graveyard advertisement for "Ruins of America, Hood Auto Parts," both likely taken by freelancers instead of regular FSA staff members.

Americans' attention was shifting in 1940–1941, away from the troubles of the Depression and toward the growing concern about inevitable involvement in World War II. RA/FSA photographers were devoting more coverage to migrant labor, Japanese internment, and the buildup of war defense industries, and Stryker was considering a new photo assignment—the effects of war on civilian life. The RA/FSA photo project was at its "peak of success," according to Jack Hurley (*Portrait of a Decade*), with a large staff, new facilities, an established reputation for quality and wide distribution of its photographs. Stryker had added new photographers, including Gordon Parks, the only African American photographer associated with the project, who had been brought on as an unpaid trainee. However, all of this was about to change quickly and dramatically.

Paul Conkin traces the sudden deterioration of the Farm Security Administration in *Tomorrow a New World*, linking it to attacks on the agency's programs for disadvantaged farmers by the persistent and formidable coalition of large farm operations, the American Farm Bureau Federation, other major farm organizations, and their representatives in Congress. In 1942, the coalition stepped up the assault on the FSA. Prominent senators spoke out against the agency, and the national president of the Farm Bureau testified against it in appropriations hearings. Congress wound up slashing the FSA budget for the upcoming year by 27 percent.

In 1943, a House select committee convened hearings to investigate the FSA. Representative Harold D. Cooley of North Carolina, who chaired the committee, actually supported the assistance to disadvantaged farmers but was bothered by the FSA's financial mismanagement, its repeated defiance of Congress, and the collectivist operation of some resettlement farm communities such as Lake Dick. The committee's final report cited the FSA on these and other issues that included deceiving clients, poor administration, and the support of industrial enterprises that competed with private business. Despite censuring the FSA, the committee recommended continuing its programs for tenant-purchase and rehabilitation but placing them under a new agency. Congress eventually abolished the FSA in 1946 and transferred its remaining functions to the Farmers' Home Administration.

According to Hurley, though Stryker had weathered budget reductions before, the 1942 cut was especially ominous. He fired photographers, pared down the staff to a minimum, and sought assignments from other agencies, including the Office of War Information (OWI). Hurley reports that by the end of 1942 the Historical Section as an entity had ceased to exist and had become the OWI photo agency. In 1943, Stryker found he was simply a custodian of the photos, providing "propaganda pictures" from the file, as he wrote Pare Lorentz, a filmmaker for both the FSA and the OWI. Aware that the project was ending and that he needed to leave very soon, Stryker began making plans to secure the photo collection by having it transferred to the Library of Congress.

Hurley writes that enemies of the FSA in Congress and other federal agencies wanted it "wiped out without a trace," including the photo file. Within the OWI there were those who disliked the work of the FSA photographers and sought to get rid of the collection. Stryker in seeking approval for the transfer to the Library of Congress skirted these adversaries by going over their heads and directly contacting the president's administrative assistant for help. He was able to secure the president's quick approval, and the photo file was placed safely under the care of Archibald MacLeish, the head of the Library of Congress and a fan of FSA photography. Stryker submitted his resignation from the FSA Historical Section in September 1943, and took a job with Standard Oil of New Jersey, a position that offered relief from the frustrations of government bureaucracy.

The controversy around the RA and FSA had pitted large farm interests against small farmers, tenants, and sharecroppers in a struggle involving class, race, and power at local, state, and national levels. Conkin writes that large farm operators sought to maintain the social and economic order that assured their political dominance and their profits. The RA/FSA relief programs were designed to pursue social and economic justice for disadvantaged farmers who lacked the political heft to fight for themselves. The agency's underlying purpose, though, was to reform the agricultural system and turn unproductive farmers into consumers who contributed to the nation's economy. At the heart of the matter, the conflict rested on fundamental differences in beliefs about the worth of human beings and the value of their work.

Large landowners operated according to a selective version of capitalistic values that drove competition and growth in the pursuit of greater financial rewards and justified a sense of entitlement and the right to political, social, and economic power. Their profits, and thus their success, in cotton growing depended on the availability of cheap and compliant labor, especially in the transition into increasing mechanization. Rexford Tugwell and like-minded thinkers viewed the landowners' variety of capitalism as perverted and responsible for an unbridgeable gap between the top and bottom in US society. Repairing it was possible only by government action to help those who had been mistreated. This required comprehensive economic planning exerting greater controls over all sectors from industry to agriculture, an approach that alarmed the large landowners by threatening their labor supply and their profits.

Race complicated the situation for the RA/FSA in the South, where the relief programs helped African Americans to some extent but never as much as white farmers. African Americans who were provided assistance always received less than whites, and it was always of poorer quality. Some RA/FSA administrators were sympathetic to the plight of southern blacks, according to Nancy Weiss in *Farewell to the Party of Lincoln*, but the management and dispersal of relief was controlled at the local level by white leaders who often were also the major landowners determined to maintain white supremacy in their communities. Administrators in Washington stayed out of local racial relations, fearing their interference could make the situation worse for African Americans. As with so many issues, however, World War II would mark the beginning of change in race relations in the South.

According to Conkin, the controversy over the FSA in the 1940s became so emotionally divisive that both sides claimed democracy itself was at stake. Opponents maintained the FSA was not only "destroy[ing] American business," but promoting communism, while defenders of the FSA declared that efforts to demolish the agency struck "at the heart of democracy." In the end the coalition of Congress and big agriculture wielded the greater power, dominating the struggle and shutting down the FSA just as the United States entered World War II to battle a sinister and very real external threat to democracy.

The RA/FSA had attempted to advance its agenda through the photography project by introducing Americans to the existence of the miseries of rural poverty and the exploitation of tenants and sharecroppers for their labor in the service of growing cotton. The Arkansas pictures, in their display of the living conditions of poor farmers and their families and the promise of a fresh start on resettlement farms, supported the agency's mission in arguing for federal assistance to address social and economic inequities by presenting a portrait of great need. The photographs served as an indictment of the intolerable treatment of tenants and sharecroppers and the view of them as mere commodities required to produce a good cotton crop. Their effectiveness in communicating this message to the public is a matter for speculation, however, as it is impossible to track publication of the photos and viewers' reaction to them.

World War II profoundly changed Americans and their sense of purpose in the world, individually and as a nation. All of those who left secure moral and cultural environments of their homes during the war for different kinds of experiences, responsibilities, and relationships, returned with changed expectations, tastes, and ambitions that challenged white male middle- and upper-class dominance. Moreover, the center of America's soul shifted from small towns to urban life. Pete Daniels, in *Lost Revolutions: The South in the 1950s,* reports that in the twenty years after the war, 11 million tenants and sharecroppers left the farm for big cities. As agriculture rapidly mechanized, the labor force moved into manufacturing jobs.

Photography changed as well in the postwar years. Although to Dorothea Lange, the change was not progress. She met with Richard Doud, the Smithsonian historian, in 1964 to talk about photographs and her memories of the RA/FSA photography project. Doud asked how she explained the success of the project, and Lange responded that in fact it had not been a success in the 1930s. Roy Stryker had, instead, had a hard time "peddling the pictures" to publications. She said that editors weren't interested: "[T]here were no outlets for those pictures. They piled up and they piled up and they piled up." But over time, the photo file gained in significance and usefulness; it became source material, she explained, important not for the immediacy of the images but because the photos were seen in a different perspective. Lange thought that "Time has given those [pictures] the value."

But at the same time Lange considered 1960s photographers who praised and revered the RA/FSA pictures to be stuck. They admired the photos but had not pushed their own work to progress to new levels beyond emulating their style. They had failed to study the RA/FSA photos deeply enough, and therefore they did not grasp that taking great images required the effort to understand people and the predicaments they faced. Instead, photographers were reacting to the emotional drama of the pictures without going below the surface. Though they were excited about photographing civil rights and poverty, both major 1960s issues, they were just "jumping on bandwagons." Lange found it "pathetic" when young photographers would ask her how to photograph poverty.

Then Lange switched gears and told Doud that she had an idea for doing another photographic survey of the country, based on the RA/FSA approach but different. After living abroad for a while, she had developed a new perspective on the United States and thought that Americans could benefit from a photographic portrait of themselves. The focus should be on urban life, and the project should be limited to five years; it would become a "resource file" on America in the 1960s.

"I very much think we need it in this country," Lange said. "No country has ever closely scrutinized itself visually that I know of." Americans could make use of such photos, she suggested, if only "we could dare look at ourselves."

ACKNOWLEDGMENTS

Writing may be a solitary exercise, but no writer puts pen to paper without a team that supports, inspires, critiques, informs, and encourages. In developing this book, I have been especially reliant on three groups of people for their contributions. Without question, the most significant person is my husband, Bill Symes, who served as a resource for thoughtful insight in his critiques as well as enthusiastic cheerleading support. His intellect and unfailing respect for the subject of this book sustained me beyond measure. Gerald Jordan, my valued colleague at the University of Arkansas, applied his sharp editor's eye, acute sense of style, and appreciation for words, and knowledge of Arkansas history to the manuscript, and was a source of constant encouragement. Other dear colleagues, Dale Carpenter, Katherine Shurlds, and Bobbie Foster, generously gave their time and advice. Arkansas historian Tom Dillard, former director of Special Collections at Mullins Library on the UA campus, very kindly supplied advice and guidance from his deep understanding of the past of this state.

Second are the many historians and other researchers who have done amazing service through their diligent exploration of various facets of Arkansas and the nation's experience of the Great Depression and its impact on the South and the agricultural economy. Arkansas owes a debt of gratitude to these people who have done the exceptionally difficult work of locating and digging through government records for the facts that underpin accurate and truthful accounts of the state's past. Special mention is due to William Downs, retired director of the journalism program at Ouachita Baptist University, for his extensive interviews with survivors of the Depression in Arkansas, published in the book *Stories of Survival: Arkansas Farmers during the Great Depression*. Gratitude certainly must be expressed to Bill Stott, who first introduced me to the FSA photography project in his graduate seminar at the University of Texas.

Close to my heart are the people who supplied the soul and inspiration for this effort, my grandparents and their five daughters, who, like so many small farmers in the 1920s and 1930s, lost their land when the cotton market bottomed out. The stories my mother and my aunts told of picking cotton, milking cows, churning butter, and finally getting indoor plumbing mirror the experiences recounted by Arkansans about those years. Their use of humor and dignity to frame stories of life barely eked out on a small farm translated the authoritative histories of shifting political and economic forces to the personal level—from the international market conditions that led to plummeting cotton prices, to what it felt like to lose the farm and one's livelihood.

This book is dependent on the hard work, knowledge, and experience of all of these people, and I am indebted beyond my ability to express to the perspectives and insights they have provided. Their spirits and ideas infuse all that is good in these pages.

BIBLIOGRAPHIC ESSAY

This book is based on wide-ranging sources in a number of areas. For ease of identification and accessibility, they are arranged by major topics including the FSA photograph collection, FSA photographers, and the program itself; the New Deal in general; and African Americans in 1930s Arkansas.

Farm Security Administration Photography Project

FARM SECURITY ADMINISTRATION PHOTOGRAPH COLLECTION

The FSA photos are located in the Farm Security Administration/Office of War Information Collection in the Library of Congress and are free and accessible online at http://www.loc.gov/pictures/collection/fsa/. The photos are easily searchable by photographer's name and "Arkansas" or a specific county or town. Copyright information is included with each photo, though the vast majority are copyright-free. Images are available for download in black-and-white as TIFFs or JPEGs. The collection includes a great deal of information about the photos and the photo project. Though the photos are digitized, many of the written documents are not and require a visit to the library or paid assistance from a researcher.

FSA PHOTOGRAPHERS

The most fascinating information about the FSA photographers resides in two sources—correspondence and oral interviews. Letters exchanged by Roy Stryker and photographers while they were on the road offer clues to their relationships, personalities, and assignments. The correspondence is located in the Roy Stryker (1893–1975) Papers held by the Ekstrom Library Special Collections Photographic Archives at the University of Louisville. The collection is not available online but librarians help with searches.

In the early 1960s, the journalist and art historian Richard Doud interviewed many of the major FSA photographers as well as Stryker and even Rexford Tugwell and his wife, Grace, for the Smithsonian's Archives of American Art. Most of these interviews are digitized and available online through searching the Archives of American Art. An oral history with Walker Evans done by Paul Cummings is also available.

A number of books and articles explore the lives and work of FSA photographers in general; others address their FSA work specifically. Ann Whiston Spirn's *Daring to Look: Dorothea Lange's Photographs and Reports from the Field* is one of the best on Lange's FSA photos and extended captions (Chicago: University of Chicago Press, 2009). Laura Katzman's article "The Politics of Media: Painting and Photography in the Art of Ben Shahn" in *American Art* (Winter 1993) connects Shahn's FSA photography to his art. In *The Photographic Eye of Ben Shahn* (Cambridge, MA: Harvard University Press, 1975), Shahn discusses his photography with David Pratt. Sources on Walker Evans's FSA work include *American Photographs* by Evans and Lincoln Kirstein (50th anniversary ed., New York: Museum of Modern Art, 1988) and Bruce Jackson's essay "Walker Evans" in the 1998 exhibit brochure for "Walker Evans: Public Photographs" at the University of Buffalo Art Gallery. F. Jack Hurley's 1973 interview with Russell Lee is the basis for the essay "F. Jack Hurley on Russell Lee," accessible online through ASX. It was originally published in *Image: Journal of Photography and Motion Pictures* (September 1973) of the International Museum of Photography and is available on request from the Eastman Museum at Eastman.org/image-magazine. Hurley also wrote the book *Russell Lee, Photographer* (Dobbs Ferry, NY: Morgan & Morgan, 1978).

I am especially indebted to Dr. J. B. Colson, former director of the University of Texas at Austin photojournalism program and Lee's close personal friend and colleague, for his insights about Lee and his work.

FSA PHOTOGRAPHY PROJECT

The work of the FSA, as well as more information on the photographers, is covered abundantly in numerous books and articles. F. Jack Hurley's *Portrait of a Decade: Roy Stryker and the Development of Documentary Photography in the Thirties* (Baton Rouge: Louisiana State University Press, 1972) is a good, general introduction to the FSA project and photographers, based to a large extent on his own interviews. John Raeburn's *A Staggering Revolution: A Cultural History of Thirties Photography* (Chicago: University of Illinois Press, 2006) places the FSA in the context of 1930s photography movements and styles and offers a wealth of detail about the program as well as observations about its cultural significance. The cultural role of the FSA photos and the range of their publication are examined by Cara A. Finnegan in *Picturing Poverty: Print Culture and FSA Photographs* (Washington, DC: Smithsonian Institution, 2003). Stuart S. Kidd in *Farm Security Administration Photography, the Rural South, and the Dynamics of Image-making, 1935–1943* (Lewiston, NY: Edwin Mellen, 2004) addresses the program's operation in the South, in particular its relationship with the RA/FSA regional offices, and how photographers were directed to subjects.

A number of essays and books assess the FSA photos as documentary and discuss the genre's development in the 1930s. William Stott's book *Documentary Expression in Thirties America* (New York: Oxford University Press, 1973) is a classic in its close examination of the term "documentary." Beverly Brannan, curator of photography at the Library of Congress, and Gilles Mora take this comment further in their essays in *The American Vision* (New York: Abrams, 2006). Along with Carl Fleischhauer, Brannan also edited the book *Documenting America, 1935–1943* (Berkeley: University of California Press, 1988), which examines the FSA photos. Pete Daniel in *Official Images: New Deal Photography* (Washington, DC: Smithsonian Institution, 1987) covers photography by other government agencies in the 1930s. Michael Carlebach dealt with the FSA pictures as indoctrination in his essay "Documentary and Propaganda: The Photographs of the Farm Security Administration" in *The Journal of Decorative and Propaganda Arts* (1988). He went further in considering the FSA photos and culture in a book coauthored with Eugene Provenzo, *Farm Security Administration Photographs of Florida* (Gainesville: University Press of Florida, 1993).

Samples of Stryker's "shooting scripts" are included in *The Likes of Us: America in the Eyes of the Farm Security Administration,* by Stu Cohen and Peter Bacon Hales (Boston: David R. Godine, 2009), and also through the Library of Congress FSA collection at http://www.loc.gov/rr/print/coll/fsawr/fsawr.html.

There are several good contemporary sources about the photos. An exceptional one is Edward Steichen's guest edited issue of *U.S. Camera 1939* (New York: William Morrow & Company, 1939), which featured photos from the 1938 International Photographic Exhibition in New York. Steichen selected about forty photos from the FSA exhibit, wrote an introductory essay, and added a number of comments made by visitors reacting to the FSA photos. Another source is Hartley Howe's article in the *Survey Graphic* (1940), "You Have Seen Their Photos" in which he addresses the accusations of propaganda lodged against the FSA images. Especially notable is the Archibald MacLeish book-length poem *Land of the Free* (New York: Harcourt, Brace, 1938), which incorporates FSA photographs.

A very personal overview of the photo project—and something of an elegy—is the book *In This Proud Land: America 1935–1943 as Seen in the FSA Photographs* (Greenwich, CT: New York Graphic Society, 1973), in which Stryker works with Nancy Wood to select FSA photos that were particularly meaningful to him and discusses his thoughts about the project.

The New Deal

THE NEW DEAL: A GENERAL OVERVIEW

Sources about the New Deal are plentiful, almost beyond counting; these sources were selected to focus on agricultural issues in the South, the Resettlement Administration, and the Farm Security

Administration. An especially pertinent source on land use and conservation is *This Land, This Nation: Conservation, Rural America, and the New Deal* (New York: Cambridge University Press, 2007) by Sarah Phillips. The book outlines the story of Rexford Tugwell and Franklin Roosevelt and the development of farm policy and its basis in conservation issues. Donald Holley's very fine *Uncle Sam's Farmers: The New Deal Communities in the Lower Mississippi Valley* (Urbana: University of Illinois Press, 1975) focuses on the RA/FSA resettlement farm program, looking specifically at its operation in Arkansas. Both of these books provide background on the Depression in the United States and Arkansas and economic events and conditions precipitating it. Nancy Weiss's book *Farewell to the Party of Lincoln: Black Politics in the Age of FDR* (Princeton, NJ: Princeton University Press, 1983) provides an excellent background on African American leaders' efforts to engage Roosevelt in their goal of antilynching legislation in Congress. The book *Plowed Under: Food Policy Protests and Performance in New Deal America,* by Ann Folino White, explores in detail the reaction to the commodity crop "plow-up" following the Agricultural Adjustment Act of 1933.

Other books that address this period include Roger Biles, *The South and the New Deal* (Lexington: University Press of Kentucky, 1994); Johnny Cash, *Cash: The Autobiography of Johnny Cash* (New York: HarperCollins, 1997); Paul Conkin, *Tomorrow a New World: The New Deal Community Program* (Ithaca, NY: Cornell University Press, 1959); Pete Daniel, *Lost Revolutions: The South in the 1950s*; Marcie Cohen Ferris, *The Edible South: The Power of Food and the Making of an American Region* (Chapel Hill: University of North Carolina Press, 2014); Margaret Hagood, *Mothers of the South: Portraiture of the White Tenant Farm Woman* (Charlottesville: University Press of Virginia, 1939); Robert Hilburn, *Johnny Cash: The Life* (New York: Little, Brown and Co., 2013); Charles S. Johnson, Edwin R. Embree, and W. W. Alexander, *The Collapse of Cotton Tenancy* (Chapel Hill: University of North Carolina Press, 1935); Lu Ann Jones, *Mama Learned Us to Work* (Chapel Hill: University of North Carolina Press, 2002); and Rupert B. Vance, *How the Other Half Is Housed: A Pictorial Record of Subminimum Farm Housing in the South* (Chapel Hill: University of North Carolina Press, 1936).

Two pertinent journal articles are Jane Adams and D. Gorton, "This Land Ain't My Land: The Eviction of Sharecroppers by the Farm Security Administration" in *Agricultural History* (2009), and Marion Clawson, "The Resettlement Experience on Nine Selected Resettlement Projects" in *Agricultural History* (1978).

Government documents include *Bicentennial Edition: Historical Statistics of the United States, Colonial Times to 1970,* Part 1 (Washington, DC: US Government Printing Office, September 1975) at http://www2.census.gov/library/publications/1975/compendia /hist_stats_colonial-1970/hist_stats_colonial-1970p1-chK.pdf; Harold D. Cooley, *Hearings on the Farm Security Administration,* 78th Cong., 1st sess. (Washington, DC: US Government Printing Office, 1943); *Fifteenth Census of the United States: 1930*

Census of Agriculture. The Negro Farmer in the United States (Washington, DC: US Government Printing Office, 1933); *Report of the Administrator of the Farm Security Administration* (Washington, DC: US Government Printing Office, 1938); *Sixteenth Census of the United States: 1940. Population.* (Washington, DC: US Government Printing Office, 1943); *Statistical Abstract of the United States, 1936* (Washington, DC: US Government Printing Office, 1936); and *The First Annual Report of the Resettlement Administration* (Washington, DC: Resettlement Administration, 1936).

Nongovernmental organizations' reports include *Housing Officials' Yearbook, 1936* (Chicago, IL: National Association of Housing, 1936), as well as yearbooks for 1937, 1938, and 1939, which provide reports on houses constructed by the RA/FSA. Also, *The American National Red Cross, Annual Report for the Year Ended June 30, 1937* (Washington, DC: American National Red Cross, 1937) addresses the flood aftermath in Arkansas and Red Cross services there.

ARKANSAS IN THE DEPRESSION AND THE NEW DEAL

Two overviews of Arkansas history are Michael B. Dougan, *Arkansas Odyssey: The Saga of Arkansas from Prehistoric Times to Present: A History* (Little Rock, AR: Rose Publishing, 1994), and Ben F. Johnson, *Arkansas in Modern America, 1930–1999* (Fayetteville: University of Arkansas Press, 2000). A number of sources address the story of the Depression in Arkansas: *Arkansas, a Guide to the State* (New York: Hastings House, 1941), reprinted in 1987 as *The WPA Guide to 1930s Arkansas,* compiled by Workers of the Writers' Program of the Work Projects Administration in the State of Arkansas (Lawrence: University Press of Kansas, 1987); William D. Downs, *Stories of Survival: Arkansas Farmers during the Great Depression* (Fayetteville, AR: University of Arkansas Press, 2015); C. Laine Gates, Justin M. Nolan, and Mary Jo Schneider, "The Politics of Traditional Foodways in the Arkansas Delta," in *Southern Foodways and Culture: Local Considerations and Beyond,* ed. Lisa J. Lefler (Knoxville, TN: Newfound Press, 2013); Thomas Harding, *One-Room Schoolhouses of Arkansas as Seen through a Pinhole* (Fayetteville: University of Arkansas Press, 1993); Lois Lenski, *Cotton in My Sack* (Philadelphia, PA: J. B. Lippincott, 1949); David Welky, *The Thousand-Year Flood: The Ohio-Mississippi Disaster of 1937* (Chicago: University of Chicago Press, 2011); Jeannie Whayne, *The New Plantation South: Land, Labor, and Federal Favor in Twentieth-Century Arkansas* (Charlottesville: University Press of Virginia, 1996).

Journal articles, all published in the *Arkansas Historical Quarterly,* provide more details of programs in Arkansas, and include Floyd W. Hicks and C. Roger Lambert, "Food for the Hungry: Federal Food Programs in Arkansas" (Spring 1978); Donald Holley, "The Second Great Emancipation: The Rust Cotton Picker and How It Changed Arkansas" (1993); Roger Lambert, "Hoover and the Red Cross in the Arkansas Drought of 1930" (Spring 1970); Gail S. Murray, "Forty Years Ago: The Great Depression Comes to Arkansas" (Winter 1970); Dan Pittman, "The Founding of Dyess Colony" (1970); Norman

Thomas, "Arkansas Sharecroppers and the Roosevelt Agricultural Policies, 1933–1937" (1965); and Keith Volanto, "The AAA Cotton Plow-Up Campaign in Arkansas" (Winter 2000).

Additional articles from a variety of sources address Arkansas resettlement, public schools, and food. They include "Dedicate Ark. Homestead Project Nov. 8: Community of 100 Families To Be Model," *Chicago Defender* (November 4, 1938); E. S. Dudley, "Report on 1937 Flood, Dyess, Arkansas," *USA Cities* (1937) at http://www.usacitiesonline.com/ardyessflood1937.htm; "Dyess, Arkansas Historical Events," *Dyess, Arkansas Historical Events* (1937) at http://www.usacitiesonline.com/ardyess flood1937.htm; Marcie Cohen Ferris, "The Deepest Reality of Life: Southern Sociology, the WPA, and Food in the New South," *Southern Cultures* (Summer 2012); "1937 'Flood Diary' & Business Ledger" (1937) at http://www.usgennet.org/usa/ar/county/greene/flooddiary1937.html; Crawford Greene, *Statistical Summary for the Public Schools of Arkansas, 1936–1938* (Little Rock: Arkansas State Department of Education, 1939); and "Lakeview Celebrates Its Fiftieth Birthday," *Phillips County Progress* (August 27, 1988). An *Arkansas Democrat* article by Gene Rutland, "FSA Seeks 'Way Out' for Negro Sharecroppers" (August 6, 1939) is drawn largely from an apparent government brochure on Lakeview titled "Lakeview: An Opportunity for Security" (date likely 1938 or 1939). Information on the Hillhouse farm settlement is given in Fred C. Smith, "Cooperative Farming in Mississippi," *Mississippi History Now*, an online publication of the *Mississippi Historical Society* (November 2004) at http://www.mshistorynow.mdah.ms.gov/articles/219/cooperative-farming-in-mississippi. Kathleen Van Buskirk discusses food and canning practices in the 1930s in an essay titled "Winds of Change Blew over the Ozarks," *Ozarks Watch* (Spring 1994) at https://www.thelibrary.org/lochist/periodicals/ozarkswatch/ow703c.htm.

AFRICAN AMERICANS IN 1930S ARKANSAS

Four books were particularly helpful on African Americans in Arkansas during the Depression and as covered by the FSA photos. Two books by Grif Stockley deal with race issues in the state, both published by the University of Arkansas Press in Fayetteville. They are *Ruled by Race: Black/White Relations in Arkansas from Slavery to the Present* (2009), and *Blood in Their Eyes: The Elaine Race Massacres of 1919* (2004). Robert Whitaker also addressed the events at Elaine in *On the Lap of Gods: The Red Summer of 1919 and the Struggle for Justice That Remade a Nation* (New York: Broadway Books, 2009). An exceptional resource on the FSA coverage of African Americans is the book by Nicholas Natanson, *The Black Image in the New Deal: The Politics of FSA Photography* (Knoxville: University of Tennessee Press, 1992). Michael Mehlman's dissertation was very helpful in its discussion of issues and conflicts for tenant farmers; it is titled "The Resettlement Administration and the Problems of Tenant Farmers in Arkansas, 1935–1936" (PhD diss., New York University, 1970).

The journal article by M. Langley Biegert, "Legacy of Resistance: Uncovering the History of

Collective Action by Black Agricultural Workers in Central East Arkansas from the 1860s to the 1930s," *Journal of Social History* (Fall 1998), provides data on slaves in eastern Arkansas before the Civil War and their postwar status. Donald Holley discusses how resettlement dealt with African Americans in "The Negro in the New Deal Resettlement Program," *Agricultural History* (1971). Information on the Rosenwald schools comes from the Fisk University Rosenwald Fund Card File Database at http://rosenwald.fisk.edu, and Diane Granat's article "Saving the Rosenwald Schools: Preserving African American History" (last updated May 5, 2011), for the Alicia Patterson Foundation at http://aliciapatterson.org/stories/saving-rosenwald-schools-preserving-african-american-history.

Newspaper sources include the five-part series of articles published in the *New York Times* by F. Raymond Daniell [*sic*] in 1935 on the conflict between sharecroppers and landowners in eastern Arkansas: "AAA Piles Misery on Share Croppers; Cotton Program Cuts Their Meager Incomes as Federal Cash Benefits Landlords" (April 14), "Arkansas Violence Laid to Landlords; Share-Croppers Charge They Foment Trouble to Eliminate Any Attempts at Unionism" (April 16), "Tenant Law Clash Roils Cotton Belt; Share-Croppers Resent Land-Owners' Evictions in Face of Protective Provision" (April 18), "Farm Tenant Union Hurt by Outsiders" (April 19), and "'Run Off Farms,' Tenants Declare; Dispossession Is Laid to Link with Union by Arkansas Share-Croppers" (April 20).

PATSY G. WATKINS is associate professor of journalism at the University of Arkansas. Her research focuses on news photography and the visual design of information.